Boris Pasternak
FAMILY CORRESPONDENCE,
1921–1960

Boris Pasternak, Moscow, 1928

Boris Pasternak

FAMILY CORRESPONDENCE, 1921–1960

Translated and with an Introduction by
Nicolas Pasternak Slater

Edited by
Maya Slater

Foreword by
Lazar Fleishman

HOOVER INSTITUTION PRESS
Stanford University | Stanford, California

www.hoover.org

Hoover Institution Press Publication No. 578

Hoover Institution at Leland Stanford Junior University,
Stanford, California 94305-6010

First printing, 2010
16 15 14 13 12 11 10   9 8 7 6 5 4 3 2 1

Manufactured in the United States of America

⊗ The paper used in this publication meets the minimum requirements of the American National Standard for Information Sciences—Permanence of Paper for Printed Library Materials, ANSI Z39.48-1992.

Cataloging-in-Publication Data is available from the Library of Congress.
ISBN 978-0-8179-1024-2 (cloth : alk. paper)
ISBN 978-0-8179-1025-9 (pbk. : alk. paper)

CONTENTS

FOREWORD

by Lazar Fleishman

Correspondence represents a most important element in any poet's literary legacy: it elucidates what is obscure and reveals what is hidden or left unspoken in lyrical utterances. It exposes the tensions between the challenges of everyday life and the writer's specifically poetic way of perceiving and confronting them. Epistolary documents help to verify a poet's lyrical statements and to identify what may be exaggerated, played-down, or distorted in verse lines.

The correspondence carried on by Boris Pasternak, Russia's greatest twentieth-century poet, is particularly important for a number of reasons. Firstly, because of the patently hermetic, complex nature of much of his poetry, which earned him the reputation of being the most difficult poet of his generation and unleashed fierce attacks on him from literary officialdom in Stalin's Soviet Union. Secondly, because—unlike the epistolary statements of many of his contemporaries—Pasternak's letters are a kind of creative counterpart to his lyrical poetry, standing on the same level of verbal artistry that characterizes his best poems. His letters are not dry, matter-of-fact biographical reports or testimonies. They are accomplished literary works in their own right; they stand on a par with his poetry in their intellectual intensity, candor, and dazzling stylistic play. The poet never kept a diary, and his letters offer a glimpse into his innermost self that significantly complements the insights we gain from his lyrical writings.

In the unusually extensive corpus of Pasternak's published correspondence—accounting for four out of ten volumes in the most complete recent Russian edition of his works—the letters to his parents and sisters occupy a very special place. His family played a crucial role in both his life and creative work, much more so than was the case for any of his great contemporaries in Russia or abroad. Much of Pasternak's work was produced in a kind of dialogue with his parents and sisters, who left Soviet Russia shortly after the Bolshevik revolution. They were people whose artistic interests and moral positions and ideals were very close to his own. They belonged to the cultural environment in which he had grown up, and to which he remained loyal all his life. Like him, they knew and deeply appreciated the magical power of art, and placed it above life, politics, and mundane concerns. They understood him better than anyone else, and were able to catch at once the meaning of his most idiosyncratic, elusive, and enigmatic utterances.

The role of the poet's ongoing intimate dialogue with his family became ever more important as the conditions for keeping it alive deteriorated progressively during the last two and a half decades of his life. The Great Terror in the Soviet Union of the late 1930s, the flight of Pasternak's parents and sisters from Nazi Germany to Great Britain, his mother's death coinciding with the outbreak of the Second World War, and his father's death just after the war's end, then a new wave of mass persecutions in the USSR, and the Soviet government's determination to eradicate the last vestiges of intellectual independence during the latter years of Stalin's rule—all this led to interruptions and prolonged suspensions of the family's correspondence. Pasternak's composition of his magnum opus, the novel *Doctor Zhivago*, was in some ways a substitute for his earlier exchanges of thoughts and ideas with family and friends in Russia and abroad. During these tragic years, this notoriously hermetic poet wrote the work that still remains, decades after its first appearance in the West in 1957, one of the most authentic and penetrating accounts of Russian life and human sufferings in the turbulent era of revolutions and wars. The dramatic circumstances of its publication, with the award of the Nobel Prize and the unprecedented international political storm that followed, make it a crucial episode of the Cold War era. The present book affords a better understanding and appreciation of these tragic events.

The complete edition of Boris Pasternak's correspondence with his parents and sisters from 1921 to 1960, annotated by the poet's son and daughter-in-law Evgeni and Elena Pasternak, first appeared in 1998 in the series Stanford Slavic Studies. It included many letters from the extensive Pasternak family collection housed in the Hoover Institution Archives. An abridged German-language version was published by S. Fischer Verlag in 2000. Now this important selection becomes accessible to English-speaking readers for the first time, together with revised annotations. It is symbolic that the difficult task of rendering Pasternak's epistolary prose into English has been taken up this time and superbly implemented by yet another member of the Pasternak family—Lydia Pasternak's son Nicolas Pasternak Slater. As a teenager at Oxford, he witnessed the storm around the Nobel Prize award. Every word, every phrase in his uncle's letters is imbued for him with double significance: on the one hand scholarly and historic, and on the other, deeply personal and intimate, reflecting the prevailing reaction to these events in the circle of the poet's close relatives living abroad. This edition will serve for years to come as a most authoritative, indispensable introduction and guide to the great poet's life and work.

INTRODUCTION

by Nicolas Pasternak Slater

The letters in this collection were written by Boris Pasternak to his parents Leonid and Rosalia, and his sisters Josephine and Lydia, between 1921 and his death in 1960. Josephine was the first to leave Moscow for Berlin to study philosophy, soon to be followed by Leonid, Rosalia and Lydia. Boris and his brother Alexander chose to remain in Moscow. The parents intended to move temporarily to Germany for medical treatment, but all four also needed to recover from the privations of years of war, revolution and famine. Leonid, Rosalia and Josephine never saw Russia again.

These letters reflect the events of Boris's life over these 39 years. They are, above all, family letters. A number of threads run through them. Foremost is Boris's unstinting admiration for his parents and their artistic gifts, which provides a running continuo to a correspondence full of family news, reflections on Boris's work and current events, interrupted here and there by emotional storms, hard words and reconciliations. Boris is the stormy one—his father (and it is usually his father who writes back) radiates an atmosphere of cool, loving detachment, often with a marked tinge of irony.

The strains in Boris's first marriage are apparent almost from the start. He married Zhenia in 1922, and in 1926, when their son Zhenichka was three, mother and son travelled to Berlin to visit Boris's parents and to sort out the marital relationship at a calming remove. Boris became frantic with frustration and anxiety at his wife's refusal to reply to his letters, until Josephine succeeded in restoring a dialogue between them. Four years later the marriage was irrevocably breaking down, with a new love on the horizon; the first inkling his parents received was a succession of cryptic letters expressing both ecstatic joy and optimism, and an urgent desire for Zhenia and their son to go to Germany again. No doubt life for Boris was too complicated with his wife and son so close to him at this time; perhaps he also cherished a naïve hope that Zhenia might manage to settle in Germany, in better circumstances than she could hope for at home.

Boris describes his second wife, Zina, in terms presaging the accounts of Lara in *Doctor Zhivago*; he writes of her beauty, her upbringing in impoverished and morally corrupt surroundings, her elderly seducer, and later his own sense of fulfilment when they share a simple, secluded life together. This time he does not trouble his parents with accounts of their later marital stresses, and when, many years later, in 1957, he introduces his mistress Olga Ivinskaya, it is almost without explanation to his family abroad, except to stress the need for discretion in their correspondence so as not to wound Zina.

Events in the Soviet Union make their mark throughout the correspondence, although with tightening repression the language has to change. In the 1920s Boris describes the housing crisis quite openly, but later on, the forced collectivisation, the savage persecution of the peasantry and the famine of the 1930s were far too dangerous to discuss so clearly, and while fully aware of the epic significance of the current events in the countryside, he dares say little about it. Later on, the arrests of close friends and relatives are alluded to in code—the imprisonment (or 'confinement') of Boris's cousin Sasha Freidenberg is cryptically referred to as 'Sashka Konfaind', as though it were the name of some exotic foreigner, and the arrest of the family friend Juvenal Mitrofanovich Slavinsky is hidden in a flourish of word-play and oblique historical allusions. The execution of the young writer Vladimir Sillov is hauntingly alluded to—'he died from the same illness as the late Liza's first husband', a phrase the parents could not fail to understand. 'He thought too much', Boris continues, 'which sometimes leads to that form of meningitis'. Terror and censorship in Germany, too, raised further barriers: the reader learns to recognise improvised codes like Boris's mention of 'your landlady's sickness' to signify the German political situation, or Leonid's proposal to move to 'Dresden', to avoid naming Leningrad.

On several occasions misunderstandings arose which threatened to put all their lives at risk. During the thirties, the Pasternak parents continually urged Boris to visit them in Germany, serenely unaware not only of how unthinkable this was for him or anyone in the Soviet Union, but also of how dangerous it was for him that they should even suggest it. Having relatives abroad, let alone contacting them, could be fatal for ordinary people in Stalin's Russia. All Boris could do was to fob his parents off with indistinct evasions. Later, when life in Nazi Germany became intolerable, the parents thought of returning to the Soviet Union, hoping also to arrange an exhibition of Leonid's paintings in Moscow. Boris now had the impossible task of expressing delight at the prospect of reunion, and welcoming his parents to come and live with him, while simultaneously persuading them, as tactfully as he could and in terms impenetrable to the censors, that an exhibition was out of the question, and that it would be mortally dangerous for them to come back. Leonid's art was no longer in tune with the Soviet cultural climate. There is a poignant irony in the way that this close-knit family, in their long separation, was condemned to endless circumlocutions, half-truths and silences.

Common humanity, no doubt, and consideration for his parents' peace of mind also restrained Boris from recounting the horrors he was living through. In his pain and frustration at the impossibility of describing his life, he is reduced to such remarks as 'it would take too long to tell', 'it's difficult to explain to you at a distance'. Yet throughout this long period of self-censorship, both parents and son somehow succeeded in keeping their communication real and alive, until it finally dwindled into the war years' sad, attenuated succession of telegrams. When the war ended and a long letter could be smuggled through, he burst out with 'If only you knew everything!!!! I can't go on, I begin to howl.'

The war began and ended with the deaths of Boris's parents, his mother in 1939 and his father in 1945. After the briefest exchanges of news in 1945–1946, the Iron Curtain descended on Stalin's new terror. So the renewal of contact in 1956, now between Boris and his sisters, breathes indescribable relief and joy — 'a festival', as Boris says. The letters of these final four years are a mutual rediscovery, enriched by Boris's new writing (including the novel *Doctor Zhivago*), Josephine's and Lydia's poetry and Lydia's translations of Boris's poems. Both sisters were astonished at Boris's uncompromising independence of spirit. It is sad to see the initial delight in their new intimacy fall victim yet again to repression. 'Things have changed in the old direction', Boris writes; and once more both sides have to watch their words.

———

TRANSLATING THESE LETTERS has been a moving and evocative experience for me. My own memories go back to wartime, when I sometimes heard subdued conversations between my mother, Lydia, and my aunt Josephine, full of anxiety both about the fighting on the Continent, and about the family in Russia, far away and beyond reach. Everyone's excitement at the end of the war in 1945 was heightened by the first real news from Moscow to reach us for years. Miraculously, the whole family there had survived. My mother (who had brought us up to speak Russian) helped my brother and me to write to Uncle Borya and Uncle Shura. In the correspondence published here Boris refers to these letters that I remember writing.

Then there was nothing again for many years, save for the Russian children's books our uncles had sent us — books that brought home to us that Russia and the Russian language weren't just an aberration of our own family and a few

Russian-speaking friends, but a real world with people and families and story-books, far away and dangerous perhaps, but a world that we might one day encounter.

And in 1956, when I was eighteen and had just left school, it suddenly all came alive. With the onset of Khrushchev's 'thaw', letters arrived from Boris and the rest of the family in Moscow, were passed from hand to hand among us, and read over the telephone to many friends.

In one of his first letters at this time, Boris enclosed a couple of photographs of himself. 'As you can see', he wrote, 'I'm still the same beauty from the Zoo that I always was'. These photographs were a revelation—neither of his sisters had any idea what he looked like now. I had always known him as the exotic-looking dark-haired young man so often drawn and painted by his father, in pictures that I saw every day on our walls—and here was a rugged old man with grizzled hair, seemingly aged by 35 years overnight. My mother replied: 'You're not at all a "beauty from the Zoo", it's an entirely different face, tormented by illness, the face of a man for whom one feels such terrible pity that it breaks your heart to look at it.' Perhaps Boris was surprised to see our photographs too—the last he had seen were also ten years out of date. He complimented us children on how unlike the Pasternaks we looked, writing (in English): 'As a non-admirer of domestic tradition, inherited nature, family likenesses etc., I was glad not to find its despotic traces in these delighted smiling figures'.

At the same time as Boris's first postcard of this year, the full typescript of his new novel arrived in Oxford. My mother mentions this very discreetly on a postcard to him: 'I'm not in a position to write you a sensible, informative let-ter—we've just returned from the seaside and I haven't had time to read almost anything yet . . . Yesterday we went to visit Katkov, who told us lots of interesting things about his trip to Moscow . . . ' The 'interesting things' included a big parcel containing two bound volumes of typewritten foolscap—the typescript of *Doctor Zhivago*. The pages were faint and difficult to read, because the typist had had to make half-a-dozen carbon copies at once. We still have these volumes, which were seized on and read over the course of several days, first by Lydia, then by Josephine. When they had finished, I too started on them, but I was a slow reader in Russian and the books disappeared. They were needed by the translator.

The dramatic events of 1956–1960, with the publication of *Doctor Zhivago*, the Nobel Prize scandal, and the relentless persecution of Boris by the authorities, weighed heavily on all our lives in Oxford. The close contact we seemed to have re-established turned out to be illusory; there were so many things Boris—or his sisters—could not write, for fear of endangering him. I myself was conscious of yet another barrier—the fact that towards the end of his life he usually wrote in English, concealing his true person (so it seemed) behind an ill-fitting linguistic mask. The constant mutual yearning for genuine contact between him and his sisters was something palpable.

When Boris lay dying, he pleaded for my mother to come to his death-bed. Travel to the Soviet Union in those days was an extreme rarity, except for diplomats; for post-revolutionary émigrés it was virtually unheard-of. Boris's outcast status, blockaded in his home and barred most visitors, made matters worse. Lydia spent an agonising week waiting at the Soviet Embassy; it was typical of the time that her visa was only granted following Boris's death.

TRANSLATOR'S NOTE

This correspondence between Boris Pasternak, his parents and his two sisters has appeared in the original Russian in two editions: Boris Pasternak, *Pis'ma k Roditelyam i Syostram*, Stanford Slavic Studies, 1998, and Boris Pasternak, *Pis'ma k Roditelyam i Syostram*, Novoye Literaturnoye Obozreniye, Moscow, 2004. The Stanford edition covers the years 1921–1960, while the later Moscow edition is more extensive, covering 1907–1960. The Moscow edition aims as far as possible at completeness, though of course many letters have been lost. The present English translation is based on the Moscow edition, but is limited to the years 1921–1960, the years of the long and continuous separation of Boris from this part of his family.

The correspondence has also appeared in German translation, as Boris Pasternak, *Eine Brücke aus Papier—Die Familienkorrespondenz 1921–1960*, translated by Gabriele Leupold; S. Fischer-Verlag, Frankfurt am Main, 2000.

Both the Stanford and Moscow editions were prepared and edited by Evgeni and Elena Pasternak, Boris's son and daughter-in-law. In addition to an introduction and footnotes, they supplied copious explanatory and contextual material to accompany the letters. This material was also translated and used in the German edition. In the present English edition, I have (with Evgeni and Elena Pasternak's permission) freely adapted, altered and selected from this explanatory material, and I take full responsibility for the resulting text. I gratefully acknowledge my enormous debt to the Pasternaks for allowing me to use their work.

The present volume represents a selection of the letters written during the period in question. In making the selection, I have chosen (for understandable reasons) to slant the balance towards letters written by Boris, at the expense of those from his family. However, enough of the letters written by his father Leonid have been included to give the reader an idea of the personality of this charming and practical-minded man. Where only part of a letter is reproduced, the fact is indicated by an omission mark, '[...].'

The approach to personal names in this translation has been pragmatic rather than consistent, aiming for easy acceptability by an English-speaking reader.

Thus Russian names which have near-exact English equivalents (such as 'Aleksandr'/'Alexander' or 'Rozaliya'/'Rosalia') have been rendered with their English spellings. Where an equivalent is less exact (e.g., 'Elizaveta'/'Elizabeth'), the Russian form has been kept. The name 'Josephine' (Pasternak) is an exception — she lived most of her life in England, where she was known as 'Josephine', and I have kept this form in preference to 'Zhosefina' throughout the book. The same applies to her husband Frederick Pasternak, who had three alternative formal forenames: 'Friedrich' in Austria where he was born, 'Fyodor' (equivalent to 'Theodore') in Russia, and 'Frederick' in England where he lived for 38 years and where I knew him. Again, I have called him 'Frederick' throughout.

Many of the family are referred to by a variety of nicknames, e.g. Josephine is 'Zhonia', 'Zhoniura', 'Zhoniurochka', Lydia is 'Lida', 'Lidok', Frederick is 'Fedia', and so forth. I have rendered these nicknames in the form used by the writer on each occasion. Spellings have again been chosen with an eye to acceptability rather than consistency. Nicknames are cited in the Index.

An important exception to the above principle relates to Boris's wife Evgenia and their son Evgeni. Both were regularly known as 'Zhenia' and either person's name could be changed to a diminutive. To avoid confusion for the reader, Evgenia's name is consistently rendered as 'Zhenia' (Boris's usual name for her), and their son's name as either 'Zhenichka' or some other diminutive, but never as 'Zhenia' — no matter what form was used by the letter-writer.

Where the letter-writer refers to a person by initials only, the reference is clarified by including the rest of the name as a clearly indicated editorial interpolation.

The letters are normally presented in chronological order, unless (where letters have crossed) such an arrangement could have introduced confusion. Undated letters have been given a conjectural date in brackets. Many of the letters and postcards were hastily composed, and often written in a tiny, cramped hand, so that copying their original layouts would have been impracticable; accordingly the presentation of the letters in this volume is largely standardised. Punctuation and paragraph breaks have been chosen so as to make the text as clear as possible. Conventional British spelling and vocabulary have been used in the translation, but letters written by Boris Pasternak in English (each separately identified as such) have been reproduced as he wrote them, with no attempt at correction.

ACKNOWLEDGMENTS

In addition to the copious and essential background material supplied by Evgeni and Elena Pasternak to which I refer in the Translator's Note, I am very grateful to Lazar Fleishman and Ann Pasternak Slater for providing invaluable further information and advice, and for reading and offering pertinent comments on the whole text of this book. I would like to express my heartfelt appreciation and gratitude to Richard Sousa, Marshall Blanchard, Jennifer Presley, Linda Bernard, Lora Soroka, and Jennifer Navarrette, all of the Hoover Institution, and to my outstanding copy-editor Janet Gardiner. My wife Maya Slater provided excellent assistance at every stage, well beyond her duties as Editor of this volume.

—Nicolas Pasternak Slater

GENEALOGICAL CHARTS

1. Boris's Antecedents

						Isidor Kaufman	Berta		Osip
Osip Pasternak	Lia								
Alexander (Indidia)		Mikhail Freidenberg	Anna (Asya)	Rosalia (Rosa)	Leonid	Rosalia		Klara (Klavdia)	
			Alexander (Sashka)	Olga (Olya)		Boris (Borya)	Alexander (Shura)	Josephine (Zhonia)	Lydia (Lida)

2. Boris and the Younger Generation

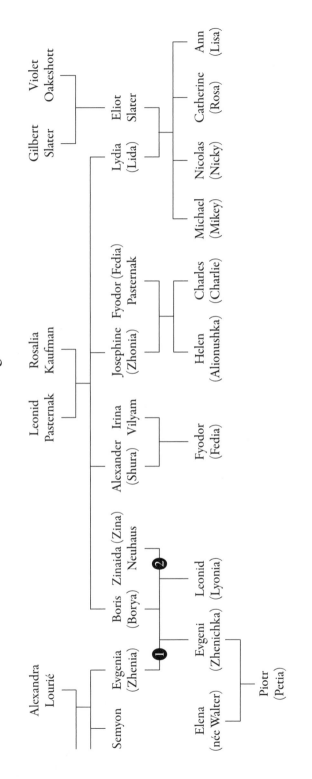

3. Pasternak and Neuhaus

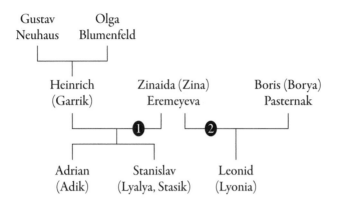

Gustav Neuhaus — Olga Blumenfeld

Heinrich (Garrik)   Zinaida (Zina) Eremeyeva   Boris (Borya) Pasternak

Adrian (Adik)   Stanislav (Lyalya, Stasik)   Leonid (Lyonia)

BORIS PASTERNAK

FAMILY CORRESPONDENCE,
1921–1960

CHAPTER ONE
1921–1925

Preparations for the journey to Germany occupied Leonid Pasternak, his wife and daughters throughout the early months of 1921. An ophthalmologist had warned Leonid that he needed surgery for a cataract, whose progression threatened his work.

Josephine left first, on 27 June 1921, to submit her application to Berlin University in good time to begin her studies in the autumn. Boris had introduced her to his and Mayakovsky's friend Osip Brik, who worked for the Cheka[1] and had obtained an exit visa for her. She travelled via Riga, where she stayed with her relatives the Hosiassons. In Berlin she was met by her second cousin Frederick Pasternak (Fyodor, Friedrich, Fedia), and on July 4th he telegraphed her parents in Moscow to report her safe arrival. He rented a room for her at the Pension Fasaneneck.

The events of recent years in Russia—the years of political unrest, the crushing death tolls of the First World War, the October Revolution and the Civil War that followed it, and the accompanying hardships and privations—inevitably conjured up associations with the French Revolution. In the summer of 1917 Boris started writing a verse drama about the last days of the Jacobin dictatorship, which involved him in extensive research on Parisian history and cartography. It was at this time that he first read Dickens's *A Tale of Two Cities*, which became one of his favourite books.

In this letter written to his twenty-one-year-old sister he carries on their game of associations, comparing her departure to the liberation and regeneration of Doctor Manette, the prisoner (and enforced cobbler) in Dickens's novel. Boris refers to the family's happy years living together on Myasnitskaya (1894–1911) and more recently on Volkhonka (from 1911 onwards). And he gives Josephine herself the name of Lucie Manette, the heroine of *A Tale of Two Cities*.

At the same time, brother and sister continue their discussion about the central elements of a writer's creative life. Boris's tone is reminiscent of a letter he had written from Marburg when Josephine was only twelve years old, a letter in which he expounded laws of literary prose which subsequently became an integral part of

---

1. The State security organisation.

his own aesthetic credo. Both Boris and Josephine shared a pleasure in subjective, introspective, rather than factual, correspondence.

Boris Pasternak to Josephine Pasternak

21 July 1921. Moscow.

My dear Zhonyurochka!

Don't be upset that I haven't written you a single letter. I did write, but I ventured too deep, and—well, in a word, there was blood all over the page. But your letters have been simply wonderful—all of them so far written from railway carriages. As to their charm, see below; but I must tell you that the only letters to arrive were those which (for lack of a more reliable route, as you very reasonably thought) you posted willy-nilly in a letterbox. There were no consulates out there at New Jerusalem or Verzhbolovo,[2] so you simply entrusted the letters to the post; and would you believe it, the post is being touchingly efficient. In fact, every detail to do with your departure and crossing is purifyingly and classically touching.

So, let me inform you that the letter and package that you handed to the train-conductor at Riga never reached us. We looked out for the conductor in a desultory way and didn't find him; and when I thought harder about you, I avoided hunting for him at all. He's tied up with the dawn of your first journey, and remains as dear and kind as he seemed to you in those first few days of your trip, despite his very pardonable and understandable lapse. The parcel perished because of its filling—the stuffing, no doubt of chocolate, that filled this cake otherwise composed of books and printed matter. Well, we'll forgive him his light fingers and sweet tooth.

Eglit[3] remembers you very well and sends his regards, and asked me to tell you that if you should want to send anything, with the mail being unreliable (and they wouldn't accept it anyway), you should send it to the Commissariat of Foreign Affairs, addressed to him for forwarding to us (write a note on the address). I've given him our telephone number, and if anything arrives he'll ring us. But letters you should send by registered post, the simple and reliable way. His name is Robert Andreyevich. He is very, very kind. *A propos des voisins*: if

---

2. Novy Ierusalim (New Jerusalem) would have been the first stop on Josephine's rail journey from Moscow to Riga. Verzhbolovo was the frontier post.

3. R.A. Eglit was an official in the Commissariat of Foreign Affairs who helped Josephine with her travel arrangements.

you want to send anything, then send books; but don't spend money, and, my dearest, don't burden your compassionate little heart. Our life here has unexpectedly eased up a bit. Materially speaking. Though one can't tell how long that will last.

But your letters are amazing. On the day you left, Lucie, at the barrier on the Vindava platform, I realised that the element of the miraculous is washed by a sea of epically agitated tenderness; that this sea is bottomless, not disturbing; almost wordless, not deafening; that the miracle lisps haltingly, without proclaiming or prophesying; that the miracle was watching from the hillocks as your train sped past; that it met you and sheltered you at Riga—and that every line you wrote was miraculous, since it conveyed that element in which you were bathed, and still are. If you think you owe any apologies, you're cruelly deluded, when you can see for yourself how these vapours of miraculousness overshadow everything else—deeds and facts, the Bashkirovs and pure reason. There's no room for any of that here, nor for apologies either.

Take Bashkirov[4], for example. I couldn't care less whether you fulfilled my errand (let's call it that) well or badly. And if I'm interested in how you did it, then it's only because on your travels, you Dickensian comet, you crossed the horizon of this person for an hour, or for ten minutes; and that you were seen on Nikolaevskaya, you and the comet-tail of your miracles, the first ones in our lives.

The errand, you say? But at the time I entrusted you with it, a day earlier, could I have known that on the next day you would be reminding us of life, and Mama of health?—and the day after, of nature, and the following day, of the non-fictitiousness of the recent war, and the real possibility of peace, and after that, of the feasibility of the best fantasies; and from start to finish, of the existence of facts as miracles in principle, if we approach them with faith, without brushing aside the things and people that surround them. And you did all that, you miracle-worker.

Do you remember, Lucie (à propos of your journey from town to town) that passage where Manette, as he sits in the stagecoach, again and again bursts out with the words 'recalled, recalled to life'?

Surely it's just this atmosphere of miraculous tenderness (unblocked ears, unrationed imagination and compassion), *de qua res agitur* for you and me. See how

---

4. K.A. Bashkirov worked at the Soviet Embassy in Riga and had opened a publishing house on Nikolaevskaya Street. Boris was trying to place his collection *My Sister, Life* with him, and had asked Josephine to contact him. (The planned publication never came to fruition.)

this *Tale*, with its wonderful spirit, echoes everything you have experienced—and now (most importantly of all) you've made us experience it too. Each of us, in his own way, is a Doctor Manette. Papa and I most of all. Passive and majestic in his ignorance of his own suffering; majestic in his helpless sterility: for one of us, the hammer tapping at the shoe is a brush painting a Sovportrait; for the other—a pen writing a Sovpoem. Mama and Shura, in their own way, are Manettes too. Lida, it seems, has been spared because of her youth.

What do I mean by this? Letting a habit become mechanical; distorting one's profession or family role to an almost insane degree; thinking but saying nothing when a fact is out of sight, letting it become no more than an empty word, while remaining heartlessly deaf to its meaning. Didn't we know what was written on the edges of those pages, and what it really meant? And now, here you are, taking this evil hammer out of our hands, and carrying our familiar cobbler's last out of the door.

It didn't happen all at once. It took a week, and another week, for your psychiatric role to work. Laughter came back to me. Now, once again, I know that there are hurdles which exist so that one can glance back after clearing them, and marvel at how low they are. It's you who bring me money and spill it out for me.

If the old cobbler-woman isn't overcome by her evil craving for the hammer, then Mama will smile more than she ever did on Volkhonka or Myasnitskaya Street. If the old cobbler's craving for his last doesn't lead him to value 'worldly wisdom' and 'common sense' higher than he has recently done, then the fearsome law of mortal peril which governed all his plans and actions will give place to the laws of a living faith in life—life which you yourself have shown to be so easy, beautiful and trustworthy. Oh my dear one, I knew all this once, and I gave the miracle a name. It's just what is meant by 'my sister life'.

And for God's sake don't adopt, *per usum epistolarem*, a dry and informative style; don't turn traitor in your tone, in the name of communicating facts and conveying information, until the vapours of miraculousness which you and your lines breathe have condensed and merged, drop by drop, with the stream of liquid facts, whose true origins they share. Very soon the time will come when your direct and precise return home from some university office, along a street which has lost the intimacy of novelty, or the planning of German affairs for the German tomorrow, will move the sphere of miraculousness even into this objective plane; and then prices, and the Berlin way of life, and the new post-war alignments, will be related by you as an actor, not an observer, that is, vaporously, preserving that spiritual balance which so impresses me in your communications.

It's possible to be too clever, at the expense of content. Schematism. Diaries in the spirit of . . . Amiel, as it were.[5] Whole stacks of emotional sauce-boats from Garrach's—profound and most deep soup-plates, gleaming in their porcelain whiteness and—waiting to be filled, to warm up their icy and empty and meaningless meaning.[6] All this is contemptible. It's all wrong. But your 'groundlessness' and 'gaseousness'—as you perceive it—is material, chemical; it gives us, in a spiritually dissolved form, the basic composition of reality, which you don't speak about directly; and empowers us to act on what you have sent us, and to reconstitute matter. And, as I have said, we develop a taste for railway lines, an eye for Latvia, ears for Berlin. Meanwhile, why write to us about factual things, when the two reports that you probably gave at the Hosiassons' and then at the Rosenfelds',[7] and to Fedia—aren't these just pages of the same *Tale* set on its feet, isn't this just the same novel? And the background to your stories, at this stage of novelty—these rooms full of gaping mouths and objects, these windows full of murmuring cities and lives—are these facts interesting for us—aren't they rather just a temporary embellishment for your accounts of what you, and we with you, have lived through? For the time being, they too are vapour, vapour, vapour.

So please, don't be afraid of being subjective: at present, that's the only objectivity for us and you. By preserving that very spiritual symmetry that you have shown, you will become truly objective, when objectivity becomes your own property and you are not obliged to borrow it. The present tense used in the letter relates to the time of your arrival in Berlin. For you, it's already long obsolete. And by now you have probably already started distilling facts, with that objectivity which, for me, still lies in the future tense. If so, then write about that too. If so, then you too will enjoy talking about it, because it too ('the trams in Berlin, my dear ones . . . ', or 'as regards the universities . . . ', or 'people here view Russia . . .') will be a confession.

When I lived in Tikhie Gory,[8] it irritated me to hear anything that didn't relate to the health of Volkhonka, or our friends, or what Papa was working on and how your studies were going. My letter is bound to upset you, no matter

5. Henri Frédéric Amiel was a Swiss writer known for his epigrammatic diary.
6. Boris is comparing the fatuity of schematic diary entries to the elegant but empty soup-plates in the Garrach brothers' fancy china shop on Kuznetsky Bridge, contrasting it with the emotional subjectivity which he felt essential in letter-writing.
7. The Rosenfelds were close friends of Boris's parents, then living in Berlin.
8. In the Urals, where Boris spent the early war years working at a chemical factory. He returned to Moscow in March 1917.

how you deceive yourself and me. Instead of bread, I'm giving you literature. It's simply become a rule in cases like this that the prose of family communications, the chewing-over of chewed-up everyday life, is regarded as worth its weight in gold. When you're living apart, that's exactly what you want to chew. But I've allowed myself to upset you, so that this rule shouldn't lead you astray; so that you shouldn't submit to it. It has its exceptions. You're one of them. Write freely, little ladybird, about how you crawl about, or what's crawling around in your little head. I wanted to write Fedia a good long letter. My dear Fedia, I smother you in embraces. Isn't this whole story just like Hamsun's mysteries?[9]

And another thing, Zhonia. I think that what I've said today expresses what we all feel. I'll give the others my letter to read. This is the best thing I could say to you, and it has been said in the very worst way, hurriedly and without pausing— and of course you understand that it's a subject for a treatise. Soon I'll write to you about myself and them. But this topic (Lucie, and the 'recall to life') had to be dealt with.

Your very loving
Borya

Once in Berlin, Josephine succeeded in getting German visas for her parents. With the support of Lunacharsky, the People's Commissar for Education, Leonid and Rosalia Pasternak and their eighteen-year-old daughter Lydia were granted permission to travel to Germany. They left Moscow on 13 September 1921, and reached Berlin three days later.

Josephine rented them rooms in the Pension Fasaneneck where she herself was staying. Both sisters entered the university, but high fees obliged Lydia to abandon her medical vocation, and take up biochemistry. Leonid sought out the congenial company of other Russian-Jewish émigrés. An ophthalmic examination showed no urgent need for surgery, although it would eventually be inevitable. He set about re-establishing himself in the artistic world of Berlin, arranging exhibitions of the works he had brought with him from Russia, learning the art of lithography and dry-point, and publishing both a monograph of his own work and a study of Rembrandt.

There was no news from Boris for a month. It was not until 24 October that two letters from him arrived, and his father replied at once.

9. Knut Hamsun, a Norwegian novelist and Nobel Prize-winner (1920). He is regarded as a pioneer of the psychological novel.

Leonid Pasternak to Boris and Alexander Pasternak

Berlin, 24 October 1921.

My dear boys!

At last, at last, at last! Hurrah! At last, dear Boryusha, you've finally given birth—and what a splendid offspring it is. A splendid letter—wonderful! I had been consoling Mama—'I promise you, they're fine! You know Borya—he's probably written us four volumes, and then burned them; no doubt he's just finishing off a new *Verlag*, and is on volume 3. Any day now we'll get two or three letters from him, you'll see.' I was just about to send off this fat letter when the postman knocked, bent under the weight of the mail to me: '*Gnädiger Herr, öffnen Sie bitte schneller—es ist mir schwer, dieses Geschäft weiter noch zu tragen!*[10] Poor man—I opened the door, and oh joy! A whole mass of registered letters [. . .]

Unfortunately Boris's letters referred to here have not survived. His father in Berlin was always on the look-out for any newspaper reports reflecting Boris's growing fame. Ilya Ehrenburg helped him to send Boris cuttings about potential publishers.[11] One of them, Z.I. Grzhebin, was transferring his publishing house from Soviet Russia to Berlin, and preparing to publish Boris's *My Sister, Life*.

Leonid Pasternak to Boris Pasternak, undated

[. . .] Yes—I must say that when you wrote that Annenkov[12] (I don't know him) had done your portrait and that you didn't like it, and were convinced—as I am—that it's not a good likeness, of course I was upset to think that I'd see your distorted image. . . . Now you see, Borya—I always wanted to draw you and you always refused and got cross, and never had any time, or got out of it somehow. If the portrait had been a good likeness and well done, I should have been very pleased, but I'm convinced it isn't—otherwise I should have heard of this man.

10. 'Please open up quickly, sir—it's difficult for me to go on carrying all this stuff!'

11. Ilya Ehrenburg was a prolific novelist and journalist who became a mouthpiece of the régime under Stalin but later played a prominent part in cultural liberalisation, first through his novel *The Thaw* (1954) which angered the official intelligentsia, and later with his memoirs *People, Years, Life* (1960–1965).

12. Yuri Annenkov, a young Soviet artist whose portrait of Boris appeared in the first edition of *My Sister, Life* (Boris Pasternak, *Sestra moya zhizn'*, Moscow: Grzhebin, 1921; second edition, Berlin: Grzhebin, 1923). Leonid Pasternak's lithograph (as described in this letter) was published in a later collection.

So that's enough about that now. If you're willing to write to Grzhebin, and if I see him, perhaps I could do a lithograph of your face for him from the 'Congratulations' picture, or the Merreküll one; I've got a very good drawing of you here—or one from a separate study for the 'Congratulations'. But only if that suits you and you want me to do it. If Grzhebin is going to be printing soon, I should like to do this. Let me know what you think.

Only one of Boris's letters from the autumn of 1921 has survived. It was written to his sisters Lydia and Josephine in response to Josephine's description of her new life in Berlin, and Lydia's account of an expedition with their brother Shura the previous year to the village of Cheryomushki, near Moscow, to collect potatoes. The sisters' ceremonial enrolment at the university reminded Boris of the traditional matriculation ceremony when he entered Marburg university in the summer of 1912.

Boris Pasternak to his sisters

23 November [1921. Moscow.]

O, Lidok!

I read your wonderful letter to Shura, where you wrote about everything including the lecture at the Institute of Pharmacology outside town. How lucky Papa and Mama are to have such inspired—no, more than that—consummately right, deafeningly first-class daughters! How near to me it all seems, when you list all the things that can be achieved by an explosive, blazing soul, evaporating, tearing upward and outward, towards God and expressiveness.

Well done, you dear, dear girl. You are so talented! And Zhonia! Her pages may be less enviable for their concrete artistry, but that's because she is projected, like a torpedo, along an elastic, integral, resilient trajectory, out beyond all the barriers of attempts, performances, trial-runs and efforts, into the sphere of consummate, self-crystallising perfection. All that's left for such a person to do is take off and fly; and, while flying, to instruct others, verbally or just by her unspoken example. Just now I remembered her first letters from her journey, and I have to say: no, she is crazier and bolder in the way she expresses herself, she alone is an expressionist, and that—trust my experience—is harder and more excruciating than your way. But—what you wrote the other day, about Cheryomushki! or what you've just written, about the academic winter in Berlin!

The words you let slip about my dissatisfaction with you all are fair enough; but you base your accusations on my first letters, and your grounds are as shaky as the letters themselves. It seemed to me that there was a specific chance for you all, in exactly the things which you identified in such a light and inspired way, in passing, in today's letter. And I was afraid that you would miss this opportunity—that the accumulated strata of four years' stagnation (the mathematics of rye rationing, the rationalism of ration-cards, the romanticism of unpredictable baths and water-mains)—all these contradictory strata, this calamitous monotony, would rise up between you, your youth and your gifts—your personal talents and your potential which you are going to university to develop. I was afraid that (1) this recent past would obscure the brilliance of the things which charged your letter with electricity; or (2) it would distort your views of the family, your brothers, your parents, the Volkhonka and the Fasaneneck. I was afraid that the two of you might draw comfort from this inexhaustible store of familiarity, and come to live by it, forgetting all those other things you ought to be gathering up in armfuls outside the inexhaustible family world—in your airy hovering as you rush around Berlin; in the university where you became so enviably flustered, I expect, when your hand was shaken. Those dear, delightful traditions *des akademischen Brauchs*.[13] It was the same when I was there. Heel-clicking and hand-shaking at matriculation, etc. etc. Will anyone really dare to tell you that all that is un-emancipated and ridiculous? And—like the organ in the Middle Ages—what a variety of ways of moving through a modern town! Overground, underground, the abrupt confluence and dispersal of these light-pulsating flights across colourful hours: misty, across-and-along-the-riverbank, heaped-coal-by-the-Hauptbahnhof, weepingly-snowy, beyond Bellevue!

This was begun about a week ago. But now: open your mouths. In a moment there's going to be—an explosion. In a moment there'll be a terrible explosion of gratitude! O martyrs, O heroines! O trousers, gaiters, O Keller and Rabindranath! O, my darlings![14]

And now: close your mouths and tuck up your trousers and skirts. In a moment there'll be a Flood. In a moment there will be a flood of emotion and astonishment!

Everything you write is marvellous, little Zhoniarhinoceros, oh no, oh my God, of course, not a rhino, no, Zhonechka, Zhonechka! Everything you write about Diushen[15] is marvellous, I completely understand, but you're wrong to think

13. 'Of academic usage'.
14. Josephine had sent Boris a parcel of books including an edition of the correspondence between Paul Heyse and Gottfried Keller, and works by Romain Rolland and Rabindranath Tagore.
15. Boris is referring to the pamphlet by Boris V. Diushen entitled 'Einstein's Theory of Relativity' (Berlin, 1921). Josephine had become fascinated with this subject when she arrived in Berlin.

that I am so much involved in concrete existence. You don't know me at all, any of you. Not only was I once just like you: there was a time when I strayed too far along that—inevitable—lyrico-ethical path. God forbid you go the same way— it's harmful and dangerous. Everything you went through, and your description of it, all these things are me myself; only you put it more expressively, crisply and successfully. Your letter about mediaeval perspective and Dante is a massive, spiritually mature and real truth. When I told Bobrov[16] about it, he thought I had invented it. About five days before your letter came, we had been talking about the same thing, but we were only scrabbling about, while you put it all crisply, exhaustively, in high relief. Silly children—if only you knew how hard I used to learn to 'behave' so that nothing should be apparent! And there you go saying 'he's different, he's this . . . he's that . . . '. Since when?

But these aren't reproaches or objections. Where could you turn to, if you were to start writing to me too? Honestly, I mean what I say. By all means, don't write.[17] As for the Frishmans, they really are dear, kind people.[18]

This letter has been lying around for over 10 days.

The correspondence breaks off through 1922–1923, partly because Boris and his young wife Evgenia (Zhenia) Lourié visited Berlin shortly after their wedding in February 1922, staying at the Pension Fasaneneck with the rest of the family. After their departure in March 1923, Boris never saw his parents again.

In September 1923 Boris and Evgenia had a son, named Evgeny after his mother. The shared name (and shared nickname—Zhenia) can cause confusion in this correspondence, and sometimes the names used are standardised for clarity in the translation.

Josephine married her cousin Frederick (Fedia) Pasternak in April 1924. He was a wealthy financier working with the Süddeutsche Bank and 20 years her senior. Both

16. Sergei Bobrov was a close friend of Boris's and the leader of the Tsentrifuga literary group to which Boris belonged for a time.

17. This passage must refer to some observation made by Josephine in her letter to Boris, which has not survived.

18. The Frishman family of five had fled Poland during the First World War and settled in Moscow. They were befriended by the Pasternaks, and particularly close ties developed between the daughter, Stella, and Josephine and Lydia Pasternak. After seven years of world war, revolution, civil war and famine, the city of Moscow had become hugely overcrowded, as people poured into the capital in search of food and work. The homeless, and particularly homeless children orphaned by civil conflict and starvation, roamed the streets. Housing restrictions were draconian. Each citizen was allowed a limited and specified area of living space. The Pasternaks' apartment on Volkhonka was certain to be appropriated by the authorities to house additional families in need, and so in 1921 Boris and his brother invited the Frishmans to move into the rooms vacated by their parents and sisters—a temporary arrangement which in the event lasted until 1940.

Boris and Alexander wrote to protest against what they regarded as an unsuitable union. Their letters have not survived, but their tone can be judged from Leonid Pasternak's response in the following letter.

Leonid Pasternak to his sons and Zhenia

13 April 1924. [Berlin.]

My dear children!

We finally received your letters today, from all three of you, with your outpourings of bitterness, hidden anger and hurt, natural from such close family members who know nothing about people's destinies, crucial life choices, and so forth. No need to be a prophet to foresee these natural reactions, which you've finally and fairly poured out and no doubt feel the better for it. [...]

Not wishing to forward Boris and Zhenia's letter to the couple (now honeymooning in Vienna) 'because of its injured and angry tone ("swine", "top-hats" and the like)', Leonid went on:

Although what you wrote was undoubtedly inspired by sincere love of Josephine and her life—you suddenly saw her as a Sleeping Beauty in her tomb— shouldn't I wait before sending this letter on to her and Fedia? Won't you come to regret what you wrote in the heat of the moment, in a flood of anger, without understanding whom you were most sorry for—yourselves, or them, or her—and then you'll have to justify yourselves and apologise and all that?

Boris's next letter is written in the spirit recommended by Leonid. He now views the couple's future as a continuation of their shared family past, from the turn of the century to Frederick's departure for Berlin.

Boris Pasternak to Frederick and Josephine Pasternak

[Mid-April 1924. Moscow.]

Dear Fedia and Zhonia!

Now you too have become proper grown-ups. One of these days, when you're out, we'll come to visit you, and we'll ask the maid whether the *gnädige Frau* is in. Please instruct her to show us over the house. It'll probably be quiet, bright, with lots of flowers and a piano in the corner. Since you're both absolute angels, you won't of course be beastly to one another, as sometimes happens to Zhenia and me. So your peaceful marriage, in the warm climate, with the windows open, won't really look like two people in shackles.

What have you dreamed up then, what's the name for the direction you've taken? I mean, you'll be almost independent? And you'll travel? And everything will be just like before? And perhaps, hidden somewhere under your divan, one might find Molodi? And Prechistenka? And a Gaston with nuts?[19] How astonishing it is that for all these decades, somewhere (like a ticking clock), life has been preserved unchanged, with that melancholy tenderness that characterises our family, sometimes seeming grey like Shura—and it has preserved everything; under its imperceptible supervision everything has survived. And now you've got it all with you. And your distant, distant childhood, Myasnitskaya, Mansbach, Pichon, Varsonofyev Alley, all the summers with all their dachas, the scarlet fever, Prechistenka, the war, Ufa, the revolution, the October fighting and the trenches, the German embassy, the iron curtain of the blockade, hunger and cold, Papa in his fur-trimmed jacket, the Polish corridor.—And all this has come together again, and most of it—if not all of it—is with you, Fedia and Zhonia. And Papa and Mama are with you, and their worlds (that's where the all-preserving tenderness has been kept warm), and Lida, and soon Shura will be there too, and it's no accident that I won't.

Alas, nothing has preserved me, and I shall never get back all that I have given away. Music has gone for good. There may still be poetry ('Luvers'),[20] but even that shouldn't be so, because I have to exist, and what our times demand is certainly not poetry. I'm going to have to give up verbal improvisation just as I've given up improvisation on the piano. It's sad. It's this same sadness that coloured all the long years of all-preserving tenderness; and it has fallen to me to express it in practice, in my own fate.

But don't imagine that my situation here is particularly bad, or that I'm tormented by some mirage, some imagined suffering. Andrei Bely[21] is in the same situation, and many others too; the age we live in has no time for what's called

19. Here and below, Boris recalls Josephine's childhood on Myasnitskaya Street, the Mansbach high school attended by her and Lydia on Basmannaya Street, their summer dacha at Molodi, the Prechistenka and Varsonofyev Alley where Frederick Pasternak had lived and worked, and the 'Gaston' chocolate cakes served at family celebrations. Then, during the First World War, Frederick was interned at Ufa as an enemy alien (he was an Austrian subject), and Boris visited him there. After the war Frederick worked at the German Embassy in Moscow. Eventually he departed to live in Berlin, travelling through the 'Polish Corridor', which separated East Prussia from the remainder of Germany and had been ceded to Poland by the Treaty of Versailles.

20. Boris's story 'Luvers's Childhood' was first published in 1922. It was planned as part of a longer prose work, which was never finished.

21. Andrei Bely (Boris N. Bugaev, 1880–1934) was a noted poet, novelist, and critic of the Symbolist school.

literature. With all the warmth I'm capable of, I congratulate you. I embrace you both very, very warmly, and kiss you.

I'm writing on Saturday of Holy Week. We've decorated everything, and Shura and Zhenia are laying out tablecloths and putting out kulich and paskha, eggs and ham. How silly! The kulich and paskha come from Einem's, which is now called Red October. And outside there's heavy, heavy snow. I'm almost in tears as I write.

Josephine, moved by this letter's mournful tone, wrote a letter of explanation. When she was 13, she had fallen in love with the 28-year-old Nikolai Scriabin, cousin of the composer, and since then felt herself incapable of genuine feeling. Boris sent a tear-stained copy of this letter to his wife, who was away for the summer.

In May 1924 Leonid Pasternak was invited to join a group of artists commissioned to spend six weeks working in Palestine. On his return in July, he found several letters from Boris, ill and lonely in Moscow, labouring over his translations of contemporary German revolutionary poets.

In late July Boris joined his wife at Taitsy, near Petersburg (Petrograd). He wrote to his father, describing frequent meetings with his father's sister Asya Freidenberg and her daughter Olga, and their tenderness towards his wife, whose health had suffered after the birth of their son.

In mid-August Boris's brother Alexander (Shura) left to visit his parents in Berlin. Correspondence at this time relates to the State's proposed purchase of Leonid's group portraits of noted politicians including Lenin, Trotsky, Rykov, Lutovinov and Karpov at meetings in the Kremlin between 1919 and 1921. They were bought by the Sovnarkom, transferred to the Tretyakov Gallery, and destroyed in the late 1930s when many of the subjects were arrested and shot. (Only studies and contemporary reproductions of these works have survived.) The purchase was managed by a family friend, Boris Ilyich ('Pepa') Zbarsky.[22]

In his next letter, Boris raises the problem of living space. The regulations were tightening. Leonid's studio had been partitioned by cupboards and wardrobes, and here Boris lived with his wife, their son and his nanny. The house committee demanded that the family 'consolidate' into less space, to make room for further tenants. Apart from Boris's family of four, the apartment already housed his brother

22. A distinguished biochemist who was in part responsible for embalming Lenin's body in 1924. He met Boris in the Urals in 1915 and became a great friend of the Pasternak family; his influential position enabled him to help them through many difficulties with Soviet officialdom. He was the model for the elder Lemokh brother in *A Tale* and *Spektorsky*, and for Yuri Zhivago's brother Evgraf in *Doctor Zhivago*.

Alexander; Vasily and Elizaveta Ustinova (shifted from the apartment below); and the five members of the Frishman family.

The risk was that Shura's room would be confiscated in his absence. The 'letter of protection' allocating the two brothers their living space was issued by the KUBU, the Committee for the Improvement of Living Conditions for Scholars, an organization created by Maxim Gorky to secure special conditions for the intelligentsia.[23] The ground floor of the Volkhonka house had been taken over by the Institute for People's Education, which wanted to expand into the Pasternak apartment.

This is the first letter in which Boris not only writes directly about the practical difficulties of living under the Soviet regime, but implies, obliquely and much more darkly, its ethical and aesthetic constraints, in a manner that should have been clear to his parents.

Boris Pasternak to his parents and sisters

20 September 1924. Moscow.

My dear ones,

[…]

We got a letter from Shura, Fedia and Zhonia wishing our boy a happy birthday—thank you very much for the thought. Although his birthday is the day after tomorrow, September 23rd, the Frishmans have already given him a woollen sailor-suit (far too expensive for a present, it must have cost at least 16 roubles); and the boy looks very funny, especially in the trousers with the waistcoat attached—then all he needs is a jacket to make him a comic and touching treasure. The suit is lovely and just his size. Anyway, as I expect Shura has already told you, Yulia Bentsionovna [Frishman] has been looking after us, very tactfully and much better than we deserve, and trying to do it without our noticing; she's always ready to help us—and always extremely helpful. When I was ill, she looked after me (she did the cooking, and their maid cleaned the room). From Petersburg we moved back into a clean, tidy flat, so impeccably neat that one could only dream of keeping it like that. Elizaveta Ivanovna [Ustinova] has just fallen very ill. She's been in bed for over a week with jaundice and is on a very strict diet.

---

23. Maxim Gorky was a major Russian writer, and a friend of Lenin (and later Stalin). After the Revolution he used his influence to protect intellectuals and writers. He moved to Italy in 1921, but finally returned in 1933 and became the chief exponent of Socialist Realism. Leonid Pasternak drew his portrait in 1906.

From the very first day that the Frishmans moved into our apartment, they and the Ustinovs didn't get on. They dislike and are jealous of each other, so as soon as the Ustinovs saw the first signs of friendship between us and the Frishmans, their relationship with us began to cool. I noticed that and took it on board. And since I'm very passive about this sort of thing, as soon as I observe how someone feels towards me I immediately become full of the same feelings myself. So I'm probably perpetuating this situation, without wanting to or even noticing, in that our relationship with the Ustinovs is now tinged with a degree of reserve. Actually there's no reason for it, apart from this character trait of mine.

This summer, the plan for next winter fell into place of its own accord. There's nothing special or unusual about it; the only novelty for me is that it's sober, strict and serious. As far as it relates to me, it was settled a long time ago by a number of very broad, general factors—the sort where there aren't any names, only social categories, typical or mass phenomena, etc. As for the part that concerns Zhenia, it owes a lot of its clarity and precision to Aunt Asya, who was talking with her usual passion, two evenings ago (we have been visiting her a lot) about how we have to live in a way that allows Zhenia to get better, and above all to work, so that she can sort out whether she's a human being or not, since she entered life without having time to get to know herself and discover herself fully.

The fact that it was Aunt Asya who raised the topic, and did so at this precise time, and kept coming back to it again and again, seemed very important to me, very significant somehow. There are things in one's life—even perhaps just a casual word—whose incomprehensible warmth and freshness—above anything else that you see or hear around you at the time—makes them seem like the very voice of life or truth, or that hidden current of times and things which carries us forwards, which is our fate itself, though we only realise it occasionally, and then indirectly. All our evenings at my aunt's were marked by this sense of her supreme vitality, and a sort of fineness of feeling that commands one's trust.

I've already told Papa how she singles out Zhenia from the rest of the family, and how she loves her. She has given her a bonnet (or hood) for wearing to the theatre, which she knitted herself, and a Parisian fan and a white Dutch jacket with edging and an old-fashioned high open collar, the sort everyone wore in the sixteenth century—an exact copy of the jacket worn by a rosy-cheeked peasant bride by Jordaens—perhaps you remember it. Asya bought it, or had it made, in Paris or Belgium, purposely imitating that style. The jacket is a delight to look at. Then she gave an amethyst brooch to Fenia, the servant girl who used to take little Zhenia to school at Mogilev and now works for us as the boy's nanny.

Aunt Asya took an excessively poor view of our financial state and my prospects, and I had trouble dissuading her from writing to you, and for some reason to Fedia too. I mention this just in case. If you've had a letter from her about this, please remember it isn't true: it's only motivated by her extreme solicitude and love for Zhenia, and her very fanciful ideas about me.

[...]

Well then, first of all, this winter we have to nurse Zhenia back to health. When the Levins come back, I want to take her to see Lev Grigoryevich.[24] And meanwhile we have to watch her diet. I'm afraid she's very disobedient, highlystrung and inclined to be silly. To get any bread and butter into her, you practically have to knock it in with a hammer. What will probably make everything come right is the fact that she can't let sickness and health be the central theme of her life, any more than I can. Letting it become a constant preoccupation is boring and stupid, and she'll probably try to avoid that. Next, we have to free her from her less pressing household duties. We don't make lunch at home—we go to eat at the Scholars' House, and bring home a lunch for the nanny too. She has to spend practically all day cooking for our boy anyway, but when we get some firewood in for the oven and stop having to use the primus, that cooking can all be done in one go and it won't take so long.

I'll probably start a job in a month's time. I think I'll have to work on statistics, and since I don't know anything about them I've decided to get the right books and do some studying. Without a regular salary, life would be too uneasy in a society so solidly constructed, from top to bottom, around the State, on the basis that everyone works for it and can be uniformly and constantly supervised, understood and monitored.

So—I've decided to get a job. I've noticed one thing in particular which has drawn me to this idea. For these past two years I've enjoyed almost unlimited freedom, life has been quite easy, and any outsider would say that happiness and success have smiled on me. At the same time I've written nothing—that is, I haven't been able to write. I'll leave this unexplained, though I think I understand the reasons for it. Perhaps a change in my way of life and earnings will alter matters. Or perhaps not. At all events, things can't go on like this. The secret behind this strange fact is something I'll keep to myself for the time being. But I want to tear myself away from freedom, happiness, success and certain advantages I have enjoyed, because in the present state of affairs all these words are

24. The Levins were close friends of the Pasternaks. Lev Grigoryevich Levin was a well-known physician who treated high Party officials. In 1937–1938, during the trial of Bukharin and Rykov, he was accused of Gorky's murder and was shot in 1938.

in quotation marks, and because I dream of a change in my social situation as though it were a real liberation.

As always happens in life, everything has come together from the most diverse and unexpected directions. And it's a very good thing that this wasn't brought about by outside circumstances alone—within myself, I had planned and decided it in advance. I shall have no obligations to the 'society' of here and now—except to give it my ordinary, honest labour. Everything else will be my own business, as it once used to be: it will be or it won't be, but at all events it won't concern anyone else. I shan't enjoy 'love', 'importance', or 'fame', any more than 'borrowed freedom' or 'borrowed rank'. I shall live without such repulsive borrowings, and have no truck with loan sharks of that kind.

And just as though all this had already happened, this autumn everything suddenly changed for me. An empty space formed around me, which will probably widen as time goes on. As soon as I arrived, I could see it at once—here a most devoted friend turning his back on me, there another treating me with unwonted coldness, here a mark of indifference, there the language of covert hostility, and there again an act of open enmity. And the odd thing is that this doesn't worry or trouble me at all. It doesn't disconcert me, indeed rather the opposite—it sets me even more firmly on my chosen path. Of course, I can't help sensing it, and it saddens me a bit. After all, I don't aim to blunt my own sensitivity.

It's strange arriving in Moscow after Petersburg. It's a mad, colourless, senseless, doom-laden city. Monstrous prices. In Petersburg they're on a human scale. Monstrous inconvenience. In Petersburg our baggage (8 items, 13 poods)[25] was delivered on a cart. Here that's not the custom. Here you have to provide a living for the chief porter, the carter, the clever rascal who makes sure someone else doesn't run off with half your belongings on the way, and another rascal to reward him for not being that someone else. Monstrous roads. I took my seat on the cart and no sooner had we driven out of Kalanchevskaya station than I bade a mental farewell to everything capable of being broken, everything constructed with the aid of screws, nuts, glass, or any other irrational foreign fancies. In my thoughts, I wrote off the 'Mallepost' (a child's pram that had cost me 50 roubles). I sat, bouncing up in the air, falling and flying up again as we jolted over the domed drain-covers; and as I watched the crowd trampling through dry plaster-dust and sand, I realised that Moscow was something inflicted on me at birth, my passive heritage, the town of my memories of you and your lives, the home of our mass of belongings, the cocoon of all that I became, my childhood years,

25. About 213 kilograms.

the ripening of three successive vocations, and in short, all my easily grasped, spontaneously interlocking past. And I realised that I was going to do everything in my power to get away—to start with, say, to Petersburg.

I must add that Moscow, with its mixture of styles and its mixed population, etc., now creates an impression of total falsity. There are times here when you begin to feel you are breathing lies, universal and all-pervading, soaking through absolutely everything around you, beginning with the bricks and ending with people's conversations.

The Revolution—whether it was a good thing or a bad one, close to me or remote—still remains a rational, unique reality with some sort of normality and logic of its own. In Moscow it even loses that logical normality. In Petersburg, you can explain it to yourself to some extent as something definite, whose definite nature links it to Peter the Great, Radishchev, the Decembrists, 1905, and also quite simply to the city itself, the sea, Kronstadt, the straightness of the streets, and all the peculiar features of the 'window onto Europe'. In Moscow it appears as the pinnacle of heterogeneity, so that the real Revolution sometimes turns into a backward look at Asia, a regression from the town to the countryside, from the worker to the peasant; any reactionary rubbish generated at the instinctual level is capable, with the help of some cheap trickery, of successfully masquerading as the 'true meaning' of the Revolution. Here, the voices of the marketplace, ignorance, narrow-mindedness, racial hatred and the like, are freely and dazzlingly blended with their opposites. This is what allows these dark undertones to acquire a binding legitimacy which they never possessed before, even in the gloomiest periods of our history. It suddenly turns out that scientific or artistic excellence is a petty-bourgeois characteristic, or in some way a quality you have to be ashamed of. The government and the party, of course, cannot think that way; but the tone and character of our lives are not imposed by the ruling orders and personalities but by the power of the masses.

The intelligentsia is under attack by a stagnant layer of society which, in its social sense (as the peasantry), represents part of the Revolution, but whose true tastes have never changed since the days of the 'German quarter' before Peter the Great. Seen from outside, from the historical viewpoint, this is all very interesting. But breathing this jumbled, slippery, duplicitous atmosphere is very hard on you. That's Moscow for you. It's much easier in Petersburg, where the spirit of the Revolution is cleaner, more unconditional and direct, where falsehood and contradiction haven't been elevated into a system.

Another good reason for leaving Moscow is that it's grossly overpopulated, and the constant anguish about the apartment will recur again and again. I don't know whether Shura was here when they published the new decree cutting living space to a strict norm of 16 square arshins[26] and 'consolidating' it, and the right of tenants to voluntary 'consolidation'. If so, he must know that all this is no joke, and that it applies very widely, to everyone who lives in Moscow. Because of the decree, people are selling off their furniture dirt cheap. There's a story (they swear it's true) that tens of thousands of relatives are advancing on Moscow from the provinces, summoned by their families to fill up their apartments. I gave up the through room (which used to be the dining room) to the house management committee, and offered them part of the studio (facing the courtyard), by moving the partition. But they took a fancy to Shura's room and the front hall. They don't want to give way on this, objecting not unreasonably that my offer doesn't suit them.

All our letters of protection now have to be re-registered at the KUBU. I don't know whether they'll accept my proposal. Shura's social position is very shaky and very bizarre—he's unemployed, and a dependant, and not a dependant, etc. etc.—and with all these apocryphal details he hasn't a hope of holding on to his room. His claim to the right to keep it for a month and a half isn't much use to anyone either. As we talk and write, time is passing and the month and a half won't last any longer than that—the end of it isn't over the horizon. And even if you take that line, the crucial fact is that the room is locked up and may stay locked for six weeks, so it's obvious that when the time runs out there'll be no grounds for us to refuse to give up the room, or think up new arguments, which would be very embarrassing. So we're fighting at the KUBU to hold on to the studio and Shura's room. The letter of protection will state that we all five (including Shura) live in the studio, while his room is my work-room. When he comes back, and if he's changed his plans (he had told me that he wanted to live with the Vilyams),[27] he'll go back to living in his room, the only difference being that I'll be working in there from time to time.

The Institute had suggested that we should move to a new apartment. We went and had a look at what was on offer. One option was part of what used to be the Gromoglasovs' place—two terminally damp rooms, black with soot, with the floors torn up, but the floor area would meet our needs. The other was part of the Davydovs' (Shura knows whom I mean): four tiny little rooms, hermetically separated from one another, with a total area of 84 square arshins.[28] In two of the

26. About eight square metres per person.
27. The Vilyams (Williams) were friends of Shura's. A year later, in 1925, he married Irina Niko-laevna Vilyam.
28. 42 square metres.

rooms, we'd need to knock a door through which would use up every bit of floor space. From the point of view of hygiene this apartment is better than the other, but even if we wanted to move in we could take only the sort of furnishings you'd have in a summer dacha.

Yet once more, the 'problem' of furniture has arisen. It's true that you authorised us to sell it all off. But even if I didn't use any of the money for myself, we'd still be bound to feel bad about it, and perhaps you would too. The fact is that when there's a sudden need to sell off furniture or possessions for some reason, it affects everyone at once—as now. And then things get sold for next to nothing, almost given away. Later on, when the period of cheapness passes, it's only because everyone has ceased to feel an urgent compulsion to sell. At such times, life is easier for us too, and then I no longer see any need to treat other people's property as my own.

Altogether, I'm depressingly conscious of being constantly enslaved by general rules. In this subjection to global, population-wide, thousand-strong processes, I have trouble distinguishing between involuntary and voluntary acts. Because in my very behaviour and in the way I organise my life, I myself often move deliberately from an exclusive and personal position towards the general position of the man in the street. What a terrible muddle it all is. Perhaps I do nothing but take false steps and make mistakes. It's amazing. On the rare occasions when I've been treated as an exception to the general rule, I've always felt that I was surrounded by an appearance of frivolity and envy, adventurism and disfavour. And no sooner did I turn my face towards genuine everyday life, which no-one exalts or debases, than I was crushed by the weight of universal, statistical, mass phenomena, which I no longer recognised as the facts of my own life, since I saw only too well that they were generalisations. These two orientations are diametrically opposite and mutually contradictory. One path leads ultimately to the person and the fact; the other, to the type and the general rule. What depresses me is that all my life I've been walking back and forth in these two directions, never getting very far on my walks. It's not only sad—in a way, it's shameful too.

Shura's letter from Munich upset us deeply. It was boring, lame and insipid. That's him when he's abroad, at the pinnacle of his aspirations. Let's speak plainly and brutally. He seems to be (and indeed he is) existing by virtue of the fact that you, his father, have charged up an enormous battery (which I've already measured, and I'll talk about it later)—consisting of a name, possessions, acquaintances, knowledge imparted to him, constant advice, financial and moral support, and so forth. In point of fact, a spendthrift rake who squanders his paternal inheritance is a brighter and loftier being on the scale of human types than Shura. The reason I write this is that if (say) you didn't exist, and everything you had accumulated was concentrated in his hands, that would still not be enough for him; he would still lack you as an adviser to explain to him how to use it all, and inspire him to do so; to push him out towards Nature, or the taverns, or women, or the railways. The reason why I've set this all out so explicitly is this. *In this respect, I am not so essentially different from him myself.* Zhonia too. Lida, I think, is an exception. But it's too early to talk about her—how is one to know whether she too won't suddenly take your line along a downhill path, a year or five years from now?—after all, we all reach maturity about the age of forty. It's a striking fact that I seem to be getting rid of all my capacity to suffer or rejoice on my own account. But I'm terribly embittered and hurt for your sake, for all that has happened to you in us.

They put on *The Alchemist* in the Komissarzhevsky Theatre here.[29] And they're going to print it in Kharkov. Both these events were unexpected for me. First of all, on the day after my arrival, a day as gloomy as all my thoughts are just now, I discovered that the play had been acquired by a publisher, and went to Lubyanka Square to negotiate terms. When I got off the tram, I saw a fence covered with a whole row of posters proclaiming the purpose of my visit in letters a foot high. I ran over to the fence and instantly concluded that this must be someone else's translation (this had already happened to me once before, with *The Broken Jug*).[30] It turned out that the translation was mine. The publication and the production have nothing to do with each other and the people involved know nothing about one another; it was all the most fortuitous of coincidences, happening within a single hour. It had all happened while I was staying in Taitsy and no-one knew my address. The event itself is of no importance whatsoever, and financially unexciting too—it's a small theatre. But the very fact of the coincidence impressed me: I arrive in Moscow, feeling insecure and forgotten by all the gods (and wondering how I'll get through the winter); then a telephone call—*The Alchemist* (publication);—then a poster on the street: *The Alchemist* (production). All this happened over a week ago. The play is on. The producer had been trying to contact me for a month, to no avail, so God only knows what he's done with my text, but the Ben Jonson has been very ably staged and it's well acted.

---

29. Boris's translation of Ben Jonson's play, published in 1931.
30. Boris's translation of *Der zerbrochene Krug* by Heinrich von Kleist, published in 1915.

Yesterday, the day before Zhenichka's birthday (he's just a year old today), I went to see the agent of the Society of Dramatic Writers to get my post-performance royalties for the week. I should have been paid by Gosizdat[31] that morning for the second edition of *My Sister, Life*, and hadn't been. I didn't have a kopek in my pockets and I was pinning all my hopes on my theatre royalties. I felt it would be a bad omen to celebrate Zhenichka's birthday empty-handed. The Society's agent lives off Karetny Row, in Spassky Lane, and sees people in the evening. I was told that he was at a meeting and would be back in an hour. The way things were, I needed to see him, no matter what. I decided to wait for him, and meanwhile went out to walk around the streets till he returned.

I crossed Sadovaya Street and soon found myself opposite what used to be the Ecclesiastical Seminary in Oruzheiny Lane. I remembered you saying that I had been born there, or somewhere nearby. I wandered this way and that, but nothing jogged my memory until I walked along the Oruzheiny extension, down Bozhedomsky Lane. Here, not far from the intersection of Bozhedomsky and Volkonsky Lanes, I saw and recognised everything. I saw the fence and the big, solitary tree above it (standing in the Seminary garden), and the side part of the garden, and the crooked lane curving off to the left: everything just as I had always seen it in my indistinct memories. It's extraordinary that I've lived in Moscow for 34 (or 32) years since then, yet I'd never been back. I walked on and on down the lane. The impulse to draw analogies was automatic. I didn't come up with any. I returned to the Seminary gates (now it's the House of Soviets No.3 and you can't get in without a pass; I wanted to walk through the garden, where I would have found treasures as rich as Mycenae).

I was standing opposite a modest house, in which you two undoubtedly once lived: where you started your career, in one of those apartments like the ones they're offering us now and we're refusing—or even worse; the place from whence you sailed your ship across Myasnitskaya and Volkhonka, and abroad, with your family; the lives you lived, in a family of six souls and on their behalf—and so forth. I was one year old then, and here I stood now, the father of a one-year-old son, as the lights went on in Karetny Row, Ugolnaya Square, the Tverskaya-Yamskaya streets, Oruzheiny, Likhov Lane; and I thought about these four souls now living on Volkhonka Streets or abroad, while their parents hold them and keep them safe; and how they crawl back to the Oruzheiny whenever the positions you've achieved for them can no longer support them. And I was

31. The State publishing house.

confirmed in these judgements and feelings by one trivial detail after another of the waning day.

The agent turned out not to have any money. That settled the form our celebrations would take. I came home for a minute, but I had to go to the theatre (for the press night). You can imagine how I felt there. I ought to have gone backstage to see the actors, but I didn't go because I was afraid I'd have a good time, and Zhenia (who had stayed at home) goes to bed early. And so forth. *The rest is silence.*

I've finally finished this endless letter. Don't be cross with me for being so verbose. Thank you very much for your letters to the boy. You ask about clothes sizes and so on. How can I say what we want? Here's a maximum list—you don't have to get everything on it. For me—two or three boxes of razor-blades, Mond Extra Gold (but definitely not 'Bebe'—those are blunt), and two or three cakes of soap (not Wolf's, but cheap unboxed ones). Big Zhenia dreams about an inexpensive warm dress (not a house-coat), something she could wear at home and when she goes out; Lydia's or Stella's size. For the boy, if possible, a woollen suit (*Bärchen* type) for going out—that is, a cap, jacket and trousers, for a one-and-a-half to two-year-old boy. I'm jotting down these requests in a hurry—the boy's out for a walk, Zhenia isn't here, and I want to get this letter off today. Maybe I'll send you an airmail letter in the next few days, and then I'll write about the pictures and about Aunt Asya and Olya.

I embrace you all warmly, and Fedia, and Zhonia, and Stella.

Finding a steady income was an acute problem. Boris had become convinced that his commissioned translations of Ben Jonson's *The Alchemist*, plays by Heinrich von Kleist, and German revolutionary poetry would never be published. He decided to translate Shakespeare, and started work on Hamlet, but these insecure activities gave place to a steady job preparing a foreign-language bibliography on Lenin for the Lenin Institute. It appears never to have been completed or published, but it gave Boris the opportunity to work in the Foreign Affairs Commissariat library. Here, for the first time since 1917, he had access to foreign journals and read about events in the West. In his verse novel Spektorsky he writes: 'The task lay in fishing for phrases / About Lenin. Attention never slept. / While fishing like an underwater swimmer / I did a lot of diving in the journals.'

Boris Pasternak to Frederick and Josephine Pasternak

25 [October 1924, Moscow.]

Some time after seven in the morning, lying half-asleep in the drawing-room, we hear the faint, quiet, mournful 'May your soul rest with the saints', it approaches along the corridor, the choir passes through the front hall, they're singing quietly as though they were afraid of waking us, they half-open our door—it doesn't shut properly, and we know that they're carrying out Elizaveta Ivanovna Ustinova, who died the day before yesterday. Outside it's probably snowing, it must be nuns in white coifs singing. Then there's the cautious, restrained noise of booted feet, they're carrying the heavy coffin.

Then the morning starts. Four families wash, go to the kitchen, boil things, run to church and come back. In the hall, which is also our dining-room now, the floor is strewn with pine-needles and chrysanthemum petals. Outside, the snow is thawing, it's a dark gloomy day, the funeral goes on for about five hours, until one o'clock; I don't go to the cemetery, but set off for the Foreign Affairs Commissariat reading-room to read foreign journals (it's a sort of job), and it turns out there was a fire at the power station last night and the trams aren't running.

When I return home, the little park is in darkness, as it was in 1919, and I hear that there's been a wake. Vasily Ivanovich fainted several times, was kind and friendly to Zhenia and brought her food.

Then Vatagin[32] comes to draw and model me; then it transpires that the house has been turned into a commune and everyone is going to be evicted. And in spite of everything, if I translate Shakespeare, my translations will be the best.

I kiss you both warmly.

Borya

Boris Pasternak to Josephine Pasternak

31 October 1924, Moscow.

Dear Zhonichka,

Thank you for your loving letter. But don't get over-thrilled about what I write. When Zhenia and I go through particularly difficult times, I think about you two with a sense of great relief. I can't stop being glad that Shura has found a

---

32. Vasily Vatagin, a well-known Soviet sculptor.

job, and seems to be working successfully and earning a living. Because if things were bad for you, or went on being bad for him, that would be incomparably worse than when something of the sort happens to me. My own life contains only the most intolerably absurd and quite unexpected barriers, which generally get erected before my very nose just when I'm getting into my stride and life is full of promise. I'm writing to you from just this kind of barrier-patterned landscape, and won't say a word about it. When one writes about calamities in a time of calamities, it's not them that one's writing about, but one's own depression; and talking about one's feelings means feeding them. A great many feelings only get stronger by being mentioned or expressed. That's why love, or a certain kind of love, is so declamatory. When I've got beyond this particular obstacle, perhaps I'll remember it and tell you all about it.

If the only problem for me were to live on a grand scale and earn a lot of money, that would have been settled long ago and the last thing you and I would have to do would be to correspond at a distance. But I'm the least free person out of the four of us. Even if it were true, as is generally said about me, that 'I don't know what I want', then in these same quotation marks, I am supposed not to know it for my whole life. By unfreedom, I mean unfreedom from my own self, the unfreedom of predestination. And yet, and yet, all this will shake down and sort itself out, and—this is what I'd like best of all—I'll spend half the day walking in the same harness as most other people (that's not in any way a burden, I like it and it diverts me), and devote the other half to my own ignorance.

My work (I'm helping to compile a bibliography on Lenin, and I've taken on the foreign bibliography) means that I have to read whole volumes of the best journals published in three languages. You simply have no idea how many there are. One sometimes comes across interesting things. I harm myself by spending time on them, since I'm paid on a piecework basis and my earnings depend on how much I find of what's wanted, and how quickly. And the interesting things are a long way from what's wanted. Today, for instance, I thought of Mama when I read, in an issue of *The Forum* (an American journal), Stanislavsky's reminiscences about Rubinstein, with a very lively and loving depiction of him. It appears that in his youth Stanislavsky was one of the directors of the Russian Musical Society, and as part of his job he used to meet Rubinstein at the station when he came from Petersburg to Moscow for concerts. Stanislavsky recalls two great men, Rubinstein and Tolstoy, and in his descriptions of them both he very successfully conveys the meaning of that concept of greatness. When you have the time and opportunity, you simply have to read the following writers: Thomas

Hardy, Joseph Conrad (the greatest contemporary English novelist), James Joyce and Marcel Proust. I'm judging their qualities on the basis of incomplete, fragmentary translations, and from what the journals write about them. Conrad and Proust are particularly interesting.

I wouldn't have written to you yet, if it hadn't been for the heartfelt intimacy of your letter which demanded an immediate reply. If you want to know—and don't take this as just a vain claim—the saddest thing for me is that I feel how much you, and Lida, and Shura and our parents, need me; and especially you, or rather your image left behind in Moscow; or all your traces, now wiped off the parquet; or that form of incompleteness which you all inevitably acquired, partly through your maturity in years and your detachment from childhood, and partly because, living abroad, you're not deeply rooted there. In short—alongside my paid work, however many jobs I accumulate, I'm constantly left with a sort of obligation of the heart, a debt I owe to the world—this world which you would have the right to forget even if you knew it. I haven't yet given up the idea of one day taking up this most necessary duty—though when I recently did so again, everything round me was turned upside-down and flung flat, barring the way to this essential and natural activity.[33]

I'm not the only one in this situation here. Bely and Kuzmin[34] are even worse off—very much worse. In its essence this isn't new, and all I want is to get rid of what's new in these difficulties. That's just indescribable. Some time in the autumn I wrote to Khodasevich[35] in Scotland. Now he's in Sorrento, living with Gorky. The things I passed over in silence, they had learned from experience; and they could easily imagine what robs us of our strength here. I repeat in all sincerity, this is nothing new in Russia. Russia will cease to be itself when it begins to notice people and single them out for any other purpose than that of slowly stifling and tormenting them.

Boris sent New Year wishes to his parents and sisters, and a letter 'with English digressions' (possibly extracts from the journals he had been reading), which have not

---

33. Boris is contrasting his mundane paid activities with the duty that he owes to his time, as a creative artist, and the political obstacles preventing him from fulfilling it.

34. Andrei Bely: see p. 12, note 21. Mikhail Kuzmin (1875–1936) was a post-Symbolist poet out of favour with Soviet literary trends.

35. Vladislav Khodasevich (1886–1939) was a poet who became closely associated with Maxim Gorky until 1925; Boris was probably approaching him about participation in Gorky's journal *Beseda* ('Colloquy') in Berlin.

survived. The following letter to Lydia echoes his mood in the verse novel *Spektorsky*, on which he was currently working:

> I was in misery. A son was born to us.
> I had to give up childishness a while.
> Assessing my age with a sidelong look,
> I noticed my life's first grey hairs.[36]

The books by Joseph Conrad which he received from Josephine on the following day are there said to 'lie in the puddles on the roadway'—an allusion to the wet pavements he describes in the same section of *Spektorsky*.

Boris Pasternak to Lydia Pasternak

25 January 1925. Moscow.

Dear Lidochka!

I'm probably going to talk to you about good things in a gloomy way. The reason is very simple. Over this last autumn, all the dental fillings that Meisel put in have fallen out simultaneously. An odd kind of solidarity, isn't it? Actually it's impaired by the fact that some of my teeth have broken, while others have remained like extinct craters. And now one of those has started to make its presence felt, particularly since the New Year. I've probably got some mild inflammation. I can't work for the pain, and if you were here I probably shouldn't think of talking to you either, any more than I've talked to the people at home these past few days. So I thought I'd have a chat with you on paper, without moving my jaws or unclenching my teeth.

We'll probably have an amazingly successful talk—the only thing I can't guarantee is that it'll keep to the rhythm of a one-step, or stick to the subject of: 'Tell me, little butterfly, how you live and where you fly.' Because, after all, I'm a melancholic—a terrible, dreadful melancholic. And because I'm a limp rag, a terrible soggy limp floor-rag. And because, *last not least*, I do have a dental abscess.

Yes, while I remember—did you get my letter with the English digressions, or did those foreign interpolations not reach you? Incidentally, you needn't be afraid to answer this, loud and clear. I'm going to see the dentist tomorrow at 7. By the time you get this letter, I'll probably be capable of blowing you kisses and even chewing macaroni and meat balls.

---

36. Introduction to *Spektorsky*, lines 5–8, composed in 1929.

Have you noticed how blatantly I've gone off the subject? I think we were going to talk about how it is that things which have been around you for as long as you can remember, appear to you when you've said goodnight to them and curled up under the blanket, and then you wake between 4 and 5 in the morning, roll over and see them from an unexpected angle and in a new (very weak and dissipated) light.

I really don't like rats, no matter how hard people try to persuade me. I have a sort of inexplicable prejudice against them, and against toothache, and debt—although, of course, there's life in everything, and I don't know anything more acutely alive than the things I've just mentioned.

'Archives' are what they call institutions where the meanest trifles are turned into documents and tourist attractions. Any old rubbish you wouldn't even glance at anywhere else, if it's in an archive it's called 'material', kept under lock and key and listed in a catalogue. The age I've reached is like that. That sounds unbelievably stupid. For other people, objectively speaking, I'm still a long way from old age. But I have a good feel for things and I can sense it from a long way off. Here's what characterises my age. Everything turns into 'material'. You start to see your own feelings—they let you look at them, because they hardly move; just one thing about them suddenly disturbs you: their distance, the way they stand in space. You discover that they're subject to perspective. Just as, when you were a child, you might be frightened by the way clothes on an armchair could look like a person sitting in the corner in the moonlight—you glance round the room half-asleep, looking to see whether your thoughts or fears or perplexities are standing over by the fireplace, whether the *intérieur* will get by without . . . problems. You enter their sphere like entering a smoke-filled room. Their presence makes the air thicker, the light less transparent. As if the room had become filled with running, feeling, worrying—the way a room becomes filled with smoke, and now you can see it: hanging in billows, chaotic outlines—these aren't shapes, of course, but emotions. Formerly they moved, dragged you this way and that, and you didn't notice them. Now they have nothing to do, they accompany you and go along with you.

It's hard to have doubts about my love for my little son Zhenechka. Could there be any comparison between this feeling and my earlier 'passions', frothy and half-imaginary, with their suspect and all-too-real links to my poetry? It would seem not. Of course not. Yet at the same time, even if the feelings are declared to be nothing but lies, those lies were flying somewhere and carrying the liar away with them. There was nothing to see there, no need to look. It was a movement, culminating in laughter, happiness, grief, tears. My compassion for my boy is something I can see—I leave it in the room when I go out of the house, and know where and how I'll find it on my return.

Zhenia has just come back from visiting various people, including the Vilyams. Tomorrow Irina Nikolaevna will come to see us. Zhenia says that she looks healthier than her sister Rita. Pass that on to Shura. Kolya [Vilyam] saw Zhenia home, and developed palpitations; and while he and I were talking about them, Zhenia looked through what I'd written. And now, as I take up my letter again, she's sitting on the sofa telling me that instead of writing you depressing nonsense I'd better go to bed too. She's probably right. She must be right, otherwise my reference to her words would be a mean bit of demagoguery. It's not likely that I'd be making fun of her, and myself, and your own high standards, in such bad faith, just to prove that I'm beyond your comprehension. There's only one possible conclusion: one can't describe unhealthy and morbid phenomena. And that includes the new elements entering my life now, which astound me by their novelty. That's something that comes with age.

A few days ago I woke up in the night, and saw many things in a strange, foreshortened light, independent and isolated from me—in a way which once used to make Zhonia cry at night, and in my case used to vent itself in music. Zhonia—Fedia's wife—living in Munich, and claiming identity with Zhonichka; and Papa, Mama, you and Shura, now sleeping in Berlin (oh, how I can see it)— you were two groups of phantoms, torn away, situated somewhere in a space that once upon a time had been my heart, but had now become a sorrowfully profound, inexhaustibly visual, morbidly contemplative vista. No, there's no expressing it.

Maybe I've started talking to you about this so that you could tell me (but do you have enough freshness and saintly directness to say it?) that my words haven't got through to you; that I've been grubbing around, limply and with no fire, away to one side of the place where I'd planned to start a sharp, fiery excavation. Then I could admit that my premises were false, which I'd very much like to do. I should very much like to think that life is uniform over its whole duration, that it's a condition of gradually slowing youth. The thought that the different ages of one's life differ more than epochs and nations—that's hard for me to bear.

As a sort of refutation, let me mention something I've repeatedly raised in my letters, which I think about endlessly at times of enforced idleness like today. Despite all the difficulties of this year, its central pith and essence are profoundly satisfactory. There are many reasons for that, and there's no point going over them all. My life has become freer and more individual. My difficulties are special ones, they don't have a collective character, as they did in the transitional years. Becoming a complete organism again is a slow process and it's not finished yet, but I'm sure I'm half-way there. I've started scribbling on paper again, and I'll make something of it; but that won't happen quickly. The fact that our life is sometimes execrable belies our opportunities: there are many of them, some of which I could take up even now, even in the field of literature (or rather journalism). All I need to do is cut down to one-quarter the effort I feel I have to make, and I could quadruple my earnings. In other words, the easiest thing for me to do would be to improve the material side of my life sixteen times over. You might say that 16 is the ratio of sense to nonsense in my case, or of spirit to matter, as they once used to say. You don't know this, but Papa will tell you that this phenomenon is as old as the earth.

That's the delightful thing—laws as old as the earth are beginning, bit by bit, to come into force once more. Outside the range of their effects, I lose my sense of touch. Now I'm getting it back again. Very recently, in Berlin, you yourselves saw me being 'anaesthetically' happy—happy without feeling. A statement about aesthetic unhappiness should obviously follow—but we'd better say goodbye, Lidok, or else I'll be up late and have a muzzy head tomorrow, which I'm not supposed to.

Kiss everybody hard, I'll show you how.

Your Borya

Boris Pasternak to Josephine Pasternak

26 January 1925. Moscow.

Dear Zhoniura,

Yesterday, out of the blue, I sat down to write Lida a letter. Zhenia and I have just been talking about you. Then I started working. Quietly the door opens, and from behind my shoulder there comes the outstretched hand of Fenia (Zhenichka's nanny), and your books fall into the puddles on the roadway that I'm describing. What's this then, all of a sudden? Why go to all that trouble? But then, what a pleasant surprise! Thank you, thank you. Now I'll never write to you about books again. Did you really take my words as a hint? I haven't read Conrad's *The Outcast of the Islands*, but I have got *Almayer's Folly* in translation. I'm sorry, perhaps I really did ask you to send it? Zhenia firmly and confidently insists that I did, and apparently she read it in my letter to you at the time. If so, forgive me, I don't remember it.

30/I. A family characteristic. The beginning of this letter has been lying around for an indeterminate reason, for an indeterminate period. Now your own letter has come. You write about your plan to come here. That would be wonderful. But you have to free this intention from some far-reaching underlying assumptions, and from its accompanying spiritual commentary. Why do thousands of people move around the globe without any reason or purpose—travelling, arriving and departing? We always require a purpose to justify us. Such a trip would be the emptiest of strolls. What could be simpler? And if you're a German citizen now, that's simpler than anything.

I'm convinced that this will be a temporary visit; at all events, until you've tested yourself and checked out your expectations, you mustn't talk or think of anything but such a flying visit, otherwise this becomes an un-serious notion, the kind that will never come to pass, however profoundly meaningful it may be. Quite apart from the joy that we and you would feel together when we met and saw one another again, you'd probably get a great deal out of such a trip.

Crossing the frontier, I've no doubt, would have a depressing effect on you. That's how it was a hundred years ago, and that's how it'll be in another hundred. Culture—a book crammed full of pictures, pages of music or philosophy, cities, Dickensian richness, and the rest—will give place to fields, beggarly clouds, beggarly jackdaws. You'll weep, and you'll be alone in your compartment, a very large and grey one. At the very prolonged and very frequent halts, the conductor will noisily fling down great armfuls of firewood from the tender, and cold, smelly air will blow in from the open ends of the wagons. But of course, this is your homeland—a great thing—and the mingled bitterness of these feelings will contain much that is exciting, enriching, and instructive.

Your home will reawaken many scenes and situations which, you will imagine, you hold in your memory, and which, of course, you don't remember. For some five minutes you won't be able to speak. Then you'll find that the rooms, the lighting, and thousands of aspects and properties that haven't found their way into the dictionary nor been classified by category, are immeasurably softer, deeper, and more mysterious than they were in your expectation. Much that can, and must, live within you, will come to life on this first day. If I were a saint and had no wishes of my own, I should advise you to come for one week.

Apart from that, you'll see our boy, and the same things that happened to you with your homeland will happen with your home. You'll experience a feeling of bursting with life, in other words a feeling that contradicts itself in every way.

This new little boy whom you don't know will inevitably appear to you as the natural focal point of the picture—not as a visitor in the world you're entitled to regard as your own, but as its master. You'll hate him, that is, you'll love him painfully, that is, with a love that's real, not imposed on you. Incidentally, he's not at all the way he's described in the letters. He's a little Chinaman, unattractive, looks like me, sometimes with an ethnic look. He's very lively, and probably endowed with good character traits (he's impressionable and receptive). He's starting to speak early, but his language has already been ruined by his nanny (a Belorussian from the Pale of Settlement)[37] and our neighbours. Perhaps that's only my imagination. At the same time, you couldn't find nicer people. It's very kind of the Frishmans to take so much trouble over him, and we don't deserve it at all. As for the nanny (Zhenia's mother's maid), she's one of the family, and more reliable than Zhenia herself. Of course, it won't always be like this, and in due course any deficiencies will be made good. But all that isn't the point.

So, about yourself. You'll gobble up some very precious things here, and return home to digest them and gain strength from them. Why deprive you of that? It's ridiculous to discuss what human beings live for. It's obvious. Purposes are illusory, one fancy creates them and the next abolishes them. But how easy it is for life itself to become illusory! I suppose that the only goal for humanity in historical times has been this: to try to prevent life from becoming an illusion; to overcome the tendency to transience of those situations that fill us with juice, weight and meaning. Those situations are entirely accessible and natural, there's no slyness or boldness or riskiness in them.

That's how your journey appears to me, and if Fedia and Papa and Mama aren't advising you the same way as I am, then—if I didn't know you—I should call their behaviour obtuse and inhuman. There's no doubt that you're bad at explaining your needs to yourself, and you're probably even worse at putting them into words. You have a habit of climbing the stairs of a five-storey house and declaring that you're going up to the sixth floor. Of course people take fright and stop you on the second-floor landing, not wishing to see you in a state of free fall, whereas there's no law against anyone going up and down stairs as much as they like, without justifying their actions to themselves or anyone else. Perhaps this is my disorder too, only in my case it's worse, because nobody stops

37. The Pale of Settlement was a region on the Western border of the Russian Empire in which Jews were allowed to settle permanently. Many parts of the Pale had a predominantly Jewish population, and Boris evidently feared that although the nanny was herself an ethnic Belorussian (not Jewish), her speech was not the Muscovite Russian he wished Zhenichka to learn.

me, and—no matter what I may assert or believe—I never get higher than the attic and at that point give up any thought of the most modest ascents, reconciling myself to an eternity on the ground floor. What a revolting comparison, and once again it's thrown me off the subject.

You'll have to go to Leningrad to see Aunt Asya. That is—Petersburg. It's a fantastic city. You have to spend some time there, live there a bit, so that your feelings about your homeland and your thoughts about it can arrange themselves as they should, and find a balance—their own special balance, unattainable without your impressions of Petersburg. There are circumstances you may be able to make use of. If Shura is planning to come home, you might go there with him. Perhaps we'll make a move too.

I'm thinking—at the moment this is the merest dream—of sending 'the grandson' with Zhenia to visit our family. She herself would only want to contemplate such a trip if it were possible for her to leave the boy with Mama and Lida for six months, while she goes to Paris to study. But that will be the subject of separate conversations, testing the ground and making oblique enquiries through Lida and Shura, so that the replies can be free and unconstrained. If this trip were to happen, it would be in spring—and then you could travel together.

But all these complicated arrangements are absolute nonsense. Don't adjust your plans to suit theirs, and don't count on them. Oh, how wonderful it would be to live a little time with you here! Zhenia and I have often dreamed about it— indeed, we've probably written to you about it.

Do you pass on my greetings to Fedia? He's every bit as close to me as you are. In the gallery of feelings established from childhood onwards, after all, nothing has shifted. Talk is just talk, but visceral attachments—it's hard to explain.

This letter will probably seem cold to you, because I'm trying to write without my innate scatterbrainedness. I've thanked you for the books. Now—thank you for your willingness to send more. Thank you. There's no need at present. I don't need Joyce at all, and Proust I'll get here.

I'm about to have a squabble with Zhenia—she'll try to hold up this letter so as to add something of her own, but I prefer to send it off now, and she can write separately. It's been lying around long enough.

I embrace and kiss you.

Your Borya

Josephine's intention to travel to Moscow was for the time being kept secret from her parents. At her request, Lydia asked Boris for help in getting official permission. The practical arrangements for getting travel documents were quickly made through Karl Radek, an influential political figure at the time.

Boris received a parcel with a reproduction of Leonid's recent large oil portrait of Josephine.

Boris Pasternak to Leonid Pasternak

19 February 1925. Moscow.

My dear, beloved Papa, my wonder-Papa!

They've just delivered the parcel and the photograph of the portrait. What a portrait! What a youthful work! What tension and spontaneity, what restrained self-control and freedom! And how full of life and concision, and what one has to call artistry in brief, since it can never be named in full. And what a likeness! It will stand before me as a wordless artistic inspiration, a mute precept which, try as I may, I can never rise high enough to fulfil. Bravo! I'm always afraid of exaggerating, but I don't remember liking anything in recent years so much as this portrait. In Shura's room, where many of your good drawings are hanging, this photograph conquers and annihilates everything else. I just can't get used to it; every time I glance at it, I experience once again my first impression of novelty, abundance, and expectations overwhelmingly, thoroughly and completely exceeded. Lucky Zhonia.

But Boris's efforts to arrange Josephine's trip to Moscow were wasted. Lydia showed his letter to their parents, and they categorically vetoed Josephine's plans.

Leonid Pasternak to Boris Pasternak

[28 February 1925. Berlin.]

[...]

It's a great pity, my dear boy, that you didn't show any interest—before making all the arrangements for this trip—in what Mama and I would think about the project. I've underlined your words—'and from their point of view, it would even be useful'. So you know some point of view of ours from which it would be useful. If this merely means that the 'true' state of affairs would show her that there was no purpose in organising such a huge and complicated trip and spending so much money (which her family so badly needs)—(the words underlined can bear no other meaning)—then the game isn't worth the candle. Neither Mama nor I can look kindly on this project, nor approve it, from any point of view. I say nothing of Fedia—I don't know, I haven't asked him—and you don't need a giant brain to realise that he's hardly likely to be happy about it, but he's too kind-hearted and honourable to be obstructive. This project could have two sorts of purpose. Either a very serious and profound one, and hence with serious and unforeseen consequences to such a special nature as hers, living as she does under the influence of 'hypnotic' notions, dimly perceived and imaginary contradictions, plus her fragile and delicate health that goes with her super-sensitive compassionate self, plus the remnants of childish imagined passions, which she feels she has 'betrayed' in some way—as happens to her even with inanimate objects (feeling pity for a worthless doll or a rag), when she compares her present life with the whole of the life which, alas, she'll see all around her, (I won't go on about this, you know Zhonia). Or it could have a second purpose—as a simple, almost unconsidered excursion—'let's go on a trip, why not' and so forth—a trip which would have been very simple before the war, when it was nothing to take off to see relatives one hadn't seen for a long time, going from Moscow to Odessa—and if one went abroad, *that* was a journey full of culture and novelty, outweighing the merely trivial interest of gazing at old friends and relations.

[...]

I've gone through the pros and cons with her; there may have been a lot that she kept back—anyway, I made it clear to her that although this would be the death of me and especially of Mama (she in particular is driven to despair by the thought of it), still I wouldn't stop her, and of course would help her on her way as well as I could—but Zhonechka didn't want to leave against our will.

[...]

But I enjoyed reading your enthusiastic postscript about my portrait. You exaggerate your 'smallness in the face of my greatness' [...]. How can you— we're all yesterday's men! But it's true that the portrait strikes everybody like that. [...]

It was difficult for Boris to earn a living from his writing in 1925. At his request, Leonid approached a Viennese publisher about the publication of *My Sister, Life; Themes and Variations*; and *Spektorsky*, whose first three chapters Boris submitted in manuscript form. Nothing came of this.

Boris's situation improved only when he began writing his poem about the 1905 Revolution. A preliminary draft, describing the bloody dispersal of the demonstration on 9 January 1905, and referred to below, was published in the journal *Krasnaya Nov* ('Red Virgin Soil'), No. 9, 1925.

Boris Pasternak to Frederick and Josephine Pasternak

[3 August 1925. Moscow.]

Dear Fedia and Zhonia,

[...]

If you're still in Germany, and particularly if you're in Berlin, and if you're interested in what I've started writing (alas, I've had to abandon it for now), you can get hold of the beginning of this novel in verse (provisionally called *Spektorsky*) from Semyon Petrovich Liberman, Rankestrasse 33, I. Ladyschnikow-Verlag (tel. Steinplatz 7960; 7927).

[...]

Parts of it have been printed here in two issues of a journal (I mean, parts of the portion that you will receive), and this same autumn the whole of that portion will be repeated in a third issue, provided all these repetitions don't cause a scandal. Please just write me your honest opinion, because this whole genre is new to me and strikes me as dubious. This is a step in the direction of prose, in the field of poetry. What do you think? Is it worth doing? Judge by your first impression. Tell me if it wouldn't be better simply to write prose. [...]

[...] This year I'm going to have to write absolute rubbish. It's the only thing that sells and brings in money. Of course they accept good stuff from me as well, though not as quickly as they accept downright trivia. But the main thing is this—you write something good, it takes a long time, you care for it, select from it, compress it—and meanwhile, at the height of my failures, and just a few days before getting the money you sent, I wrote something in two evenings—I felt absolutely ashamed when I showed it to Zhenia, it was so thin and hackneyed and jejune—and as soon as I submitted it (I had gone straight from the station to the editorial office), I instantly made 150 roubles. When I got the money next day, I immediately phoned the editor to say that what I had given him was terrible trash—please wait a bit, I said, and I'll change it for something more worthwhile. And he says 'Honestly, what are you worrying about? What a neurotic fellow you are!', and more in the same vein. It's terrible that this is how things are supposed to be. How good it would be if life itself imposed and sustained genuine standards. How joyfully one could work, at a steady pace, with a constant head of steam, without interruptions and cold showers. Oh, what is one to do with them all?

Zhonichka, my darling, Tsvetaeva said in a letter that Rilke was dead, but she just mentioned it in passing as though everyone knew about it.[38] When did it happen, and what do you know about it? I can't tell you what I felt when I read the news. And there was I thinking that I'd one day go to visit him in Switzerland, and I was living for this dream.

I embrace you both. Thanks for everything.

Your Borya

The erroneous rumour of Rilke's death reached Pasternak from Marina Tsvetaeva in Czechoslovakia; Leonid also heard it in Germany. Its wide diffusion was all the more surprising since Rilke spent January to August 1925 in Paris. Josephine wrote denying the rumour, and enclosing Rilke's recently published *Sonnets to Orpheus*. Rilke's 50th birthday was celebrated throughout Europe in December 1925.

In September 1925 Boris's brother Alexander (Shura), now married to Irina Nikolaevna Vilyam, returned to Moscow. He told Boris that Josephine had abandoned her plans to visit them there.

Boris Pasternak to Josephine Pasternak

Autumn 1925. Moscow.

Dear Zhonichka,

The beginning of your letter greatly saddened me. The main thing is that you don't say anything, and it's impossible to guess the reasons for your state of mind. So I'm saying nothing about it. There's no point asking Shura about anything. He's dear to me, as the most powerful embodiment of our family, and above all

---

38. Marina Tsvetaeva was a great Russian poet, contemporary and friend of Boris Pasternak, Mandelstam and Akhmatova. She emigrated in 1921 and lived abroad until 1939, when she followed her husband Sergei Efron from France to Moscow. He was arrested and died soon after in prison. Her daughter Ariadna was also imprisoned (until 1955). With the outbreak of the Soviet-German war in 1941 Marina was evacuated to Elabuga, where she committed suicide the same year.

Rainer Maria Rilke was the greatest German poet of the century. He visited Moscow in 1900, where Leonid met him; Boris later included a childhood memory of him in *Safe Conduct*. Shortly before Rilke's death, Boris corresponded with him through the intermediary of Marina Tsvetaeva; *see* Boris Pasternak, Marina Tsvetayeva, Rainer Maria Rilke, *Letters: Summer 1926* (London: Jonathan Cape, 1986, and Oxford: Oxford University Press, 1988).

of its weaknesses. He doesn't find the essence of things in the same place as me, and perhaps he doesn't seek it at all. Corresponding about one's personal life and spiritual state is very difficult, and in your case it's impossible. As for me, I'm probably perfectly happy, because I never think about my fate even in my sleep, and I scarcely understand any longer what it means. Letters can't replace an actual meeting. The fact that you won't have come this winter is not only a great deprivation for me; objectively speaking, it's part of how you are. Taking this fragment of your existence together with Shura's opinion of the idea of your trip, which indirectly allows one to sense the atmosphere surrounding him in Berlin—the whole thing comes to seem so mysterious and contradictory that I simply daren't try to understand it. But that isn't why we're close to one another. A conversation between us would in any event have by-passed personalities and homes, and happiness and unhappiness as isolated concepts. All times are epochs, and in any epoch the existence of homes and personalities is astonishing. Even if we hadn't spoken directly about this topic, we probably would have been walking about in that kind of atmosphere. What you say about Venice is wonderful. On a cursory look at Rilke's book, what struck me was that—despite finding himself, seemingly, under the influence of totally different forces and conditions from us Russians—he, like us, has begun to write worse. That's a very big subject. You can't even imagine how timely and appropriate your present to me was. More than anything you've ever sent me, this little book will become the most intimate and fruitful part of my life.

Warmest thanks for everything. I kiss you and Fedia.

A letter from Boris to his parents around the turn of the year, evidently recounting his shock at the 30-year-old poet Esenin's suicide, has not survived. This event, which Boris linked to the death of Alexander Blok and the execution of Nikolai Gumilev in 1921, persuaded him that poetry had no place in Soviet society.[39] His mother replied on 5 February: 'Your letter is so beautifully written that it's stupid to praise it . . . I was in tears as I read it.' Leonid wrote at the same time:

39. Sergei Esenin was a popular lyric poet who initially welcomed the Revolution but became increasingly disillusioned with it; he finally hanged himself in a Leningrad hotel. Alexander Blok was a leading Symbolist poet who wrote mystical, romantic verse. His great poem *The Twelve* is a visionary celebration of the Revolution. He died broken and disillusioned. Nikolai Gumilev was an influential poet who founded the Acmeist movement. After the Revolution he returned from France to Russia, but made no secret of his anti-Bolshevik views. He was arrested and shot in 1921.

Leonid Pasternak to Boris Pasternak

[...] But be a little more 'epic', not in what you write but in your everyday life. Don't get excited or angry, don't rage at yourself or other people. What is needed is a rational victory over the absurdities that surround you . . . because you need strength for your continuing, serious, creative work. Esenin's tragedy is an integral part of the landscape, and a natural one—and what's more, it's characteristic and, yet again, demonstrative. It's a terrible and deplorable thing that fate considers another such demonstration necessary, and such a dear and precious one. I understand how you must have reacted to it. [...]

oris Pasternak at Merrekül on the Baltic (in present-day Estonia).
)il painting by Leonid Pasternak, 1910.

Leonid Pasternak in his studio in Moscow.

onid and Rosalia Pasternak.
ouble oil study by Leonid Pasternak.

Alexander Pasternak.
Pencil and charcoal sketch by Leonid Pasternak, 1927.

Albert Einstein playing the violin.
Sketch by Leonid Pasternak.

Rainer Maria Rilke.
Sketch by Leonid Pasternak.

Facing page:

Top left: The composer Alexander Scriabin.

Top right: Pavel Ettinger (Pavetti).

Bottom: Leonid Pasternak with biochemist
Boris Zbarsky, in Leonid's studio, 1917.

Farewell picture in Moscow:
Leonid, Alexander (Shura), Berta Kaufman, Boris, Rosalia, and Lydia (left to right),
September 1921 (Josephine was already in Germany).

Boris Pasternak.
Oil painting by his wife Evgenia (Zhenia).

Josephine Pasternak (left)
and Ida Vysotskaya, 1912.

Zinaida as a young woman.

Lydia Pasternak, about 1921–22.

Lydia Pasternak walking
in Berlin, 1927.

Left: Stella Frishman, 1922.

Below: Portrait photograph of Rosalia, Lydia, Josephine (in front), and Leonid Pasternak in Berlin, 1921.

Frederick and Josephine
Pasternak, wedding photograph
outside Berlin-Charlottenburg
registry office, 1924.

Frederick and Josephine
Pasternak, 1924.

Vladimir Mayakovsky,
Boris Pasternak, Lili Brik,
and Sergei Eisenstein (left
to right), 1924.

Boris with Zhenia and little
Zhenichka. Studio photo by
M. Nappelbaum, 1924.

Zhenia and Zhenichka.
Studio portrait, 1926.

Zhenichka in a
knitted suit, 1926.

Boris, Zhenia, and Zhenichka, aged 3,
in their courtyard in Moscow, 1926.

Rosalia, Lydia, Josephine, and Leonid Pasternak in Berlin, 1926.

For information about illustration sources, please refer to pages 421–4.

CHAPTER TWO

1926

Boris decided to send his wife and two-year-old son to spend the summer in Germany, for her to recuperate from a suspected recurrence of the tuberculosis she had suffered in her youth.

Leonid Pasternak to Boris and Alexander Pasternak

Berlin, 17 March 1926.

[...] And now—for the first time in ages—we've had a whole succession of letters from you two. Thank God that you, Boryusha, and you too, Shurka, are a bit less weighed down by money worries. Please God things stay that way! Well, and how we'll celebrate and rejoice at the arrival of the youngest member of the royal line, the Prince of Cornwall—our wonderful grandson—I don't suppose any chronicler has ever succeeded in describing our feelings at this time, we just can't tell you! Well, God be with you—send Zhenia and Zhenichka off and we'll treat them well!

[...]

Now—I have some good news for you. I have had a very pleasant and precious letter from Rilke—particularly so for you, Borya. The thing is that we were wondering whether he was alive at all, and then, not six months ago, the newspapers announced that the literary world was celebrating his 50th birthday, and messages of congratulation were appearing in the press, etc. Having thus assured ourselves of his happy 'existence', and rejoiced over it, I one day decided to make the effort and write to congratulate him myself—to send him a few warm and sincere lines, even putting part of the letter in Russian.

In recalling our previous meetings, I incidentally told him that you—my children—and particularly my elder son—'a Russian poet who has already achieved a fine reputation'—were sincere and passionate admirers of his. Not knowing his address, I sent my letter via Insel-Verlag. It reached him only recently (he's in Switzerland), and now I've just received a long, informative and gratifying reply from him—gratifying because he writes enthusiastically about you, Boris (and the beginning of his letter is in 'Russian' . . . but he's got a bit rusty, he puts soft signs instead of hard ones)—and had recently read Valéry's translation in a Paris periodical. Next time we write to you we'll send some extracts copied out by Lidochka—I'm afraid of sending the original in case it goes astray. I'm just going to send it to Zhonia—she'll be thrilled.

Your Papa

Boris's next letter crossed with his father's, and continues the story of '1905'. At this time he also read Marina Tsvetaeva's 'Poem of the End', which led him to reassess his preoccupation with the revolutionary events of 1905 and the epic genre in general.

Boris Pasternak to Lydia Pasternak

[20–21 March 1926. Moscow.]

Dear Lidochka,

In one of his letters Papa asked me to send him something I had written. Periodicals that publish something of yours generally only give you a single copy, and I seldom keep hold of these. What's more, there's no sense in sending a whole brick by post just for the sake of a single page. I'll make copies for you occasionally. Here are two fragments from '1905': Father Gapon, and the beginning of the Potemkin mutiny. I doubt if you'll want the continuation. It's unexpected, isn't it? But just think for whom, for whose comprehension one is supposed to write!

[. . .]

But do read it seriously, not just sloppily. For one thing, this is a 'creative drama', and for another, there's 750 roubles worth of material. This isn't an easy job— that's what you have to do to earn the money. I break the material up into stanzas of 10 or 11 lines. There's no help for it, it's not my fault if fees nowadays are only paid out after you're dead. Ask Papa to forgive me for using such tiny handwriting, and read it aloud to him nicely, once you've understood it yourself. It's important to understand the precise sense here—every single word counts. [. . .]

Boris Pasternak to Josephine Pasternak

23 March 1926. Moscow.

Dear Zhonichka,

Our parents told me about Rilke's letter, which has so thrown me that I haven't been able to work today. What excited me wasn't what probably pleased Papa and Mama, since after all I only got to hear of it by ricochet—that someone, somewhere, in France or England, knows me, is translating me, mentions me—but naturally I haven't seen any of this with my own eyes, it's just that Tsvetaeva said so, or Akhmatova told someone about it.[1] But you need to know what Rilke was for me, and when this all started. This news was a short-circuit between widely separated extremes of my life. The incongruity of it shattered and devastated me, and now I don't know what to do with myself.

On top of everything else, you need to know who Valéry is—assuming this really is Paul Valéry, which is totally unlikely!

If Papa hasn't invented all this, then please copy out the whole of Rilke's letter, from beginning to end, because it's probably amazing and I want to read all of it. If Papa has been telling stories, I mean if he's exaggerated, then of course I'll forgive him, but he can't know what he's done to me. He says that 'R. writes enthusiastically about me'. I've translated that from Bayreuth-speak to my own Scriabin-speak.[2] A breath of closeness and love, Platonism, the equality of the spiritual with the divine. And if that's all fibs, then [may the fates forgive Papa].[3]

I embrace you.

Borya

Leonid's summary of Rilke's words did slightly alter their tone, and he misremembered the fact that Boris's poem had been published in a periodical edited by Paul Valéry, but had not been translated by him.

1. Anna Andreyevna Akhmatova was a major Russian poet who survived political hostility, the execution of her first husband Nikolai Gumilev, and the death in prison of her last husband Nikolai Punin. The arrest of her son Lev Gumilev in 1938 inspired her great poem *Requiem*. Her works were proscribed in the Soviet Union for most of the time from the mid-1920s until Stalin's death in 1953, and *Requiem* was only published there in 1987. See also below, p. 238.
2. 'Bayreuth-speak' is not a reference to the National Theatre in Bayreuth, but to Bayreutherstrasse in Berlin where Leonid and Rosalia had lived. The term no doubt refers to their propensity for emotional, enthusiastic language, as opposed to terse, dry 'Scriabin-speak'.
3. The words in brackets were deleted by Josephine out of superstitious fear for her father.

Boris Pasternak to Josephine Pasternak

28 March 1926. Moscow.

Dear Zhonichka,

You're robbers and cannibals, the whole lot of you out there!

Well, where's your imagination? They just mention, in passing, the bare fact that Rilke has written a letter to Papa—no more than that; and then the letter gets forwarded to you, with the idea that afterwards, when the family has had time to make full use of it at home, it can be sent to me for my own family use—only in part, naturally, just what relates to me, in the napkin-ring engraved with 'Borya'—like any of those other famous bits of 'happy news'—'Olya has been praised by Marr', say, or 'Shura—by Mendelsohn', or even, or even, 'Papa has been painted by Corinth'.[4] To promise me such a table-napkin (and I haven't even seen it:—I can just imagine how much it looks like Hamlet's shirt-front—for Papa wrote to say that I'm 'a Russian poet who has already achieved a fine reputation'—I wonder how fragrantly that came across in German!)—to promise me that napkin, and then expect me to wait and smile with delight (I was in tears and couldn't sleep for three nights running, because this isn't about Corinth or 'praising'), and expect me to go to the lavatory and 'worrk' (pronounced in the appropriate way), and be thrilled with my son, and love my father and mother, and so on and on, and—and they'll send it to me in their next letter. How kind! And a cake from Gaston's? And we'll all sit down to tea, and Yakov Maximovich[5] will be there.

I don't know what would have happened to me if this source of excitement, so subtly flaunted by you and then immediately and lovingly concealed again, hadn't been joined by another one, more open and direct—the same element, but from a different place. By chance I received a typescript of one of Tsvetaeva's latest works, the 'Poem of the End'. Happily, this excitement wasn't suppressed by anyone or anything, and it has managed to find expression. I have her address, and I wrote to tell her who she is and what she's doing.

Oh, what an artist she is—I can't help loving her best in all the world, just as I love Rilke. I'm not telling you this in order to confide in you, but to say: read her. You (or Fedia) must have acquaintances in Paris. Ask them to send you

---

4. Boris's cousin, Olga Freidenberg, a specialist in classical antiquity, had recently been praised by the distinguished Soviet Academician N.Ya. Marr; Alexander's latest architectural project had pleased a leading architect, Erich Mendelsohn; and Leonid's portrait had been painted by the German artist Lovis Corinth. (It now hangs in the Hamburg Kunstmuseum.)

5. Yakov Romm, an amateur musician and family friend.

everything there is by her, and read it. You must hear a lot of the same things in it that I do. Amongst the riot of imperfect stuff of modest worth, one repeatedly comes across pieces of real, great, perfect art, revealing a talent that often rises to genius. The only other people to excite me like this have been Scriabin, Rilke, Mayakovsky and Cohen.[6]

Unfortunately I scarcely know anything of what she has done in recent years. Someone brought me her Russian tale 'A Fine Fellow', which is dedicated to me. It's a beautiful piece of romantic writing, but not up to the standard of the best parts of the 'Poem of the End'. That has something of me in it. But good God, into what miraculous hands did that something fall! You absolutely have to get it, not for me but for yourself. Even if you did send it, it wouldn't arrive. And then you can feel—oh, what a sorrowful but what an honourable tragedy we are acting out here, and paying for it with our very souls! There's nobody here who could write such a thing. Oh, how depressing it all is, how depressing. How terrible '1905' is! What uninspired genre-painting we go in for!! What's it all for, what am I doing it for? But I won't always be like this, you'll see.

Your Borya

[…]

Boris sent four more impatient postcards demanding to see Rilke's letter, all on the backs of reproductions of his father's works, as a propitiatory gesture.

Boris Pasternak to his parents

[29 March 1926. Moscow.]

My dears!

So where's the promised Rilke? How kind you are! 'We didn't know it would excite you so much'—? Papa wrote about Rilke's letter in a brief postscript (I quote

6. Alexander Scriabin was a great composer and a friend of the Pasternak family; they spent the summer of 1903 in neighbouring dachas. Boris was much influenced by him as a young man, as he recounts in *An Essay in Autobiography*.

The poet Vladimir Mayakovsky (see also p. 1) has been described as 'the antipode of Pasternak'. He had a strong personal, romantic voice in his pre-Revolutionary poetry, but later dedicated his creativity wholeheartedly to the service of the Revolution and the State. From 1922 he was a leading figure in LEF, the 'Left Front of Art' movement, with which Boris Pasternak was briefly associated (he broke with it in 1927). Mayakovsky committed suicide in 1930, but was posthumously promoted by Stalin as 'the best and most talented poet' of Soviet times.

Hermann Cohen was the Marburg philosopher with whom Boris had studied in 1912 and who influenced him profoundly.

it word for word) ... 'a gratifying letter—gratifying because he writes enthusiastically about you, Boris ... and he recently read, etc.' So? Does that mean that he had read something else of mine previously, perhaps in the original (which would have been more precious for me)? A thousand riddles—and then silence. And then it'll turn out that there was just some phrase or other, meaning something entirely different from what the family fanfaronade made of it! Were you wanting to give me pleasure? How clever, how skilful, how well you understand the secrets of an artist's being, modest, fathomless and loving! Thanks a lot.

Boris Pasternak to Lydia Pasternak

[1 April 1926. Moscow.]

Dear Lidochka!

Today Stella got a letter from you. I asked her whether there was any message for me—and received a surprised look. Can Papa really have thought that I'd note his statement about Rilke's enthusiasm, and calmly carry on living with it? I mean, he needn't have written it in the first place. Or else he could have written properly, quoting Rilke's actual words, which are precious to me. It's just as if someone were expounding Lermontov: 'There's something about love. About a twig. About Arabs ...' It's a document! A document! We quote actual lines, and value them. Translated enthusiasm is worthless!

Yesterday I got a letter from Zhonia. The same ideas on life, and the human spirit, as everyone else's. A mountain of hospitality—and not a word about Rilke. Are you purposely making fun of me, or what? Is this your April Fool's joke? But why pick on such a topic as this!

Or else, if (as I'm convinced), 'Rilke writes enthusiastically about you' is something Papa has inflated out of some entirely meaningless sentence with the idea of 'giving me pleasure'—well, I haven't lived a single minute of my life for that sort of 'pleasure', and he should be ashamed of demeaning me so!!! The main thing is that this is playing a game with intimacies of a high order, of which you all evidently have no understanding whatever.

Boris Pasternak to his parents and sisters

[1 April 1926. Moscow.]

My dears!

I've just enclosed a postcard to Lida in Shura's express letter. I feel miserable and bitter about this one-week quarrel with you. However much I'm in the right, I should have bottled it all up or overcome it. I love you all very much, and what I said about Papa, what has burst out from me over these last few days, bears no relation to my constant feelings for him. Forget about everything, as I have forgotten his deadly little postscript. Nothing has happened, I know nothing, I remember nothing. I'm entering a grey, austere, indifferent period of my life, from which I had briefly escaped into a realm of great emotion. A chance event has shown me how right I was to toughen my character and keep it in the state of equilibrium that age brings with it. And how terrible of me to attack you for the fact that you are modern people—as I probably am too.

Forgive me for everything. I kiss you all warmly.

Forget about my postcards. I wrote them under the stress of extreme emotion. I'll take myself in hand. I don't expect anything. But how you have tortured me—what you have laid your hands on—if you only knew!!! Anyway, forgive me, and let everything be as it was before. Papa, I'm sorry.

It was not until 3 April that Lydia's copy of Rilke's letter was finally despatched. Rilke had written saying how vividly Leonid's letter had reminded him of his visits to Russia in 1899 and 1900. During the previous winter in Paris, he frequently met Russian émigrés, and was moved yet again by his love for Russia and pity for her destiny. 'From various sides', he went on, 'I have become aware of the early fame of your son Boris. The last thing I tried reading when I was in Paris were his very good poems (in a little anthology edited by Ilya Ehrenburg).' In a postscript he added that 'in the winter issue of the good, heavy-weight Paris periodical *Commerce*, there is a very eloquent poem by Boris Pasternak, translated by Elena Izvolskaya.'

The extracts from Rilke's letter sent to Boris in Moscow omitted some critical passages comparing the tragic fate of present-day Russia to the Tartar yoke—passages which would have fallen foul of the Soviet censors.

Leonid Pasternak to Boris and Alexander Pasternak

[1–2 April 1926. Berlin.]

My dear young falcons!

You first, dear Borya. The Rilke affair is closed! I've taken your two postcards straight on the chin—one of them addressed to the entirely guiltless Zhonichka, and the other special supplementary one aimed at us two. Neither postcard contained anything new or unexpected for me, or any of us.

[. . .] Then, today (again as usual!) we received your first 'penitent' postcard—'Papa, I'm sorry' and so forth. I know that tomorrow or the next day there'll be more, when you've had time to read the extracts from the letter. My dear fellow, we haven't got time—Mama can't always be writing and copying out letters, Lidok is revising intensively for her exam, and I too have to work, though I often have to 'raise my pencil in mediation', as I do now. I thought that you were grown-up, that you could wait a couple of days . . . until the letter was copied out (there were some 'old-fashioned' turns of phrase in it that prevented us from sending you the whole thing, as we could to Zhonia . . .). Yes, I repeat: I know, I'm sure, there's bound to be either a postcard or else a full-length letter of 'penitence and forgiveness', full of merciless self-flagellation—well, that was why I started this letter, to avoid any such lengthy explanations. The Rilke incident is long ago exhausted; it's not for you to ask me forgiveness, but for me—and I've already asked it of you in my last letter, for the torments of impatience and so on that I caused you. As stupid as Krylov's bear,[7] I thought that I would share some good news with you, 'provisionally', in the hope that you would believe that I hadn't invented it, and that as an adult person you would suppose that something more detailed would follow on (it wasn't on fire, was it?), probably, or at worst you might have asked, like anyone else: 'So what did Rilke write to you—for God's sake let me know'—but no, little Boryusha flings himself on the floor and ro-o-o-oars—so loud that there's no calming this Lyovochka, this curly-headed little lion-cub—and drums his little feet on the floor, and the neighbours come running round, but he won't be pacified, he's screamed himself hoarse, his face is covered with dribble, he won't let his nanny near him, he's roaring louder and louder, and all that. That's why he's called Lyovochka!—And then it's all over, and of course as usual it's the fault of the parents who spoiled him, and now they're cross with the child they themselves spoiled!

So, my dear Boryusha, I haven't ever been cross, not even in the days when it was worse than this—and certainly not now. So don't write us any letters of penitence or forgiveness, since I know that 'once the fit is over', it's bound to be followed by repentance, self-flagellation and all the rest of it. The incident, I repeat, is closed. I've written more about it than it merited, because if I had passed it over in silence, you would have concluded that I (and Zhonia, and all of us here) had been bitterly offended and hurt, and you would have been tormented by pangs of conscience—and I repeat, all for nothing! All of us—without a word

7. A reference to a fable by the Russian fabulist Ivan Krylov (1769–1844), after Aesop. A hermit befriends a bear and they become inseparable. One day as the man is sleeping, a fly settles on him, and the bear tries to swat the fly with a heavy stone, smashing his friend's skull.

being said—just looked at one another, smiled our accustomed smiles, and we're all—myself in particular—very grateful to you for your nice, heart-warming postcards with my sketches on them! [...]

Rilke's letter, and the fact that he had read Boris's poetry not only in French but also in the original Russian, acted—in Boris's own words—like a 'short-circuit'. 'I couldn't have been more astonished', he later wrote to Rilke, 'if I had been told that I was being read in Heaven. Not only had I never imagined such a possibility in all the twenty-odd years that I have revered you—it was ruled out from the start, and now it ran counter to my ideas about my own life and its course. The arc whose ends had become ever more widely separated year by year, and should never have met, suddenly touched before my very gaze, in the twinkling of an eye. . . . For the first time in my life, I realised that you were a person, and that I could write and tell you what a giant, superhuman role you had played in my existence. Such an idea had never once occurred to me before. Now it found a place in my awareness. And soon afterwards, I wrote to you.'

Boris's letter to Rilke is dated 12 April 1926. He sent it to his parents' address, because the USSR and Switzerland did not have diplomatic or postal relations. To circumvent these difficulties, Boris asked Rilke to answer him via Tsvetaeva's Paris address. The triangular correspondence between Boris, Tsvetaeva and Rilke continued through that summer.

Boris briefly thought of travelling to see Tsvetaeva in Paris, and visiting Rilke with her. However, he changed his mind and decided to stay in Moscow for another year, to complete his long poem 'Lieutenant Schmidt'. He also continued his efforts to arrange for his wife and son to visit Germany.

Once again, it is evident that Boris's and Leonid's letters have crossed.

Boris Pasternak to Leonid Pasternak

[5 April 1926. Moscow.]

My dear, dear Papa!

I shan't calm down until you tell me that you're not cross with me, that you've forgiven me and love me. Don't write me letters, that's difficult—just write those few words: I've forgiven you, I'm not cross, I love you. Oh, the everlasting collisions between these two sides of life: the fairness of an emotion, in other words its correct motivation, and its mistaken direction! You dear, great, beloved man, who have achieved the devil only knows how much—what fault is it of yours that

I'm such a villain? Please write and confirm that you've forgiven me. I warmly embrace you and Mama.

'How many scenes, how many tears, valerian drops and promises!!'[8]

And it's happened again. I kiss you, my little sisters! O, life, life!

Boris Pasternak to Josephine Pasternak

[13 April 1926. Moscow.]

Dear Zhonichka!

I still haven't begged your pardon for the rough things I think I said to you during that hellish week (something like 'Holy Week', eh?). They've announced new rules for getting passports. Instead of costing 30 roubles, they now cost 200, not to mention visas, additional fees and the rest. 500 marks, just imagine! But I'm not abandoning this idea. Zhenechka will come to you. This summer and next winter I'm going to have to work like a slave. Not for the money—God forbid. But there's so much still to do! I've become afraid that I'll die this year, before I've had time to finish *Spektorsky* or write all the other things I want to. But my mood has changed sharply. I'm going to subordinate everything (even what nowadays passes for 'accepted behaviour') to my freedom of imagination.

Your B.

Leonid Pasternak to Boris Pasternak

13 April 1926. Berlin.

My dear children!

Thank you, dear Boryusha, for the poetry you sent, which we liked very much—the only pity is that it was short and there wasn't much of it (besides the fact that it was fragments); it would have been good if. . . but maybe that's the secret of its virtues. I certainly understand, and so do we all in the family understand, a brief allusion—a detail of your childhood and its environment—but the question is how it would strike a stranger (but perhaps everyone would understand). For us, an allusion in two words is enough to conjure up a whole living experience, an epoch, a slice of life!

8. A quotation from Boris's poem '1905', which he had just sent to his father.

The departure of Boris's wife and son for the West was linked to a crisis in the marriage. Boris did not accompany them, and Zhenia said that she would not be writing to him from Germany—a resolution she kept for some time.

Written on the eve of that departure, Boris's letter shows how for him the spring of 1926 was coloured by the new possibilities of free contact with the West, and by the excitement of the friendship between himself, Rilke, and Tsvetaeva. This friendship was to be one of the happiest and most significant experiences of his life.

Boris Pasternak to his parents

17 June 1926. Moscow.

My dear, warmly beloved Papa and Mama!

The passport has come through, thanks to Pepa[9]—an exceptional event these days when everyone's applications get turned down, and the more official a personage is, the quicker it's refused. Soon, soon you'll meet your daughter-in-law [. . .] Zhenia, whom you already know, though she's changed such a lot that she may be unrecognizable. And your grandson whom you don't know at all. He's been represented to you in excessively and undeservedly glowing terms, nothing like my view of him; such praise would be bound to prejudice your first impressions of him even if he deserved it. And he never has deserved that much praise, least of all now that he's reached the age at which a child becomes vulnerable to being spoilt. He's a little tyrant, a screamer, an egoist and a usurper. Perhaps he's not responsible for these faults.

I don't want you to be put off by your first, probably unfavourable impression of him—I don't want you to feel that you're being harsh on him, in fact—so let me admit to a feeling that invariably comes over me every time I see him again after even two days' separation. I felt it very recently, last week, when he and Zhenia were staying at our friends' dacha and I didn't see him for five days. It's such a powerful feeling that it can't be fortuitous or peculiar to me. I'm sure that when I describe it I'll awake memories in Papa of feelings which, if they weren't precisely the same, were similar to mine. After a short separation, when I first look at him, my heart is oppressed by the feeling 'Not mine! Not mine!' This is accompanied by an overwhelming, unbearable feeling of pity for him (as if being 'mine' meant being the son of God), and a much weaker feeling of pity for Zhenia and myself. Let me explain. 'Not mine' doesn't in any way mean that I

9. See above, p. 13, n. 22.

don't acknowledge the fact that he's my son—in fact it's accompanied by a feeling of terrible physical likeness between the boy and myself. There's something different here.

At least half of this deeply wounding feeling is subjective, linked to the very structure of my imagination, since imagination plays the primary role in my life. But part of it—just because of my almost clairvoyantly mistrustful nature, which dreams infallible dreams—is objective too. In little Zhenichka's case, it's a chaos of linguistic and other influences shaping him, most of them pernicious through and through—pernicious because they are lower and worse than his own innate characteristics, his origins.[10] This is nothing to do with the Abrabanels.[11] There's no snobbery here.

It's surprisingly difficult for me to talk—particularly at a distance—about matters of prime importance: about physics, the indisputable facts that constitute the human world. Every word one says imposes another reservation. The terminology is the same as that of everyday speech, but everyday speech doesn't give the direct meaning. In my vocabulary, the word 'lavka' means 'a bench', but in everyday language it's a shop. That's how far away verbal usage has taken us. Like 'die Bank' in German.[12]—Anyway: so it's nothing to do with the Abrabanels. Parental involvement is something like aviation. A vocation that carries people upwards. Too rarely during the course of a day does the boy see human legs being swept through the air. He's spent too much time squeezing his way among legs that were marking time on the same spot where the previous generation had placed them. Yet it was the intertwining of those same limbs that called him into existence.

When my soul is cut and split to its foundations by such discontent with what is supposedly mine, or supposedly me, then my yearning for what is genuinely mine or genuinely me is accompanied by a hurried realisation of what is most important in a person—the divine, essential element. It's no accident that one's first juvenile convictions are confirmed, ever more clearly, by the conclusions we reach during our gradual maturation, or perhaps even at the onset of our old age.

---

10. Boris appears to be uneasy about both the general materialism of Soviet culture—but censorship prevents him from being explicit—and the influence of the Frishman family, who were probably spoiling the little boy. His additional anxieties about Zhenichka's linguistic environment have been voiced earlier—see above, p. 32, n. 37.

11. 'Abrabanels' refers to the Pasternak family's reputed descent from the distinguished Sephardic line of Don Isaac Abrabanel (1437–1508), a Talmudic scholar and royal adviser to Alphonso V of Portugal, then to Isabella and Ferdinand II of Spain.

12. 'Die Bank' means both 'bench' and 'bank' in German.

It's no accident, because our juvenile froth, as it boils off, forms the very essence of what we forget, while what we retain and call to mind is the unique insights of childhood, those inspired ideas, those idealistic theorems of life whose demonstration over the course of many years (even the most apparently nonsensical of them) makes up the whole of our later life. I would say this: when a living person dies (if death hasn't already overtaken him before that time), what does death catch him at? An uncompleted, complex and prolix demonstration of his childhood, once expounded in succinct, conclusive and categorical terms.

So don't be surprised by the resemblance to the past in the position where I now stand. There is no truth and no goodness—since we are dealing with a living being or a combination of many beings—there is no humanity outside a thoroughly considered aesthetic. No, there cannot and must not be any instance where something within the soul winces, instinctively and unaccountably, while 'duty', or 'fairness', or 'pity', appear to be prompting some different reaction. In all such cases, one's conscience, as it yields to the arguments of the words in quotation marks, is simply being hypocritical—dodging the harder and more heroic deeds that are dictated by the feeling that's wincing. (Try to discover it, and you'll find column after column of injunctions; try to obey the injunctions, and you'll find tenfold greater fairness and pity!)[13]

There's only one thing that needs to be said, when we remember the destiny of this truth, which is not new. We need to add that the aesthetic we are concerned with can only be an active one, the aesthetic of a person who loves for the first time and therein sets an example to others; the aesthetic of a prophet and not a false prophet, the aesthetic of a poet who has invariably, throughout his life, felt and spoken things fresh and new. It's an important corrective, the essence of thought! Aesthetics at their peak, in full spate, represent a quintessence of superhumanity—which incidentally includes a quintessence of truth and goodness and thousands of other virtues which don't have names because we know them by heart; whereas in a state of decadence most of these qualities are forgotten. That's the only reason why a passive aesthetic (even Wilde's aesthetic, that is to say even Nietzsche's aesthetic,[14] let alone a class aesthetic or a hereditary or retrospective one) is dangerous and base and inferior to the words I put in quotation

---

13. In this rather obscure passage, Boris implies that ethical imperatives that lack an aesthetic dimension are wrong and misguided.

14. *[Marginal note by Boris in the original letter]*: Nietzsche and Wilde are the true authors of the thought adduced here. Their truths—are true. But being obliged to speak in paradoxes, they delivered the thesis of an active aesthetic into the power of the aesthetes and of aestheticism, that is to say, for the first time in history they gave impetus to a passive aesthetic which, before them, had been impotent.

marks earlier. A passive aesthetic is an upside-down aesthetic, in other words, it's life stood on its head, life whose content has dropped out.

I've written at length about this for the following reason. As far as the boy (your grandson!) is concerned, let your immediate feelings be your guide. They won't betray you. Don't be indulgent. Give expression to the aesthetic *daimon* within you: that's something the boy will understand in you more readily and more gratefully than any sweetmeats. A fairy-tale, Papa's humour, Mama's caress—in other words, Papa's artistry (as an actor) and Mama's lyricism—let those be your chocolates and your *Grosselternthum*[15] for him. How unconsciously he always reacted, ever since he was a small child, to my mood when I came to his cot—whether I was in an excited state, straight from writing good poetry, or just in the trousered animality of fatherhood!

I admit it on the spot. I have always had a selfish motive for dreaming of his meeting with you. I'm now living through the apogee of this selfishness. His closeness to you must liquidate and extinguish the non-aesthetic influences on his life in Moscow. How can I isolate him here? And am I to blame for everything? My and Zhenia's influence doesn't make up more than one-tenth of his whole, contradictory, mollusc-like environment. What am I saying!—not more than one-hundredth. On my word of honour, there was no other way. Nor is Zhenia to blame for anything either.

A word or two about her. Thank God, she's a Nietzschean in the best sense of the word. In other words, she would sign up to the truths in this letter, if only I weren't the one expressing them. I don't know whether she is as deep (that is, as well equipped with an intact spiritual reserve) as I am. But at all events she's more stubborn, more even, more consistent in her convictions, which are close to what I've just described. Life with me has for her been a sentence to hard labour, simply because of my long-standing, protracted betrayal of aesthetics.[16] Since both the name and the idea of 'half a life' are absurd, this existence hasn't been a life at all. There was no alternative. I am an un-free, non-civilian person. I am a particle of the state, a soldier in a small army consisting of three or four, or anyway not more than ten, real, non-fictitious persons, and thousands of phantoms, shadows and false claims. I've been obliged, unwillingly and unwittingly, to re-enact that whole army's diversionary movement towards the ABC, universal literacy and the worship of sacred commonplaces. Perhaps I'm deluded in my belief that this

15. 'Grandparenting'.
16. Presumably because Boris felt he had been writing to order, betraying his own aesthetic conscience.

pilgrimage is accomplished, and that each of us is now free to return to his own star, his fate and destiny. Even if this feeling is premature (there's no objective foundation for it), its onset coincided for me with a number of circumstances which called me loudly back to life.

This last half-year has resurrected me, it's the start of a new birth. It's a strange fact that in the moments of my deepest tenderness towards Zhenia (mother), the rarest moments of keenest power and purity, I invariably feel myself an absolutely free man—that is, I feel that I myself am an entirely chance phenomenon, and so is she. Once again, this feeling (like my feeling for the boy, that he's 'not mine') is so astonishingly powerful, meaningful and reproducible, that it can't possibly be mine alone; it must remind Papa of something.

A range of themes and plans, and of my own emotions, progressing from the Revolution through a sense of history, or of myself in history, has become intimately identified for me with the fate of a whole generation of Russians. This happened before I started hearing, ever more frequently, how the two extremes of that generation were again becoming well-disposed towards me. Shakhovskoy, Sviatopolk-Mirsky, Izvolskaya, and—the Komsomol.[17]

It would be an exaggeration, a distortion of the truth, to represent me as a well-known or popular figure. That's not the case, and I hope it won't be. What cheered me was precisely the fact that this present wave of goodwill accurately represented me—myself, my character and my aspirations. It would be true—though not the whole truth—to say that my distinctive characteristic was that of encompassing wide latitudes and quantities and abstractions in my own closed personal circle; the intimisation, previously of the world, and now, of history; the assimilation of a collective, granular infinity into myself. This happens in a confident, youthful way, almost superstitiously, without affectation, with no loss of proportion, and unknown to anybody. I don't know what modesty means, in its hot, living form, if it isn't the general fusion of these feelings. I love the same peculiar quality in Marina [Tsvetaeva]. I love her altogether, and I should never be able to prove in words that this in no way conflicts with my devotion to Zhenia, nor threatens her in any way, until I can prove it in deeds, until it's proved

17. Prince Dmitry Shakhovskoy edited the journal *Blagonamerenny*, which printed favourable reviews of Pasternak's work by the critic Sviatopolk-Mirsky. Elena Alexandrovna Izvolskaya's French translation of two Pasternak poems was published in Paul Valéry's journal *Commerce*. All three were independent representatives of Russian émigré culture. The Komsomol (the Communist Youth League in the Soviet Union) wanted to print extracts from '1905' in the paper *Komsomolskaya Pravda*. Thus a readership from two political extremes coincided in its estimation of Boris's work.

by time, as a gift to me and her—time that is entrancing, pregnant with discoveries and inspiration, time that is always beautiful when it's not being prompted and its movements aren't being interfered with.

Just as it's impossible to breathe by only inhaling all the time, or only exhaling, so I, too, refuse to accept the features of my present life, from the Volkhonka to my love for Mayakovsky, as the characteristics of my biography, the *mise-en-scène* of my full earthly existence, unless I can tear myself away from all of this for a year and escape to a cycle of other destinies and other difficulties. If I had cast off from my native shore this spring, as for a while I wanted and planned to do, that would have been a hysterically impulsive act. There would have been more of a destructive element in it than of truth. And yet the whole sphere of my thoughts, decisions and tendencies is subordinated to a desire for creation and longevity. I wasn't able to do that this spring. The necessary resources (incidentally including financial ones) aren't yet available. Most important of all, Zhenia herself isn't ready for it. And without that I can't do it. Only when I had exhausted every last resource could I have brought myself to risk her temporary incomprehension. I love her, or want to love her, more than any other individual person in the world, and if she understands me less well than Marina does, that's a serious disorder. It has to be cured, and it is curable.

Zhenia has all the instincts of a great and independent person, a person who is growing expansively and can blend qualities within herself today, which yesterday were not susceptible to such fusion. Involuntary difficulties created by the nature of our life and times have cast a shadow on these instincts, and partly atrophied them. Since it was I, above all, who came up against the false and difficult aspects of our times (in earning money etc.), the harmful influences appeared to be reaching her from me, passing through me to her. And that was indeed the case, though not through any fault or wish of mine: a great person, or the embryo of one, was diminished and circumscribed by me. I very much want her to get to Paris in the full awareness of her freedom and of the prospects open to her. That itself will be a preparation for my own journey next year; and for our continued life in the future.

You may be appalled by the profound egotism of my argument. You may all—particularly Mama—be astounded by the freedom with which I evade the question of the boy, as though I were tossing him into your or Zhonia's arms while devoting myself to all sorts of untrammelled activities. But would you be arguing in those terms if I were going off to war? And I repeat, I'm not a free man, I'm a conscript. That's the first point. Secondly, I haven't told you this before. I remember very well how distressed Mama always used to be at my predatory behaviour—for instance the way I stole cigarette-papers during the famine years. We all remember those scenes. The scenes and the cigarette-papers and the years are gone and forgotten, but the poems remain. That was an event in the life of a great poet, not a trivial detail in a family chronicle.

Never mind whether the next year or two turn out as my profound, far-reaching egotism dreams them, or as your sacred altruism directs them. It's not the sweetness of my existence that depends on it, nor the fate of my well-known gluttony and my desire for a calm and comfortable life. What does depend on it is the outcome of a divine, superhuman lottery: it's the question of whether I am going to write my novel, or whether it'll be written, on the basis of widely disseminated hints, by some disciple of mine whom I've never met. The hand at work is no human one, and all it knows is that the cards are being shuffled; this fact alone means that there can be no insisting or imploring. Even a hint of disagreement seems to be a falsification and distortion of destiny. I seem to see before me, in the system of forces carrying me onwards, my family abroad (you or Fedia or Zhonia) as those near and predestined people who will carry out the difficult but feasible task, and by doing so will help the impossible to come about, to take shape and survive.

But who can prove to me that my vision of these great matters and movements is correct? Perhaps what I need here isn't you at all, but—let us say—a tragedy; and perhaps without one, nothing will work out for me? Here I am, writing to you—writing and thinking. Can it be that there's no-one among you who can hear and understand that the voice of this letter is speaking of love (including love for you); the most intense love of which I'm capable—I, a man in trousers and a tie and with a permanent address. Do you have any notion of that?

But for the time being there's no question of any 'proposals'. Any day now, a piece of densely freckled life, very unlike its photographs but not like anything else on earth either, is going to enter your field of vision. That's all. There's nothing else to discuss for the moment. The rest will be decided by fate and the personal peculiarities of all the characters in the—I was going to say, the drama, but no—the family.

It's impossible not to let oneself run on too long, when in a single evening, in a letter, one touches on the sort of deep and dark strata that determine one's life. But it'll give you a general idea of my standards, my pretensions and my potential. Please don't reply. Especially not in detail. Be outspoken, free and unconstrained. Answer: 'You're a villain'. Or: 'Little Lion-Cub'. If that's the sort of thing you mean. If you find it unacceptable. Just don't saddle yourselves with the laborious torment of persuading me point by point. I've already told you that for me, there'll be just one noun governing all your predicates—the words of fate: 'Not them: find a different path, await a different force!' That's why it'll be enough if your answer is succinct and laconic. Its message could even be mimed, if one could convey that in a letter. A simple phrase like 'You're a fool' would be a whole region in which the banner of fatality could wave in freedom.

My dear ones, I'm writing without reading over what I write—I'm in a hurry. Don't fail to send this letter on to Zhonia. She'll separate the essence from the shell, the formulae from what's half-unsaid or repeated. All those dear eyes that will slide over these unworthy lines, I kiss them long and lovingly. Of course, I'll give my travellers a physical message of this kind to transmit, and they'll do that. Need I say that they're the dearest thing in the world to me? But they have to cease for a time from being everything (in a small world), so as to become everything again (in a larger one).

Anyway, enough of metaphysics. Pepa gave the required guarantees that Zhenia wouldn't be carrying any money. That was the only way she could get a passport. What exactly this means, we'll discover from him; we keep arranging to meet in the evening, and it keeps not working out for him. But it means that his undertaking, and his understanding of that undertaking, is binding on us (over and above the laws themselves). Zhenia wants to take a few things with her, which Shura has chosen. If Pepa and the Museums Directorate give her permission, she'll take them. Tomorrow I'll go and apply for the permits.[18]

It's excruciating and terrible that I still haven't replied to Rilke. But that's not because my love and admiration for him are insufficient. They are infinite (one can't say they're 'excessive', for to love him too much is impossible, and to love him infinitely is only just enough). The fault lies in a misunderstanding which has lasted a month. When Marina forwarded his letter to me, with understandable tact she didn't add anything of her own to the letter; she left the two of us, as it were, in the room alone. And I didn't know how things had gone with the two of them. Only now, some two weeks ago, has she sent me copies of his first two letters to her. I don't have the right to quote the second one (it's his reply to her, when she did as I had asked and sent his letter on to me). I can't quote it because of its power and richness, the letter of one poet to another, in which he calls her familiarly 'Du', and includes a new, uncompleted part of *Malte Brigge*, full of rare feeling. Only then did I pluck up courage, realising that I hadn't been wrong in

18. It would have been impossible for Boris to obtain passports for his wife and son without the influential support of Pepa Zbarsky, who had to guarantee that no money left the country with them. He did get permission for them to take a number of Leonid's pictures for a forthcoming exhibition at the Galerie Hartberg, Berlin.

my feelings and presentiments. The bond between us was what it had to be. I copy here what I can, justifying myself by his repeated and unchanging warmth towards Papa, whom he writes about in his first letter to Marina. So:

[Original in German]

3 May 1926

Dear Poetess,

I have just received from Boris Pasternak an infinitely moving letter, overflowing with a torrent of joy and feeling. All the emotions and all the gratitude that his letter excites in me, if I understand him rightly, are to be directed in the first instance to you, and then through your mediation to be transmitted on to him! The two books (the latest of mine to be published) which will follow this letter are for you, they are your property.

Two further copies will follow, as soon as I get them: these latter are to be forwarded to Boris Pasternak, if the censorship allows it. I am so overcome by the richness and power of his letter that I can say no more today, but please send the enclosed page to my friend in Moscow. As a greeting. Must I explain? You know that I have counted Boris's father Leonid O.P. as a true friend of mine for over 26 years.[19] After a long, long interval, a letter from him reached me from Berlin at the beginning of this winter—and I replied with all the joy that our mutual rediscovery aroused in me. But I would not have needed a message from Leonid Osipovich to tell me that his son was a great and famous poet; friends of mine had already provided me with proofs of this (last year in Paris), which I was moved and excited to read.

—He goes on to regret that he didn't meet Marina and get to know her during his stay in Paris. It seems he hadn't known her at all. Then she wrote to him (in answer to this letter), and they began the correspondence I've just described.

Here is his letter to me, in his own hand (the page he mentions in the letter copied above).

[Original in German]

Val-Mont, Glion (Vaud).

My dear Boris Pasternak,

Your wish was fulfilled in the very same hour that the letter you sent me had wrapped itself around me like the breath of wing-beats: the *Elegies* and the

---

19. Leonid met Rilke when the poet visited Moscow in 1900 and subsequently painted his portrait.

Sonnets to Orpheus are already in the poetess's hands. Further copies of these same books will soon reach you too. How can I thank you for allowing me to see and feel what you have so wonderfully multiplied within yourself? Your ability to turn the great richness of your spirit in my direction is a glory for your fertile heart. May all blessings fall on the paths you tread. I embrace you.

Yours, Rainer Maria Rilke

I am painfully aware that it's exactly a month today since I received this letter (and before that it had already made three journeys, since Marina was already by the ocean, in the Vendée, and it was sent on to her from Paris). But I have to be entirely myself, and collect my thoughts, before I can answer. For God's sake, Papa, don't correct my gaffe and don't think of thanking him on my behalf. Don't mediate in any way. And don't be jealous of anybody. You have no idea what you are to me, Papa, and how I think of you, and—when I can—write and speak about you. But it's only in absolute solitude that my voice can be pure. Well, goodbye. I must get money for their journey. Please receive the better part of my existence (Zhenia and our child) with unforced, open-hearted tenderness.

I kiss you. Borya.

We'll let you know the day of their arrival by telegram. They're travelling through Poland (via Aleksandrovo, through Warsaw, as in the old days).

Zhenia and Zhenichka's arrival in Berlin began painfully—the frightened two-year-old warded off his grandmother's welcome, because it had been severely impressed on him that she didn't like naughty children. A potentially hurtful moment that in no way diminished their enchantment with their grandson.

Leonid Pasternak to Boris Pasternak

30 June / 1 July 1926. Berlin.

Dear Boryusha!

I've already described in my postcard the joy with which we greeted our dear little grandson, who has become a great friend of mine. Unfortunately he was stupidly set against your mother (out of a desire to 'do good' to the two of them); she was very upset, and I'm doing all I can to convince her that all this is trivial, it'll all change, he'll forget it and get used to feeling that his grandmother is someone who loves him most of all, who is as endlessly devoted to him as only such a grandmother can be! Unfortunately I have been infernally busy these last days and I haven't been able to attend to my enchanting little grandson as much as I should have liked; but even in this short space of time, we've become friends. Oh, what a dear, lovely little boy! One could write a whole volume about him and our impressions of him, and all I can do is write a couple of words—he's a dear, lovable, intelligent boy, with a voice full of intimate and appealing intonations, boundless curiosity, and thousands of similar characteristics—all of which say little about him. God grant you bring him up to adulthood in happiness!

I embrace, kiss and bless you.

Your Papa

I kiss dear Shura and Ina a million times.

Boris was deeply troubled by his wife's persistent silence, and over the summer his letters to Josephine returned time and again to this topic.

Boris Pasternak to Josephine Pasternak

12 July 1926. Moscow.

Dear Zhonichka!

Yesterday Stella got a letter from you with a lot of news that was important for me. Only there wasn't much about Zhenia. Is her health improving? Thanks for that letter. But for God's sake don't write and answer me—I know how busy you all are, and their visit means you have even less time to spare. I don't expect an answer and there's no need for one, I'm not asking any questions. That's enough about me.

My constant feeling for you, which you well know, is strengthened and altered by the fact that you see Zhenia every day, while I never see her at all. I feel through you, as though you were me, if you see what I mean, and I'm writing to you with that subtle and indefinable pain which we experience when a forced analogy, the need to feel the same things as someone else, reveals to us the hidden elements of our makeup turned inside out by the effort; when the naked inward form begins to speak. Such a feeling overcomes me when (knowing Zhenia's tender feelings for you) I picture to myself the actual friendship, or at least the insistent possibility of a friendship which I can't resist imagining, between her and you. I envy you both, particularly you. It's the envy of a lower being for a higher one, of black for white. Being friends is easier than loving one another and living as a couple—which means living with a need for continual transformation, while surrounded by relations and loved ones, circumstances (always wretched), and people. People, people, people, whose greatest desire is this: to nail both of you firmly to one thing, preferably some stock cliché or trivial anecdote, so that they can know you as that one thing, labelled once and for all.

I love Zhenia terribly, more than anything in the world. I don't tell her that now, and I shan't write it (indeed, I don't know how I'm going to write to her at all), because when she hears it she makes the mistake that people always make in such situations. Who is proof against that?

She doesn't realise that one person's feelings aren't enough for two people to live on. Why is this error so common? It's provoked by the proximity of another truth, no less simple but opposite in meaning. This second truth, which glitters and casts the first into the shade, is as follows: love is born in the exclusiveness of a solitary feeling, in the victorious preponderance of one person's love over another's. People always confuse these truths, which use the same voice and the same words to talk about different things. The message of the first is about two people living together, in other words mainly about re-smelting and welding together the disorganised chaos one encounters on one's way, every minute of one's life, no matter how long. The second is about the meeting of two organic forces or worlds, about the heart, about heartfelt feelings in their pure state. These are different things, or different stages of the same thing. The electrical 'anti-pole' is called into existence only by a sympathetic effect of the first pole when it appears. But useful work requires an integral current, and if that's lacking it can't be remedied by dragging an inert raw material into the process.

Forgive me for these ignorant analogies, which will make you laugh and would make Lydia laugh too; try to find the proper sense in this Okeno-Novalisian heresy.[20] I've put it obscurely. I should have liked to express it clearly and comprehensibly. I'm writing about things that are important to me. Sometimes when I tell Zhenia about this, she replies that 'my letter hasn't got through to her'. It won't get through to you either.

But if only you knew how beautiful, how altogether splendid she was, in body and spirit, that winter when I called her and she came. How bold, and how ready to give—more than ideas, people, memories or words can express. I mustn't tell you everything; but what a lot of transforming and wounding torments she endured and accepted at that time! When I'm parted from her I keep picturing that time; and I can't call it to mind without suffering fresh and terrible pain for her self-respect. I behaved vilely. How many un-named and nameless crimes,

20. A reference to two German Romantics: the philosopher Lorenz Oken (1779–1851) and the poet Novalis (1772–1801).

crimes unrecognised by the rules of morality, each of us has committed against the beauty and honour of the moment! That was one of them. Has it been expiated? Objectively, in the time and space of life, it has indeed been atoned for with interest, through the life of our son, if he's really half as good as he's painted. But even subjectively, it would all have been redeemed absolutely, if Zhenia had been able to love me; if, this summer, she had suddenly become a great, great friend to me, believing in and excited not by me, but by her own belief. That will never be, as she has repeatedly said quite clearly. This hopeless admission of mine is no great discovery. And I wouldn't be saying any of these sorry things, nor grasping at a faint shadow of hope (see what expressions I'm reduced to!), if she hadn't restrained and stopped me this spring when I had almost decided to leave her and the boy.

I'm sorry that I never left, but it's not a lost happiness that I regret. Oh, no. I regret it as a rare opportunity for me to have done something that was in any case inevitable, and to have done it with less pain than at any other time. The inevitability of it creeps up on me out of her total silence, or out of her letters when she does write to me. The inevitability of it rises up out of the recent past, when—finding myself by chance at our last year's dacha—I suddenly remembered, on one beautiful evening, all my journeys to town, and how I used to return and meet her on the porch. How much humiliating, unheard-of cruelty there is in the past! And she doesn't know that she's like this!! And here's what reinforces that inevitability: every time I return from a trip to town, with the vague hope of finding something at home to soften the misery of my memories, I find that there hasn't been a letter today, as there wasn't on any of the previous days, and won't be tomorrow either.

Why did she hold me back in the spring? What is irreparable can yet be repaired: that was what I always thought. She used to see things more cleanly, coldly and rationally. And yet, she suddenly held me back. The impulse came from her. Consequently, something had changed in her. She must have known that there was something new for us both to expect—from her, not from me; for it had been she, not I, who held me back. That was what my feeble hopes and expectations rested on. But they're disintegrating before my eyes. During this separation, she has given me nothing new. In her actions, in her incomprehensible empty-heartedness towards me, she's absolutely the same as she was in the summer of 1924. But I'm not the same, I mustn't be the same. She shall not hear or see any more of those things that I used to tell her, straight out, on a first impulse, about herself. I can think about her as much as I like, but I shall either bury all that within me, or you shall hear about it, or some other woman will, some day—but not she, not she any longer. I'm tired of speaking and feeling all on my own, I know that all that is pointless, so long as she makes no higher demands on herself. I shan't write to her. If you know of anything that can quickly, surgically, cut short this long torment, let me know at once. Do you know what I mean? Perhaps you can see her character clearly, and can read her heart. Her capacity, or incapacity, to feel as a human being, and be carried away by her own feelings, is more important to me (that is—more frightening, sharper, more painful) than . . . a possible infidelity.

In the springtime, she was put on trial here by people, and blind chance events, and prophetic coincidences. They all drove me away from her; they all said no, there's no room for hope here. They all condemned her. I didn't know that the separation I had firmly decided on would hurt her. She said: stay. The sound of her voice influenced me more than all that chorus of well-wishers. I put my faith in her, more than I did in destiny. If you see any way out, let me know. I desperately want her to be magnanimous, kind and adult. I can't not love her. I can't love anyone else as I do her. But that's irrelevant to her. It's all up to her now.

Please, love her with all your heart. She's an unhappy person. But do you understand me? There's no jesting with life's opportunities. I want to have a good, real life with her. But that won't happen. For her, I am distant and strange.

Forgive me for this letter. It's hard to read, but it was harder to write. I shall write to you again, many times, and tell you many things. Nothing can make good this loss. Although my conviction that we must separate was shaken by her plea last spring . . . but what hope is there for me? And I no longer have the strength to bear any more hostility or indifference.

I can't write anything to the little one, I feel so bitter and distressed.

Boris Pasternak to Josephine Pasternak

[Mid-July 1926. Moscow.]

Dear Zhoniura.

Thank you very much indeed for the photographs. Naturally I'm still concerned that there's no word from Zhenia. On the rare occasions when I feel calmer, I can't call that calmness satisfactory, because at such times I'm assailed and shackled by the way she keeps me in complete ignorance—ignorance of what we are to each other and of how she views herself and what her intentions are. It's her turn to speak; I've already written to you to explain why.

[. . .]

My heart aches at Zhenia's loss of weight. You can't imagine how that distresses me. It's not just that she needs to get better. So long as she's emaciated, she's not Zhenia! It's difficult to express this without making it look like a joke, or provoking indignation; but there are forms in which a person is his real self, an embodiment of what he is, and these forms are different for each individual. I, for instance, or Shura, or Papa, could be skinny without any moral damage to ourselves. I won't go on piling up examples—but Zhenia remains morally distorted so long as she fails to put on any weight. I'm not joking; at worst, I'm only out by a matter of ten pounds or so. Zhonechka! People get better in sanatoria, don't they? Is that really impossible to achieve? In the photographs of her as a child or a schoolgirl, and in my memory of her, she's plumper, warmer, more harmonious and less clear-cut. Her present frailty is my fault. I'm obliged to talk about her outward appearance, because it's transparent and allows me to see the roots of her bitter, awkward, unhappy cast of mind, which was never in the Creator's plan and was never her true self. I'm tortured by the idea that I'm the one who has dried her out, eaten and drunk her up. Yet I'm not a vampire at all.

I beseech you—when you have a little free time, do something about this. There are many ways of getting round her infuriating unwillingness to do herself any good. I know that it's simply maddening, this stubbornly clinging anaemia that shuns good health and pushes away a glass of milk or a plate of scrambled egg; as maddening as anything that obstructs you from working a miracle and doing good. But you have to overcome this feeling. Anyway, you should arrange it all through a servant. Apart from that, she's probably exhausted by little Zhenichka—she probably spends days on end with him. Shouldn't you hire someone for him? Couldn't you work out something like that? Remember that for all Mama's self-sacrifice, which was her chief character trait, we still had nurseries and nannies just like all the other homes at the time. So that any hasty generalisations and judgements about Zhenia, on the lines of 'other mothers manage . . .', would be unfounded, cruel and unfair. After all, the whole notion of her trip started with the idea of her resting and recovering. Remind her that she has a winter at Vkhutemas[21] ahead of her and she'll need all her strength.

Please don't be angry with me for giving you advice and asking you to do things for me. It's true that it's tactless and pushy of me; I ought to be thanking you for all you've already done—more than I've asked of you—rather than giving you further instructions. If possible, don't show letters of this kind to Fedia. To a male eye, they're ridiculous. In reality, I'm not a pathetic wreck.

I kiss you warmly. Hug the boy. [. . .]

---

21. The Higher Institute of Art and Technology, in Moscow.

Boris Pasternak to Josephine Pasternak

27 July 1926. [Moscow.]

Zhonichka, how can I thank you? I was reading and re-reading your letter in the bus and in the long queue at the Moscow Finance Department, where (as every summer), I was paying in my income tax, with fines for lateness, in the stifling heat.

'Boris Leonidovich!', our old postman called out to me—you'll remember him—and thrust a letter into my hands at the very bus-stop, right in front of the bus. The letter made me happy, firstly because you love her so much and stick up for her. Go on doing that. You must know one thing: she's an unusual person, but also a terribly damaged one. There are many things you don't know about her that make her deserve your love. Another joy is that you agree with me how overwhelmingly important it is for her to recover and get some rest. It was marvellous of you to scatter here and there in your letter, in passing, by way of illustration, some living details that soothed my eyes: so that, for instance, I saw her in the sun, laughing; I saw her in the kitchen; I was persuaded that she eats eggs in the mornings; I realised that little Zhenichka was real with a Munich reality; and that my mother and my son are friends and as much a part of your German flat as Fedia and you, instead of being isolated in a dense conical shadow cast over them by me, the culprit of a continuous series of eclipses.

And another joy is what you say about her work: it means she has been talking to you in the way she dreamed of doing, and that you and she are sisters and accomplices and friends. I can't tell you what a happiness it would be for me to know that she was putting on weight, and feeling calmer, and had an opportunity to paint for three hours or so every day. When Papa comes to Munich, it wouldn't be a bad idea for her to do some drawing.

Of course I'm not talking about this minute, when so many urgent things have piled up around you, but about tomorrow. Today is the 26th, and Lidok is probably in the thick of her final exams, if they haven't been deferred. Although I have unshakable faith in her, I can still imagine her feverish anxiety, and I'm infected by it myself. Let me know the good news by air mail. So—she's going to be a scientist. I've been at ceremonies of this kind, and I'm proud of her. Just think of the struggles she's been through, the apparent setbacks, the haste, the hopes and despair—and now here it is at last, this long-awaited hour. When my letter arrives, Lida will probably already be in a state of collapse and surrender, like a railway engine at the terminus, or an over-watered horse. She'll already be finding that everything seems terribly far-away and grey, and she won't have any strength left for the celebratory cake she's been promising herself through the last few weeks of cramming and self-discipline. But that will soon pass. Gradually the clouds will clear from the horizon, leaving one central idea: that she's a person with precious knowledge, that her future is assured, and she has many paths wide open before her. Congratulations to her, congratulations, congratulations. Make sure you include both my children, my daughter and son,[22] in her celebrations and the general quadrille. Joy and laughter are the best thing for both of them. That's your idea too.

It would be wonderful, too, if Papa could arrange to go to Paris, and if he went together with Zhenia. That's something she and I have often dreamed of. I'm sure it would be a wonderful trip for her, and he'd enjoy himself too. But I daren't imagine such happiness. I'll transfer money for her journey by September.

So—I absolutely agree with you that the top priority is to restore her to health, and everything else has to be sacrificed to that. As far as that goes, I submit unreservedly to whatever you decide. I say unreservedly, because what I'm going on to say isn't in any way a reservation, but a point of prime importance which has to be expressed, and achieved. It's already found expression in a letter I wrote to Zhenia, which I've sent by registered post and which she's no doubt already received.

Well then, I don't take back a single word of it, however much I agree with you; and I'm glad I managed to write it before your letter arrived. Even if I'd had your letter, I should still have written everything that I did, but it would have been even more difficult for me to set all that out for her, clearly and concisely, like a commandment for myself. It's all about precisely those things that you advise me not even to think about, let alone write about to her. This is what I ask: that she doesn't answer that letter yet, in fact doesn't write to me at all, but gives herself over entirely to the sunshine, her happy talents, and your love and care. For some time—and particularly since your letter came—I've been thinking more optimistically of the possibility of all kinds of improvements for her. Let my letter stand on its own, just in case. Let her forget about it, and then suddenly, never mind when, let her remember it again. But neither for her sake, nor for my own, can I cancel the meaning of that letter, nor its binding nature. I told her that she might remain oblivious and silent, never mind for how long. But that period isn't limitless. She has to have a clear and ready answer to it, as absolute as a religion, by the time she decides to return home. No, I'm sorry—I'm imposing

---

22. Boris is referring to his wife as though she were his child.

too much on myself; I too am human. I'm expecting her back by October. So there—by October she has to have sorted herself out, and drawn the inescapable conclusions from whatever she decides. I'm saying nothing about myself, and making no promises. I'm aware that my tone seems harsh. That's because when taking this step, I stop passively dreaming and telling my story. I'll just say that I'm talking about a hope, cherished and supported by my will, which desires a corresponding will on her part. Her will would be listened to, it would become a constant theme, a constant voice, sustained through all the vicissitudes of everyday life. I want that feeling of hers to be fixed in a decision, in words spoken by her to herself, so that there's something to come back to at times of breakdown and beastliness, something to act as a threat and a guide for her.

I want her and me to have a very good life, or none at all. During her current absence and my absolute solitude, it's not just her presence (whatever it may be) that I want, but the presence of her emotions, which must be equal to my own wish for a life with her, and no weaker than that wish. I'm deliberately not discussing the continuation of that letter, in which I explain many things. I don't want to seduce or persuade.

I shan't write any more about this. Tell Zhenia not to hurry about answering my letter, and to forget its sharp tone.

I kiss you all warmly.

I kiss my dear Fedia; I'll write to Zhenia and Zhenichka in a couple of days. Evictions have started again; the Frishmans have received an order, like everybody else in the house. I'm being left alone for the time being.

[…]

Boris Pasternak to Frederick Pasternak

[Late August 1926. Moscow.]

Dear Fedichka!

It's been a whole age since I wrote to you. My constant silence towards you is based on a misunderstanding. I'm almost convinced that you must be reacting to my interminable, 20-page letters with the justifiable prejudice of a man for whom life is no joke, and who values every minute of it.—At the same time, I can't for one minute forget how much tenderness and warmth you have shown towards Zhenia and little Zhenionok, and—putting it more simply and crudely—how much you have done for me and them. Words can't express my gratitude to you.

Even if both those hangers-on had been angelic beings from an Andersen fairy-tale, rather than living humans, and therefore sources of noise, overcrowding and complicated inconvenience, as they actually are—even then, I would have given you due credit for your warm and generous hospitality and intimacy. Having set up your home without any Andersen angels, you could have gone on living quite happily without them, in the peace and quiet you chose for yourselves and adopted as your way of life, and which has now inevitably been disrupted.

But I'm particularly grateful, and particularly to you, for the strong affection that my boy feels for you personally, over and above his friendly feelings towards the whole family. Zhenia has mentioned it several times in her letters. That's something priceless and immeasurable. So—a particularly heartfelt thank-you for something I can't evaluate or measure: some kind of childhood secret between him and you.

I know that you can't regard me as an idler. Yet at the same time I don't believe you can begin to understand the difficulties besetting me, by no means all of my own making. Those difficulties, as yet insuperable, are the only reason for the apparent and probably irritating light-heartedness with which I seem to have disposed of you all, and Zhenia, and the boy, and many, many other things besides. Never mind—I'm your everlasting debtor, and you're my saviour in the most precise and unaffected sense of the word.

In general, I can't complain of my fate. But it's not a daily delight either: I can't enjoy it every day, and it doesn't provide the practical relief one needs every day, just as we need sleep, money and all the rest of it. It can't be a source of recurrent satisfaction or of a calm sense of self-worth in a self-respecting person, because its reality doesn't lie in diaries and dates, or even here on Volkhonka, but in some steep, exalted region where the higher you go, the quieter and more inaccessible and more responsible and more simple everything becomes. It takes infinite labour, and provides almost no joy. Joys are things that happen on specific days, on Volkhonka, on the earth, on the floor.

In moral terms, I'm very glad that the essentials of recognition, fame and all such trivia lost the attractions of novelty for me long ago, and now have lost them for other people too. So that this attraction, which has been the undoing of many artists, has ceased to be something I feel emotionally, and is now nothing but an ordinary, mechanical part of my existence. It's only in my capacity as a person whose earnings depend on publishers and editors, someone who has made his family dependent on them, that I feel anything but indifference to the question of whether people love me or hate me.

, But I'm thirty-six years old, and I haven't achieved anything yet. The ultimate misfortune was to be born as a human being, subject to chance events and illnesses, with no magic protection against fire and the knife, sooner or later doomed to die. A serious inconvenience was being born a Jew—a remarkably dumb thing to do. If that had to be, then I should have been born at the time of the Maccabees, and learned the language of camels and palm-trees, as my racial travel-documents dictated. But to land up in the depths of Russian birch-forests with that sort of distinguishing mark, even in the happiest, most profound fairy-tale (as in my case), was a very silly thing to do. And finally, I have to say: there was one last blunder. My choice of family was brilliant, I'll never tire of praising it. My parents, my home, all of that was an outstanding success. So much so that they counterbalance my mortality and my Jewishness. But there's just one thing wrong. In this family, I should have been the younger son. However, what's done can't be undone, and that's enough of that.

Most of the summer hasn't been too good. I couldn't see any sense in the way I organised it, or myself. I felt that everyone was a burden to everyone else—I was a burden to Zhenia, Zhenia to me, the two of us—to all of you, the boy to Mama, the trip—to the travellers, and loneliness—to the man who stayed behind. And it wasn't until recently, when nice letters started arriving from you, that I cheered up and everything suddenly changed. The summer started to make sense; I'm happy, and both my children[23] will benefit from that. And I'm writing to you with a smile on my face, with a feeling of the tenderest love towards you and everyone around you.

Kiss them all from me. Think of something funny and loving to say to that curly-top, my darling curly-headed Zhenichka. Kiss Lidok for her lovely letter. And grown-up Zhenia too. By the way, if you remember, please tell her that her nanny Fenia hasn't put on 12 pounds as I told her, but 15; she recently visited the bath-house, and can't deny it. All concerned must draw the appropriate medical conclusions.

I embrace you warmly, my dear brother. Thank Zhonia for her letter with the photographs—everyone looks totally alive. But the most alive thing of all is what she says about the little one.

And another thing. When cataloguing the fatal inconveniences of my life, I missed out what is probably the most ticklish one of all. Time. I suppose the time one lives in is selected even more unthinkingly than one's ethnic origin. But probably I'm not exceptional in this; what makes people into Andersen angels is simply the fact of being born contrary to their own wishes and to common sense. That's probably the *principium individuationis* of earthly diversity, and if carp

23. See above, p. 67, n. 22.

didn't have their well-known and legendary urge to get into the frying-pan, they wouldn't be carp. There you are, see how much of your time I've wasted.

Your Borya

As Boris wished, his wife was admitted to a sanatorium in Possenhofen on the Starn-bergersee, while their son stayed with his grandparents at Josephine's apartment in Munich. Rowing on the lake and riding in the Bavarian Alps improved Zhenia's health, and gradually the couple opened up the dialogue they needed so badly.

CHAPTER THREE
1926–1927

In early September 1926 Leonid and Rosalia returned to Berlin, and on the 28th Zhenia and her son set off home to Moscow. Boris travelled as far as Mozhaisk to meet them, and they completed the train journey to Moscow together.

Boris Pasternak to his parents and sisters

4 October 1926. Moscow.

My dears,

Once again, endless thanks to you for everything. Have you forgiven us for our disgracefully late telegram? For the first two days I seemed to be in a dream, forgetting everything as soon as I remembered it. We meant to send you a wire from the station, then we planned to send it as soon as we got home, then we realised to our horror and shame that it was the next morning, and we finally sent it off that evening, with a message of apology. As you see, even my handwriting has changed. I've probably forgotten how to write and how to work. That's a supposition which I haven't had time to test yet.

I started out that day at six in the morning and spent the first half of it in a horrible compartment on the Mozhaisk train. A lot of things had happened to me by midday, when I stepped into the fabulously clean, warm and well-appointed 'international' coach. I won't try to describe the wave upon wave of emotions that came over me on that cold autumn morning, by the misted-up window of the immaculate compartment, seamlessly upholstered on all sides with the nonchalant poetry of the Sleeping-Car Company. I found little Zhenichka looking nicer (he was asleep at the time), and Zhenia looking stronger and somehow perfected. The patina of Germany, so dear to my heart, lay on them so securely that first day that it only needed my lively and over-excited kinship with them and two hours' travel in the welcoming arms of the *Sleeping Car* for me to step out onto the platform with the unshakable illusion that I had just come back from visiting you, and being close to Rübezahl.[1] It was a joy to find that even without such links as Marburg, Rilke, Romanticism, knowledge of the German language or German history, and all the rest—the miraculous workings of sympathetic coexistence made this German patina palpable on them in exactly the same form in which I once bore it myself. I mean, it was the patina of exactly the same country that I love so much, and in such a special way. Zhenia talks about you a great deal, and very well—better, more deeply and more maturely than I myself am able to think about you.

That indescribable meeting was best embodied in the scene of little Zhenionok's awakening (that's what his nickname is to be, he's announced). He didn't immediately realise what had happened (any more than his mother did, actually), but an unhurried smile gradually spread over his face, and he clambered up to give me a hug. His next words (after his first exclamations of 'Papochka!') were: 'Zhenichka is riding to Papa, and Papa is riding out to meet his son!' Then he started entertaining me in a very touching way, leading me up and down the carriage and pointing out everything and everybody, making me sit down by one window and then another. It took me a long time to get used to the novelty of my first impressions. He's grown bigger, and infinitely more dignified, and completely changed in some elusive way. I'm terribly grateful to you all, particularly Zhonia and Fedia: this is the fruit of your loving care and concern.

All that first day until night-time he was like that. By next morning he had begun to fall under the sway of old memories, recalling his old, uncontrollable habits, one by one. On the first day, for instance, he greeted 'Babulya', Stella and the rest of them very nicely, and then ran back to our quarters for lunch. But by next morning he was back in his old ways, seeing the corridor as a strip of space that can transport the furtive fugitive into the forbidden territory he treasures with unnecessary (that is, unhealthy) passion. It's very vexing. His nanny, who comes to look after him for the whole day, is a real find, a wonderful person, and very experienced. Zhenia and I do all we can to blunt and smooth over the intense longing he has for those other quarters—a passion that's premature, too intense for his years, and which he carefully hides and dissimulates. We don't forbid him to go there; but as soon as he goes, his relations with his nanny for the rest of the day become un-childlike, insincere, ambivalent, as if he were only putting up with his family surroundings until the next possible escapade. The Frishmans, beside all their good qualities, are adults too. I hope they'll help us establish a calm and sensible way of life for the boy. He's a nice boy. I agree with

1. A legendary German mountain spirit.

you. 'Romanchenko—that's what Dedushka calls me.' He remembers all of you with great love, particularly his grandmother Rosa.

Zhenia's mother had a very serious operation (tumours on her spinal cord) just the day before Zhenia left Berlin (Saturday 25th). The operation was a success, and for several days she felt well. Now, she's had a high fever for three days and the doctors have no idea what's wrong. She's in the surgical clinic on Devichye Polye. Zhenia goes to visit her, but hasn't been allowed to see her yet. At the moment her condition is very grave.

It's hard for me to write to you. I've been knocking around doing nothing for almost a week now, enjoying Zhenia's company and the chance to play with the boy. I can't wait to sort out my work somehow. There won't be any need to set up barriers. If it hadn't been for Zhenia's letter to you, which she wrote God knows how long ago and I have so far failed to send off, I shouldn't have got round to writing to you today. I'd like the year ahead of us to be brighter, more sensible and satisfactory than its predecessor. There is some hope that this may happen. Have you recovered from your summer guests?

I kiss you warmly. Borya.

And a message from Zhenionok: 'Tell them I love them a lot and want to see them very much, but they have to come here, I won't go there, I can't just now.'

Leonid Pasternak to Boris Pasternak

[29 October 1926. Berlin.]
My dear children, Borya, Zhenia, and a certain other wonderful acquaintance of mine!

[. . .] I've been reading, my dear Borya, your recent letters (including those to Zhonia and Lida), and I like their style and language—you're very *sachlich*[2] in them, astonishingly serious, you exhaustively define and characterise the things you describe; sometimes I detect your hypertrophied sensibility (which I know all too well)—particularly where you describe your meeting with Zhenionok and Zhenia—I could see you, and your innermost self, and your expression— when the soul, while rejoicing, still aches and floods with tears . . . and utterly dissolves in a sort of boundless compassion (I regard this as an essential feature of a great writer—Tolstoy was filled with it). It's too early, my dear boy, for you to come unstuck (though you have all the prerequisites for it); but apart from

2. 'Objective'.

that, it's clear that life, your whole geography, latitude and longitude haven't treated you over-indulgently. They rip open, even wider, the boundaries of that 'anatomically' disposed sphere of compassion, sensibility and all kinds of 'neuro-psycho' etc. which even an artist is assumed to possess. In a word—my soul sometimes weeps as I read between your lines and see your feelings and moods, and the life that you and those around you lead! Reading your letters gives one pleasant minutes—and we've found ourselves reading them a lot, particularly recently—but at the same time there's a recurring theme, as you've mentioned: 'I can't do any work', or 'I haven't done any work recently.' So if you write a lot of letters, which is very nice for us, that means that you aren't working; so we'd better not look forward to getting letters from you, because if we don't, the presumption will be that 'he's busy working'. I don't know if you understand me.

Yes! I'd been meaning for the umpteenth time to write and tell you that we've all been reading the books you sent. Your poems are beautiful, and of course we understand them—particularly touching is 'I'm fourteen years old . . .' which contains so much precious, intimately lived experience—only for us, I think, that is for the family . . . They're very good! And we liked 'Lieutenant Schmidt' very much too.

I recently happened to see a little book called *Autobiographies* (or *Biographies*—I don't remember which) of Russian writers, and of course I looked for your entry at once. It's a splendid article, written with great tact, serious, succinct and lucid, an impressive autobiography, and its form and conciseness raise you above the chatter of all the other writers who were 'glad of the opportunity' . . . Of course I was moved to tears by the exaggerated importance you ascribed to me and Mama! The unexpectedness of it hit me in the face like a burst of hot air from an oven (I can't find the right words for it—when it comes out— gakhhh!—straight in your face), and I was embarrassed! [. . .]

And this autobiography—its form, and the tone of someone who knows himself (alone amidst the multitude) to be seriously indebted to others, once again showed me how you—or rather life—has 'made you grow up'; it has made you serious beyond your years, as you are obliged to be by the ascetic duty and labour of a Russian writer, and particularly a poet, 'whom nobody out there needs'. Yes, I didn't know that when you are born, you have to be careful not only in your choice of parents, but also—as life has taught us all—in your choice of the time to be born in . . . What's to be done? Perhaps Zhenionok's birth-date will be an advantage to him in the future—I profoundly believe it and wish it from the bottom of my heart, for him and both of you. I often think of you, when I see and read about the success enjoyed in all countries by our composers—the young ones, I'm not speaking of Stravinsky, but for instance of Prokofiev—successes everywhere, their works are put on and performed—their language is understood by everyone—they can travel and live where they like, etc.—in a word, they're non-Party people. Not that you could beat him hands down—well, the latter one perhaps you might—but life might have spared you a great deal, and lightened your load. Well, one could dream idle dreams about a lot of things. And my old age would have been different. [...]

The autobiography that excited Leonid Pasternak was included in the collection *Writers: Autobiographies and Portraits of Contemporary Russian Prose Writers*, published in 1926. Boris's autobiography began with the words: 'I was born in Moscow on 29 January 1890 (old style). I owe much, if not everything, to my father, the academician and painter Leonid Osipovich Pasternak, and my mother, an outstanding pianist.'

Many of Boris's letters to his parents dating from the autumn of 1926 have not survived. They must have included one that described the 'unpleasantness' surrounding the publication of his poem 'Lieutenant Schmidt' in the journal *Novy Mir*. The censors took exception to some lines in the second part of the poem, and held up the print run for several days.[3]

In early January 1927 Boris received a letter from Marina Tsvetaeva telling him of Rilke's death. His letter of enquiry to his father is lost, but Leonid's reply survives:

Leonid Pasternak to Boris Pasternak

19 January 1927. Berlin.

[...] Dear Rainer M. Rilke's death threw me into despair for several days—it was so unexpected. Only a few weeks earlier his secretary sent me a nice letter and a

---

3. This is a scene in which the hero faces a delegation of sailors and resolutely refuses to lead their revolt.

But the doors are open, and standing there:
'I'm here. And I'm an enemy of bloodshed'.
—And see the horror of the moral dwarfs:
'Then what kind of a politician are you?
You, a revolutionary? People don't
Set off to fight a battle in ladies' gloves'.
—'I'm on my way to Petersburg.
No arguing. I'll not give way'.

card, which I forwarded to you. Incidentally—don't return it. I asked her to send me another copy, and she was kind enough to do that. I exchanged letters with her, and in the last one she told me the cause of his death—leukaemia.

Naturally I could read your despair in the few lines you enclosed with Zhenia's letter. Of course I understand what a loss this is for you, but you can't build your whole future on that—'the pointlessness of life' and that sort of thing. That's going too far—knowing you, one might think that you were on the point of falling into needless dejection, and letting yourself go [...]

So—in accordance with the personal request and desire of the late Rilke, addressed to Mme Bassiano, editor of *Commerce* (his secretary is now living with her just outside Paris, as her children's governess), Mme Bassiano has asked me, through the secretary, to let her know your address, so that she can send you 'a certain sum of money' for having published your poems (in translation). I'm just going to write to her, and she'll send you the money either directly or via me. That's very nice of her. 'Tell your son Boris that R.M. Rilke loved him very much and often talked to me about him. And he talked about you too, just as often, and recalled your meetings.' Don't be cross with me that I can't send this letter on to you. [...]

The question of a trip abroad arose again this spring. Raisa Nikolaevna Lomonosova (a Russian émigrée with whom Boris carried on a lively correspondence) pressingly invited him to visit her at Sorrento (she had also met Zhenia in Berlin in 1926). Boris felt bound to refuse because of a profound ideological rift in his relations with Mayakovsky and Aseyev.[4] In their journal *Novy Lef* they advocated the complete subordination of art to the needs of the socialist state. Boris felt it so essential to combat this position that he rejected any temptation to travel. 'Breaking with people whom you're always being brought into contact with is impossible when you're abroad', he wrote to Lomonosova on May 17th, 1927. 'There's something insuperably awkward about it.' His grave differences with Mayakovsky and Aseyev recur in the next letter to his sister.

4. Nikolai Aseyev was a poet in the same futurist group as Mayakovsky, and a close friend of Boris in their early days as writers.

[This opening paragraph was dicated by Zhenichka.]

Boris Pasternak to Josephine Pasternak

6 May 1927. Moscow.

Dear Auntie Zhonichka!

We had some pussy-willow, and we've still got it, because it's standing in water. But now I have to tell you that they've thrown it away.[5] We painted eggs by the stove, Mama and Anya, and I watched. Has Frau Stiegler's kitten grown big? Frau? Frau? So everything grows, and everything goes upwards, does it? Upwards? Frau Stiegler?

———————

At this point he ran away, and I didn't repeat the attempt to record his mediumistic states. It's difficult, anyway, to get him to concentrate his thoughts in a letter. But what beautiful photographs you sent him! And thanks from us, too, for your postcard.

Zhenia wants to write something to you, she's worrying about you again.[6] And because I don't follow suit, but keep detached, she says that I think and care only about myself. That may even be true. What can I say—these things happen. Sometimes life works out like that, for decades on end: personal experience, attempts to interfere in other people's worlds, attempts to arrange one's own life, and so forth—and in the end all you can do is think of yourself and look after yourself. But naturally that isn't straight egoism. It's the complex, compounded form of all life's experience.

Now, as if in confirmation of this—a few words about myself, if you're interested. There was a tempting opportunity—a letter from Lomonosova, the contagious effect of a whole horde of people travelling to Paris, eviction with a grant of several thousand roubles to buy a new flat, and some money accumulated for me at Gosizdat—there was a tempting opportunity for the three of us to go abroad this summer. But a journey for the purpose of refreshing oneself, relaxing and gathering impressions, is something I can't yet understand: I couldn't say that either my activity here, or its future prospects, are entirely normal yet. But going on an excursion presupposes just such a feeling of home and normality. And this half-destroyed home hasn't even been half rebuilt. So if I were to go, it could only be for a long visit, for work. And that's not convenient, for many reasons. For a

5. On Palm Sunday, Russian Orthodox Christians carry pussy-willow twigs symbolising the palm-branches spread before Jesus on his entry into Jerusalem.

6. Josephine was pregnant at the time.

whole number of reasons which are too complex to spell out, I'm going to have to start dealing with topics which are regarded here as contentious. Addressing this tricky business from abroad would be inappropriate. It would affect the weight of those truths, in other words their value.

'The Year 1905', whose retrospective theme used to protect me, is finished. Once again I have the present before me. I understand my total insignificance in the face of its real and indisputable historical foundations. But I have a quarrel with their embodiment in everyday life, and time hasn't changed that. It's the difference between two world-views. That's something one can't give way on, without making one's life meaningless, because the meaning of life doesn't lie in breakfasts and dinners, nor in royalties. What a pity I'm not a musician or a painter.

I'm going to have a difficult year. Automatically and inevitably, I'm going to break off relations with my true friends Aseyev and Mayakovsky, particularly the latter. Their feelings towards me, and above all Mayakovsky's, have been especially warm this last year—his ideas about '1905' are pure exaggeration. That makes this inevitability all the more painful for me. But it can't be helped. They don't in any way measure up to their exalted calling. In fact, they have fallen short of it for all these years, but—difficult as it is for me to understand—a modern sophist might say that these last years have actually demanded a reduction in conscience and feeling, in the name of greater intelligibility. Yet now the very spirit of the times demands great, courageous purity. And these men are ruled by trivial routine. Subjectively, they're sincere and conscientious. But I find it increasingly difficult to take into account the personal aspect of their convictions. I'm not out on my own—people treat me well. But all that only holds good up to a point. It seems to me that I've reached that point.

I embrace you and kiss you warmly, and I'm not worried about you. Life is sometimes cleverer than we are.

[The letter ends with a postscript from Boris's wife Zhenia.]

In the summer of 1927 Boris rented a dacha in the village of Mutovki, on the Northern railway line out of Moscow, in the same area as the village of Raiki, where Leonid and his family had spent happy summers from 1907 to 1909. In this letter Boris recalls the names of the railway halts that he and the family remembered well—Pushkino, Kliazma, Tarasovka, Mytishchi. Josephine had just written a poem about the night violet, evoking memories of their childhood in the countryside near Moscow; wanting to get the name right, she had checked with Boris, once seriously interested in botany.

Boris Pasternak to Josephine Pasternak

24 June 1927. Mutovki.

Dear Zhonichka,

Those flowers are called just that—'night violets', in common parlance, as well as in the shops and in the eponymous poem by Blok ('. . . and the night violet blooms'). In Russian botanical terminology they're called *lyubka* [wild orchid]. And a warm thank-you for your letter about that, and us, and yourself. I've been in town, and I saved your letters for dessert. For five hours I was in such a rush, sweating in such a summery, cloudless noonday way (sunshine, asphalt, sand, flies, and Okhotny Row[7]) that several strips of postage stamps in my outside waistcoat pocket stuck together like a thick plaster, and the next day I had to steam them apart over the samovar.

I didn't open your envelope until Pushkino, when there was a bit more room in the carriage; the shadows were lengthening, the air smelt of rotted birch-leaves, and the train got up steam for long stretches, full of a feeling of relief, like a long-distance express. Our parents remember this railway line from their summers at Raiki, and it hasn't changed a bit.

Papa hasn't changed either; I'm terribly exhilarated and gladdened by his vigour, that of a great man with the great richness of an expansive nature. All this, from the garden wheelbarrow and rake wrapped up in brown paper for Zhenichka, or the crease in my forehead from the peaked cap pulled over my eyes, from the jostling crowds at Kliazma and Tarasovka, to the contents of your letter and the conditions under which I read it, are so typical of the whole of our lives together! It's a sort of constant, composed of transient chance events; and with Nature's help, specifically in that urban setting, it repeats itself point by point, almost unchanged. It's beginning to look as if this is the style we've adopted for our current edition, otherwise known as life on earth. Its aching attraction resides in its conspicuous randomness (why this one in particular, out of a thousand other possibilities?), which is empirically illimitable—in other words, if the poet was suddenly to turn into an explorer and geographer, he'd find himself somewhere like Borneo, still carrying with him the night violet and the sound of the name 'Mytishchi'.

If you're to think through this quality of fortuitousness, with its fearful loneliness and anguish, and if at the same time you're to stay in harmony with the logic

7. A large street in central Moscow.

of life and with your own heart (I had a few minutes of time, and from all life's possibilities I bent down and picked up that horseshoe lying on the ground next to me; perhaps I ought instead to have cast a lightning look around, and selected the most worthwhile thing of all, in all that mad rush!) . . . if, I say, you can distinguish properly between the many shades in this planetary stand-and-stare, then of course you must be alive—somehow, never mind how;—and you must have an idea of immortality.

The most important correction that the idea of immortality introduces here is this: it affirms that time exists in infinite quantity, and no matter how fortuitous your style may be, it is the first and last style that has fallen to your lot under the sun;—but it's neither the first nor the last in the living sequence. Or, to put it more accurately and honestly, in a sort of philistine paraphrase of Kant: the very discussion of your style's alarming nature requires and brings with it, as a lived-through presupposition, the successive change of these styles, one of which is the fortuitousness of your existence on earth.

This isn't a good time for this kind of metaphysics. One day people will invent conventional signs to represent this selection of five or six crucial feelings, signs such as a handshake or a kiss. They would constitute a remote approximation of a hint, allowing the feeling to be individualised to fit each case and each person, rather than being distorted into obtuse scholastic nonsense as happens with dogmatised verbal expressions. Perhaps I've been pushed towards topics like these by Papa's praise for my 'wisdom', as he calls it. Perhaps I'm instinctively seeking a repetition of that praise. Of course I'm joking, but there is another, serious side to his comment, and maybe it indirectly forced me to 'have my say on this topic'.

I haven't aged, and yet I've more than aged. I don't think I'm going to live as long as I should like. But there are other reasons too—I'll explain them below—why I've started behaving and feeling—in my consciousness, in my spiritual being, without reference to my biological self—as if I were in the final stage of my life. The main reason is this: that it's the only way to live in Russia at the present time without being a hypocrite, or wasting effort to no purpose—or worse, provoking horrible catastrophes while achieving nothing whatsoever—wasting the explosively personal creative fire of mature middle age, these years so utterly and deservedly devoted to the love of freedom. I don't want to let myself go on this subject. I'll leave it at that.

[. . .]

Forgive me for this somewhat lifeless letter. I had meant to write something quite different. I embrace you and Fedia.

Your Boria.

Boris's summer at Mutovki resulted in a short cycle of poems. He sent Josephine the one called 'Lyubka' in its original version.

Boris Pasternak to Josephine Pasternak

13 July 1927. Mutovki.

Dear Zhoniura,

It's a hot summer noon. As so often in recent days, we got up before 7. After our tea, Zhenichka and I went off into the woods beyond the neighbouring village. It's on a ravine, the place is called Malanya Mountain. It's haymaking time now, so you can imagine what the wind smells of. The path from the station passes through that wood, and this morning we were expecting Margarita Vilyam to arrive from town along the path. We set off to hunt for berries. Can you remember your early childhood? Call it to mind, and you'll see a living picture of Zhenichka with a little basket on his arm and passion in his eyes, sitting on his haunches, sinking out of sight in the thick succulent grass that's overgrown the tree-stumps and hummocks on this strip of ground where the trees were felled last year. And amongst it, no less dear to you—the large grainy rubies of wild strawberries, melting with ripeness.

We were so engrossed with picking them, that although we were only twenty paces from the path along which a packet of surprises delayed in town was being delivered to me (including your present and your letter), we missed Margarita as though she had never materialised, and we were quite invisible to her too. It's true that the strawberry field is hilly and overgrown, and the thick birch-wood in which all this happens is so dazzling in the sunlight at this time of day that there's no material or colour that wouldn't look like part of its burning greenery. Can you picture it? It's congealed in the stubborn whiteness of the birch-trees and the watery ripples of the young, seemingly waterlogged foliage of the oaks, the palest thing in this incomparable sea flooded with blue. We're walking barefoot, stepping right onto the warm round paws of the shadows warming themselves on the path. Suddenly the path twists steeply downwards through the thickening undergrowth, as though through the night, and there is the river. The alder leans over it, so low that right from its roots upwards, it's lying on its own reflection. This woodland mirror is completely in its power; you could dive into it, but there's no way to swim up to it.

At home, there's your letter and a writing-block, a letter from Tsvetaeva, and the July number of *The London Mercury*. I'm answering you first of all, straight away, and starting with a proposal that's directly related to the *Mercury*. While our parents are staying with you, please get that issue. I don't think there'll be any need to subscribe to it—I'm sure you can get it at the library. So: it's *The London Mercury*, July 1927, vol. XVI, No. 93. Read it, and if you have time, give them an oral translation of the article 'The Present State of Russian Letters'.[8] That will please them, and give you particular pleasure. You have your own views on a lot of what's said there, and you'll compare them with the author's. And Papa's and Mama's pleasure will also make you happy. I don't need the journal myself, of course—I already have a copy.

As you see, I've received the writing-paper. It only got very slightly crushed. Thank you very much indeed for it. And even more thanks for the books you've promised me. If the book dedicated to Rilke and published by Insel-Verlag is *Das Inselschiff*, April 1927, VIII. 2, then I don't need it—Ernst sent it me as a gift a long time ago, and I thanked him for it at the time.

As for *Orplid*—you'd better not read it. What a disgrace! The *Letters from Tula* are a mess even in the original. What was the point of translating them?

But you're wrong to refer to your own letters as 'scribbles'. I love them, and I'm always interested and excited when I read them. Kiss Fedia and all the family. I wrote to Lida recently. Is she with you?

What can you do, after an article like that English one! I'm able to work, and I want to, and I'm full of hopes—but what an exceptional way of life you need if you're to succeed. No going out in a threesome to pick wild strawberries.

Boris Pasternak to Leonid Pasternak

17 July 1927. Mutovki.

[. . .]

Dear Papa!

Has Zhonia read you the article in *The London Mercury*? The author spent a year trying to get my address out of Tsvetaeva, but she wouldn't give it; so he wrote through her, and she sent me a covering letter imploring me to correspond through her and not to give him the Volkhonka address. She says she was afraid of the evil eye—afraid that his enthusiasm would tie me down, that he'd be standing looking over my shoulder, fettering me with his expectations. Incidentally, she told the story of the centipede: 'Someone asked him—How do you manage

---

8. In this very positive article the critic Dmitri Sviatopolk-Mirsky introduces Boris Pasternak as a poet of 'overpowering influence . . . Pasternak's experience is new. . . . Our current critical language has not yet found terms to describe it.'

not to get muddled, how can you ever remember which of the hundred comes next?—And straight away—stop!' Those are her words, she's always that laconic, like Aunt Asya. Anyway, she was worried and wanted to protect me. As things turned out, I didn't obey her. I can't say that her fears have come true in every point. S[viatopolk]-M[irsky] is a marvellous person, and while knowing him has had its price, that doesn't make his heart any less precious to me. Besides, even without him there are plenty of such riddle-solvers and expectant onlookers. But her observations are remarkably true. I'm thoroughly tied down on every side.

I've already told you that this place is so incomparable, and the summer so beautiful, that even a wooden block would be filled with gratitude to fate and providence. But I've no reason to expect any joy from the memories that article awoke in me, nor any right to promise any. Oh, if only I had a little money! Then I should know what to do. But as it is—when my work is measured out on a fine centimetre mesh, and I'm forced to match it up to my regular but intermittent earnings, inch by inch—I have to spend my time finishing off things that were started during this washed-out time. I can't just abandon them—there's no sense writing off my 'capital outlay'. And I'm going to try and finish *Spektorsky*, a prose piece in verse, a genre that's fundamentally and categorically pointless and compromised, that's possible only in a period of cultural godlessness, that is to say when art is transferred to secular status and never, anywhere, rings out from the belfry of genius. That period is drawing to a close now, but in material terms I can't yet benefit from my liberation.

[There follows a postscript from little Zhenichka; Boris's letters at this time often contain dictated messages from his son, relating recent events and recalling life in Munich.]

Boris Pasternak to his parents

[7–17 September 1927.]
Mutovki. a very long time ago.

Dear Papa and Mama,

Only yesterday I asked Zhonichka to tell you not to be cross if you don't hear from me for some time. But my heart isn't made of stone, and despite the fact that writing letters is quite simply bad for me, because I ought to be doing something else, it's better if I warn you of this temporary interruption myself. I haven't seen Pepa yet, but I already vaguely know through Shura about the new alpine avalanche of innumerable presents from you. You can easily imagine my feelings, not only of happiness and gratitude, but also of profound embarrassment, when I get to stand under this landslide. But that isn't what I wanted to write about.

A few days of hard north wind have changed the landscape, our circumstances, habits and everyday life beyond recognition. It's autumn, little Zhenichka is ill (tummy and throat), and it's beginning to look like a move to Moscow. As always, since a move like this takes place all in one go, switching from one season to another within a day, this new season seems like a solid block, as though the whole of the coming year were meeting us on the first day, all at once, with all its Decembers and Januaries. Well, never mind, so long as there aren't any unexpected illnesses or misfortunes. I must say that it looks unusually propitious—particularly from the financial point of view. I think there's no rubbish of mine that they wouldn't accept for publication; and of course, being aware of this new danger, I'm going to be even stricter and more careful with myself. It's no longer any good trusting to obstacles, however blind, to filter my work. However inwardly unstable the demands of editors may be, even their constraints are being withdrawn from my writing, so much so that I'm beginning to suspect that my reputation is hypnotising people and turning black into white. I repeat—I shall simply be even more cautious about my work. But I shan't have to sign contracts for kopeks any more, in the immediate future; I'll be able to set my own conditions and insist on them. I say 'in the immediate future' because I know how changeable all this is, how much it depends on a thousand chance occurrences, even the nearest of which—one's own life and work—can hardly be foreseen or controlled.

My morale is fine as well. As far as that goes, Fate has always been kind to me. But just now it has all become much denser, somehow. I don't want to go into details here—but I believe, in a way, that the same accidental chance that brings these waves of affection to me, sometimes from unexpectedly far away, brings them to you too—not necessarily the same ones, but something like them, and sometimes without my knowledge.

And I don't want to write a lot about my plans: I'm rather superstitious about that. But since it appears that only presentiments—that is, ideas about something that is to happen in the future—are subject to the influence of fate, while awareness of duty and necessity is part of even a superstitious person's spiritual rights, there's one thing I can say right now. The time is coming when the writing of great and absolutely free works will become (subjectively) my most immediate and sole task. The objective fate of those attempts won't be predetermined by anyone, not even myself. But this uncertainty can't in any way alter the fact that I shall have nothing left to do except what I've just said.

I'm going to try to devote this winter to setting things up in such a way that I can embark on this purest of tasks. Achieving it may even involve plans for a prolonged stay abroad. Not that I regard living abroad, generally speaking, as one of my life's ideals. Quite the contrary—unlike Shura and (now) Zhenia, who is always yearning to go abroad, I myself, in the depths of my being, could live only in Russia. But that's how things are now; the only conceivable way to accumulate large amounts of money for future use, or make any long-term plans, is through the outward symbol of a passport for foreign travel. Not to mention the fact that I miss you desperately and have to see you. For that, all I would need to do is take a month's trip to Germany. Who knows, perhaps that's all it will amount to, if I discover on arrival that I can't work there. Our meeting itself promises me such utterly incomparable joy that I need fear no disappointments; whatever they might be, they'll be outweighed a hundredfold simply by meeting you. But all that is still a long way off, and it's too soon to speak of it.

Need I remind you that fully ten years ago I was standing on this very same threshold? It was only the need for that extensive diversionary movement which occupied the last ten years, that prevented me from pursuing all these natural aims at the time. Only now can we appreciate how far we underestimated the war, the abolition of war, and its aftermath and effects. That was all an integral, indivisible process, and all of Russian society is contained wholly and integrally within it, whatever it looks like on a short-sighted view. The labour service of the War Communism years was only a partial expression of what all those years were, and had to be. I served my term and discharged my obligations to that service with my book *1905*.[9]

[...]

17th, morning, Moscow.

My dear ones,

However outrageous the gaps in our correspondence may have always been, on this occasion we've really outdone ourselves. This letter has probably waited at least 10 days. The reason is that the latest visits by the Vilyams and Shura were rounding-off ones before our departure, quite unlike their summer visits, and they shook us out of the rut of our usual dispatches to town. And so I absent-mindedly missed three chances. And another important reason: I had run out of envelopes and stamps at the dacha, so I didn't have a letter for posting, in the ordinary sense of a letter as depicted on postboxes and mail-vans; yet to ask

---

9. The 'diversionary movement' refers to Boris's composition of historical works (such as *1905*), which he regards as less the product of inspiration and more of a service to the state.

someone to buy an envelope and stamp seemed too much of an imposition. Yesterday night we moved out of the dacha back to town. The move had been planned for today; but ever since being promoted to the 'nobility of this world', I have increasingly despised fuss and bother as 'themes' of existence, and yet at the same time they remain exclusively my responsibility. So having begun to pack, I took it up without the slightest respect for what I was doing, in a bestial rush, with no empathy or psychological relish. It suddenly came to me that all this nonsense wasn't worth my attention for a whole day, and no sooner had I filled myself with this idea than everything got done in 4 or 5 hours, and the fantastic load—needing two carts—went to the station a day earlier than we had expected, and we ourselves with it.

At the moment I have a bad headache, with attacks of dizziness every now and then. It's due to lack of sleep. It's also the effect of the city and the flat. I haven't felt the slightest fatigue from the move, the packing, the rushing around, the expenses—and I'd rather do all this every week, in the open air, in the enviable surroundings of a large modern peasant's cottage, and on open station platforms . . . sooner than endure the indescribable senselessness of our modern city.

I wanted to go to the bath-house, and travel to Petrograd this very day to see Aunt Asya. The first of these aims I probably won't achieve, since I'm afraid my dizziness may make me faint in the soapy steam. But I'm just off to buy my train ticket. I'll write to you from there. I can't go on—the letters are dancing before my eyes. I kiss you, and so do all of us.

Borya

Boris Pasternak to his parents

[30 September 1927. Moscow.]

Dear ones,

There's a point at which tenderness and kindness overlap with laziness. The fact that I'm thinking about you is always an expression of tenderness; but I often write to you out of laziness—what I ought to be writing, of course, isn't letters but books.

Yesterday I came back from Leningrad. My only purpose in going there was to visit my aunts and cousins. You can see that my trip was intimately reflected in the name I've used for the town—it's difficult, after my everyday experiences with trams, publishers and railway-tickets, to remember that this is Petrograd—or Petersburg.

In Moscow, even high earnings leave you living crowded together in cramped and cluttered apartments—absolutely indescribable, and yet babies get born, nannies and servants move in, crowds of visitors keep coming round, and so forth. So it's not surprising that the spaciousness and cleanliness of every single one of the apartments I saw in Petersburg produced the depressing effect on me of tidy, genteel poverty—much in the same way that the more golden and peaceful an autumn is, the sadder it feels. Wherever I looked, my Muscovite eyes took in vistas of rooms filled with a tranquillity that Muscovites aren't used to. It felt as if want was wandering through the rooms, in greying hair and clean underwear—just at the precise point where our Moscow neighbours' primus stoves would have begun.

But objectively, aside from this compassionate view, they're coping with difficulties there too. The ghostly, unearthly aura simply arises from Petersburg's advantages which we don't have.

I checked up on Yeta's impression last spring that Babushka's (physical) health in her old age is something we could all envy. She wasn't exaggerating. Aunt Klara, too, is still in splendid form.[10] I went to see them straight from the railway station. I arrived unexpectedly, and she rushed out to greet me, beautiful as ever, in a whirlwind of smiles and exclamations. I said as much to her, and later, while I was in the bathroom washing and shaving, she managed to make herself look ugly and aged, with powder and such. Anyway, she's a marvel. It looks as if she's holding on to everything, not only materially but emotionally too. You probably know about her trip to the borders of Central Asia, sixteen days' journey from here, and how they were robbed on the way, and all her other adventures. Mashura is being drawn along behind her on the same dramatic path.

[…]

One thing happened in Leningrad which would have seemed insignificant to anyone, and which can't be described. It was of profound and decisive importance for me. For me, or even more narrowly, for my heart—it was the end and resolution of my long-standing quarrel with Esenin, which he had forced on me when he was alive. Perhaps I'm anticipating, perhaps the quarrel will develop further and become more entrenched, but I feel that it's already played out, and that happened just now through the same boy (a young poet) to whom Esenin wrote a poem in blood before he died. I met him and spoke with him.[11]

10. Yeta (Genrietta Dailis) was Rosalia Pasternak's first cousin; she had been visiting Berta Kaufman, Rosalia's mother ('Babushka'). Klara Lapshova was her daughter, Rosalia's sister; and Mashura was Klara's daughter.

11. Esenin's poem 'Farewell, my friend, farewell', written on the eve of his suicide, was addressed

Did you get the book I sent you, and didn't you find it disappointing? Warmest thanks for your letters to Zhenia. Thanks to you and Zhonia too. I embrace you all.

Your Borya

Marina Tsvetaeva's sister Anastasia, who arrived in Moscow from Paris on 10 September, told Boris about her sister's illness and extreme poverty. Boris's immediate response was to send her money. To avoid time-consuming formalities he asked Josephine and Frederick to send Tsvetaeva money from Germany, and undertook to repay them in Russia by taking on himself their regular gifts of money to his grandmother in Leningrad. This form of exchange became a regular practice in the family.

Boris Pasternak to Josephine and Frederick Pasternak

[Mid-October 1927. Moscow.]

My dear Fedia and Zhonia!

Endless thanks for carrying out my request so quickly. But the twist you gave to it, Fedia, generous and touching though it was, was quite unnecessary. It's too early for Zhenichka to be having a money-box, and the amount is too much for a present. But I would still suggest you bear this current account of Zhenichka's in mind, as a potential way of transferring money, in case Babushka or anyone else should need it.—At all events, I thank you very, very warmly.

Zhenia and I went up in an aeroplane for the first time in our lives today. I believe that isn't a new experience for any one of you, so I won't describe anything, you can easily imagine our feelings and reactions from your own first impressions. Actually, Zhonia, I believe you don't take too well to flying. We were taken up by an amazing pilot, and although Zhenia suffers from all possible forms of seasickness, she was every bit as thrilled as I was.

Thank you very much for your letter, dear Zhonia. Perhaps it's an idiosyncrasy of mine, but I read *The London Mercury* in July, and I can hardly imagine that the article still means anything now, when the first snows have fallen. You were five when the first revolution happened, and you can't remember anything about it. But the author is the son of Witte's predecessor, a very important and upright

---

to Volf Isidorovich Erlikh, who was with Esenin in his last days. Boris's acquaintance with Erlikh was of great personal importance to him.

man.[12] Of course Papa will remember the name. This Sviatopolk-Mirsky is now a professor of Slavonic literature in England. I've been corresponding with him since last winter. I'm delighted that we agree about his qualities. You picked out the same parts of the article that I did—about poetic experience (or cognition).

A couple of weeks ago I sent our parents a copy of *1905*. I expect it's arrived. If you're well enough, ask them to send you the book to look at. If you don't like it, scold me about it—don't hold anything back. The book is a link in a chain of inevitabilities. That conviction absolves me from any thoughts or worries about its qualities. I don't think Gorky liked it. When I sent him the book he replied with a brief note of cordial thanks, without a word of comment. The essence of his letter was to tell me that 'Luvers's Childhood' had been translated into English and would appear in America. I'll write back and ask him to forward the fee to the same address to which Fedia's rare and incomparably generous response was sent.

I've also heard that 'Lieutenant Schmidt' is to be translated into Czech and German. I don't know what for. There are forces at work in relation to this book that aren't an intimate part of my own destiny and don't belong to that living, narrow circle in which it operates.

I've been unable to do anything for a long time, a very long time, not out of laziness or tiredness but because of the incessant flood of drivel that has poured over me like a tidal wave through the past month and a half. I'm now paid more than any of the other poets, and being thus deprived of the resolute support that poverty brings, I don't feel entitled to send visitors packing or refuse to answer the telephone. But I shall have to. I want to write a piece called 'An Article about a Poet', about Rilke, viewing him not as an exception but as a law.

Zhenia was astounding, in the aeroplane and then on the ground. She felt everything in her very flesh, as she should have. But my affection is oddly inhibited and even paralysed by the fact that she feels herself to be in competition with Marina Tsvetaeva, and Marina feels the same about her. If only they could forgive one another! This is a great sadness for me.

I embrace you. Kiss Fedia.

Your Borya

---

12. Piotr Dmitrievich Sviatopolk-Mirsky, who was Minister of Internal Affairs, 1902–1905.

CHAPTER FOUR
1927–1928

Boris sent his parents a copy of his book *1905*, inscribed: 'To dear Papa and Mama, with deep feeling, of which filial love is only a small part. Borya. 20.IX.27. Moscow'.

Anastasia Tsvetaeva had recently visited Gorky at Sorrento, and reported that he had responded coldly to *1905*, which Boris had sent him. Gorky quickly contradicted this impression in an enthusiastic letter, received in late October. Boris saw Gorky as the personification of the 1905 Revolution and its true hero, and felt that Gorky's approval vindicated his book.

The English translation of 'Luvers's Childhood', for which Gorky had written a preface, was never published.

Leonid Pasternak to Boris and Alexander Pasternak

5 November 1927. Berlin. Motzstrasse 60, W.30.

My dear Boryusha and Shurka!

Never mind anything else—today I have to write you a couple of lines at last! It's been so long since I had a chat with you, and it's such misery to realise what a long time has passed and I still haven't written to you. All the worse because you, Boryusha, have recently been writing quite often—and wonderful and touching letters too. [...]

And another thing, Boryusha—we haven't thanked you for the *1905* book you sent us, with its moving dedication. You really do spoil us more than we deserve, particularly with such unexpected words as you put in your autobiography (I wrote to you about that at the time). Incidentally, that's the main topic of M[arina] I[vanovna] [Tsvetaeva]'s letter, which is written in the most beautiful literary French (even Fedyuk noticed it and was touched and delighted by it; I know that Zhonichka wrote to you about all that).[1]

1. Tsvetaeva's letter of 11 October thanked Leonid for the money she had been sent and praised Boris's tribute to his parents in his *Autobiographical Note*, which she compared to the opening of Marcus Aurelius's 'Meditations'. She added: 'In our time, which I hate, when any fledgling that drops from its nest thinks it's descended from heaven, such an admission in the full sense of the word is unheard-of, and only confirms the author's heaven-sent nobility. Greatness never ascribes its origins to itself, and

So how did I like your '1905', you'll ask. I think that if I say that I found genuine enjoyment in reading the verse itself, in its form—well, it was just pleasant (almost as a visual experience) to take it all in, to absorb it from a visual to an inward experience—I can't exactly formulate my impression or put it in words for you—but strange as it may be, this rigorous compactness of style, this laconically polished (parsimonious?) style, is something I'm already used to, and I found it easy to read, not experiencing the tormenting difficulties that I once did when I tried to penetrate the sense hidden behind your words and formulations—and so, I repeat, having said all this, I'm telling you of my approval and appreciation—although I must admit that I have a feeling of something incomplete, unsaid or not understood (which is my fault) when I finish reading the whole poem and shut the book . . . 'Where's the dog buried?'—not a dog, but our doggishly run-of-the-mill minds that prevent us from understanding you. Even Mirsky, after all—a very learned exponent of your craft—even he admits it'll take another generation before people acquire the necessary critical method and interpretative skill which they still don't possess, despite being professionals. Understanding you, my dear beloved boy, is difficult—and how much more so for us aged academicians and professors. But joking aside, he probably understands better than the others anyway, doesn't he?

What I would say to you is that having written this poem (think of your poor readers!), you ought to have included one or two historical notes at the end of the book; that would have simply made it easier to understand the sequence of events and the historical facts which your contemporaries will have forgotten (while future generations won't understand anything at all about them). Just the way it's usually done, at the end of a book—a few notes (as they do for Dante—it's the same thing, after all). I don't want to go on about this, but let me just say that though I haven't yet read your confession in your last letter to Zhonia, I said more or less the same thing. How to put it—it's part of the landscape. [. . .]

6. 11. 27 (evening)

Mama and I have just come back from the Einsteins. You must congratulate her—she played two sonatas with him (Mozart and Beethoven), and, of course, just as she used to do, thank God!![2] He's a good violinist. He's indefatigable, thank God.

---

this is undoubtedly right. Whether the father is an earthly or a heavenly one, the important thing is to acknowledge one's sonship.'

2. Boris's mother Rosalia Kaufman was born in 1867 and gave her first public concert in Odessa at the age of eight. She studied under Ignatius Tedesco, and at the age of thirteen met Anton Rubinstein, who arranged several concert tours for her. On his advice she later studied with Leschetizky in Vienna,

Boris Pasternak to Leonid Pasternak

12 November 1927. Moscow.

Dear Papa!

I thank you warmly for your long letter.

I ought to have done this long ago. One of the ladies on the staff of the Tret-yakov Gallery asked me to ask you for some information on the points overleaf. They're re-issuing the gallery's catalogue, and will be providing brief biographical data in summary form, Baedeker-style. She's already compiled your entry from available reference books (e.g. Sobko), and asked me to check and correct it. I thought it would be better to send it to you for editing and amendment.

So, for the question about your origins (i.e. social and material situation), since the answer is to be so brief, it's better for you to answer it; you'll do it more accurately (e.g. 'what guild', or other points in relation to Babushka). The same goes for your principal works, i.e. which ones you yourself rate as most impor-tant, etc. Remember that the compilers have exhausted the reference works that existed in your day, some of which you no doubt knew; so don't burden your-self with the whole task of writing an autobiography. It's just a matter of adding data, of answering a questionnaire, which can be done in 10–15 minutes. What's more, if for any reason you find it an annoying burden, then let it go hang, as I do myself with impunity in all these bio-bibliographic situations. But if you do answer, then do it now—they're in a hurry to publish the catalogue. Their direc-tor at the moment is Shchusev.

Don't use fancy language, confine yourself almost to nouns,—what I mean is that since the editors will inevitably be condensing all their material, you too can use laconic formulations if they help make your answer shorter and easier.

I have a sort of premonition that this letter will reach you just when Zhonia's time is upon you, and will be overtaken by our telegrams; so I don't want to talk about anything else. Everything that you (you and Lida) wrote to me about '1905' would have been absolutely fair, if only the factual background of the year 1905 were not an elementary historical ABC for every literate young person today. Of course, I could have bypassed this Mother of God that everyone knows by heart, and provided my own pragmatic commentary; but then my book would have fallen foul of the censors and never seen the light of day. I think the book is having some success. I have grounds for thinking (though I'm afraid of speaking

---

and continued to give public concerts until her marriage in 1889. After this she mainly performed for her family and friends.

too soon) that it may be an even greater success abroad, among those émigrés with connections to the year 1905. Gorky wrote me a wonderful letter about the poem, soon after I suggested to Zhonia that he hadn't liked it. A few other people have written too. Last summer, before the proofs were corrected, it was easier to understand; but I eliminated all the clarifying water from it—about a fifth of the whole.

Pardon me for writing so small—this is the last page of my notepad. I hug you and Mama warmly.

Well, Mama, what partners you have! I felt for you, and lived through it with you!

Embraces.

Borya

Biography

[Questions in Boris's hand, answers in his father's]

Surname, forename, patronymic.
Pasternak, Leonid Osipovich

Exact date of birth (date and month) (use old style for dates before 1918)
22 March 1862

Place of birth.
Odessa

Origins (nationality, social class, material situation)
Russian Jew, bourgeois, over a long working life saved up some funds 'for my old age', but that was then . . .

General and artistic education, indicating time (beginning and end), place and teacher. Years in parentheses. Distinguish between 'pupil' and 'follower'.
Novorossiisk University (Jurisprudence). Munich Academy of Arts 1883–85. Herterich, Liezen-Mayer.

Travels—in brief.
Germany, Paris, London, Munich, Berlin, Dresden, Düsseldorf, Kassel, Belgium, Holland: Amsterdam, The Hague, Haarlem.

Exhibitions. Indicate what part was played—permanent or incidental (organizer, member of society, etc.)
From 1888, took part in Wanderers' [Peredvizhniki] *exhibitions; in World of Art* [Mir Iskusstva]*; founder member of '36' group and the Union of Russian Artists, in which I played a permanent part. Outside Russia, participated*

in international exhibitions abroad (Vienna, Munich, Berlin, Düsseldorf, Cologne, Paris, London, Copenhagen).

Principal works (where situated, i.e. in which museums or collections, other than in the former Alexander III Museum or Tretyakov Gallery).

All principal metropolitan and provincial museums in Russia, also Paris (Musée du Luxembourg), Berlin and Dresden.

Leonid Pasternak to his children in Moscow

18 November 1927. Berlin.

My dear everybody!

So, our Zhoniurochka is a Mama, thank God, and since you all know about the happy event already, your Mama and I congratulate you all, our dear ones, jointly and severally (not severely . . .).

We get news from Lidochka and Fedyuk by telephone every day, and everything is going splendidly, thank God, and the 'mama' and 'daughter' are very well indeed and everything is going as normal (including feeding etc.).

And how are you all? I wrote you a letter recently, my dear little falcons; now I want to ask you a favour. I've just discovered that Pepa is coming here in a few days, so please don't forget to get the cartoon from Lili, and give it to him—I want to exhibit it. Have him pick up the portrait of Al[exei] Iv[anovich] too, since it didn't get sold anyway.[3] [. . .]

Leonid Pasternak's exhibition was to open in Berlin on December 18th.

Boris Pasternak to Frederick and Josephine Pasternak

18 November 1927. Moscow.

My dear Fedia and Zhoniura!

I congratulate you and kiss you endlessly. Now, time will be turning its face in your direction too, and watching as a little burning dot grows into a circle, the circle into a lisping face, and the face into the luminous story of a woman, unutterably new from beginning to end. And as if on a signal, our own good wishes and transports of joy are flying to join you. Thank you for our little niece, for

3. This refers to a sketch of Lenin (done from life), and to a portrait of the Soviet politician A.I. Rykov, which had failed to sell in Moscow.

this precious new life of ours; it's thanks to you, Zhonichka, that the dark, half-dissipated, oppressed and failed cargo of family blood, outworn inclinations and hopes, has been granted the opportunity of turning once more into something absolutely new, expanding into a potential that no amount of guessing could ever have foretold.

An insuperable, vital feeling tells me that writing to you just now, Zhonichka, would be insensitive, clumsy and blasphemous. Because right now you have no relatives, and shouldn't have any. Every movement of theirs declares that something is continuing, whereas (as you're entitled to say), before yourself on the 15th there wasn't anything, and nothing has ever before begun in just this way. But what would everyone have said (yourself included, perhaps), if I hadn't written for a month? I can just see you, lying there in all your beauty! Hurry up and recover! I warmly embrace you and Fedia, Papa, Mama and Lidochka.

Boris Pasternak to his parents

22 November 1927. Moscow.

Dear Papa and Mama!

I've just got your postcard, and the news that Zhonichka had such a difficult delivery has worried, distressed and frightened me. Above all, it was completely unexpected, and when I was writing to her, for some reason I never even thought of the possibility (although of course neither Zhenia's letter, nor mine in particular, had so much as a shadow of everyday 'merriment' in them anyway). It's all the more frightening right now for me to imagine her sufferings, since the mere thought of a trivial sprained ligament sometimes drives me out of my mind—let alone the pain she has suffered.

As a matter of fact, for the past two years I've been aware of this as a regular feature of my life. Whether it's my teeth, or something surgical—whatever it is, time and again it almost makes me faint with the shock of the associated pain. And every time, this physical suffering provokes a sort of mental irritation which at times grows into something like insanity. At such times I forget that I'm a father, husband and son; I'm abandoned by everything bearing the simple name of 'Borya', and my brain—my train of thought—is taken over by something so chaotically bitter and insipid that it feels like nausea or heartburn. When I'm in bed and can't find even a barely tolerable position to lie in, there are moments when I'm capable of getting into an ice-cold rage with my pillow because it won't turn over of its own accord, although it can see that my hands are tied up in bandages and I'm suffering unbearable pain.

And if I don't apply the simple laws of proportion to judge of Zhonichka's pain, then it's merely because the superhuman torment that she suffers is alleviated by the fact that it's devoted to life, while my own sufferings of the past few years have had nothing to relieve the frank process of dying. I'm not personally a hypochondriac, nor fearful for my nearest and dearest. The more acute my suffering, the more I experience it as suffering inflicted on some conceptual world related to me, my future in some form, or I don't know what, but not directly on me. That accounts for the indignation that goes with all these pains. Just writing this has made it all come back ten times worse.

That's all. I embrace you warmly.

Your Borya

Boris Pasternak to his parents and sisters

5 December 1927. Moscow.

My dears!

Whenever you write to us, make sure to tell us how Zhonichka and Alyonushka are. This letter is addressed to all of you, in Munich and Berlin. All your letters and photographs have arrived. The baby's face looks extraordinarily human and fully-formed for a three-day-old. We thought she looked a bit like Fedia, though of course it's too early to tell. Mama's postcard also arrived yesterday. It made me realise what a hellish task Papa has taken on himself, and one full of anxiety too; but at the same time it showed me once more that he's managing to cope with problems that would completely defeat me. Shura and Irina have done everything he asked them to. We've finally got hold of Lenin, and the official order for it has arrived; permission has been granted for sending all the other items, and everything has been packed up and delivered to Boris Ilyich [Zbarsky]. I expect that Shura has written to tell you all this, or will do so.

Zhenia asked Frosya (Bubchik's wife, who will be accompanying Pepa together with her husband) to buy some paints for her—the ones you can get here are useless. But since it's even more difficult than before to export currency, they're not willing to take the money to buy the paints. So they'll have no choice but to bother Papa. It'll be a matter of 60 to 80 marks (we think) that we'll ask him to give Frosya, and we'll refund them to Babushka or Klara here. I'm writing about this in good time so as to make sure that no money is sent, and we'll immediately pay out some 40 roubles here instead. I find this all very unpleasant, I did everything I could to avoid bothering you, but it's the money transfer that's the stumbling-block, and there's no other way round it.

What I thought was a sprained ligament has dragged on and on. I consulted a better surgeon, who said it was a torn ligament with a haemorrhage. The pain is mild now, but I'm completely unable to use my hand and will remain so for some time. All that is quite natural and doesn't worry me.

This has been a very difficult time for Zhenia. Our maid strained a tendon in her foot at the same time, and Nanny was ill and off work, and finally little Zhenichka fell ill with a high fever and no apparent cause. We supposed it was measles, but his temperature fell without any symptoms whatsoever appearing, then we thought he had recovered, and then a few days later he went down with the same mysterious fever again. Dr. Balander suggested it was malaria with attacks at long and progressively lengthening intervals, but now tests have shown that he was suffering from pyelonephritis (which he calls 'pile of frightful'). All this is nothing terrible, but it needs meticulous and exhausting care, and Zhenia got so tired that she has fallen ill herself now—she's caught a mild flu. I wanted to have her admitted to a sanatorium for the Christmas holiday, but it's not likely Zhenichka's health will allow it now, he needs such careful nursing.

[. . .]

Boris Pasternak to his parents and sisters

19 December 1927. Moscow.

My dears!

Warmest congratulations to Papa and all of you on the opening of his exhibition yesterday. I can easily imagine how you all worried about it, each in their own way but all with equal intensity, since even we succumbed to worry, despite our distance and lack of involvement in all the fuss and bother and in the whole event in its palpable reality, and despite the fact that the Sunday morning in question was already past. I expect it was a frosty one, already smelling of the approach of Christmas; I expect there were flowers in the exhibition room, and friends present among the slowly gathering public, and all this reminded Papa of the openings of past winter exhibitions, and many other things besides. The fact that all this has been collected together, realized and brought to pass, and set up in the year 1927 in a huge foreign city whose very name summons up memories of the vicissitudes of the last thirteen years and their distant and tragic beginning—this alone is something immeasurably great. I can see the exhibition in my mind's eye. But Papa, I'm sure you'll photograph it, won't you, and send us snapshots of the picture groups and the corners of the rooms? And once again there'll be articles about it, and some of the authors will be fools and ignoramuses. All this

is intensely interesting to me, and although I've always asked you to confine yourselves to postcards or not to write to me at all, but just get Zhonia to pass on your
news, this is a radical exception to the rule. Like it or not, Lidok, you're going
to have to write to me from time to time to tell me how the exhibition is going,
and what the news is about it. As far as I know (from what I've seen and heard),
Papa's most interesting and serious works are the most recent ones. I only know
two or three of them, from reproductions.

It's very naïve of you to think that Anatoly Vasilyevich [Lunacharsky] would
have passed anything on to me—even the live greeting that Papa mentions in his
postcript.[4] Perhaps it might have been easier for him if I lived differently—if I
went out to the theatre, attended debates, parties and so on. When chance brings
us together, no more than once in three or four years, he asks me in amazement
whether I'm in Moscow. He's so inordinately busy that I simply can't believe that
men of his kind live on the same time-scale as I do. I wouldn't have the time to
do a hundredth of what he does. I think he's a very good and exceptional person;
I should very much like to know what it was like for Papa to meet him, and
what they said to each other (about the paintings and so forth). Was there any
mention of commissions, Lenin and the rest? He can't have told Papa anything
worthwhile about me. He doesn't know me, and knows too little about me to say
anything interesting.

As I write, they're airing Zhenia's part of the apartment. Little Zhenichka is
pottering about next to me, and despite my groans of indignation he keeps shov-
ing his curly head right under my elbow. I offered to put him in the envelope
and send him to you. 'What nonsense. You'd never find such a big envelope.
That's not how to travel.'—But supposing I found an envelope? 'Then put somebody else in it first. And then somebody else again. If they arrive, then I'll get in
myself.' According to his latest version, he's a lion-cub, his Mama is a lioness, and
I'm a lion; so I told him he had to leave me alone, the lion needs to write. 'Where
would a lion find a quill? Now a hen—that's a different matter. She can think and
think, and then yank a quill out of her bottom and write it all down.'

He's had a mild inflammation of the kidney calyces (I think it's called pyelitis);
Balander reckons it's a complication of a cold and that there's a lot of it about just
now. He's out of bed now, but of course he's very pale and has lost a lot of weight.
He's not being taken out for walks yet, because it's twenty below zero outside.
Christmas is approaching, with all the usual chaos.

4. Leonid's old acquaintance Anatoly Vasilyevich Lunacharsky was now the People's Commissar
for Education. Leonid hoped he would help publicise the 'success of Russian art in Berlin' (as the German reviews put it) in the Soviet press.

You misunderstood my postcard—I wasn't annoyed in it, nor anywhere else, and see no reason why I should be. But I'm fiendishly busy! I embrace everyone, in Berlin and Munich.

At the same time, I send you my best wishes for Christmas, and hope you celebrate it in perfect health and appropriately good moods. Zhenia and Zhenichka kiss you all tenderly.

Leonid Pasternak to his sons in Moscow

[16 January 1928. Berlin.]

My dear children!

I actually wanted to say—my bl.... children! I sent you newspaper cuttings about the success of my exhibition, didn't I?—One or other of you might at least have answered! Now the exhibition's closing tomorrow, after a whole month (instead of three weeks)—I've had a staggering success, thank God, beyond anything I hoped for—I suppose Pepa has told you all about it—or will do—go and see him, ask him—he's an observer and eye-witness of this event, which is so tremendously important to me—at a time like this (and at my age!). A lot of pictures were sold, thank God (about 22); there's a crisis in the art market at present, and my exhibition has probably carried off the biggest prizes. All the newspapers have carried superb reviews, and the illustrated supplements are going to print reproductions. Ask Pepa how happy my entrepreneur Hartberg is with this 'harvest'—he was very doubtful about arranging the exhibition—felt uncertain about it—after all, I'm a foreigner, and unknown here, while he has nothing but famous young artists on his books—how dared I go and 'push myself forward'? [...]

I gave Pepa the synopsis—keep it for the press. I absolutely have to delight my 'friends and comrades', with at least a brief report and extracts from the principal reviews which I sent you, and Pavetti too (at the same time as you). Ring him up—it's got to get into the Moscow papers!

Of course Boris and Alexander were delighted by their father's success. Unfortunately, though, Boris's congratulatory postcard was lost in the post, and apart from a brief, botched note by his friend, the art critic Pavel Davidovich Ettinger ('Pavetti'), the Soviet press ignored the event.[5]

5. Pavel Ettinger was an art critic and collector, and a lifelong friend of Leonid Pasternak, with whom he corresponded until the latter's death.

Boris Pasternak to Leonid Pasternak

19 January 1928. Moscow.

My beloved Papochka!

Zhenia wasn't in Moscow on the day Pepa arrived—she was in a sanatorium out-side town, and is only coming home today; so I've left the whole consignment of goods from you intact, still in its packaging, and put it in a safe place until she comes. The pleasure of unpacking it all still lies ahead. But because of that, I've deviated from my usual practice and not written to you at once about all the things Pepa told me, or rather about my feelings on hearing his account. The most important thing was that he had found you both very cheerful and youthful-looking, and this (and particularly the fact that Mamochka 'est encore verte') has made me happier than I can say.

Then he told me about the meetings you arranged with him at a restaurant, and how you went to see the exhibition, and many, many interesting and gratify-ing things about the exhibition itself—its success, the pictures that were sold, and the plans to take the exhibition to other cities. And I was in tears over your enqui-ries about Shura and your readiness to help him recover (going to the Caucasus etc.). In parentheses—the only Caucasus for him (subjectively) would be on the Motzstrasse, and if he owned any geographical, objectively necessary treasure such as Kislovodsk or Essentuki,[6] he'd pawn it or sell it to a Tartar for the sake of seeing you, and the *Untergrundbahn*, and all the rest.

But when he told me how Frosya had suddenly remembered Zhenia's list, at the last minute, and how you yourself rushed off to get that eight-kilogram bundle of confusion and importunity, I was delighted, moved and astonished beyond anything, I'll never be able to describe my feelings to you, nor ever be able to respond with anything comparable. The main thing is this: over and above the confusion that your generosity throws me into, I'm overcome with happiness: your instant readiness to help brings you irresistibly to life before my eyes, youthful, impulsively helpful, with a lock of grey hair emerging from under your hat, on an echoing German pavement. God grant you may always be buying these paints for Zhenia! And, as is the way with such things (everything happens at once), I recently bumped into An[atoly] Vas[ilyevich] [Lunacharsky] too. He spoke of you with emphatic enthusiasm—your freshness, your wonderful old age, which one could wish for anyone; the joyful liveliness of the walls hung

---

6. Spas in the Caucasus region. What was wrong with Shura at this time is not known.

with your paintings and drawings; he was particularly delighted with some roses of yours.

It's not the fault of the very intelligent and sharp-witted Sviatopolk-Mirsky that his article has some comical absurdities in it. The fault lies in a letter I wrote him last autumn, after his English article, a letter in which I unwittingly tied him down emotionally. I sent him '1905', and wrote that his opinion of the poem would become my own, in the expectation that he would write personally to me, and all the more freely after my expression of confidence. But my openness forced him into hyperbole, and he treated me like an eager, importunate woman. This saddens me, not for my own sake of course, but for his. 'A great revolutionary and reformer' . . .

> In his next letter, Boris continues the discussion about getting the Soviet press to report on Leonid's exhibition in Berlin. Two of Boris's immediate difficulties were that his father was quite unaware of the political constraints affecting every aspect of Soviet life, and that Boris himself no longer had friends among Soviet journal editors. A recent official attack on the political opposition had triggered a change in editorial staff and the adoption of a hard ideological line. V. Polonsky was dismissed from *Novy Mir*, and A. Voronsky from *Krasnaya Nov*. Boris suggests approaching the art critic Yakov Alexandrovich Tugendhold, an acquaintance of Leonid's who was now head of the art section of *Krasnaya Niva*. A year earlier, Tugendhold had asked Leonid for a drawing of Berlin at night, for publication in his journal, but Leonid demurred. Subsequent discussions brought in Pavel Ettinger ('Pavetti'), Pepa Zbarsky, the artist Olga Alexandrovna Bari-Aisenman, and Boris's acquaintance Yakov Chernyak, a literary critic working for the journal *Pechat i Revolutsiya*.

Boris Pasternak to Leonid Pasternak

3 February 1928. Moscow.

Dear Papa,

Has Pavetti written to you? He telephoned me recently about his report of your exhibition. The invariable chaos here, plus certain peculiarities of the newspapers themselves, means that I hardly ever read them, so I hadn't seen his note in *Vechernyaya Moskva*, and now it's too late for me to get hold of it. Has he sent it to you? He complained that it had been cut down to just three lines and placed where no-one would see it, and since (which is true) he has no access to either *Pravda* or *Izvestia*, he suggested he might talk to Pepa about getting reports into these major papers. I believe he even wanted Pepa to appear as the author. Needless to say, that struck me as totally pointless.

So—what can I do now? Not only as your son, but for many other reasons besides, I'm acutely conscious of the importance of your success, and proud of it, and I'm nourished by its spiritual meaning, and ready to impart it to anyone you like. But I don't entirely understand how you would like to exploit it. Here again you have all the advantages—you're more vital than me, and the ground above you is clearer (I mean that you don't have a father, let alone such a father as you are to me); and so forth. But my intuition tells me that I mustn't on any account be the one to submit notices about you. Ettinger himself considers that I mustn't get involved, either in this way or even in a way that would seem to me natural, unprejudicial, and above all in line with my own feelings. If you want notices to appear here, and if you allow me, I'll take the three cuttings you sent me and show them to Tugendhold, quite simply, directly, and with my blood up from the start; or I can enclose them in a letter to Lunacharsky; or even send them straight to the newspapers. It's not a good idea for you or any one of us here to edit what we submit. Nor can we expect art critics to write long articles—they write about what they've seen, not about hearsay. In other words, all we can achieve now is to convey the fact that an exceptional exhibition has taken place and has been a great success; that's what newspaper notices are for.

All this would have come about of its own accord, and I wouldn't be troubling you with my enquiries, if it weren't for a whole series of unpleasantnesses and upheavals with the opposition which have brought new people into the newspaper offices. In a year or two I may re-establish the straightforward relationships I had developed, over many years, with the previous generation of editors and writers, but at the moment it's not like that, and I can't allow myself any sort of familiarity with them without demeaning you, and perhaps myself too.

Two postcards from Leonid, which have not survived, arrived after Boris started this letter. Its continuation on 13 February answers the distorted report Leonid had heard of Boris's telephone conversation with Ettinger, where his attitude to his father's request was said to be one of 'indifference'. Boris's rejoinder also suggests that Leonid thought his son's reluctance to intercede with the Soviet press on his behalf was prompted by a sense of false modesty. Boris remains constrained in what he can and cannot tell his father.

Boris Pasternak to Leonid Pasternak

13 February 1928. [Moscow.]

Dear Papa,

I started this letter a long time ago, but I was waiting to meet Pav[el] D[avyd-ovich] [Ettinger] at Olga Alexandrovna's in order to finish it and send it off, after having further discussions with him. Now I've received your two postcards, which greatly upset me. Things aren't at all as you imagine, and in particular the 'I' that appears in your imaginings bears no resemblance to the real me. I don't know whom it is that you love and whom you are writing to, but . . . but it isn't me. The present situation, and my own feelings, tell me that the first thing to do is precisely to see Tugendhold. Besides which, he's one of your (quote) friends, whom you would like to (quote again) delight. Unfortunately I can't do that today, since I've already passed on the three cuttings I had, to the journal *Pechat i Revolutsiya*, for publication as a news item. They would be very happy to publish an article about the exhibition, from a graphic arts angle—I mean an article about your new drawings (this journal deals with books and bibliographies, and they're interested in the figurative arts in a graphic context)—if someone over there in Berlin were to write an article like that and enclose photographs. [. . .]

If you find such a simple interpretation of my character appealing, if you think that's the true key to my actions—that's up to you, of course. But that's the very thing that upset me in your letter. Don't be angry with me, think better of me. There are things that are more powerful than me, and perhaps they have a simple explanation. I'm everlastingly aware of the gulf between my absurdly high reputation and the insignificance of what I've achieved; it's something that haunts me, embarrasses me, and has shaped my character. My modesty doesn't adorn me, on the contrary—it often degrades or disfigures me. And yet the causes of my modesty are so ever-present that I can't shake myself free of it. Perhaps it damages my relations with you too, in this whole business. In which case please forgive me.

I kiss you and Mama warmly.

Your Borya

The disappearance of one of my postcards has worried Zhenia. Did you get her letter after the sanatorium, or don't you know how grateful she was to you?

Probably the same (now lost) postcards carried news of Josephine's nervous break-down, which frightened the whole family. Rosalia and Lydia Pasternak immediately left Berlin to join her in Munich.

Boris Pasternak to Leonid Pasternak

14 February 1928. Moscow.

Dear Papa,

I have three cuttings: from the *8 Uhr Abend Blatt*, the *Berliner Tageblatt* and the *Vossische Zeitung*. Send me some more, if there are any worthwhile and interesting ones. Also, if you can, send me some photographs of the best and most important pictures (the portraits of Corinth, Harnack, Einstein and others). I'm not talking about drawings now, but about the best of your new works that aren't known here, those that the art critics have particularly noticed. The journal *Krasnaya Niva* is going to publish an extended report, something like a review, so it would be a very good idea to have some photographs. It's going to be written by Yakov Zakharovich Chernyak, one of my best friends, if you remember him, the one who has the etching of me that was copied from 'Congratulations'. He's more of a literary critic, but he's very cultured and gifted, a pupil of Gershenzon. If it's not a foolish request, please don't send too many Jews—the two that fate brought into the world in the persons of you and me are enough for me. The proposal relating to *Pechat i Revolutsiya* still holds good too, but that will need an article from Berlin, one mainly devoted to graphic art. I terribly want to see you, particularly now—to get over there to you.—What I'm going to say now is in stark contradiction to my last request. Yesterday I read *Sunset*, a play by Babel, and almost for the first time in my life I found that Jewry, as an ethnic fact, was a phenomenon of positive, unproblematic importance and power. But that's not likely to alter my destiny, which isn't shaped by my individual impressions. I should like you to read this remarkable play, but the issue in which it appears also contains a long article about me, and if I cut that out you'll notice from the contents page that it's missing, and be offended. But I can't buy a second copy now, we're gradually getting into debt again, though that's just a temporary difficulty and doesn't worry me in the least.

This letter has been lying about for over three days, and now it's time to send birthday wishes to Zhonia. Do tell her that I don't forget her for a single minute, and from all my heart I wish her a quick recovery and a return to full, healthy strength of mind, to look after her home and all around her, meaning yourselves.

I can't imagine a recovery without that, because I can explain her illness to myself only as an excessive dislocation of her own central focus-point, the one which sustains her life.

Another reason I'm not writing to her is just that all this is too acutely serious; or rather, it's all so morbid because of the dense muddle, which is only aggravated by each new piece of advice. If I were there in person, there might perhaps be a lucky moment of understanding which would resolve everything; but a letter can only make matters worse. Out of all of us here, I'm the one who least understands from your letters what is actually happening with her, because 'nerves', and 'a little better', and 'thank God, thank God', tells me absolutely nothing whatsoever. But I'm not asking you to tell me the name of her illness either, because even if you were doctors you'd only cite me some (understandably) inaccurate term instead. Don't get me wrong. In cases like this, letters are powerless and pointless, that's all I mean to say.

I embrace you and Mama, and trust that Zhonia will manage things herself. It's a remarkable thing that the people with the strongest characters are the most weak-willed in everyday life. It's an enormous task, bringing together one's widely diverging intentions and performance.

In response to the 'offended tone' of the above letter, Leonid Pasternak wrote back, saying that he had good reason to believe that his old 'friend' Tugendhold would never accept an article by Chernyak. Instead, he offered the following text of an 'article from Berlin' for *Pechat i Revolutsiya*:

Leonid Pasternak to Boris Pasternak

25 February 1928. Berlin.

SUCCESSES OF RUSSIAN ART ABROAD

An exhibition of works by our artist Leonid Pasternak has just closed in Berlin. Judging from the enthusiastic reviews in all the Berlin papers, the exhibition was a resounding success. We present here, in literal translation, some extracts from articles in the principal Berlin papers by such renowned art critics as Fritz Stahl, Max Osborn and others. [...]

I'm intentionally including the beginning of a journal article (with reproductions), as an example of how they do these things here: first they give a 'news item' which records the bare facts of the event, and then the article follows—the 'literary padding', as I call it. Show this to the Signor who writes the 'information', and he'll see that it's no invention of mine when I refer to '*ausgezeichnete Kritik bei der ganzen Berliner Presse*'.[7] That'll ease his conscience when he comes to 'report' it.

Well, that's enough of that. I must confess that I'm heartily fed up with all this—just think—in order to get a simple objective report into a newspaper, based on submitted material, with a literal translation or a couple of review extracts, as a record of the factual 'success' of 'our Russian art' (to gladden the hearts of my well-wishers)—I've had to set up Pepa, write to Pavetti with reviews and information, and then motivate you to undertake this great enterprise, and carry on an immense correspondence with explanations and so on and so forth.—Isn't it odd? Apparently, that's how it has to be. Anyway, I'm sick to death of it now.

But I'd be very interested to read Babel's *Sunset* which you wrote about, saying that it's 'in stark contradiction' to what you say about the word 'Jew'. What a strange fellow you are—you didn't mention where it was published, or in what journal. I made enquiries at the library yesterday and today, but they don't know when or where it was printed. Tell me where to find it—I'd very much like to read it.

And I very much want to see you too, and it's significant that you mention the fact—perhaps you'll succeed—but for the moment, of course, all this is 'dreams, dreams'. [...]

As regards Zhonichka, of course, you're not far off the mark, and you're right to say that her illness can't be diagnosed through letters, 'even if we were doctors and could name the illness'—because it both is and isn't an illness—Anyway, she's getting better every day, thank God. According to her, she's had something like this before (though neither I nor Mama knew about it)—some two years ago; and in her childhood too, do you remember?—The only new thing is that she now has nervous nausea, and sometimes vomiting too, but not of a gastric kind—it's purely nervous—but it passes, and I'm convinced (and the nerve specialist and a well-known psychiatrist have reassured us) that it will pass, gradually but completely—she has to cure herself by herself. [...]

In an earlier letter dated 23 January 1928, Boris responded to his father's anxieties about Lydia, who was considering a marriage proposal from Ernst Rosenfeld.[8] Her parents advised against the match (Ernst was a live wire, and also badly off). In her

---

7. 'Enthusiastic reviews in all the Berlin papers'.
8. Ernst Rosenfeld was the nephew of one of Leonid's friends; he visited Moscow in the summer of 1926 and helped Boris and Alexander organise the paperwork and transport of a number of pictures for the forthcoming Berlin exhibition.

uncertainty, Lydia wrote to Moscow for advice. Despite Boris's sympathetic encouragement, the marriage did not take place.

Boris Pasternak to Lydia Pasternak

15 February 1928. Moscow.

Dear Lidochka,

Please don't answer this; you can see how long it takes me to get round to writing to Zhonichka and Fedia. A reply from you would tie me down: it would be painful for me not to start a correspondence with you. But I've read your letter to Shura and Zhenia, and the main thing I want to say to you is very simple. Why would you want to justify yourself to everyone else? There's no such thing in the world as a totally justified action. Any new step is always risky. The best and most vital ones are those whose justification lies in the future. Lived-through reasons and arguments pump out our feelings down to the dregs; life isn't a syllogism, it doesn't wait for conclusions or consequences, nor does it save up its ammunition to meet them. What struck me to the heart in your letter wasn't so much that you go in for vivisection, mercilessly turning yourself this way and that in search of greater conviction; rather it was the way you found yourself obliged to mix your intentions and wishes into the unyielding dough of discussion and certainty. Decide for yourself, don't discuss—that's what I wanted to tell you. Decide lightly: marry Ernst on the Rhine or near Basle, but not in general terms, not in an awareness that everything is decided once for all. Realise with your whole being that in order to fulfil your own wishes, you have to forget the general chorus for a moment; and then hang on to the memory of how light your decision was, so that one day you can turn it to account when the chorus is singing in Ernst's favour, while you, perhaps, have once again turned your back on the choral version of your life.

With all my heart, I wish you true, impetuous recklessness; this question is unthinkable without it. In a year's time you'll remember what I said, not because Ernst is bad (which he isn't at all), but because this year will be a re-birth for you, and you'll want to swallow the planet whole, precisely because of the upbringing we've both received—but that's something one would have to write volumes about, and I'd better stop.

And another reason why one can't listen to good advice from living people these days, is that our whole epoch is nothing but a failed marriage, a huge, all-consuming one, and this tragedy becomes a comedy when we hear the actors on stage uttering pronouncements about happiness, assumptions about happiness, recipes for happiness. At the present time, my dear, we shouldn't listen to anyone, apart from the voices of the radio, the Balzacs and the Tolstoys of our world. Because the people who will, one day, keep up verbal communication and build a sensible bridge from the last happy individuals of our own time to the first happy members of a new line—these people live terribly modestly, they don't press advice on one, nor expect happiness in this sunken path. Saturated as they are with the logic of misfortune, they love their time for one thing only: for the fact that they are gradually, and with great pains, humanizing it by learning to understand it.

You need to see the squalid slum from which Shura dredges up his teachings and judgments about happiness. You have to see the 'joyfulness' of Zhenia's inner life, faced with years of silence from me, to believe in her competence too. You have to consider the 'brilliance' of Fedia's spiritual balance, or Papa's—biographical—balance, to say at once: here are the professors of true eudaimonism.[9] You'll say—and what about you, Borya? Yes, but I have no illusions about myself, and I keep my mouth shut.

I think that Ernst is a man with an independent mind, and convictions of his own. He's light—he's not dragging a train of prejudices from his milieu and family behind him. I think that—having already learned lessons from life—he won't ignore its teachings in the future, if any are offered. And that's the most interesting and vital path to follow. I'm probably not without merit myself, but I'm an altogether inflexible sort of person;—the most important thing for me, given my inclinations, has always been to reinforce all my qualities, with all their negative aspects too, because the point wasn't to reform myself but to build some sort of structure on the foundation provided, *quelle qu'elle fût*. Well, yes. Certain trivial things did bother me about Ernst, and this probably does me no credit—there was something indefinable. Besides which, I was having a difficult summer.

Vas[ili] Iv[anovich][10] has died. Once again, like three years ago, trunks and wardrobes were shifted so that both halves of the door could be opened, and once again the requiem was sung to the accompaniment of people waking up and children crying, and they carried his body out, lifting their collars when they were on the stairs. If anyone thinks of writing to Pasha, her name is 'Praskovya Petrovna'.

9. Eudaimonism is a theory that the pursuit of happiness is the highest good. In this bitterly sarcastic paragraph Boris implies that none of the people he cites, nor he himself, have achieved much happiness.

10. Vasily Ivanovich Ustinov, co-tenant of the former Pasternak apartment, whose wife had died three years earlier. Their maid Praskovya became his second wife, and now she inherited their room.

Kisses to Fedia, Zhonia and Alyonushka. I didn't mean to write to you the way this letter has turned out. I embrace you warmly.

Your Borya

A year earlier, Rosalia had written to Boris that Olga Serova, widow of the artist Valentin Serov, had—shortly before her own death—asked Rosalia's permission to send some of her late husband's works to Berlin to raise much-needed money. Pessimistic about the prospects of success, Rosalia had asked Boris to try to interest the Soviet state museums in acquiring these works, and she also asked him for the address of Serov's daughter Natalia in Paris. (In the end, Leonid managed to sell some small drawings to his friends; Josephine and Frederick bought some, and so did Leonid himself.)

Boris Pasternak to Rosalia Pasternak

6 April 1928. Moscow.

Dear Mamochka,

Zhenia will write to you about everything to do with your needless anxiety. Natasha's address is: Natalie Seroff, 3, Rue Albert de Lapparent, Paris VII. And Olyushka Serova asks me to send you very warm kisses. Don't be cross with me for not writing. As time goes on I'm dissolving more and more in my work, and the years have started living themselves out one after another faster than I can plan them ahead. I had thought I might complete something by springtime, and until that's done I don't want to go away even briefly. But over the winter I achieved unbelievably little, and once again—as every summer—all Raisa Lomonosova's invitations have been sent in vain. I don't know why, but as I wrote those old-fashioned words my electric light-bulb flared up with incredible brightness— they were probably switching generators at the power station. My dears, don't on any account send money here—if you want to help anybody, let me know the precise details. I have some debts abroad, and sometimes I feel the need to settle them, but transferring money from here is fraught with enormous difficulties and (above all) loss of time. I've already asked you this (not to send money) before, but it was probably on the same postcard on which I wrote about Papa's first press cuttings. By now I've even worked out why it never arrived: I probably covered half the front of the card as well, and that seems not to be allowed, though the layout of the markings suggests otherwise.

Papa once wrote about Rilke's letters and their publication. But they are probably stored together with his entire archive, in one of the impossible piles of
boxes here. It'll be hard to find them.[11] You probably have no idea of the cramped
conditions in which we live.

I sometimes write to you indirectly, either by ricochet via Lydia, or little
Zhenichka will suddenly succeed in getting me to write to his Babushka at last,
at his dictation, or I hang a letter onto Natasha Serova's address. Have I written
to say how good Papa's portraits are? But Chernyak's daughter has scarlet fever,
and for the time being I can't talk to him about an article. And please don't be
cross that we haven't written to you both to send birthday greetings, and aren't
sending any now. Although it's loutish behaviour, of course.

Your B.

Boris Pasternak to his parents and Lydia Pasternak

21 May 1928. Moscow.

Dear Papa, Mama and Lida,

[...] And you haven't merely been clothing us (I do that too);—from some
incomprehensible fullness of your hearts, you love us as well. I don't mean that
I'm entirely heartless, or that I'm in some kind of 'drama'. But everything that
happens at home, even in those frequent cases when it's done by my own hands—
stowing things, tidying up, etc.—reaches my consciousness as though in a dream,
through a space of distant quietness and absent-mindedness, which I always carry
with me and spread about me. The house doesn't terrorize me, and I'm not scared
of work or bother, although I have enough and to spare of all that. The reason
I have no time is something entirely different. As with money, and with objects
that I don't know how to value and am always glad to give away, I would probably be glad to share the most precious treasure that I know, which is: free time
(perhaps that's the very thing that all religions have deified under the name of
God). I mean the pure interval in which one can see the boundless fullness of
real life, as real as the life of trees and animals. And incredible as it may seem, I
would be able to find enough free time to share with anyone you like, because
everyone always manages to get hold of and store up the thing he values most

---

11. Insel-Verlag had approached Leonid about Rilke's correspondence with him, for their planned
edition of his complete works. The letters from Rilke were soon found, but it took a year to make and
send copies to Berlin.

highly. But, more than anything else in the world, this is something reserved for the connoisseur. An understanding of art, however rare it may be, is much more widely distributed than a feeling for and understanding of free time. I'm talking about something that's far greater than mere 'leisure'. I'm talking about living time, in freedom.

This is something that I would be willing to share (as I have done on occasion), but only with someone who knew the meaning of the word 'an instant'. Why is there so much beauty in a thunderstorm?—Because it piles space upon space, making them flash, in other words it shows how fathomless the instant is, and what immense distances it can absorb and give forth again.[12] But since there aren't many people who know how inexhaustible and capacious an instant is, there's almost no-one to share it with—yet an instant is all that free time is. It's in this sense that I never have time—I don't have time for those who don't know what time is.

[…]

Pavetti recently gave a lecture at the Academy of Fine Arts about you as a graphic artist. He spoke warmly, with understandable and proper feeling; so there's nothing to reproach him personally with—but his lecture was very unintelligent and naïve. Needless to say, this last is between ourselves. But if he prepares his lecture for the press, then in one way or another it's bound to pass my way, and perhaps (without his knowledge, so as not to hurt his feelings) the necessary corrections will be made at the necessary time. His mistake lay in the fact that he played a sort of gipsy fiddler's lament over the fact that you're somewhat undervalued, uttering the stupidest and most sentimental clichés. In his striving to 'explain and solve' this 'problem'—this, if I may say so, unheard-of wonder and novelty of the undervaluing of an artist (as if it weren't a constant law of history with nothing unique or exceptional about it), he floundered into the most banal babblings about Jewishness, rights of residence, persecution, and the like, which Olga Alexandrovna, for instance, or Aristova, or Ekat[erina] Vasilyevna[13] felt had nothing to do with your true profile at that time, while people who didn't know you, young people and the new generation, were given a false impression of you (but one which from P[avel] D[avydovich]'s viewpoint presented you in a 'tragic' or touching light). But one can't be angry, because half of that evening

---

12. This idea echoes Boris's poem 'Groza, momental'naya navek', translated by Lydia Pasternak Slater as 'Thunderstorm, instantaneous forever'.

13. For Olga Alexandrovna Bari-Aisenman, see above, p. 104. Anna Ivanovna Aristova and Ekaterina Vasilyevna Goldinger were friends and pupils of Leonid.

was devoted to P.D.'s own personal recollections (not that he was talking about himself, that's not what I mean, he didn't say a single word about himself; but in talking about you, he was involuntarily recalling the best and most precious period of his life); and all his simple-heartedness suddenly spilled over. If he were more of an egoist, of course, he'd be much cleverer.

Finally, there's been a letter from Aunt Asya, a terribly nice, inconsequential letter full of interesting things, in which she presses me to her heart—astonishing—but also mentions that she's been to see an oculist who found a cataract in her right eye; she has asked me to let you know about this. Incidentally she also told me about your absent-mindedness, and how (on your envelope) you had once again promoted her from a Freidenberg to a Pasternak. She asks very warmly after all of you. I answered her yesterday, and you should write too.

Zhenia Genikes,[14] with her husband and child, is lurking somewhere near Moscow. She's been here once. She seems a perfect fool, and her husband is a blatant, arrant parvenu. I didn't ask for her address, or her surname either. We have no need of each other.

I embrace you all warmly.

Your B.

Leonid Pasternak to Boris Pasternak

28 May 1928. Berlin.

Dear Boryusha,

Thank you for your letter of yesterday, a wonderful one as always (where you tell about Pavetti's lecture—well, one has to know what to expect from different people. I can just imagine it!)

We've just written to Aunt Asya. Of course I was very upset by the oculist's diagnosis. My theory—of family traits and heredity . . . But it's not so tragic for her. Not a pleasant subject.

What you write about 'free time' and the 'instant' (thunderstorms) is very good—as always, it comes across very beautifully and well. I'm very sorry that people waste a lot of your time—and I don't at all include myself among those who rob you of it, so I didn't take what you wrote as aimed at me, but regarded it entirely objectively as a true and beautifully expressed view of 'free time' and the 'instant'. If I had felt guilty, I would have taken it as an admonition—but since

14. A great-niece of Leonid Pasternak.

it was a cry from the heart, raised in an academic way and directed 'to one side', I took it all coolly.

It's strange for us to read that you, poor boy, are surprised at us, and wonder how it was that we had enough strength and time and attention to devote to you, our children, etc. etc. Incidentally, while I'm on the subject: for God's sake, Boryusha, and you too, dear Zhenia,—however irritated you may be (you in particular, Borya, are often very quick to let everyday unpleasantnesses drive you to exasperation)—have pity on dear little Zhenionok, and remember that one must always keep one's will and one's reason under control. It's only reason—alongside natural love—that can help you to maintain a high degree of insight—to see that if your irritation tells you that he's a such-and-such and a so-and-so, then the fault lies not in him, but in us, from his nearest to his furthest relatives. [. . .]

Altogether, Borya, you should take care to control yourself, learn to control yourself; for unto whom much is given, of him shall be much required. How clumsily Lev Nikolaevich [Tolstoy] attempted to control the demons that thwarted his self-improvement. Of course, nothing of the sort applies to you, and there's no need for it—but what little Zhenionok needs is something quite uncomplicated, possible and achievable by both of you—simply for you to think of him more often, without hostility or irritation. [. . .]

CHAPTER FIVE
1928–1929

Boris remained alone in Moscow while Zhenia and Zhenichka spent the summer in the Caucasus. He was preparing a new edition of his collections of poetry from 1910 onwards, and continuing *Safe Conduct*, begun in the winter. The opening of this autobiographical prose work describes his decision to abandon his first vocation as a composer—a difficult choice mirroring his mother's sacrifice of her career as a concert pianist, in order to raise her family. Boris's unprecedented recognition of their spiritual consanguinity is triggered by the chance observation with which he opens the following letter.

From mid-July to the end of August he joined his family at Gelendzhik on the shore of the Black Sea.

Boris Pasternak to Rosalia Pasternak

24 August 1928. Gelendzhik.

Dear Mamochka!

Just now, for a joke, I put on some spectacles, and it turns out that I look so much like you that Zhenia even asked me not to take them off, so that she could look at you a bit longer. I suppose our long silence needs some explanation, and I ought to give one, but if I were to list the reasons for it, I wouldn't say anything of any importance or interest, so it's better if I don't. Our contact with you has naturally been interrupted by the uncertainty in which we lived here for a time. Initially we intended to move deeper into the mountains, and wrote to Moscow to stop our letters being forwarded to Gelendzhik until further notice. But then, having decided to keep a 'base' in Gelendzhik and only go on occasional excursions without Zhenichka, we failed to notify anyone in time, so it's no surprise that we're not getting any letters here. However, I have indirect reason to believe that all's well, because a postcard came from Stella, and of course she would have written differently if anything alarming had happened to you.

The fact that this letter is addressed to you is something that happened all by itself. I've explained to you how it came about, but this chance event is in strange harmony with the way I've been feeling in the last few days. It's a very good feeling—just in case you think there's anything wrong—and like every good thing, it's irresistibly trying to burst out, and doesn't admit of any sort of communication, which in many ways is unthinkable.

In the autobiographical piece that I started last winter, and which you'll read one day (its continuation is my next task, waiting for me when I get back to Moscow)—well, in this autobiographical piece I describe my parting from music in exactly the terms that would have been appropriate to my present situation. Anyone who hasn't experienced this kind of crisis, culminating—somewhere—in the bitter harmony of a universal reconciliation, has lived unaware that he too possesses a soul.

It was with such feelings that I recently wrote an immensely long letter to you, 32 pages of it, about myself, the Caucasus, Zhenia, the sea, our journey, and many other things; but it didn't come out right, and in its place my life is now filled with great tenderness towards you, a burning likeness to you which I've just discovered through the medium of glasses, and a mass of kisses and greetings to all of you from us. Best wishes.

Your B.

This letter will be posted in Moscow by our neighbours, who are just about to leave.

The centenary of Leo Tolstoy's birth in August 1928 prompted Leonid to write his memoir article 'How *Resurrection* Came About', describing his friendship with Tolstoy, who chose him to illustrate *Resurrection* as it was written. Extracts from Leonid's recollections of the painter Vasily Dmitrievich Polenov and the philosopher Nikolai Fyodorov, written at this time, are included in his collected reminiscences, *Zapisi Raznykh Let*.[1]

Leonid Pasternak to Boris Pasternak

6 September 1928. Munich.

Dear Boryusha,

It's 100 years since I wrote to you—around two or three days after Tolstoy's birth!

1. L.O.Pasternak, *Zapisi raznykh let* (Moscow: Sovetskiy Khudozhnik, 1975); *The Memoirs of Leonid Pasternak*, tr. Jennifer Bradshaw (London: Quarter Books, 1982).

You absolutely have to send us that 32-page letter, if it hasn't been destroyed—
or did you merely think that you had to write 32 pages? Have you already
started wearing spectacles? Or who is it that's wearing spectacles in your home?
Zhenia?

I'm very glad to hear that you've gone to the Caucasus—it'll be useful to you.
One day, like Leo Tolstoy, you'll tell some Pasternak of the future: 'Once upon
a time I too was young, and the Caucasus was young, and the pheasants were
young...'

That, my boy, comes from my recollections of Tolstoy, some of which I've
contributed for the Jubilee celebrations at the request of *Literarische Welt* of
Berlin. It's been over 20 years, and I still haven't found the time to write my
'memoir' of Tolstoy. Unforgivable!! But there's never any time!! But now—
chance has forced my hand, and I've written something. Only a fragment—
about the time when *Resurrection* was being written. But now they ought to
be sending me the proofs of the translation (there was no-one here to translate
the piece—Lida is at work, Zhonia is too busy at home, and in the end I had to
submit the Russian version). The family liked it; but whether it'll be printed,
I don't know.

As a matter of fact, my boy, I'm planning to take the bread out of your mouth—
I've *umgesattelt*[2] and become a 'writer'. I had already written my recollections
of Polenov—do you remember, Mme Polenova was asking for my address. She
wrote me a long letter asking me to record my recollections, for the forthcoming
anniversary of his death on 18 July (she's collecting materials, and probably wants
to publish a monograph later on). Well, I summoned up my courage and wrote
some 30 pages, and sent them to her in time. I got a touching letter from her,
how much she liked it and so forth (and, damn it, I still haven't answered her...
ever since becoming a 'writer' I've stopped writing letters)... Oh yes! before
that, I wrote a little piece in German about Nikolai Fyodorovich Fyodorov[3]—the
Germans don't know him and aren't interested in him, so the *Epochische Zeitung*
didn't print it. But I'll get it published somewhere. Do you know anything about
Fyodorov? You must have heard of him. I wrote to you about him, and even
wanted to send you a little pamphlet about him (it was sent to me from Harbin,
in China)—but somehow or other you never responded.

2. 'Changed saddles'.
3. N.F. Fyodorov (1829–1903), an idealist and utopian philosopher who preached self-perfection
of mankind, control over nature, and the attainment of personal immortality and resurrection of the
dead by scientific means. He greatly influenced Tolstoy, Dostoevsky, and Vladimir Solovyov (1853–
1900), another idealistic philosopher. Leonid Pasternak painted a group portrait of Tolstoy, Solovyov
and Fyodorov.

Incidentally, do our press cuttings get through to you (we occasionally send you some)? Including today, as it happens. Two words about you ('*der Russische Rilke*') say a lot. It's a *feuilleton* by a German journalist, Heartfield,[4] about his impressions of Moscow. [...]

I'm sorry to be writing in pencil—it's a very hot summer, and all the ink in Munich has dried up ... Start making notes straight away—before you can turn your head, you'll find you're having to write 'recollections' about me.

Meanwhile—are you better? Have you managed to rest? I like your 'autobiographical project'. God grant it works out. How's my little Zhenionok? Looking better? And Zhenia, I expect, is bowled over by the landscapes in the Caucasus? Well, we kiss you all, my dears, and God preserve you. We're going back to Berlin soon—around the 15th.

Your Papa

Rosalia Pasternak to her sons and daughters-in-law

18 September 1928. Berlin.

Dear Zhenia, Ina, Borya and Shura!

Pavetti will soon be coming here. Take the opportunity and send us Rilke's letters. When the volume of his correspondence is published, and the ones to Papa aren't included (Papa is very anxious that they should be), then your consciences will prick you and you'll feel sorry for him, but it'll be too late! You're always writing 'how sad and ashamed we are, Papochka, that you're such a busy man, and yet you drop everything and carry out ... all our requests' ... Well, now you have a chance to thank him. When we left, I bundled up all the letters and left them in perfect order: Papa's to me, letters from deceased relatives, and 'facsimiles' from famous people (including Rilke). [...]

Mama and Babushka

After a long interruption due to her severe nervous illness, Josephine resumed her correspondence with her brother. He wrote in reply:

4. John Heartfield (Helmut Herzfeld), a German graphic artist and stage designer who visited the Soviet Union in 1931–1932. He was one of the founders of the Berlin Dada movement, and also co-founder with his brother of the Malik publishing house (see the letter from Leonid Pasternak, 21 May 1929, below, p. 141.

Boris Pasternak to Josephine Pasternak

28 October 1928. Moscow.

Dear Zhonichka,

[...] What is your news, and how is Alyonushka? Is everyone in Berlin well? They haven't written for a long time, but I rarely write myself, and I only listen to life with half an ear, not because I'm conceited but the reverse. At present I'm in a state of extreme embarrassment, which isn't false or imaginary but provoked by a real disgrace, though I'm not directly at fault for it. Someone at some time told unnecessary tales about me, and then a long time went by, and the rumours are growing like an avalanche and will go on growing unless I can divert or arrest the avalanche myself. The interest shown by foreigners who seek me out or ask questions about me is absurd and inappropriate. I ought to have been Heinrich Heine or Khlestakov,[5] so as not to lose my head or start lamenting over all this. But I'm neither of them. You know me, and probably remember me; and I haven't changed. It's a different matter if approaches are made directly to me, for some specific reason; then my own conscience and strength see me through. When foreign publishing houses approach me about translations, the answer has always been, and remains, a very simple one: there's really nothing to translate, and that's what I tell them. It's too early, other people's enthusiasm and goodwill is premature, let's wait and see, and when there's something to talk about, we'll be in touch again. But this opportunity (of talking with the world) doesn't lie around waiting to be picked up; and in principle, spiritually, it's not alien to my own nature or my psychological experience. All that's needed is for me to feel the opening up of this conversation. And that involves a certain change in the character of my work—its nature and scale. Oh, if only I didn't have to talk or write letters, but could take you by the hand, or Olyushka,[6] or another of those real women whom I sometimes like just in the same way, just as indefinably and impossibly, as I do the two of you—and if I could, without using any words, pour into your minds the instantaneous nature of my 'dreams' and plans, just as they sometimes pass before me, in the mornings while I'm dressing, or going downstairs on my way out! Anyway, I'm longing to live and work as never before, quite

5. Heinrich Heine (1797–1856) was a leading German romantic poet and satirist. Khlestakov is the fraudster hero of Gogol's well-known satirical comedy *The Government Inspector*.

6. Boris's cousin Olga Freidenberg. His intense and extensive correspondence with her was published: *The Correspondence of Boris Pasternak and Olga Freidenberg 1910–1954*, ed. Elliott Mossman (New York: Harcourt Brace Jovanovich, 1982).

indescribably so; and as I think this to myself, it may be that some of it will pass before your eyes too. Of course I'm longing to go abroad, and write a great and unheard-of work (unheard-of by me, or unrecognised in me—what does it matter: don't I live, like everyone else, constrained by this Fichtean 'Not-I')[7]—yes, this great work, I say, I should like to write it abroad. But in order to do that, I have to finish and sell everything that's so far unfinished and incomplete, and that'll take a year or two.

Warmest kisses to you and your husband and daughter, and warmest thanks for everything.

[. . .]

Boris wrote to congratulate Josephine on her daughter's first birthday, and went on to describe the death and Jewish funeral of Alexandra Nikolaevna Lourié, Zhenia's mother. The scene of Zhenia at her mother's death-bed is echoed in *Doctor Zhivago*, in Tonia's lamentation over the body of her mother; but the perfunctory ritual of Alexandra Lourié's funeral is replaced in the novel by the exalted music of a Russian Orthodox requiem.

Boris Pasternak to Josephine Pasternak

14 November 1928. Moscow.

Dear Zhonichka,

Today you're getting congratulations by telegram, but nevertheless I warmly kiss you and Fedia and the birthday girl, and wish you a full and long life with her, and to her I wish an easy and peaceful time, during which conclusions are drawn rather than dissipated in unfulfilled beginnings.

I have less leisure than anyone here; but by the law of contradictions, I'm the only one to write to you from time to time. I've just received an envelope from you containing a page with a reproduction of Rachmaninov.[8] Perhaps there was a letter to go with it, but if so it's disappeared without trace.

You've probably already heard that Zhenia's mother has died. The nature of her death, her last words and so on, emphasized and at the last moment reinforced the resemblance that there always was between her and Zhenia; and Zhenia's

---

7. The German philosopher Johann Gottlieb Fichte (1762–1814) developed his idea of the dichotomy of "I" and "Not-I" in *The Science of Knowledge* (*Grundlage der gesamten Wissenschaftslehre*) (1794–1795).

8. Leonid's portrait of the composer.

own tears, shed over many days, particularly on the first, grasped this impalpable connection and further strengthened it. She wept, stroked and embraced her mother's body, adjusted the pillow under it, and furtively—in the midst of her tears and her conversations with visitors—sketched her. All this was fleeting, transient, childishly full and direct, it was all fused into one—death and grief, an end and a continuation, fate and the possibilities within it; it was all, in its evanescent nobility, beyond words.

But one word would suffice to name and define what followed next. Something fraudulent burst in, something which—in a way that's beyond my comprehension—passes as religion for a whole people, and has been preserved, with its heartlessness, almost unchanged for centuries, while alongside it the human heart, through music, philosophy, the plastic arts, romanticism and the rest, has been winning an ever-growing place in history. The rituals before and during the burial were like an unceremonious summary execution. I felt it all as a blatant abomination, and when an aeroplane roared low over the cemetery, having taken off from the nearby aerodrome, it was the only thing in which I found some support for my instinctive need for some elevating truth and sublime purity, the only thing that testified to a true and living religious tradition, the highest note that once sounded in remotest antiquity, and that carried on from generation to generation in a resounding voice (developing as it went, as inevitably happens in true life), right up to our own day. And I don't care where it was hurled on its way, into science or technology or somewhere else. Because the expression of religion over a fresh grave (and perhaps only there) is always a reminder to us that it was born as something whole, and at some time probably even had to embrace such things as the invention of the wheel.

19.XI. This letter has been lying around a long time. I have long wanted to talk to you seriously about many things, but there's no way to get round to it. But it won't go away, each new occasion hits the same spot, and the only essential point is my feeling that my friendship with you is something that I'll preserve longer than my friendship with anyone else. How naïve everything is around me, how naïve my friends and the people near me, how naïve the interpretation of itself that time provides. There are more and more topics about which I have to swallow my indignation and remain silent; it would be easier than easy to expose their stupidity, but one can't do it without running the risk of being regarded as . . . very youthful, and being misunderstood. Only a false understanding could give rise to the things I observe and encounter; only a false imagination could approach me with certain particular requests and commissions, as even

Olyushka has done; only a false fantasy could have made the proposal to me that Mamochka has made haste to delight me with. You see, she writes to tell me that Ida[9] has asked her to pass on to me that if I come to Paris on my own (without Zhenia and the boy, that is), she can offer me her sitting-room, but in case I might get the idea that 'the grass is greener over the hill', Mama makes a point of adding, in her own words, underlined, 'and this isn't a *manière de parler*, but the genuine truth', etc.

Naturally neither I nor anyone here was offended at Mamochka, but of course everyone laughed. But the point about this nonsense, for me, is that it's symptomatic of Mama's ideas about why and how I need Paris. And in its own way, that's touching. But Ida astonished me. Of course she's alive in me and for me, like everything that I've experienced, where every part is dearer and greater than the whole. But the real Ida, the one who gave Mama the message quoted here, would of course have done better to write to me, or even just pass on her address in response to the book that I once sent to her by a roundabout route. But if I even attempted to say anything of the sort, they'd decide that I . . . have 'inappropriate ideas about myself', or at least that my thoughts are moving along this conceited path. That's why I tell less and less about myself in my letters.

I embrace you

Your B.

Warm kisses to Fedia. I expect he too will be delighted by the note about Ida's delicacy and hospitality.

I've written this letter in a hurry; I know I ought to have been more careful in what I said about Mamochka, but of course you'll know how to read it, and know that it mustn't be shown to her. The main thing isn't her, of course, but Ida.

Boris Pasternak to Josephine Pasternak

20 November 1928. Moscow.

Dear Zhonichka,

Take no notice of the letter I sent yesterday. I was longing to talk to you but there was no time, and I failed to realize that the need for haste couldn't help distorting

---

9. Ida Vysotskaya, daughter of a rich Moscow businessman and art patron. Ida had been a close friend of Josephine's. Boris fell in love with her, proposed, and was rejected—experiences that are described in his early poetry and in *Safe Conduct*.

both the tone of the letter and the very thoughts expressed in it; yet I still dashed it off and sent it without re-reading it.

First of all, everything I said about Mama is unfair. Older people, and parents in particular, are entitled to see younger people and everything related to them in the light of their own lives; indeed, they're obliged to see and think in that way, unless they are acting young, trying to be modern and putting on a style. I only mentioned Mama as the purveyor of someone else's stupidity; but I didn't formulate the thought carefully enough. I wrote to you on a day when I had been annoyed by a visit from an expansive, loud-mouthed lady who treated me like a doll or some famous tenor, as she introduced me to an American composer. On the same day, I poured out half of this to the French poet Charles Vildrac, a delightful man who's staying in Moscow; and all that came out in my letter too.

The following letter to Josephine was prompted by the news that her sister-in-law Lina Pasternak had committed suicide. She was the wife of Albrecht (Alyosha), the younger brother of Josephine's husband Frederick. Albrecht visited Moscow in 1925, staying with Boris on Volkhonka. He later died in a Nazi concentration camp.

Boris Pasternak to Josephine Pasternak

31 December 1928. Moscow.

Dear Zhoniura,

The year is ending, it's after nine at night, they've rung the bells, soon it'll be time to dress and go out to celebrate the new year. So I wish you a happy New Year, you and Fedia and your little girl, and please embrace and kiss all our family.

Do they know, in Berlin, what has happened in Vienna? As a precaution (Zhenia thought of it, and warned me and Shura) we haven't mentioned this terrible story. But how dreadful it is! Poor Lina! [...]

I've had a bad autumn, for many reasons. I've become idle, because it really has been difficult to get over the obstacles that prevent me from working calmly and confidently. I'm waiting impatiently for the end of the holiday on January 2nd, when I'll lock myself up for a long time, just as I did once before. I'm terribly tired of this stupid week of drinking, Christmas trees, outpourings of talk, and constant lack of sleep. I can hardly put the words together to write to you, I've got such a headache and I'm so sleepy, but we have to go to Petrovsky Park to visit Pilnyak.

L[ev] Grig[oryevich][10] has arrived. I'll meet him tomorrow or the next day, and he'll tell me about you. He says he's got some pullovers for us—I'm thanking you straight away, who knows what's coming? The bells have gone silent, it's time to shave and change, I'm sorry for the rush.

Warm kisses to you all, all, all.

Your B.

[…]

The end of 1928 saw an abrupt change in official policy towards the smallest signs of independent thought. Official speeches announced a campaign against 'Right deviationism', whose suspected manifestations were sought in all aspects of life, particularly literature. 'The atmosphere, which force of habit had made tolerable over the years, reminds us with fresh vigour how intolerable it is', Boris wrote to his friend the poet Sergei Spassky.

He expressed his alarmed indignation both in print and in his letters of the time. However, he felt compromised; up to this time of increased state pressure, he had received generous recognition for his revolutionary poems. The state authorities now wanted him to be a different kind of writer, and confidently stated they knew better than he how he should express his gratitude for 'the trust they put in him'. 'It's difficult to live in constant awareness of one's own black ingratitude', he wrote to the émigré poet Vladimir Pozner. 'The mildest complaints about "incomprehensibility" (while signs of favour continue unchanged) affect me like the unfounded jealousy of someone who has sacrificed everything for you. And I'm not a monster; when all's said and done, you do have to listen to these nice people, so to hell with truth if it's so difficult to live with.'

Boris Pasternak to his parents

12 January 1929. Moscow.

My dears,

As promised, I sent off the money to Babushka on the 9th.

I've been living off advances for over a month—it's a capricious and devilish art, especially in some unrepeatable situations, and especially in our time. I haven't been able to work since spring—nothing to be done about it. And of

10. Dr. Levin. See above, p. 16, n. 24 for more about the Levin family.

course it isn't that I wasn't in the mood, or was . . . waiting for inspiration. No, things here are not velvety-smooth and inspiring, and we can't help passing through periods of distressing enforced sterility. And sometimes you're forced to turn aside and devote yourself to unproductive work and thoughts which have no direct relevance to yourself, because you're swayed by rumours and gossip. You listen and obey, because this isn't 'Roscius' speaking, but the State.[11]

And I can't help obeying it. I'm not afraid of it, but I respect it, because I believe in its future more than I do in my own. But one day soon I'll get down to work—I can't go on like this, with everything on credit all the time; it gets very awkward. So don't rely on letters from me. And anyway, you ought to distinguish between me and Shura, not in your love and warmth, but in your notions about what we can do. It wasn't heaven that dropped my role down on me, and when I'm called to account, it won't be by my family. For the Manfred question, for instance, you ought only to have approached Shura.[12]

Boris Pasternak to Josephine Pasternak

16 January 1929. Moscow.

Dear Zhoniura,

Two days ago I got down to work, and the fact that I'm abandoning it to write a letter is explained by two requests. As you see, we're true to ourselves in this, and I'm no better than anyone else. But you'll see for yourself that they're not binding requests, and please only do what I ask if it's no trouble for you to get hold of the things I want—otherwise don't bother.

A month ago I was visited (after a telephone appointment) by a person with the physical type and stature of Lydia (but that's very approximate—perhaps I'm flattering her*), who—amidst repeated blushes and mysterious fits of embarrassment—asked whether it was possible and permissible to ask a private person to translate her favourite German poet—whether, in fact, such a commission was conceivable. She wanted a translation of some poems from the *Stundenbuch*,[13] and I turned her down because I was too busy, and also because I'm paying my

11. 'Roscius' (a celebrated Roman comedian) was the nom de plume of the art critic Abram Markovich Efros, who wrote hostile articles on Leonid's work in 1910. Leonid was distressed; Boris thought they should be ignored.

12. The Kahns were Germans living in Moscow; when war broke out in 1914 they had to leave hurriedly, and entrusted Leonid's large commissioned portrait of Manfred Kahn to the Pasternaks' safe-keeping. Now the family sought its return.

13. 'Book of Hours'.

debt to Rilke's memory on an entirely different plane and in a more comprehensive way. I mumbled something about how it would be a different matter if the proposal had come from a publishing house; but she interrupted to ask if it made any difference to me—she could offer me the same terms as a publishing house; and then I smiled, not only because literary patronage is materially unthinkable here at present, but also because this had all become particularly touching in view of her worn-out shoes and more than modest jacket.

At all events, I made a note of her address (she's from Leningrad); I discovered that she teaches at the Leningrad Conservatoire, and needs the translations to bring R[ilke]'s poetry to the attention of Russian musicians and Russian music, something she considers essential. Her name told me nothing. However, I must add that I spend most of my time at home, and I'm no judge of whether today's names should be telling me anything or not.

Some time passed, and one day I got to know one of our best pianists here, Heinrich Neuhaus, one of whose concerts I'd attended in the past. And he, declining my compliments, started pressing me to go to a concert (not yet advertised) by a Leningrad pianist, compared to whom (he said), he himself was a nobody—she was a magnificent musician, with certain peculiarities— mystically inclined, wore iron fetters under her clothes, and performed in them; and, interestingly, was of Jewish origin; and so on and so forth—and he named my visitor.[14]

She played Bach, the *Kreisleriana*, some pieces by Hindemith, then Bach again—mostly his organ chorales. In the interval I sent her the only one of my Rilke things that I could bear to part with and that I had to hand: a juvenile collection of stories—weak compared to the later Rilke—called *Am Leben hin*,[15] with an appropriate inscription: 'I'm sorry that I didn't know who you were. Write to me from Leningrad, and I'll translate anything you want.'

14. Maria Yudina (1899–1970) was an outstanding Russian pianist who graduated from the Petrograd Conservatoire. She had a chequered career, her notable artistic successes being interrupted by periods of disgrace because of her outspoken criticisms of the Stalinist régime, her uncompromising Christian views (she was a Jewish convert to Orthodoxy), and latterly her support for Boris Pasternak. His friendship with her lasted a lifetime. His first reading from *Doctor Zhivago,* in February 1947, was given in her apartment; and in 1960 she played at his funeral. In 1961, as a concert encore, she read from his poems, for which she was banned from public performances for five years.

At the time of this letter, she was seeking to extend the Russian vocal repertoire, particularly by a performance of Hindemith's *Marienleben*, a setting of some Rilke poems; in the previous year she had collaborated with the poet Vsevolod Rozhdestvensky on translations of Rilke. Beautiful editions of the books 'to her taste' which Boris requested from Josephine were quickly dispatched. Later Boris translated some poems by Goethe for her compilation of Schubert Lieder.

15. 'On the Rim of Life'.

Now I've had a letter from her, just the sort of letter that was bound to follow. But I shan't be in a hurry to do what she asks—it's less feasible now than ever. But I'd like to send her some real, worthwhile R[ilke], and—something to her taste. There are two books like that: *Buch der Bilder* and *Geschichten vom lieben Gott*.[16] Please send them to me, if it's not too difficult. I need to do this, specifically because I want to leave everything on the same restrained sort of spiritual level as before. I may not even answer her when I send the books. Maybe, as part of the same pattern of economy, I'll send her the last (chronologically) of my old musical manuscripts, if I have time to find them. But I'm more likely to give them to Neuhaus.

What's the news with you? Yes, you'll be wondering about my second request. I've only made one so far. I'll limit myself to that one; the other was my own, I mean it was for me, but I've changed my mind and we'll forget about it.

Levin talked a lot about you, including the Burgundy for Alyonushka's dowry. Kiss her and Fedia from me.

I embrace you

Your B.

* the visitor, that is—not Lida

A close friendship developed with Heinrich Neuhaus and his wife, which was to shape the course of Boris's life. As intended, he gave Neuhaus the manuscript of his 1909 sonata, secretly hoping that Neuhaus might perform it one day.

He was becoming increasingly absorbed by 'A Tale' (also known as 'The Last Summer')—a prose sequel and conclusion to the verse novel *Spektorsky*—and by the autobiographical work *Safe Conduct*, the fulfilment of his 'debt to Rilke's memory'.

Boris Pasternak to Josephine Pasternak

25 January 1929. Moscow.

Dear Zhoniura!

You leave me no peace—or rather, you're tearing me away from my work. No sooner had I written to you, castigating myself for my distractions, than those two bundles of underwear arrived, which I suppose (failing future explanations

16. 'Picture-Book, and Stories about God'.

or refutations) I have to thank you for. And you'll appreciate how sincere and cordial my gratitude is, although the machine-gun tempo of your gifts arriving one on top of the other gives me no chance to differentiate between them— and you'll understand my gratitude all the more easily and fully since it's all I have to offer you, or any of our family, in return for this flood of generosity and kindness.

I'm quite carried away by my work, which I took up so tardily that I'm now having to get on with it at a back-breaking, exam-like pace, probably right through to the autumn. It's true that in this respect I'm a man of extremes, I can't work in any other way, and this is all predestined, it seems.

Having picked up my pen, I want to tell you about Pilnyak,[17] or rather to pass on his greetings to everyone, especially you. You probably know that he's one of our four or five best known writers; he's been translated into many languages, and you may even have read his *Das nackte Jahr*,[18] or seen it in a bookshop window. We meet a great deal now, that is, we often go to visit him at Petrovsky Park where he has a beautiful little *cottage*, a magnificent Great Dane he brought from Egypt, a fine collection of old books, mahogany furniture he's picked up over the years for next to nothing in remote spots like Uglich or Putivl, where he's off to at the moment, only hesitating between that city of Yaroslavna's[19] and Kasimov where our Uncle Osip is. He knows Osip from my stories, and only last night was urging me and Zhenia to go and visit him, taking with us Pilnyak's wife and even Panait Istrati[20] whom we've met there, etc. etc.

Pilnyak's family, I mean his children, are at Kolomna with his first wife; he himself has been married for over four years to his second wife, a very sweet, simple and affectionate woman, a young actress from the Maly Theatre. His mother-in-law is agreeable, and probably a wonderful person too, and I remembered her name and patronymic straight away because she's called Elizaveta Ivanovna. And that's appropriate, of course, though transposed into a different genre (gentry/intelligentsia).[21]

17. The writer Boris Pilnyak met Boris Pasternak in 1921, and a temporary rift that had developed between them was now repaired. Pilnyak often travelled abroad, to Egypt, Japan, and also to Germany where he met the rest of Boris's family. Among the foreign visitors visiting Pilnyak in Moscow, Boris met young prose writers including Andrei Platonov.

18. *The Naked Year* (*Goly god*, 1922), a novel depicting the chaotic situation during the Russian Civil War of 1919.

19. In the Russian epic *Slovo o polku Igoreve* (*The Lay of Igor's Host*), the Princess Yaroslavna stands on the ramparts of Putivl, bewailing the fate of her husband Prince Igor.

20. A Romanian 'proletarian' writer, initially promoted by Gorky, who became deeply disillusioned with Soviet socialism after visiting the country in 1927.

21. In 1931, when Pilnyak was in America and Boris left his wife Zhenia, he was welcomed into Pilnyak's home in Petrovsky Park for nearly three months. He became very fond of Pilnyak's wife, Olga

I've just thought that Papa (or even Fedia) will read about the cottage and all that, put two and two together and feel sorry for me. And of course, it could be upsetting, but it doesn't mean a thing. I know I've achieved immeasurably less than Pilnyak, and never will achieve much (although I do seem to be writing something genuine at the moment, but I've only thought it out very briefly). I don't measure myself up against anyone, I can contemplate other people's gifts lightly and accurately, and I think particularly warmly about the merits of people whom life has brought close to me. All the same, I do think I deserve his friendliness, and deep down we're equals—except that we visit him, while I have nowhere to invite him to, neither him nor those foreigners whom he sometimes asks me to meet. So, all that's *à propos du cottage pour le cas qu'on en souffre.*[22]

Apart from that, Pilnyak talks about you more and more often, and told Zhenia about you and about how he was in awe of Leonid Osipovich, and has often asked to be remembered to you.

I'll stop here, since this is just an overgrown letter of thanks for what you sent; I mean—all the rest was by the way. And in a contrasting outburst of impertinence, as I cross this fold to the last page, I'm going to ask you to pass on a message to Lida. When she was in a sulk with us, or rather, when I thought she was in a sulk with me, I got someone to ask Malik-Verlag to send her the volume containing a translation of *Aerial Ways.* I haven't seen it myself, but I've heard that the edition is sold out and my order will no doubt be filled in a month's time when there's a second edition. Well then, 'on the allotted day', when she has the book in her hands and has read it, could she please send me, printed paper rate, a block of writing-paper,* as she used to do. But, please: it must be she that does it, and only at the time that I've specified. It's a trait of mine, to set up this kind of exchange, with its whisper of cajolery, so please don't deprive me of this—what shall I call it?—wheedle-*Freude.*

And now a storm of hugs for Fedia, Alyonushka, Papa, Mama and Lidok, and for the benefit of the two men here named, will you two sisters please both stand up and defend my dignity (*re* cottage etc.), so that I can sleep easily.

Loving you all,
B.

* By the way, we have a paper crisis here, and it's difficult to get hold of writing-paper.

Sergeyevna Shcherbinovskaya, and her mother, Elizaveta Ivanovna, who reminded him of his deceased neighbour, Elizaveta Ivanovna Ustinova.

22. 'About the cottage, in case anyone is upset about it'.

Boris Pasternak to his parents and Lydia

[End of February 1929. Moscow.]

Dear Papa and Mama, dear Lida,

[…]

Today I'm getting down to copying out the Rilke letters. Oh, there are no words for this. How wrong it was of me not to have realized until this instant—when I felt it with tears and agonizing pain (as a child does, as with Mama about Braz,[23] or as with my feelings towards Mama)—how guilty I am before *you*, not before literature or R[ilke]'s memory.

But I'm so frightened that the letters will get lost (and frightened for you, that you'll be deprived of them), that I can't simply hand them over. They say Stefan Zweig will be coming again; I'd be happiest sending them with him. One could do it through an Embassy, but ours … do you remember what happens there? And the regrets that Gorky was a Social Democrat? Or perhaps the German Embassy? But that'll arouse gossip—why should he go there, what are all these papers then? It really would be best to use a live courier. Reassure me, tell me yourself that it won't ever be too late (I mean up till springtime, no longer than that). Even if the book has already come out, they'll be reprinting it with additions, and they might publish this material in *Neue Rundschau*. But don't tell me—I know it myself. And how to keep pace with the passage of time? I mean, I've gone without everything, everything—all I want is to finish my writing before I'm 40 or 41, because I always have this feeling that I'm going to croak about then. I'll try to materialise before you with something substantial on the 11th.

The next letter was written on Rosalia's birthday, and her and Leonid's 40th wedding anniversary.

Boris Pasternak to his parents

5 March 1929. Moscow.

My dear, dear ones!

Congratulations on a day on which, more than ever, I long and need to be with you; I'm writing to you and not seeing you on this day (and feeling glad? and can

---

23. Osip Braz was a Petersburg artist (originally from Odessa), a member of the 'Mir Iskusstva' (World of Art) group. As a child, Boris had been jealous of his closeness to Rosalia Pasternak.

you believe me?). Oh, you wonderful, wonderful people! In his postcard of congratulations today, Papa has given me 10 more years (of life)—twice as much as I was counting on. Oh, how murderously long it is since we last saw each other, and how much we need to talk about so many things! And of course this will happen; I'm doing everything I can to bring it about. If only I had half the confidence in myself that I have in you!

An unexpected pause for rest. The next-door neighbours' girl has gone down with measles. Yesterday Zhenia instantly carried Zhenichka off to stay with her family. My work was interrupted, and today is even worse. Before that, someone reminded me that I've been living without a letter of protection[24] for four years, my union expelled me two and a half years ago for defaulting on my subscription, and altogether I don't possess a single valid unexpired document. So I made the best of a bad job, and went the rounds of the offices; it was a beautiful spring day, there was no need to think about anything, and writing out my applications— what a pleasure!—straight onto a fair copy, briefly, with a clear aim, and a predetermined effect! I hope you understand that I'm not being ironic, I'm telling the honest truth.

Then I went to the Metchnikov Institute to give blood for Zhenichka for a measles vaccine. At once I remembered how we had the measles in 1903, or was it earlier? and Papa was in Paris (no, I'm wrong, that was before Zhonichka's birth, wasn't it?)—anyway, Braz came to visit Mamochka, and probably kissed her hand in the Petersburg manner, and I was probably already reading story-books, gripping ones with involved plots, and my word, how jealously I defended the soul of our family against him, and how I hated him! In short, I was prepared for an abduction, and the ruin of the whole family. It was midday, and we had high temperatures—well, it was all like a dream, like the summer poisoning in *Hamlet*. Nowadays I sometimes hark back to this memory. It's wonderful, it expresses in a delirious form all the wild atavistic despotism that characterises family life. Now, remembering that young woman, I'm rather sorry she never allowed herself anything in her life; and the only thing I find fearful and repellent is the tyrannical fervour that took possession of the child.

I'm writing with a bandaged arm (after the Institute), which isn't too easy. So long as I'm wearing a jacket and tie, my vague diction comes across as a living idiosyncrasy, or even a capricious mannerism. But as soon as I take my clothes off, the same characteristic has an entirely different effect. All the call-up boards I ever attended asked me whether I could read and write—when I was naked, all the gloss of twelve years' schooling fell away without a trace. And even today,

---

24. An official document guaranteeing immunity from having one's apartment confiscated.

though I'd only taken off my jacket and bared my arm, the same thing happened again: the nurse checked out my name on the form and didn't believe that I was related to my own self.

I've said that today felt to me like a day of rest. Of course, I couldn't say that about Zhenia, who gets worn down by all these bothersome moves. She's quite unable to look after herself—at the slightest thing, she gives up.

I'm sending the money to Babushka, and tomorrow, when the letter to her has gone off, I'll enclose the receipt, so that'll all be finished and done with. Once again, thanks for your trouble and for making these exchanges possible. Incidentally, I've forgotten my credit, I mean I've lost the sheet of paper where it was noted down; so when you can, let me know how much it comes to in German marks after adding in this payment for March. And if you can and need to, send me further instructions. Excuse this boring letter, which will arrive on the day of a double celebration—Mama's birthday and your 40th wedding anniversary.

So now I'm the same age as Papa was in 1902. How young he was then, and with what an appetite, and a justified appetite, he looked to the future!—while I'm thinking about things that I'd like to be able to finish in a year or two, so that I can then peacefully look forward to death. This isn't just words—indeed, it's a source of a kind of borrowed happiness even in these times.

Your B.

Boris was able to send presents for his parents' wedding anniversary and order them flowers with the help of the writer O.G. Savich, who was about to go to Berlin. At the same time Boris finally sent the autograph versions of Rilke's letters, by registered post.

Boris Pasternak to his parents

6 March 1929. Moscow.

My dears,

I've started to write to you, and it seems that I can't tear myself away. If you find a short note from me together with the presents, then you should know what happened. It was all done in such a rush that even the things I sent weren't what I wanted; but the main thing is that as soon as I had sent it all off, I remembered that I hadn't signed for Zhenia and Zhenichka, as I had meant to and should have done. For God's sake put this mistake right, add their names if not in my hand then in your own, please do, and include them in your answer. But actually there's no need to reply, I only need information about two points. Did Rilke's letters arrive; and what is the total amount owing after adding in the enclosed receipt? But only the first question bothers me.

Once again, congratulations to you both and Fedia and the girls.

Your fortieth anniversary almost coincides with the thirtieth anniversary of the first letter.[25]

Leonid Pasternak to Boris Pasternak

10 March 1929. Berlin.

My dear Boryusha,

I hasten to inform you that I have received, to my great joy, the two Rilke letters. Enormous thanks, also for your anniversary greetings. What a fateful coincidence. Yesterday, half an hour before getting your registered letter, I was at the home of a lady artist where—after many many years—I met again with her friend: Mme Rilke! And I started telling her how—to my shame—I was completely unable to get hold of his extant letters to me, and struggled to explain to her the reasons for this (it's difficult for a cultured European to understand this, since it's unforgivable: 'Papa, it's hard to find anything now in all this jumble, and we can't think of sorting it out'—that's the sort of thing that Shura wrote me at the time . . .), while you remained somehow deaf to all my requests and letters—but thank God that the letters are here, and that you yourself began your letter by saying 'there are no words for this . . . How wrong it was of me not to have realized until this instant', etc. Well, it's too late now, but thank God the letters are found, and you've admitted your fault.

So, I left her, reassuring her that the letters might still be found and then I'd send them to her (she knew that he had written to me). I get home, and half an hour later the postman hands me your registered letter with the Rilke originals. I was so happy to get them (it was a good thing that you copied them, and please do the same in future, and send me your letter too, for the collection). I telephoned her straight away (today is Sunday, we celebrated our fortieth anniversary yesterday, though it was actually on February 28th. Not a word from any of you . . . It's a good thing that you remembered and mentioned it in connection

25. The note accompanying Boris's package still survives: 'I embrace you both warmly and kiss you endlessly. Borya.' Then, in Lydia's hand, 'Zhenia and Zhenionok'. The first letter from Rilke to Leonid Pasternak is dated 20 April 1899.

with Mama's birthday). She'll be with me in an hour's time, and I'll hand them over to her. So, thank you again, and I look forward to the next consignment. The girls came to the celebration—we'll write more about that. I kiss you and Shura and your families, and God preserve you.

Your Papa

We've got the letter from you and Zhenionok!!! Kisses.

Leonid Pasternak to Boris Pasternak

[11 March 1929. Berlin.]

Our dear Boryusha!

This morning we got your postcard with a request that we should not 'take against' something you were sending. And an hour later, we received some absolutely beautiful dark-red roses, redolent of perfume and nobility, with your touching note, which Zhonia and Lida, as moved as we were ourselves, immediately signed with the names of 'Zhenia and Zhenionok', which had been forgotten in the haste and fervour of your sacrificial filial love, but—as you see—were immediately restored as inseparable! Well, my dear boy, and you, dear Zhenia and Zhenionok, we embrace you warmly and have no words to express our gratitude for your touching thoughts and attention. I guessed at the person through whom you had arranged it all—was it Kozintseva-Ehrenburg? This supposition is based on an invitation we have received from her to her exhibition of pictures (judging from the printed invitation, the opening of the exhibition was yesterday, in one of the private salons. I'll go there one day soon . . .)

Yesterday I sent you a postcard to tell you that we'd received two Rilke letters; I hope you've got it and are reassured, and that you'll go on doing the same (copy them first). His wife Clara visited us yesterday, and met Zhonechka and Lidok and Mama; she had tea with us, and everybody liked her very much, and she brought a very good photograph of him as a present for me, and showed a lot more photographs (some including him) of their daughter and grandchildren (two girls). It may be that the letters will get into the edition. I had the idea of painting his portrait—based on a variety of sources but mainly on my recollection of him (there are a lot of features of our family in him, particularly my bust at Aunt Asya's). We're now in a period of weeks of celebration, and delight at our precious guests Zhonichka and Lidok (Zhonia is going back home again today, God willing). Lidok has some things to do here for another couple of days, and then Fedyuk will come for a couple of days on business. Baskets of fruit, flowers, gifts, bouquets—splendid silver (from the girls), a beautiful antique vase (baroque) for confectionery, from Rosalia Alexandrovna (and some handwork of her own too), flowers, and endless 'festivals' . . . As for your request to let you know how much Mama owes you—here it is (Mama notes it down, and Zhonichka puts it in the savings book): (Yes! Mama wanted to write at this point, but she has guests, so I'm doing it).

[. . .]

Your Papa and Dedushka

Boris Pasternak to Leonid Pasternak

15 March 1929. Moscow.

Dear Papa,

I've got your card and enclose another instalment—five letters from R.M. Rilke that follow chronologically after the ones I sent you. I hope these reach you safely too. Then I'll only have to send the last two letters (of the ones I have here), one dated 25 March, the other 10 December, 1906. I haven't copied them yet, but all the ones I've sent have been copied. As regards the copies, I thought of hanging on to them as keepsakes. If you don't agree with that, then naturally I'll do as you wish and send them to you. But it seems to me that they wouldn't have the same documentary value as copies taken from the originals and notarized or some such thing, on the spot, in Berlin. Are they really going to deprive you of the originals, without leaving you any trace to show that they were once written to you?

Incidentally, the last two letters that I haven't yet copied contain a lot of things that will be precious for his widow; there's a postscript from her, and above all, in the other letter, when they were living in different cities, signs of his concern for her. I myself know certain things, and can guess a lot. Besides, it's all painfully similar to my own life, right down to the finest details, but it's best not to speak of that. Once again, send me a postcard to let me know you've received this.

Warmest kisses and embraces to Mama.

Your B.

Leonid Pasternak to Boris Pasternak

20 March 1929. Berlin.

Dear Boryusha,

Simultaneous thanks for the five Rilke letters delivered yesterday, and the last two that arrived today, and thank you also for copying them out. Today I telephoned his widow, and she was overjoyed and will come to see me tomorrow or the day after, to take copies of them. I hadn't even suspected how interesting their contents were for his biography! What a lot of water has passed under the bridge since then, and what a special feeling of 'a different age' they convey when you read them; it's hard to believe that they were written to me . . . Tempora mutantur . . . one might translate it, but it's all muddied now . . .

Of course, have the copies as a keepsake. Naturally I'll get the originals back— would I ever give them away?[26] [. . .]

Boris Pasternak to Leonid Pasternak

26 March 1929. Moscow.

Dear Papa,

I've got your postcard telling me that the letters have arrived. Well, thank God for that. I'm writing this with my mouth full of sage tea, blowing out my cheeks and sipping mouthwash from a cup. It's the old story—an attack of my annual pyorrhoea, when my teeth, evidently striving to escape from my gums, tear at the gold bar that Meisel put in, and as they're unable to shift it, they take out their revenge on me.

Please (you or someone else) let me know two addresses. One (I've already asked this before) is Uncle Osip's. Is this enough: Kasimov, Ryazan Province, Dr. I.I. Kaufman? This is holding me up from sending the letter. The other (which I'm asking for the first time) is the address of Frau C. Rilke. Incidentally, please don't tell her that I've been asking for it, since I'm not sure that I shall be writing to her, and don't know exactly when. I may have to, but only if it's absolutely necessary. I may perhaps translate a particular poem by him, in which case I may find it essential to have some information which she can probably give me. But I have such a vast amount to do at the moment—on top of my teeth playing up

---

26. In the event, only one letter from Rilke to Leonid Pasternak (dated from Capri, 10 December 1906) was included in his published correspondence (*Rainer Maria Rilke: Briefe aus den Jahren 1906 bis 1907*, ed. Ruth Sieber-Rilke & Carl Sieber [Leipzig: Insel-Verlag, 1930], pp.114–117).

again—I can scarcely believe I'll be able to do the translation in the foreseeable future; so you mustn't say anything. Unless you yourself would like to ask who Wolf, Count von Kalckreuth was, to whom 'Requiem' is dedicated? By the tone of the poem, he must have been a poet with a raw, emotional style, the opposite of Rilke's, probably with a colourful life and passions, who ended by commit-ting suicide. Or else I can ask her myself, in a suitable letter, naturally. How, and where, and what. And the information has to be reliable.[27]

Warm kisses to Mama and Lida and you.

In a postcard dated 31 March, Leonid tells of Josephine and Frederick's trip to the Riviera. Leonid and Rosalia were delighted by her 'wonderful artistic descriptions of sailing along the Mediterranean shore'.

Leonid Pasternak to Boris Pasternak

31 March 1929. Berlin.

[...] In a word, we'll have to publish a 'family chronicle'. What a family! Thank God for it! But your dental abscess—Boryusha, that's not like us! You poor miserable boy!

Well, Mme Rilke has copied out all the letters, and the originals are back with me, and even some of the copies. I'll find out everything for you when she comes back here. She's a lovely person. [...]

Boris later characterised 1929 as the year when 'literature and 'poetry died'. In *Safe Conduct* he calls it 'the last year of the poet': 'Suddenly, ideas that could never reach a conclusion come to an end. Often nothing is added to their incomplete state, save for a new certainty, permitted only now, that they are complete.'

His sense of the end of his career as a writer, and his urge to finish what was begun, is voiced in many letters to correspondents at this time. His intention to translate Rilke's 'Requiem', dedicated to a poet who had killed himself, is particularly signifi-cant in this context. (The translation was published as an addendum to Part I of *Safe Conduct*, which was dedicated to Rilke, in the August 1929 number of *Zvezda*). The same valedictory impulse underlies Boris's translation of Rilke's second 'Requiem', 'Für eine Freundin' ('To a friend'—dedicated to the artist Paula Modersohn-Becker),

27. Wolf, Count von Kalckreuth (1887–1906) was a poet and translator from an aristocratic fam-ily. He entered the army, but could not endure the rigours of military life and committed suicide at the age of nineteen. Rilke's 'Requiem für Wolf, Graf von Kalckreuth' was published in Paris in 1909.

completed in the summer of 1929. And it suffuses 'A Tale' (whose English-language edition was titled 'The Last Summer'), in which Boris's unfulfilled intention had been to describe the First World War and the Russian Civil War. Instead, it ends in 1914, with the last summer of peace.

Boris Pasternak to Leonid Pasternak

3 April 1929. Moscow.

Dear Papa,

I'll probably get a postcard from you in the next few days in reply to my last one, and I'm wasting my time writing to you now without waiting for it.

I've got better and started going out. I work a lot every day, as I have done all this time. I've probably already said that I'd like to spend a year, or a year and a half, getting the best of my writing more or less rounded off, so that I can draw a line under it, temporarily or permanently, partly so as to draw breath, and partly, perhaps, to undertake something different—not a different text, I mean, but a different field, obviously a related one. But that means I have to finish writing and working on a great many things, and it'll take more time than I've allowed myself. This spring, in about a month and a half or two, *Over the Barriers* will be published—a book that you'll fail to recognize, not only because it's twice the size of the first edition, but because everything good in the earlier books, with a few exceptions, has been rewritten.[28] The girls will be upset at first, as everyone has been, but then they'll get used to it and change their minds.

Is Lou Andreas-Salomé still alive? Is it possible to find out, and if she is, then could someone discover her address?[29]

At present I'm working on a prose piece which I won't be able to show to either Walter, or Pepa, or the Sinyakovs, because although it doesn't say anything bad, it'll be obvious what it's all drawn from.[30]

The prolonged application of poultices has irritated my chin, and it itches terribly.

I kiss you and Mama.

B.

28. *Over the Barriers* included substantially rewritten versions of poems written in the period 1913–1916, and new sections devoted to the 1920s.
29. Lou Andreas-Salomé (1861–1937) was a Russian-born psychoanalyst and writer who was Rilke's companion and lover.
30. 'A Tale' exploits autobiographical material from Boris's time as tutor to Walter Philipp; it includes the two Zbarsky brothers, Boris and Yakov, under the fictitious surname Lemokh, and it gives some details of Boris's relations with the Sinyakov sisters.

Leonid Pasternak to Boris Pasternak

21 May 1929. Berlin.

My dear Borya,

At last I'm able to write to you—I can never get round to it. I might have found time in the evenings, but for guests. Here's what Mme Rilke wrote to me for you the other day:

[Original in German]

'Then you asked about Count Wolf von Kalckreuth, and I'll be happy to tell you what I know. I myself never knew him, but a good friend of his told us about him shortly after his death. He was, as the Requiem makes clear, a particularly gifted person, and a book of his poems was published after his death. He must have suffered from a pronounced imbalance in his personality, which sometimes elevated him to heights of spiritual experience, and sometimes left him suffering from depression. His father had hoped that his year of military service, just then starting, would give him some equilibrium and stability, but instead it depressed him even more, leading him to the fateful decision that is the theme of 'Requiem'. This is more or less what I was told about him at the time; how far it is true I cannot say. I later got to know his parents and siblings, and became friends with the family. His father was the painter Leopold Kalckreuth, now deceased.'

That's all—then she goes on to ask how everyone is, how Mama is doing, and so forth. I'm not sending you her whole letter, because she writes in a terribly large, sweeping hand, filling three big pages—there's no point in stuffing the envelope so full. Evidently she forgot to write about Lou Salomé; tomorrow I'll try to find out about her from the lady artist at whose house I met Mme Rilke.

The other day I received 80 marks from Malik-Verlag, whom you had instructed to send me your fee for printing your story 'Erde an den Händen' in their collection *30 neue Erzähler des neuen Russland*.[31] They sent a letter enclosing a cheque for that amount. The letter ends: 'We are hereby settling, in a global payment, your fees for inclusion of the story, release, and subsidiary rights e.g. offprints, radio broadcasts, or translations from the German.'

---

31. 'Earth on One's Hands' (not in fact by Boris) was included in *30 New Writers from the New Russia*.

I've made a point of copying out this text for you because you need to know these conditions. At the end of the letter there's an NB: they promise to send a copy of the collection, but I'm afraid I haven't received it yet. Tomorrow I'll telephone to remind them to send it.

[...]

Boris Pasternak to Leonid Pasternak

26 May 1929. Moscow.

Thanks for your letter and everything. Malik-Verlag has created some sort of mix-up, which has probably already been sorted out at your end after causing you yet more trouble. 'Erde an den Händen' is not a story by me, but (if I'm not mistaken) by Pilnyak or someone. To my annoyance, I can't check this with the book itself, because a nephew of Rud[olf] Mosse has been here and came to see me. Like most of these peripatetic sky-gazers, he was planning to write an article on Russian literature without having the faintest understanding of it. And I made him take away this volume (*30 neue Erzähler*), so that he could at least skim through it, rather than simply retailing what he's been told by the obliging journalists who always swarm around such travellers (who themselves deserve no better). On this occasion I wasn't concerned to do myself justice, but to preserve my guest's honour: it transpired that he didn't know the name of a single one of my fellow writers, who are the glory of their time. Well, he took the book, and probably left the country with it—I hadn't insisted on his returning to see me and give it back. My own story, I think, was called 'Wolkenwege'.[32] I expect that the sum owing to me will be a lot less than 80 marks, because the fee for the first edition has already been paid to Yu. Tynyanov on my behalf. He was in Berlin for medical treatment and needed money, so he did an exchange with me, Leonov and Kataev. Couldn't you ring them up? I wouldn't want it to appear as if I had pocketed someone else's money. But it may be that the amount is correct, only it's all for 'Wolkenwege'.

Your B.

32. *Aerial Ways.*

Boris Pasternak to his parents

31 May 1929. Moscow.

My dears,

[…]

Everything has fitted in very well. Zhenia has been away for a whole month, and it was only yesterday that I handed the typist the first part of my novel (in prose).[33] So my temporary liberation coincides to the day with Zhenia's arrival, and I'll be able to devote two days to her without thinking about anything else. This is the first time for many years that I've felt (as I did ten years ago) that I've achieved something, and that something is going to happen to me too, inevitably, and on the same great scale.

All this has another side to it, a fateful and alarming one. The thing that I have most feeling and understanding for is Nature; and I understand human society when it comes closest to subjection to the laws that govern it, that is, to the state of dull silence that precedes an explosion—the state where it resembles a vast, miserable living body. And my success, that is, the seriousness of what I have done, frightens me as though it were a collateral historical symptom. I understand this all very well, and can't change anything. So perhaps I'll send Zhenia and the boy over to you, but I myself will have to stay here all year. There's no chance of my finishing what I've started before another year is out. Remember that every great work of creation carries a tragedy within it. Well—this is mine.

But I'm the biggest fool the world has ever seen. Why should I cause you needless anxiety? I had forgotten one thing which ought to reassure you. There are many people here who love me dearly, more than I deserve. And misfortune and love are the only two forces that still remain, on a stage cleansed of trivia, a stage worthy of us. I can't finish my work abroad. No point talking about it.

For the part of it that I've completed, I've been rewarded a hundredfold. Last Tuesday I read it at Pilnyak's, to a group of young beginners, some of whom were gifted writers. Probably we all hypnotised each other, and just dreamed that night at Petrovsky Park. This very dream is my lavish reward. It's been a long, long time since I last experienced this—there hasn't been one such time since you left here. It reminded me of many things. But this same happiness has also called up some dark parallels.

[…]

33. 'A Tale' ('The Last Summer').

Boris's impatience to finish 'A Tale' ('The Last Summer'), which was supposed to be only the first part of a novel in prose, was aggravated by his existing contracts for the still unfinished *Spektorsky* and *Safe Conduct*. He was anxious about the inevitable catastrophe that the forced collectivisation of agriculture would bring. A sense of impending doom pervades the 'Tale'. All this prevented him from joining his family on a journey abroad. By this time, in any case, such travel had become extremely difficult for ordinary people.

Leonid Pasternak to Boris and Zhenia Pasternak

21 June 1929. Berlin.

My dears,

[. . .] I've been meaning to write to you for some days, Borya, but I haven't had time. Meanwhile we've had two letters from you, the second of which contained a receipt for the 150 roubles you sent Babushka (and today we've had confirmation from Aunt Klara in Leningrad that the money has arrived); and also an indescribable joy for us—three photographs of our wonderful grandsons.[34] You, dear Zhenia, deserve our particular gratitude for this, since but for you, this event that we've all been longing for, for such a long time, would probably never have come about. Mama will write about everything from Munich; at the moment, the apartment is being cleaned and our bags packed for our departure—I just wanted to write you a few words about this great joy for us all. Oh, what a special little boy Zhenionok is! How serious he is, and how painfully sorrowful on one picture! What a beautiful group with Fedyushonok—splendid! Endless thanks, dear Zhenia!! Welcome back home, and thank God you're better!

[. . .]

As regards Malik-Verlag, you probably already know everything from my letters. There hasn't been any 'instead of', or any mistake about Pilnyak: the money is for you, and the story is by you (I think we read it in Russian a couple of years ago in an anthology), and the title isn't 'Erde an den Händen', but (I think) 'Die Wolken'[35]—I'm not sure—as soon as we'd read it, we sent the book to Zhonia.

Uncle Osip is alive and still living in Kasimov, but just now he's about to go (or has gone) to Kislovodsk.

Just two words more: we're terribly glad that you've started a big work, and

34. Boris's son Zhenia and Shura's baby son Fyodor (Fedia), born in 1927.
35. Not 'Earth On One's Hands' but 'The Clouds'—a reference to 'Aerial Ways' (the Germn title is 'Wolkenwege').

have had some time to work recently—it's a pity, of course, that your visit to us is being postponed, but there's nothing to be done—the time will pass quickly, God willing.

Messrs Architects[36] don't write, for some reason. [...]

Boris suffered from intermittent excruciating pain in his lower jaw. In June 1929 a bone cyst in the jaw was at last diagnosed and surgically removed, to his great relief.

Leonid Pasternak to Boris Pasternak

7 July 1929. Munich.

Dear Borya,

Your letters here, to Zhonechka and us, have contained very mysterious and worrying news about your illness and an operation on your jaw. What have you got? How are you now? If it's difficult for you to write to us at the moment, please get Zhenichka to write—just a couple of lines to say how you're recovering, and what sort of an operation it was anyway. We hope the person who did it was a very reliable expert—? No matter how you try to gloss over it in your letters— just barely touching on 'the surgical thing'—a single look at the photograph you sent is enough to show how much suffering this illness has caused you! You look terrible . . . one can't look at the picture without lamenting—'Poor, poor Borya!! Whatever has happened to him? What a terrible misfortune!!'

How can things have got to this pass?!! 'And just my luck'—you write—'the sutures separated and they're having to pack the wound'. My God—whatever is up with you? For God's sake, don't leave us without any more news!

However sad it is to look at your photograph—it seems ridiculous to say this—it's a comfort that (if it's true that it was taken on the fifth day after the operation) even a close inspection doesn't reveal any 'sutures' or any structural changes whatsoever . . . Well, God grant you a rapid and complete recovery, and please take better care of your health. On top of all your sufferings, it seems, you also have a problem with 'visits'*; and worst of all, 'relatives' have started to turn up—for while visits from 'strangers' are to some extent limited in time, these 'relatives' unmask themselves as tireless and importunate satellites, planets that will circle round you for the rest of your life . . .

[...]

36. Alexander and his wife Irina were both architects.

*You, dear Zhenichka, have got to act as the bouncer, and get rid of these people! This Russian habit of visiting writers to have 'just one minute's heart-to-heart' with them, which turns into 3–4 hours!! What hell it is!

Boris Pasternak to his parents and sisters

15 July 1929. Moscow.

My dears,

At first the doctors thought that I'd need to go for a check-up by mid-July. But Zhenichka has anyway spent longer in town than he needed to this year, and then my operation held everybody up. Last week, when I was already out of all danger, I insisted on their moving to the country. Now they are near Mozhaisk, with Dm[itry] Petr[ovich] Konchalovsky, whose wife runs a *pension* for holiday guests in the summer months. I haven't been there and don't know her, nor what it's like. Zhenia is coming to pick me up in a few days and I'll join them there.

[…]

I got your letter yesterday. There's absolutely nothing to worry about. The operation had to be done, and it was splendidly done by the best surgeon in this specialty; the cyst was non-malignant, so it's to be hoped I shan't develop another, and the one that's gone can't come back. I'm writing at length about this because of your interest—otherwise the whole subject isn't worth a moment's notice. It may have been excruciatingly painful, but that's all in the past now, and if anything deserves to be mentioned it's Zhenia's self-sacrifice—for two weeks she didn't stir a step away from me, and throughout the one-and-a-half-hour operation she suffered every bit as much as I did.

[…]

Although it's a dreadful responsibility, once I finish my own work I'll probably start translating *Faust* for the new Jubilee edition of Goethe, or else revise and rewrite the old translations (Fet, Bryusov and others). Of course it would have been very convenient and pleasant to do this on the spot, in Germany, but it can all be done here too—this isn't Afghanistan, after all, and we do have libraries. And I may be overrating the spiritual attractions of being abroad. There are many reasons for that—firstly all of you; then my friends in France and England, most of whom I don't know personally; and finally, my whole Germanic yeast of fellow-feelings and memories—Marburg, Rilke, music, philosophy. And if you want to help me in this, that's very easy—just give up transferring money here, and get me to look after that side of things. The more you do that, the better.

Don't be deceived by the tone of my letter—it's my usual one. There are some professional defects that develop over the course of time, and I'm probably not immune from them. I'm not capable of being witty, of laughing, or of being moved in a way that is . . . visible. I'm calm and serious with myself, with Zhenia and little Zhenichka, and it's only in this spirit of calm seriousness (which I don't always achieve) that I feel myself replete from within with kindness—universal, not family kindness—and feel that I can and must become even more replete with it.

Rilke's Requiem 'Für eine Freundin'[37] is very good—do you know it, Zhonichka? With its laconic clarity, it's probably the most powerful and moral statement that was ever made, with a socialist note, in recent pre-war art. It incriminates philistinism without even mentioning it, *par défaut*, without any loud declarations, in spheres to which, in any event, philistinism can't penetrate. And as with every great work, the thesis of this Requiem, if one can draw any conclusion from it, runs up against an absurdity. An even bolder absurdity than in *The Kreutzer Sonata*.

I can't even think of writing about Alyonushka,[38] until the miserly and offensive element always present in any pre-prepared expression of familial tenderness at a distance has been replaced by that inevitably great thing that exists within her and in everything around her, and that I shall see. And—why should I be shy of saying it—I have eyes and heart enough not to diminish her enormous and mysterious charm, and her right to an enormous and mysterious acceptance of her manifestation and her existence. Why, when I haven't ever looked at her, should I start including her in the cheap repertoire of exclamations without which no family feeling, as a genre, is complete? And you, Mama, don't be cross and don't think that I'm complicating things—God knows, as they say, that my complication is simpler than many simplicities.

I embrace you both warmly, and Fedia, Zhonia and Lida. Dm[itry] Petr[ovich] [Konchalovsky] sends his regards.

Your B.

Little Zhenia, since you write about him, is a sly, clever, ugly little boy all covered with freckles, who seemingly has no intention of ever learning anything in his life. At the moment he has, as a French governess, an intelligent, ironic 60-year-old lady of very exalted origins, from a family related to Lermontov's.

37. 'For a Friend'.
38. Josephine's baby daughter Helen, born in 1928.

Zhenichka's French pronunciation is that of a soldier. '*Le kut*' (*le coude*), says he in measured tones, in order to get to put his elbows on the table (which he isn't allowed to do)—but here it's an illustration: '*Le kut*'—and elbows on the table. While big Zhenia has turned out to be a splendid person and a wonderful friend.

[…]

In the summer, Josephine successfully submitted her doctoral thesis in psychology (on acoustic aspects of communication) at Munich University.

Boris Pasternak to Josephine Pasternak

[Early September 1929. Moscow.]

Dear Zhoniura,

Hearty congratulations to you and Fedia on your academic triumph. You may have been surprised and hurt at my long silence, and these belated congratulations won't put matters right.

The reason is that life under our present conditions is very difficult—difficult for me, I mean, and that's probably my own fault. One ought to be completely different, one ought not necessarily to earn more, but to earn more easily; one ought to love reality not at a distance, but in a more ordinary closeness to it, and somehow participate in its progression; one ought to be able to bring up one's family, and—by simplifying one's share in it—place it in a more difficult, but at the same time a more living situation than the one in which my own family is placed; and all this is beyond my power.

And all these senseless difficulties generally manifest themselves in town, in our neglected and overcrowded apartment; and more so year by year. That's why I selfishly cherished every hour of happiness that I enjoyed in the countryside, far from the gloom and dirt of town:—I paid the whole summer's rent in advance, and not only didn't try to work there—I was even afraid of writing letters, because that too would have reminded me of town, where most of my letters were written—and town was just what I didn't want to be reminded of.

On this occasion, this happy oblivion was not brought about by Nature alone. Beautiful as the place was where we lived, I didn't go for any long walks there.

All these delights turned out to have a great rival in the shape of the Konchalovsky family. I got very fond of them.

In July, there were more than 20 of us at table, and all this housekeeping (with the nearest food supplies over 6 kilometres away) was kept up just by the Konchalovskys, with the help of a single girl who did the washing-up. I don't want to go on about this, but you'll understand how close I felt to this atmosphere of keen, hard-working simplicity, bathed in sweat and redolent of efficiency and profound enlightenment. I was shy of them at first, but soon found myself drawn into their group, and took part in it myself.

But now I'm writing to you from my flat in town, in a great hurry because I have a lot of urgent things to do. Needless to say, it isn't only my correspondence with you all that has suffered; all the delays have led to complete chaos in my domestic affairs. The only reason I'm saying this is in order to persuade you to grant me some days' grace, up to the 15th, if you have any requests for me— though so far there haven't been any.

But I'll probably send the money to Babushka before that, around the 8th. Please note, incidentally, in case anyone is travelling this way: we can't get hold of tea, and if anyone could bring some (which is the simplest way, after all), I'll be extremely grateful. I needn't add what a lot of it I get through.

I embrace you and all your family, and love you and kiss you warmly. Since I'm going on to write to our parents below, and since I'm afraid someone might forward the letter to some distant place if you're away, I'm addressing the envelope to Mama. The parents will open it and read the letter, and then send it on to you.

[...]

The collection *Over the Barriers: Poems of Various Years* was due to be published in the spring of 1929, but publication was delayed and the book only appeared at the end of September. One of the first copies was sent to Boris's sisters on 25 September, with the inscription 'To Zhonia and Lida from their poor brother'.

Boris finished working on *Spektorsky* in October 1929. The final chapters were delivered to the journal *Krasnaya Nov*, which had published the earlier chapters a year before. In accordance with his contract with the Lengiz publishing house, Boris sent off the full manuscript to Leningrad at the beginning of November. To his surprise, the end of the novel was judged to be ideologically unsound. These chapters depict the disruption of everyday Moscow life in 1919, reflecting on the vast shift in the social and political order which allowed no space for the individual and his story. The publishers demanded a revision, which Pasternak refused outright, and the contract was cancelled.

Boris Pasternak to his parents

3 December 1929. Moscow.

My dears,

Yesterday we got your parcel, endless thanks, our joy is infinite, we're hurrying to let you know how delighted we are. I'm just sorry for you—you don't have the opportunity of experiencing this as we do. What an enormous amount of tea—and what tea! We'd forgotten the taste of tea like this. Big Zhenia is hopping around on one leg: she's got stockings, a beret, gloves, everything she might have ordered.

I'm enclosing your grandson's letter, which has been lying around. His mother took his dictation in pencil, and it's been given to me to copy out. I'm sorry it's handwritten instead of being typed. Knowing my weakness for it, Shura has most nobly renounced his share of the tea. I'm extremely touched, but look to the future with foreboding: I'm afraid it wasn't pure altruism, and there will be consequences. Before you know it, he'll ask you for a barrel of coffee, and I'll be the excuse—and so much for your tea.

They don't write because they really are busy. So am I, but since all my drudgery is an outpouring of ink, it reaches you in the form of letters or my inability to write them. Tomorrow I'll take a fat bundle down to the mailbox in a wheelbarrow. And all the letters are for abroad. London, Warsaw, you in Berlin, a letter in Russian to Paris, a letter in French to New York, one to Pasadena (in California)—and all of them, since I have no time, are some ten pages long. That's what makes me laugh—this is my second day of letter-writing. Half of them are to the people I'm fondest of—I haven't written to them for a year, and now they've just found out about my summer operation.

Suddenly I'm thinking of music. I got to know Prokofiev at the Meyerholds'.[39] Or have I already told you? . . .

The row of dots is because it's a long story, but there's nothing ambivalent or sad behind the dots. I was absolutely right to give it up. I ought to have been a pianist, not a 'natural-born genius'. If I hadn't given it up, I'd be walking about now as a hopeless . . . cripple.

---

39. Vsevolod Meyerhold (1874–1940) was a famous Russian theatrical producer and director. (Pasternak had written a poem dedicated to him in 1929.) In the 1930s he ran his own theatre in Moscow, but in March 1936 he was fiercely attacked in the Soviet press, in 1938 his theatre was closed down, and in 1939 he was arrested. Shortly after his arrest, his wife was murdered. He himself was tortured in prison, and executed in 1940.

They say one ought to repay one's debts. I was granted a 500 rouble loan by the Gosizdat Literary Fund. Recently I was supposed to receive a contracted payment, and another one was due from Leningrad, by post, for a manuscript I had just sent off. It seemed a favourable conjunction of circumstances, and I decided that I wouldn't get another chance like it. So I paid back the 500 roubles. What happened then?—Next day a letter comes from Leningrad to say that the manuscript has been held up due to the ... uncertainty of social trends—and there isn't going to be any money. Hmm, hmm, the 500, the 500, the 500, the 500, etc., etc., etc. So far this is just the *entremets*, the outright refusal will come for dessert.

I'm enclosing a postal receipt for 115 roubles, which I've sent to Aunt Klara. That's 50 for November, 50 for December, and 15 for the lady who looks after Babushka. Mama, you didn't write me anything about this, but I got a postcard from V.I. Lapshov in which he mentioned this projected transfer of 25 R. and thought that it was too much, so he asked me to send only 15. Which I did.

For the second Gosizdat edition of my poems (counting all the 'Sisters', it's the fourth), I provided your portrait of me, without your permission. They reproduced it as well as they could—they can't do better here. And insisted on my signing the picture right away, 'on behalf of both father and son', as you'd put it; and—blast them—they handed me a thick crayon, and for all I begged them, they couldn't come up with anything better. It looks as if I'd wanted to overwrite you. I enclose it. Please don't veto it—it's too late anyway. Everyone is thrilled, they hang it on their walls and are amazed at how—having such a portrait by you—I could have put up with all kinds of photographs, let alone those ... 'creative solutions'. He didn't say a word about money, but it would have been a paltry sum anyway, and even that won't be paid.

Now please, don't latch onto this theme of the ungrateful son—the lackey and the great man, and all that. Both you and Mama used to enjoy catching me out in just this way. There's nothing of the kind here. Let me remind you of the autobiographical note you once found so moving, where I wrote more fully and powerfully about you both than about myself. It's just that my style is such that not everything is apparent straight away. I could say a lot about that. I'm not in the least boastful or vain, and superficial slurs like that can't hurt me. But I do need to have some sort (God knows what sort) of objectively accumulated recognition of merit in me and my life, if I'm to start writing about things that I could have spoken of long ago.[40] This isn't a sidelong look at other people, it's

40. This rather obscure reflection seems to imply that there are things Boris feels he must write about Russia's fate, as he was later to do in *Doctor Zhivago*, but in his diffidence he feels in need of

something physical, something like the way that aerial vapours need pressure in order to form clouds and discharge themselves as rain, snow or hail. Needless to say, all this is much more interesting than my analogy, but as I say, it can't be explained in a couple of words.

I warmly embrace you both.

B.

Leonid Pasternak to Boris, Zhenia and Zhenichka Pasternak

13 December 1929. Berlin.

My dears,

We finally received your letter, Boryusha, and Zhenionochek's, with the enclosed reproduction of the portrait of you. How pleased we were! And how grateful we are!!! Well, thank God that you're all well, and—if I'm to believe you—Shura and Ina are too—but 'they're busy'! Of course, you're the only one who's not 'busy', any more than I am—all my life long! You sit out there scribbling away— what sort of an occupation is that?!—and I daub away here—and what sort of an occupation is that? So we have to write each other letters on everyone else's behalf. Let's start with the parcel. We did tell you before that the only thing from us in the parcel was the tea; the rest was from Zhonia. All we did was go shopping according to her instructions, or rather—it was because it's easier to find things here and send them from here. Well, we're pleased that Zhenia liked everything—wear it, dear Zhenia, and may it bring you good health, and may you hop around on one leg for joy, and when you've worn through your soles with hopping, we'll send new ones! You told me in your last letter how your painting was going, and your School affairs (you were explaining why you had worn out your dress), and how you were going to a factory to sketch the workers. From this I infer that you must be painting a 'programme' work, as they say here—something for your final assessment at the School, is it? One could say a lot about this, but there isn't enough paper, and it's difficult for an outsider. But the main thing is that the sooner you're done with the School, the better. God grant it happens soon.

And now, my dear little grandson, a big thank-you for your dear little letter, lots of kisses and don't forget to go on writing to Dedushka and Babushka! We're

---

encouragement, in need of the sustained pressure of objective approval—and (as he says) God knows where that can come from, since public and State support is non-existent or suspect, while private individuals will increasingly become silenced.

very glad to hear that you go to eurhythmics lessons and have fun there with the other children. Give your best love to Alexandra Andreyevna and tell her that we often think of her. Soon you'll be having a great treat—a Christmas tree, and all kinds of presents hanging on it! And you'll probably have your friends coming to parties round the tree, and there'll be Betty, and big Zhenia, and Galia, and Tania, and Arkasha; and you'll be dancing and singing round the tree as the music plays and people sing. Then you can write us a letter and tell us all about it. Well, keep well, my dear little grandson, and grow up clever and obedient, and kiss Mama and Papa from us, and I kiss you warmly.

Your dear Dedushka.

And now—Boryusha—I'm entirely at your service—your dear Papa (that's a wonderful expression of Zhenionok's!).

As far as the reproduction of your portrait is concerned—apart from giving us great joy, you haven't done us any harm. [...]

We're glad that you're fanning out in all directions (I don't envy you—your 'I'm not busy—all I do is pour out ink')—to London, and Warsaw, and Paris, and New York, and the Papuas—I mean Pasadena, sorry—and then suddenly you remembered about music. You didn't write about your acquaintance with Prokofiev. Is he an interesting man? Out here he's become very famous over the last two or three years. Stravinsky and he—nobody else gets into the leading articles. Even so, I don't agree with you: if you hadn't given up music, I'm convinced you might have achieved even more, perhaps, in that field. At least it's an international language, and foreign countries would have celebrated you with no need for a translator, as they celebrate Stravinsky and Prokofiev. Of course, it's a shame you weren't a pianist, and you're right—and I agree with you—that without that ability, without the chance to be your own publicity agent, it's more difficult to be a success. So—thank God, then, that you gave it up. Incidentally, do you ever improvise—anywhere? [...]

You poor boy, how stupidly it all turned out when you suddenly decided to obey the injunction that 'debts must be repaid' ... How will you manage? Evidently fate is against you! And yet they do say that debts should be repaid ...

On your half-page postscript about 'please don't latch onto this theme of the ungrateful son', you mention, speaking of your style, that 'not everything is apparent straight away', and later you say 'I do need to have some objectively accumulated recognition of merit' and so forth. Wasn't I the same, and am I not still? Can't I see now what I could have said as an artist long ago? This character trait in you is a hereditary one—alas—(and you have even more of it from Mama);

it's not in fashion now, and it's probably harmful; but on second thoughts not: could it be that this very thing is your salvation and your strength, in the midst of modish modernity? Have I understood you aright, or am I mistaken?

I often want to talk to you, heart to heart, about a lot of things—but everyday concerns and 'business' take up so much time there's none left for anything else. And my constant anxiety about my advancing age, which I fear more than anything, gets in the way of everything. […]

Boris Pasternak to his parents

15 December 1929. Moscow.

[…]

Here the winter has started, very late.

About a month ago, a final-year art student in V. Favorsky's class asked me to look at her diploma project for the Graphic Art faculty; this turned out to be an 'external formulation' (as they term it nowadays—in other words, a book decoration) for my '1905'. I didn't know her; her surname is Pokrovskaya.

Nowadays, even well-known people don't know how to draw. There was no way I could show myself indifferent unless her drawings had been completely talentless or bad. She brought me illustrated endpapers (seemingly woodcuts) which weren't bad at all, some of them in fact quite nice. So how could I refuse, later on, to support her application for a grant from Gosizdat? That means that there's now a second illustrated edition of '1905'. It's a very odd, fortuitous outcome, since there are other serious graphic artists (not to mention yourself!), such as Kravchenko, Kupreyanov and others. And quite apart from those, what will a lot of other people say to me, such as Ada Engel perhaps, who might have done this in a more individual and delicate way? But why should I have deprived a final-year student of her chance to earn some money, when she had for some unknown reason selected me for her diploma project? I had a look at it—it's not brilliant, but nor is it ugly. Just good average, then. It would have been a piece of outright hostility on my part if—with her drawings already available—I had gone and engaged someone else.—But that's how everything is, with me— fortuitous and home-grown. My life, my earnings, my family.

Yesterday I had a telephone call from the Society for Cultural Relations with Foreign Countries (VOKS). They had received a letter from Poland—I'm invited to Warsaw, they'll get me a passport and pay my travel expenses. I refused, of course, and of course they couldn't begin to understand why.

Zhenia is going through a very difficult and worrying time. In three days' time she has to hand in her diploma project in painting. Her subject was work in the foundry of a metallurgical works (a theme like Menzel's, with the colour palette of your early oils, e.g. 'On the Bridge'). She was working in the actual factory, but moving about made it difficult, and the days were dark, while at home she has nowhere to stand her easel. The work is unfinished; some parts have come out well, in the midst of large areas of preparatory daub. We'll see what comes of it; but in our apartment there's no room to move, the working conditions are appalling.

Borya

Leonid Pasternak to Boris Pasternak

16 December 1929. Berlin.

Dear Boryusha,

Further to Mama's letter with stockings and tea, which she wrote a few days ago (the letter went to Zhonia 'for information' and has just come back), I want to take this opportunity of writing you a few words—since we never write to one another. Pavetti recently sent me Loks's review of your book *Over the Barriers* that appeared in your *Literaturnaya Gazeta*—whose size (the Gazette's) terrified me: well, I thought, what a lot of all sorts of things they've printed there! But when I read it (after summoning up my courage), it all turned out quite *vis-à-vis*!

Loks wrote a very nice and friendly review—but (as I wrote to Pavetti too), I've read more ecstatic ones (in *The London Mercury* and elsewhere).

I recently read, in a review of the first volume of Rilke's letters which has just been published (the ones to me will probably appear in Volume 2) something very flattering that I hadn't suspected: in one letter he mentions two very important and happy events for him (!) (I don't recall his exact words—I sent the article to Zhonechka), the second of which was his meeting in Rome with the artist Pasternak. It seems to have been well put in the original. When I have it, I'll tell you exactly what he said. [...]

In his review of the second edition of *Over the Barriers*, Boris Pasternak's erstwhile fellow-student Konstantin Loks recalled the powerful impression that the slim first edition of poems written 1914–1916 had made on him in the winter of 1917.

Literaturnaya Gazeta, the independent organ of the writers' union, was only six months old. It had already shown itself to be a powerful agent of literary despotism. September 1929 saw the opening of a fierce campaign in the Soviet press against Evgeny Zamyatin and Boris's close friend Boris Pilnyak, who were accused of publishing abroad without permission from the Soviet censors. This marked a sharp tightening of Party and Government control over literature and culture in general. Loks's review, published in *Literaturnaya Gazeta* on 28 October 1929, reflected the narrow constraints on supposedly objective assessments of literature. Only strictly positive or negative verdicts could now be formulated, with no attempt at serious analysis. This was in striking contrast to the free expression of views in Sviatopolk-Mirsky's 1927 article in *The London Mercury.*

The urgent work involved in completing *Spektorsky* caused a break in Boris's correspondence with his parents, who became worried by the absence of news from Moscow.

Zhenia and Boris Pasternak to Josephine Pasternak and family

29 December 1929. Moscow.

[In Zhenia Pasternak's hand]

Dear Zhonichka, Fedia and Alyonushka,

Once again, Happy New Year to you. I'm so fond of your daughter (from the photographs you sent to Stella), I just can't tell you. Her little face has so much character and temperament, and her eyes are so expressive. Zhonichka, you're going to have a very gifted daughter. I very, very much want you to write to me about her; tell me everything you can. It's very good that you're getting a playmate for her. What I regret most of all is that Zhenichka doesn't have one (it's too late now), it's very sad for him to grow up by himself, without a world of his own. Once again, kisses to all three of you, and I wish you good health.

Your Zhenia.

Warmest greetings to Babushka, Dedushka and Lida. Put me down as a great admirer of your favourite person; everything in her is so full-blooded—her frown, her seriousness, her sleepiness. I kiss her tenderly.

[In Boris's hand]

I'm very glad that Zhenia has put all this down in writing. She has been talking about Alyonushka so often these last few days, sharing her delight in her with me and all our household, that I was really afraid this would all remain between ourselves and not come to your ears. Naturally I share all her feelings, and echo her comments. Moreover, everyone here is convinced that our niece seems to look a bit like me (in those of her features which rather remind me of Aunt Elena).

Happy New Year to you all and to the parents in Berlin. As usual, our seasonal wishes are late, but on this occasion that's excusable since this winter we ourselves won't be celebrating or recognising the New Year in any form.

I've had all sorts of unpleasantnesses and setbacks, which aren't worth going into.

I kiss all three of you warmly.

Your Borya

Is Lida with you over the holidays? I kiss you warmly, dear Lidok. How long-drawn-out all this is, how long it is that I've been a grown-up elder brother to you, someone on the other side of life, like Papa and our family friends; how many years have passed without anything being achieved, and what rubbish it all is! [...]

CHAPTER SIX
1930

An official decree of 1929 abolished the 'religious propaganda' of Christmas and New Year celebrations, and prohibited Christmas trees—an irony poor Leonid was quite unaware of in his Christmas greetings to his grandson. The chimes of church bells which had for centuries marked the hours of the day and night throughout Moscow, and which echoed through Boris's letter to his sister a year ago, were now also forbidden. Boris had always cherished the winter festivals, redolent of his childhood, and they figure large in his lyrical poetry. Now churches began to be closed and bells taken down. At the same time, the countryside was forcibly collectivised, kolkhozes were created and the wealthier peasants, the 'kulaks', exterminated. Everything which had hitherto sustained Russian agriculture and the Russian countryside was destroyed, and once again the country was threatened with famine.

Boris Pasternak to Lydia Pasternak

9 January 1930. Moscow.

Dear Lidochka,

As soon as I got your letter, I replied with a postcard. It lay around here for a week or so, or rather I carried it in my side-pocket when I went out. But the newspaper kiosks didn't have the extra stamps I needed, and after three days I tore it up since it had lost all its point, not that it ever had any.

Now I'm writing to you so that you don't feel hurt, and the parents don't feel worried. I didn't reply because there's absolutely nothing to write about.

We've had cruel frosts here, with the usual miseries in the apartment in such cold weather. The corridor that ran past Papa's studio has for many years been divided in two by a partition that goes up to the ceiling. If you remember, it was never heated even in the old days, and was always cold; but now when there's a frost, it's like being out of doors. The more you heat inside, the sharper the difference between the room and the corridor. So we've all been going down with colds and at various times we've had flu too, but fortunately in a mild form without complications.

Please send this letter on to Papa. The last one I had from him was very long and substantial, relating Olya's misfortunes.[1] It's true, they are of Homeric proportions—but they're not in any way as exceptional as they must seem to you. Everyone nowadays lives under very great pressure, but the burden weighing down the lives of town-dwellers is a positive privilege compared to what's going on in the countryside. Measures are being imposed that are of the most far-reaching, epic significance; one would need to be blind not to see the unprecedented consequences of all this for the nation; but I think one needs to be a peasant in order to dare to discuss it; I mean that one must experience these surgical transformations on one's own body. Singing about them from the sidelines is even more immoral than writing about a war from the rear. And the air is full of that.

[. . .] There's positively nothing to write about. The fact that food, drink, and other essentials can still be found here, just as in real life—that's something you can probably guess for yourself. Everything else is unlike our usual notions. It's like the window-display of a big sewing-machine store. There's a row of dummy seamstresses, each with her hand on her sewing-machine handle, and the handles are going round and round, driven by a dynamo, noiselessly and smoothly—because they're idling. That's the true picture of our life, assiduous, smooth and uninterrupted. But I'll tell you about all that one day—we're going to meet, after all, and there will be a time for it.

Now I must hurry to embrace you and send off this letter, in case the family get anxious because there's been no news from us for a long time. Ask Mama to tell me when I should start my regular mailings of money to Babushka, which have been temporarily interrupted.

Kiss Fedia, Zhonia, and Alyonushka.

B.

Boris Pasternak to his parents

10 January 1930. Moscow.

Dear Papa and Mama,

Your Borya turned up, and I went to see him. His telephone call distracted me from a (belated!) letter I was writing to Romain Rolland.[2]

---

1. This probably relates to an attempt by the Leningrad authorities to evict Olya and her mother from their apartment.

2. A French novelist and poet, who won the Nobel Prize for Literature in 1915.

This was because (through a conjunction of circumstances I had done all I could to prevent) Rolland had sent me a New Year gift of a book, which arrived on January 1st, with an inscription which he in his generosity could have written to anyone—I mean an inscription entirely unsuited for boastful quotation (which you love!), but one whose universal humanity, whose exaltation high above any sort of vanity, binds me and constrains me and enslaves me.

For if your room contains a book whose title-page carries the inscription

'A Boris Pasternak, Au jeune frère de la rive du ciel où le soleil se lève, le vieux frère de la rive où se couche le soleil. Bon jour, Bon an et Bonne traversée, de l'un à l'autre bord!
Romain Rolland, Villeneuve, l'an qui s'en va'[3]

—then of course that not only subordinates you, it distresses you and torments you too; and moves you to tears.

All the worse was the impression your debtor made on me. He owes you money, and was supposed to repay it to me; but around this trivial matter he flaunted so much intolerable elegance that the mere fact of his conversation made it difficult if not impossible for me to go on writing to Rolland. That was more than I could bear, so the next day I went and gave the money back to him. Then Shura went to collect it, and I eased Shura's task by suggesting to the gold-toothed popinjay that he should moderate his air of mystery. These cultural philistines love to play at hide-and-seek and shadow-puppets, they'd find life boring without it, but I can't stand that sort of nonsense.

May I ask you in future not to send me people with whom any conversation is incompatible with my approach to life—people who presume to offer advice to me, when I am older than they by a whole universe; people, worst of all, who subject me to their ignorant mystery-making in situations where it's neither necessary nor appropriate. I have no secrets from my time: I have a love-affair with it, I am part of it myself.

Your Borya

I've passed on your greetings to Stella, transferred 100 roubles to Sonia, everything will be done. But you don't love me. You mustn't entangle me in a spider's web of preposterous and unnecessary half-hints. Why couldn't you have sent him to Shura? He's a free man, while I'm a slave.

3. 'To Boris Pasternak, the young brother on heaven's shore where the sun rises, from the old brother on the shore where the sun sets. A happy day, a happy year, and a happy crossing from one shore to the other! Romain Rolland, Villeneuve, in the departing year'.

Boris Pasternak to his parents

[January 1930. Moscow.]

My dear, dearest ones!

I'm sorry I forgot that you're alone in the Berlin apartment, without the girls—and I wrote you such a letter. Not a word about it; it's probably reached you, but the fact that I forgot that you were alone, with nobody near you to soften the blow a little—that was unforgivable and dreadful! For God's sake forgive me for the pain I've caused you, and forget about everything except my request in the letter. Never force me into contact with philistines—they're death to me.

As you will have guessed, the very next day after sending the letter I regretted the loud voice that would have reached you in your quiet apartment. Do I need to tell you how much I love you, and how much I'm tormented by my rebuke? But you have an astonishingly strange notion of my duties, my responsibility, and my peculiar, non-philistine lack of freedom.

I embrace and kiss you warmly.

Your Borya.

When forwarding this letter to his daughters in Munich, Leonid Pasternak added at the foot of the page:

Well, isn't your Papa the clever one? Only yesterday, Zhoniurka, I wrote to you and predicted today's missive! It's very sweet and touching of him, and I'm sorry for him—I'll write to him straight away.

Leonid Pasternak to Boris Pasternak

20 January 1930. Berlin.

My dears,

Let me start with you, dear Borya! I wasn't in the least offended by your raised voice—and I was sincerely sorry for you, since I knew that you would be lacerating yourself and repenting, and the next day you would write to send me your sincere regrets etc. When I got your first letter with Rolland's dedication, which we were so pleased to see, I immediately forwarded it to Zhonechka and even added a postscript: tomorrow we'll get Borya's 'letter of repentance'.

What a strange coincidence: I once wanted to send Rolland my engraving of Tolstoy, with my '*hommage*' etc., but in the whirlwind of other activities I postponed it—until fate turned in my son's direction. Well, congratulations on this acquisition.

Boris Pasternak to Lydia Pasternak

26 February 1930. Moscow.

Dear Lidochka,

For some unknown reason, I sent you an issue of a journal with part of my *Safe Conduct* and an offprint of the first part of my planned novel, which was printed separately in the spring as a short story. Read them if you have time. And if I've got the dates wrong, and Zhonia still has leisure to read, give them to her.[4] And send them to Berlin—Papa and Mama, I think, would be glad to remember some of these events.

And if you can, write me an intelligent and serious letter.

For that purpose, you must give up for a time the idea that everything is a hop, skip and jump, shine and glitter, in what I and Papa do, and above all Olya,— and that the family bottle is fizzing with soda, noisy, foaming and festive. That's not what I want, and there's not the faintest smile on my face as I send you these pieces.

Quite the contrary. This is the most tedious of tragedies, and one I can scarcely cope with. You'll tell me whether I'm coping with it. And you won't keep anything from me, will you?

Safe Conduct was started in 1927. True, times were different then. But even then, they already contained something that has since been growing bigger year by year, and is killing me. I have begun to load my art with theoretical, valedictory interpolations, something like testamentary truths, because I can't rid myself of the presentiment of my imminent end—either total and physical, or partial and natural, or, at least, involuntary and symbolic.[5] Isn't it all the same? But don't you be upset by my moods—just look and see whether all this is readable, or whether the commitment to a knowledge which I speak of doesn't weigh down my text and make it completely indigestible. There's no happiness behind these writings, as there was behind the pages of 'Luvers's Childhood'. The reasons for that are, of course, neither personal nor family ones.

Warm kisses to everyone in Munich and Berlin.

Your B.

---

4. Josephine was expecting her second child.
5. Boris is alluding to the possibility of his suicide, natural death or arrest.

Boris Pasternak to his parents

1 March 1930. Moscow.

My dear, beloved ones,

[…]

I should have remembered on the 22nd about your anniversary on February 27th. I did know and remember it, but there's a big difference between an abstract awareness in one's memory of a forthcoming date, and paying attention to the real days of our lives, which might pass without being numbered in any way, monotonously grim as they are, so many thousands of versts[6] from any kind of festivity. I had in my mind the last possible date for sending you a letter of congratulations to reach you by the 27th, and went on carrying the date with me and waiting, while the 27th itself had long come and gone. So you can see that I don't read the newspapers.

And if you only knew how many times I cross out and destroy my letters to you before I ever send them!

I've sent Lida something of mine to read. It'll reach you too. You, Papa, will see, and so will you, Mama, even more quickly—how my style is affected by the very thing that makes me fail to write in time to send my best wishes to the nearest and dearest people I have in the world. I'm afraid that an oppression which no language can overcome, and a darkness against which the heart can hardly prevail, have so strongly affected me that there's no art left in me. But will you perceive, in my writings, the things that I wanted to say?

Anyway, something or other is bound to come alive for you in them. If you write to me, say something about that. I'm adding a postscript to Zhonichka. I warmly embrace and kiss you.

—I wanted to say (about these pieces), but forgot: a sort of hopeless autobiographism, not of the lyrical, youthful kind, but an ossified, proliferating autobiographism, is exerting an ever-tighter hold on everything that I do. And that's where art ends.

The annual series of family anniversaries began with the parents' wedding anniversary on 14 February (old style) or 27 February (new style).[7] This date always reminded the family of the parents' silver wedding celebrations in 1914, a few months before

6. A verst is just over one kilometre.
7. There was a difference of thirteen days between the calendar used in Tsarist Russia and that used by the Western world. The Western system was adopted by the Soviet government in 1918.

the outbreak of war. Leonid commemorated this event in a large picture known as 'Congratulations', portraying his four children bringing gifts. According to the new style, 18 February was Josephine's birthday, 22 February—Alexander's, 8 March—Lydia's, 11 March—their mother's, 4 April—Frederick's, and 9 April—Leonid's. The change in dating systems brought a great deal of confusion and made the timing of birthday greetings difficult to remember.

Boris Pasternak to Rosalia Pasternak

6 March 1930. Moscow.

Dear Mamochka,

Although in my last letter I wrote about dates, and haven't had a reply from Lida, I still remember them all (without much confidence), and I know that the day you get this letter, the 26th (or 11th) will be your birthday. I send you my sincerest good wishes on this day, and wish you health and long life, leisure, a happy and carefree spirit, and for Zhonia—an easy delivery, and for Papa—success in his work.

[. . .] I never, or rarely, write anything about myself, and when I do I write very little, because it's difficult and pointless. I'm very tired. Not because of the last few years, nor because of the difficulties of living at this time—I'm tired of my whole life. And this is to be understood exactly as I say it. I'm not exhausted by work, or by the circumstances of family life, or by any anxieties; in a word, not by the way my life has turned out. What has exhausted me is just the things that would have remained unchanged no matter how it had turned out. That's what's sad and exhausting—that these two sides can be separated from one another, and that almost the whole of my being has been useless all my life, and will remain so. It's not my fault, nor anyone else's.

Shura and Irina have been working day and night recently, and are very busy. I recently saw A.S. Shor at a concert, and he asked to be remembered to you all. And Nemenova-Lunts too—she's quite grey-haired, but as cheerful and full of joie-de-vivre as ever. And Gnesina. And greetings to Papa from Koenemann too, who met him at Safonov's when he was a student at the Conservatoire.

The only bright spot in our existence is the very varied performances by my latest friend (for the past year), Heinrich Neuhaus. We—a few of his friends—have got into the habit of spending the rest of the night after a concert at one another's homes. There's abundant drink, with very modest snacks which for technical reasons are almost impossible to get hold of.

Last time, he played with Koenemann on two pianos, and it was intriguing to see that the mere difference of a player's touch can transform two pianos of the same make into two instruments of radically different timbre. Without ever diverging from one another in rhythm, they constantly diverged in their music, and even Zhenia and Irina could tell with their eyes shut when Neuhaus came in, injecting into the brisk-running finger exercises a sudden flood of sonorous meaning, and a devilish sense of rhythm and temperament.

Then we went and drank till 6 a.m. (without Koenemann, of course), ate, played, recited, and danced the foxtrot in Shura's and Irina's room, while little Fedichka was carried to Zhenia's. Little Zhenichka is so highly-strung that any minor departure from his regime keeps him awake until 11 or later.

I embrace you all warmly. Everyone joins wholeheartedly in my good wishes.

A few days later Boris added a postscript to a letter from his wife, in gratitude to Lydia for her serious reply after reading his 'Tale' and the first part of *Safe Conduct*. He was very pleased with her response. Journal offprints archived in Oxford carry an authorial note at the end of the 'Tale': 'Continuation follows. Planned and will be written after completion of *Safe Conduct*'. This intention was sustained during the early 1930s, after Boris's visit to the Urals where the action of the 'Tale' takes place, but the 'Tale' was never completed.

Lydia was moved by Boris's two prose works, and wrote to him on 1 March, 1930. Much of what she had read, she said, called up memories of shared times long ago:

'You liberate life, and me, and all experience as a whole. This is what I feel, with impossible acuteness: liberation (from the oppression of time), and joy, and gratitude for my liberation.'

Boris Pasternak to Josephine Pasternak

11 March 1930. Moscow.

I take this opportunity of adding a postscript. My wishes for you only grow and gain in strength.

I've just had a letter from Lidochka—sincere thanks to you, Lidok. You said a number of things that were irreproachably relevant and profound. Even if they can't be directly related to me, they still retain their laconically definitive quality in relation to any great art. You're wonderful, I kiss you warmly.

When you speak of the liberation of life by art, you hit upon the core of that fundamental feeling by which I live, both in my work and in my relations with those currents that my work later brings me. And your fear that I'm being pampered with friendly overtures on account of my past—that's well-founded and correct. You're not deceived, that's just how it is. But so what? There's nothing shameful in that. My youth is long past, it's not in my power to prolong it indefinitely.

But don't think of showing the 'Tale' to Walter. He'll misinterpret it and be hurt.[8]

Finally, I kiss and embrace both of you, and Fedia. And I take Alyonushka in my arms for the same purpose. All yours, and with you,

B.

If you send the pieces on to our parents, warn them about Walter too.

Josephine Pasternak gave birth to her second child, a son named Karl (or Charles), in mid-March.

Boris Pasternak to Josephine Pasternak

22 March 1930. Moscow.

My dears, I congratulate you and myself with all my heart on this new victory of the unknown and infinite over our superstitious fears, which—I can say it now—I myself shared, so acutely and painfully.

Splendid, Zhonechka, I kiss you reverently and am mortally jealous of you. There you are, you women, wailing about how this is wrong, and that is wrong, and how you're being passed over, and get no glory. But giving birth, being a sergeant in that divine victory—how much that alone is worth! There you are, lying in your great white bed (all right, I grant that you've been up for quite a while now), lying and feeding your child, and receiving congratulations, presents and nonsenses from every side—all that serene and touching commotion. And how irrefutable he is, the profoundly lovable and wordless reason for all this! For the main gifts—no, the only ones—proceed from him! In the first place, he gives you the opportunity of loving with the uttermost fervour; but that's not all. The destiny of the tenderness you will be pouring out on him is in those very hands of his. Not to love him is impossible, loving him is easy; and no matter how you

8. Spektorsky's life as a tutor in the well-to-do home of the Frestelns was based on Boris's own employment in the Philipp family. Margarita Leopoldovna Philipp, the head of the family, now lived in Berlin with her son Walter, and they were friends of the Pasternaks there.

love him, he'll grow up as the embodiment of your feeling, a personified echo transformed into sound. But this isn't the main gift—it's the way he invisibly inhabits the room and the house where he has appeared. He lies in his cot and composes the future, near and far. Where there used to be nothing more than bored and formless air, frightening no-one and setting no boundaries to vague caprices, there now appear resistant outlines (one day it'll be like that here too), there appears a variant of that same definite quality that has just gained its victory. And now we have new fears, which it will conquer once again; we are afraid, but the air is joyful, it loves and believes in the new forms. What joy to give birth to a creator, to feed him and depend on him; and how worthless to give birth to creations, feed on them, and detest them for their dependence on you!

Lastly, I kiss Alyonushka all the more warmly because I've been treated just as unfairly as she has. This letter has turned out a bit wounding to her. Why wasn't it written when she was born? Why isn't there a footnote to my words about Karl Alexander, to say that the shapes that he has placed all around you have their predecessors: that Alyonushka's shapes stand beside them, and he won't be composing your future all on his own, but following in her footsteps? That's right, dearest girl, take comfort from my hurt, let's sulk and cry together.

I kiss you all, and my parents and dear Lidochka, very, very warmly.

The next letter refers to the Second Moscow Art Theatre's adaptation of Tolstoy's novel *Resurrection*, by Fyodor Raskolnikov. Boris was reluctant to see it, because it was part of a sweeping ideological campaign to 'rectify' and reconfigure Tolstoy's thought by stressing his critical attitude towards the Tsarist régime. Fyodor Raskolnikov later defected to the West, wrote an open letter critical of Stalin, and was promptly assassinated.

The central topic of the letter is the arrest and execution of Vladimir Sillov, whose death 'from the same illness as the late Liza's first husband', refers to Leonid's niece Liza Hosiasson, whose first husband was executed by firing squad in 1918. To talk openly about such things would have endangered both the speaker and his hearers and readers. Regret was considered 'tactless'. In a chapter of *Safe Conduct* dealing with Venice, Boris wrote that at times of political terror any mention of persons who had disappeared without trace became 'a sign of bad manners . . . in those cases where the authorities themselves had not expressed regret on the subject'. In this way he voiced, obliquely, his own resistance to such political imperatives.

Boris's horror at Sillov's execution echoed his presentiments of his own end, 'total and physical, or partial and natural, or at least, involuntary and symbolic', as he wrote to Lydia on 26 February. Sillov's death shook him profoundly, and exerted a strong influence on the content of *Safe Conduct*. It laid its stamp on Pasternak's attitude to contemporary life.

Boris Pasternak to Leonid Pasternak

26 March 1930. Moscow.

Dear Papa,

Many happy returns of your birthday. What a wonder you are, how splendidly you live, what a journey you have behind you! I kiss and embrace you warmly.

I've long meant to write and tell you that the Second M.Kh.A.T., that is to say the former studio of the Moscow Art Theatre,[9] is showing an adaptation of *Resurrection* whose staging is clearly linked to your illustrations. I'm using this cautiously vague circumlocution because I haven't seen it yet myself, but people who have seen it are unanimous in their enthusiastic praise for it, and say that your illustrations have been brought over from the museum (?) and are hanging in the foyer. Naturally you'll be surprised that I haven't yet been to see it, and you'll be right; but you'll be even more surprised to discover that I ought to have gone to this show (which promised nothing but enjoyment) for another reason too—so as not to offend the author of the adaptation, who had invited me to the première. I didn't know at the time that you had played such an important part—in spirit, invisibly—in the production, otherwise I would have gone in any case. But I not only missed my chance—I had to apologise for not being able to use my ticket. I had been sent a single ticket, but my Zhenia is . . . touchy; little Zhenichka was ill with something or other; and the day before, in a similar situation, I had gone out with a lady friend (Zhenia couldn't go out because of Zhenichka's cold, and her ticket would have been wasted) to see the dress rehearsal of a new production of *Kabale und Liebe*.[10] It would have looked as if I was going out to the theatre every night, while she remained tied to the house. The outcome would have been sombre, and there's little enough light around us and in our home as it is. Be that as it may, *Resurrection* is on my list, and as soon as I've been to see it, I'll write. I remember that you yourselves used to go to the theatre a lot, and spend ages there—and how much easier those times were than now!

Just listen to this. Here's an example of how I live. I used to know a man, with a wife and child, a wonderful, cultured, talented man, a progressive to the highest degree, in the best sense of the word. In age he was a boy compared

9. The famous theatre company in Moscow founded in 1897 by Konstantin Stanislavsky and Vladimir Nemirovich-Danchenko, who was directing this adaptation of Tolstoy's *Resurrection*.

10. *Intrigue and Love*, by Friedrich Schiller.

to me; we often met between 1924 and 1926. By virtue of his work (he was a lecturer in literary history and theory at Proletkult[11] and a number of workers' clubs), but principally by virtue of the purity of his convictions and of his moral qualities, he was, I suppose, the only one of my many acquaintances whom I felt to be a living reproach to me that I wasn't like him—not a Marxist, and all that.

I don't meet many people nowadays. Recently I found out by chance, a month after the event, that he had died from the same illness as the late Liza's first husband. In the light of everything I've just explained, you'll see how dreadful this is. He was 28 years old. They say he kept a diary—not just the diary of a man in the street, but the diary of a supporter of the revolution—and he thought too much, which sometimes leads to that form of meningitis. When I heard about all this, I went to see his wife, who was once a great friend of mine. She had a deep scar over the whole of her arm—the result of her first attempt to throw herself out of the window (she was restrained and only managed to break the glass, severely injuring herself in the attempt).

That's theatres for you.

I'm working a lot at present, but it's very slow and difficult. The further I go, the harder I find it to determine what it actually is—philosophy, art, or something different. In artistic composition one isn't required to refine one's thoughts down to the precision of a formula; while in contexts where a formula is appropriate, one can't achieve the vitality of an artistic image. Yet I subject myself to both these requirements and many others too, which monstrously delays my work and affects my earnings.

Don't forget to pass this request on to Lida. As soon as she's finished with the copy of *Zvezda* that I sent her, she's to send it as printed matter to the following address: Prince D. Mirsky, 17 Gower St., London WC1.

There's no need to send the 'Tale', they know it there; only the journal with *Safe Conduct*. If she's written any comments on it, she should rub them out, but of course that doesn't apply to proof corrections, which there's no need to erase. That's all.

Yesterday I wrote to Zhonia and Fedia and Alyonushka to congratulate them. And I congratulate you too on your new grandson.

I embrace and kiss you both.

Your B.

11. The Proletkult was a network of organisations for the advancement of proletarian culture established in Soviet Russia after the October Revolution.

Boris Pasternak to Rosalia Pasternak

9 April 1930. Moscow.

Dear Mamochka,

I hasten to reassure you that the 75 roubles have been sent to Babushka, as shown on the enclosed receipt. I sent my own money, and not 50 but 75, because Shura's reserve is finished and the 25 of your money that you wanted him to send isn't there. I think you must have forgotten about your present to Fedichka, or overlooked something else, because your accounts with Shura disagree by precisely 50 roubles; you've recently been overestimating his resources by just that amount. I hope he's already written to you about this misunderstanding, and you've remembered what you had forgotten, and seen your mistake, so that now everything is sorted out. So please add these 75 roubles to the rest—I'm talking about my own money, of course.

I was upset that neither of you said a word about the prose pieces you must have got from Lida.

We're all fine, except poor Fedia who has a sore throat, but he's getting better.

I've recently been indulging in an orgy of work—I've started working on *Safe Conduct* again and continued it a bit further than what's already been printed— about Marburg, Cohen, Ida V[ysotskaya], and Venice. I ought to go on, and really I shouldn't interrupt my writing since it's so difficult for me to get back on track again. But in the heat of composition I forget about everything else so completely that it makes life difficult for those around me. To work without interruption (the only way for me to produce something truly extraordinary) is denied me, it's impossible.

As every previous year, this winter Raisa Lomonosova sent us a pressing invitation to visit her. They are in Pasadena (California), and sent letters full of rare generosity and tenderness, with photographs of the intense tropical light.

I've long been intending to go abroad for a year or a year and a half, but every year I've given up on the plan. You probably remember that last winter I was invited to Poland, and—as usual—everyone here was astonished when I refused to go. But since I've decided that I will go abroad all the same, and R[aisa] N[ikolaevna]'s invitation is so embarrassingly touching and tempting, and since we're all worn out here, and above all since I can't everlastingly shrug off this whole question, sooner or later I have to address it. So I've given Zhenia my word that when the next chapter of *Safe Conduct* (which I mentioned above) is written, I'll finally get to grips with this idea and set about realizing it. Incidentally, as regards writing this chapter, one friend of mine, Ir[ina] Serg[eyevna] Asmus, has shown extraordinary understanding in working out how to help me. In Zhenia's presence, she commissioned the chapter from me by a particular date, her birthday (so that the date of completion was fixed, and not by me); and—which was an even greater help—she asked Zhenia to paint her portrait, took her out for walks, etc. So Zhenia and I made a pact that on the 7th I'll read the chapter aloud, and on the 8th I'll start applying for a passport.

The reason I'm writing to you about all this is to ask you to set about getting entry visas for Zhenia and Zhenichka. I'm not mentioning myself because at the moment I can't begin to think about travelling. *Safe Conduct* is and will be a work of decisive significance. Its importance lies not so much in the fact that people will henceforward judge me mainly on the strength of it, but that it'll be the main reason why people will follow me. One could do a lot of harm here. That's why there mustn't be anything unconsidered in the writing of it, either in its length or in the range of topics it embraces. There is a particular part of it that has to be written here, a part whose composition can't be transferred out of the country. This is the part that reviews the foundations of my ideas, my most un-contemporary and—in the superficial view of people here—most controversial ones. To write about these things in other, easier, surroundings would be ignoble; it would introduce into my text something that isn't there. I'm intending to come later, in half a year's time; but I'd like to send Zhenia and Zhenichka off earlier. They won't stay with you long, but will probably go to visit R[aisa] N[ikolaevna]. But since you won't be running out for their visas tomorrow, and it may not be you who go for them anyway, there's still time to talk about this. That's the explanation for my tone, neither imploring nor apologetic, which may upset you.

I embrace you warmly.

Your B.

The money was sent on the 7th. Nevertheless, please forgive me for broaching the subject of the visa with you, rather than trying to act through someone else, as I used to do. That's become awkward now, and of course it's disgusting of me that my unwillingness to exploit connections and intimate friendships makes me follow the line of greatest intimacy (as I see it, it's probably Zhonia who'll have to go to all the trouble, and that's why I'm purposely writing to you in advance, in case that's not possible and you advise me against it).

Leonid Pasternak to Boris Pasternak

26 April 1930. Berlin.

My dear Boryusha,

These last few days I've very much wanted and needed to chat with you, naturally not about the usual everyday matters and all kinds of family topics, but about your two prose pieces. As soon as we got them from Lidok, we immediately started reading them whenever we had a free minute. First we had to read *Zvezda*, so as to send it off to the address Lidok had given us as soon as it was finished, and that was done a long time ago.

So, you've already heard the main thing from Mama—we liked both the pieces very much. I must admit that the 'Tale' made—for the first time—a 'real' impression on me, as if I wasn't reading 'my son's work', but reading objectively, and there were passages that moved me to tears of joy at this real work of art! Mama is wrong to write that 'Papa knows how to use words' and all that. Papa doesn't know anything, and doesn't plan to write a 'detailed criticism'—all I want to say is that this is a serious, very subtle and very distinguished literary and artistic work. And astonishingly enough—I recognised myself in days gone by, for instance in the scenes with Sashka—it's very, very good, real and true to life, like a portrait! And this purity, this spiritual chastity, a quality that's completely lost nowadays—these days when authors prefer to savour all sorts of piquant erotic descriptions which they can flaunt in their writings—that quality is especially precious. And I won't be wrong if I say that it's precisely your sincerity and spiritual purity that raises you head and shoulders above your most extreme 'competitors'—the show-offs—who 'strip people naked' and use 'nudity' as something to flirt with. Not to mention the reader—even the most avid one must feel, in his heart of hearts, that purity is superior to filth, that a pure artistic style in literature is superior to the 'breathtaking eroticism', bowling the reader over with nudity, that's typical of modern literature (so-called).

Sometimes your descriptions of Nature, or your comparisons (nowadays usually much more vivid than they used to be) show far greater simplicity and surprisingly successful imagery. For instance, the way that Seriozha's longing ran ahead of him like a dog, tugging him after it (I don't remember the exact words, but I think that was the sense of it). Yes, so some of your descriptions of Nature still leave me dissatisfied because of their artificial, futuristic impressionism—well, maybe that's just how it appears to me—but you seem to be trying to find the most peculiar jarring images that you can—a simile, a comparison: 'the dusty windows were grey, poured a quarter-full with rounded cobblestones'(?)—to take an example at random. Actually, I must say I quite like it, and in places this absurdity, this anti-aesthetic quality (I don't know what to call it—the contradictoriness of the features of a given object or phenomenon) is very successful and original—although I think the reader won't understand. Still, to hell with the reader.

Ah, Borya, I take the original and try to find passages to support these quibbles of mine, and instead, at every step, I keep running into beautiful passages of great quality and particular interest and begin . . . to read on, instead of carrying on writing to you.

How well he sketches out this tale (this drama)—peculiar, strange, fanciful (a brilliant idea or undertaking—absolutely like Hoffmann!)—

Imagine, Boryusha, I skim on and read about the arrival of Mme Fresteln with Walter after the rain—and I can't forget how, the day before yesterday, after many years, the lady herself, the original of this character, came to see us and it was so weird—as if she had come to find out whether her portrait had been drawn correctly and whether she could now be reassured?

All in all, I have to tell you—interpret this how you will—that what you have drawn from life is splendid, lively, artistic; and however odious the words 'reality, realism, nature' may be, they all represent an eternal value (of course with a grain of art in it, in Tolstoy's sense). And I remember that you complained in one of your recent letters that everything you're doing nowadays is 'autobiographical' and so on. Well, thank God for that! What could stand higher than the task of drawing an artistic portrait, and what could be more eternal? The Egyptian portrait busts have never been surpassed, as great works of art, to this day. Their vitality, their truth to life, belong to the immediate present and will live for ever and ever. While every stylised invention is transient from the very first day, and is alien to us, the people of a later time.—I'm in a hurry, that's why I'm getting tangled up in this 'critical abracadabra'. Producing a polished, rational formulation of these ideas that flood into one's mind takes time, leisure and labour—all those things that you writers employ, you Flauberts who chisel out every word.

Yes! I must confess, I prefer your 'Tale' to *Safe Conduct*. Though that too has powerful passages. The bit about Marburg is magnificent. You're a subtle writer, my friend—but who will understand you? It seems to me that only I and Shura will understand and appreciate the beauty of your allusions, the almost impalpable single pencil-strokes and the hints they convey.

You've grown up, Borya, grown up a lot. Thank God. And how glad I am that I have seen you at this height!! What a great height it is, and God grant you sustain it in the future.

I'm sorry that I don't have your latest letters to hand (they're with Zhonichka, not yet returned), and I can't go through them line by line, but I remember that in the last one you wrote about your invitation to California—about your coming here, but mainly about the fact that you can only complete the continuation of your 'Tale' and *Safe Conduct* on Volkhonka, and have got to do that. Yes, of course. Of course, that's a difficulty, and writing is a difficult task, but nevertheless, don't ignore a piece of wisdom which is so essential for you in your creative work. Just before your last letter arrived, I was saying to Mama that you have to refresh your observations by travelling, that you should see more things and broaden your horizons with new impressions [...]

So—we, your readers with more of an interest in you than the rest, look forward to the further fate of Margarita Leopoldovna and Walter and his mentor Vinovata Ivanovna,[12] and something about Marburg. This Marburg is a very perceptive bit of writing. Pearls before swine, eh? I suppose it's not much understood or appreciated? And which do you prefer, the 'Tale' or Marburg?

I'll stop here—it's late—time for bed—although I'd like to write so much more.

And Mama didn't write anything about your trip (your letter is still with Zhonia), apart from 'outpourings'—but I seem to remember that there was a practical part, about permission etc. But I suppose that's all just 'in prospect' for the time being, or, as they say, 'pie in the sky'!? [...]

On 14 April, a month after the news of Vladimir Sillov's execution, Mayakovsky committed suicide. For Boris, this was a shattering blow. It signalled, objectively and incontrovertibly, the end of all his hopes for the recognition of art and the artist's role in contemporary life. Filled with anxiety and gloom, longing for news from his family, he telegraphed Munich:

24 APRIL 1930. MOSCOW.

WORRIED BY SILENCE WIRE TRUTH. BORIS.

Josephine replied the same day:

ALL WELL HAVE WRITTEN TWICE. LETTER FOLLOWS. JOSEPHINE.

12. 'Vinovat' is a form of apology. This is a piece of linguistic wordplay making fun of Boris's habit of including profound apologies in his letters.

Boris Pasternak to Rosalia Pasternak

[Early June 1930. Moscow.]

My dear, dear Mamochka!

The sad news of Babushka's death will, I suppose, already have reached you. I search for words to comfort you, and don't find any. Particularly as this news was more of a blow to me personally than I would have expected. The pangs of conscience usual in such cases have overwhelmed me, and oppress me. Imaginary ones, of course, for what guilt could I have towards her?

But the main thing is this—people used to depart from this life, leaving behind others who were definitely alive. And grief was more clear-cut, and the riddle not so nebulous and hurtful. How can one name what dying people leave behind now? They write that she felt well during her last days, and nothing pointed to her imminent end. All this finds me distracted and stupefied. The existence from which we will all, one after another, depart, itself bears little resemblance to life. I've probably grown old and tired. And I'm oppressed, too, by the repetitiveness of things. Once more there are queues, and once more I stand in them. I've already been through all this before.

[...]

Your Borya.

Please forgive these attacks of groundless bitterness. This often happens to me, quite suddenly, directed against everybody, and then my nearest and dearest are first in line.—It's over, I kiss you, forget about it.

[...]

Boris's gloom at the death of his maternal grandmother Berta Samoylovna Kaufman chimed with his forebodings about the tragic hopelessness of the times he lived in, the material difficulties of his life, and his own imminent death.

The terrible year of total forced collectivisation threatened the country with epidemic disease and famine. It became known as 'the black year' in the history of the Soviet Union.

Boris's attempts to get permission to travel abroad with his family met with insuperable difficulties. The Party activist Karl Radek also tried to help, without success. In the next letter he is obliquely referred to as a 'well-known personage' (deleted), a 'joker and cynic' in order not to endanger him. On 31 May 1930 Boris wrote to Gorky:

'I have made a number of attempts, and from the very start I was persuaded that without your intervention I have no hope of getting an exit visa. Please help me—this is my request to you.'

Gorky replied with a refusal: 'I shall not fulfil your request, and strongly advise you not to solicit permission to travel abroad—wait a while.'

The published correspondence between Gorky and Genrikh Yagoda, head of the GPU, shows that Gorky was afraid that Pasternak's gentle character and 'lack of will' would render him susceptible to 'alien' influences while abroad. There had been a flood of defections of Soviet diplomatic and trade representatives abroad in the autumn of 1929, provoked by worsening conditions in the Soviet Union.

Boris's letter to his mother also mentions his sister Josephine's reaction to the 'Tale', which hurt him. She wanted the work to show greater breadth of scope; she found the 'attractions of the subject' insufficient, and his 'attempt at a Tolstoyan novel' unfulfilled.

Boris Pasternak to Rosalia Pasternak

12 June 1930. Moscow.

Dear Mamochka,

Thanks for the telegram. I've sent the money to Aunt Klara, and enclose the receipt.

Everything depends on Gorky's support. I wrote to him in Italy on the 5th. I'll await his reply in Irpen, where I'm going on the 14th—the day after tomorrow. I'll write to you from there. There's no call to interfere in this, naturally—in case Papa thought of doing so.

For all these years I've dreamed that when we meet, I'd not only be happy to see you, but finally turn out worthy of you—I and my past life and my family. And now this all seems to be unachieved and probably unachievable. If we do meet, I shan't arrive as the person I had hoped to be; I shall have completed nothing, done nothing.

And now Zhonia has been measuring me with a yardstick that I don't possess. I'm frightened, and envious. Where does she get that from? And how coolly she uses it!

This isn't how I wanted it to be—I didn't mean to hurry, all I needed was another year. But Zhenia is restless, Zhenichka has grown bigger, and so on and so forth.

I've had a letter from Sonia. If you like, I'll send her some more.

Now I'm off to the dacha, quite far away, with no clear idea of what will happen next. It's quite possible that I may have to return to Moscow soon, to make arrangements and talk to people. The summer will be fragmented, all in little bits, shot through with anxieties and doubts. Yet summer is the time I really rely on for working. Because even in these rural log cabins, the accommodation is more spacious and comfortable than the overcrowded conditions, with families on top of one another, in which we spend the winter. In summer—it's as if you finally had a quiet, peaceful roof over your head. Like all previous summers, this one has been paid for in advance. But my time won't be my own. Well, maybe everything will sort itself out. And this is the first summer that I've been given all the money I wanted, on credit. And I might have spent the time calmly and profitably. But perhaps Zhenia is right too—one can't always postpone everything.

Please, I ask you, be more understanding with me. Remember how ridiculous I once was, and how I didn't come up to your expectations, and sometimes seemed a burden and a trial to the family. And yet that didn't all turn out to be true; I mean, my subsequent existence hasn't disgraced you. Oh, I'm so afraid, so afraid of you—if you only knew! Afraid of your pride, your judgments, your advice. And yet I creep back to you. What am I to do? This is the first in a series of illogicalities and tactless actions that I'm probably doomed to commit, if I move from this spot, this indescribably fatal and highly . . . unusual one, but nonetheless—my own. Don't ponder too much about what I've said. There won't be any more of these morbid letters.

So—see you in Irpen.

The same joker and cynic who once arranged Zhonia's proposed visit to us has now been interceding on my behalf, and has been refused.

I embrace you all warmly.

B.

Everything can be accounted for by the fact that I'm deathly sad and unreasonably hurt. I can't get Babushka out of my head. And I see no difference between her death and my own indeterminate but imminent one.

My summer address is: Irpen, Kievsky district, South-West railway, Irpen, Pushkinskaya 13.

Leonid Pasternak to Boris Pasternak

17 June 1930. Munich.

My dear Borya,

Your last two letters—heartfelt thanks for both—are written in such a gloomy mood that we have to respond to them at once. I say 'we', because Zhonia yesterday (before leaving with Fedyuk on holiday to Switzerland), and Lidok, and needless to say Mama too—we're all equally amazed—what is actually wrong with you, what is it that's causing you to have such sorrowful thoughts? Just the postscript to your letter says it all (although in the letter itself you instruct and request us not to mind its content—'There won't be any more of these morbid letters'): 'Everything can be accounted for by the fact that I'm deathly sad and unreasonably hurt. I can't get Babushka out of my head. And I see no difference between her death and my own indeterminate but imminent one'...—?!

How can you write such nonsense, my dear Borya—what's up with you, how is it you aren't ashamed of yourself? What about me—what can I say after everything I've written you recently, just slightly lifting the curtain from my own none-too-rosy prospects, which aren't at all the product of idle fantasy? And then, my age. At this age, shouldn't life have allowed me to join the ranks of those who live out their days in carefree contentment? And have I achieved all this?

But all this talk is pointless. I know that your next letter will reproach us—why do we take any notice of your transient utterances, etc. etc., and then you'll start hiding things from us. Well, it's better if you go on being open with us, and write what's on your mind. One thing I do know—when you're out there in the midst of Nature, with your family, you'll cheer up and you'll see your gloomy moods as morbid and unfounded. And why do you take such a morbid (and, for us, rather unpleasant) attitude to our future meeting? And is it really true ('Please, I ask you, be more understanding with me') that you're such a burden and trial to us ('Remember how ridiculous I once was, and how I didn't come up to your expectations and sometimes seemed a burden and a trial to the family')? And then you go on to say you're afraid of us, afraid of meeting us—'your pride, your judgments and advice. And yet I fly back to you. What am I to do? This is the first in a series of illogicalities and tactless actions...' etc. Borya, dear boy, what is wrong with you? As they once used to say—Christ be with you! And the main thing is that not everything you say is always clear to us; of course, it's not possible to express everything... and the more subtle it is, the harder—I know that, but I'm in the same situation myself... When all's said and done, one has to follow your advice: 'Don't ponder too much about what I've said'. So that's what we do. And maybe, if it raises your spirits, then '*dic et animam leva*'[13] (did I garble that correctly?); we'll manage to work out what to put down to degrees of latitude and what to rate as subjective. [...]

God grant, we'll meet again. And we'll rejoice, as always—at you and your family, who are every bit as dear to us! And don't worry if things don't turn out easy straight away—now is a particularly difficult time. There's no need to go mad if it doesn't happen at once—have patience a little longer, we've waited longer than this. The most important thing is to give your spirit and your nerves some rest—and let Zhenia and Zhenionok rest and recover in the countryside too. Then you'll see things clearer, and everything will appear in a new light.

Boris Pasternak to Lydia Pasternak

20 June 1930. Moscow.

[...]

Our parents have probably told you about my recent plans. I was so certain of success that I had already started living on this probability, and was with you all in my thoughts. But I've received refusals on all sides, and yesterday I got a reply from G[orky], who very strongly advises me to wait, in other words he refuses to support my application. So, for the time being we have to give up this idea. In the autumn I'll renew my attempts for Zhenia and Zhenichka, since the main obstacle, seemingly, is myself. My request to Papa not to get involved in all this still holds. And another request too—that any help to our relatives should not bypass me. I'm trying not to lose hope, at least for those named.

And my calculations about the dacha have also turned out wrong. I've twice 'set off' for it, and twice remained behind—the second time with my suitcase packed and my ticket bought, and I was supposed to board the train in two hours' time, and at the last minute I had to rush off to the city booking office to get my ticket refunded, forfeiting half the fare. And once again, as with you, I had been with my family in my imagination from early morning on, so that when I returned home from the Sleeping Car Company (no other tickets were available), I saw Moscow with the eyes of a new arrival or someone who had been away for a month.

13. 'Speak out and lift your spirits'.

The reason was a jaw prosthesis [. . .]. They've made me a thing which, on the very first day, cut into the cavity below my tongue, causing a deep wound in the living tissue; and when I put it in for the journey—what else could I do?—I felt that I couldn't travel with it, and that it needed to be corrected on the spot. And I've got some sort of eczema on my chin, which I simply can't get rid of.

The worst thing is that my illnesses drag on incredibly long, I never seem to get rid of them. None of them are serious or dangerous, and they're all physically bearable. But over the years they increasingly terrorize me by their remorseless presence. It's as if some unpleasant person had attached himself to you at the very height of your hopes, or your work, or your conversation with the family; you have to throw up everything, and take him to see the doctor, and stand on your head for him if the doctor tells you so, and worst of all, you have to live all your life with him, under his unpleasant sidelong gaze.

But don't you grieve about this, and if any of the family read this letter, advise them not to take what I say too seriously. When it gets so bad that I want to cry like a child about how nasty life is to me, I remember my everlasting escape route, which cannot, cannot be taken away from me. Of course I can never forget your wonderful, manly letter—how rightly I guessed to whom I should send my most essential one! But naturally Zhonia is right too—I'm the first to judge in the way that she does. But she can't imagine my life. Which is something you didn't forget, when you called all this a liberation.

And now I have to spend the summer revising two piles of trash for publication—the book of prose, and my ill-fated novel in verse. If I manage this (and I have to), it'll only be after surmounting a mountain pass similar to the revision of *Over the Barriers* in 1928, when I was rejoicing in the midst of more or less the same illnesses that now leave me in despair, and when I didn't notice the things that now fill my eyes. So, I hope for happiness. But—a 'good life'? My dear, please explain to me what that means. I've never seen it, or not for a long, long time, and I daren't dream of it. I don't know how. [. . .]

Boris Pasternak to Josephine Pasternak

15 July 1930. Irpen.

Dear Zhonichka,

I ought to have written long ago to reassure you about my health, and to say how much I love you and how stupid it was of me to frighten and upset you so. So what stopped me? It's better not to mention the reasons, they're so trivial. But this delay now finds me completely recovered and rested. And probably that'll show in this letter, to our mutual advantage. There's just one unpleasant thing. You probably already know that Gorky, out of excessive caution, refused to support me, and that equates to the complete destruction of all those hopes. Well, what can one do but accept it, maybe it's all for the best. At the end of a very difficult winter full of disappointments and losses (just think of Mayakovsky alone!), Moscow in the spring, at the start of the season of repairs, has taken on an absolutely delirious appearance. As always happens with us, having sailed through some major difficulties almost without a murmur, I was driven out of my mind by two or three absolute trifles. I got particularly furious with some stupid eczema that came out on my lip, seemingly with no intention of ever leaving it again.—But now all that's over.

I've been here since late June. I've got your *L'Âme enchantée*,[14] which I started gulping down, volume after volume, from my first day here. When I finished the fourth volume, it was as if I'd been separated from a great and thrilling world whose presence had become essential for me. And I feel very empty without it. Actually, the last two books form a single volume, Volume III. This summer, R. R[olland] is writing, or has already written, the fifth book, Volume IV. You're in Switzerland, aren't you? Here's his address, just in case: Mr. Romain Rolland, Villa Olga, Villeneuve (Vaud), Suisse. I'm not saying you have to contact him, but I'm not hiding him from you, because no matter what you do, you can't fail to have an impulse that's better and fresher than mine. Through a series of happy chances, I have the completely undeserved right to think of writing him a letter—such an intimate right that it would be embarrassing not to make use of it. This right is very awkward. It's entirely undeserved. An acquaintance of mine, M. Kudasheva, a talented French poetess and a very, very good person, is R. R[olland]'s closest friend (and perhaps more). She's French on her mother's side, a Muscovite, lives permanently in Moscow and has been in correspondence with him for a long time. Incidentally, she had been anxious that the Swiss wouldn't give her an entry visa, and if that happened they were planning to meet in Freiburg. And then, having heard from me about you, she asked me in advance if I could help her. It might have turned out that you, Fedia, had to intercede on behalf of someone who was close to R[olland]. Well then, this Kudasheva, in her kindness, told R[olland] something about me; besides which, my name is now well known in Russia—a circumstance all the more accidental because my

14. 'The Enchanted Soul'.

reputation is completely outdated, it hasn't been renewed in any way, and by its long standing has become burdensome and false.

But—a few words about Irpen. This is a winter dacha; the house, like the one in Raiki, has three rooms and a veranda; the tall, light rooms are divided by real walls. In short, and without exaggeration—compared to my Moscow situation, this is a real palace. There's a large garden. By the time I arrived, all the flowers had faded. Storks, cranes, orioles, hoopoes. The thought that we'll soon have to leave here fills me with terror. I should like to stay here always. I got down to work from the very first day. Even worse than my observations on the thickness of the walls and the number of rooms is the fact that here my thoughts can be ten times more wide-ranging, and I can achieve, qualitatively and quantitatively, some twenty times more. I'm scared of the comparison, because this relief is short-lived.

Dear Zhonichka, I'm asking you for books again. But reading R[olland] was such a delight! And I could never have allowed myself to do so in town. If you can, please send me (here—but if so then without delay) two volumes of Proust, the 1st and 3rd; I already have the 2nd, *A l'ombre des jeunes filles en fleurs*. What I need is: Marcel Proust: *A la recherche du temps perdu*, tome I, *Du côté de chez Swann*, and tome III, *Le côté de Guermantes*.[15] Up till now I've been afraid to read Proust, he's so close to me in every respect. Now I see that I've nothing to lose, I mean there was no reason to protect or treasure myself. There's no longer anything in me for Proust to influence. But please remember that this letter is a cheerful letter and a request—not a sorrowful one!

Dear Fedia! I kiss you warmly and love you. Once upon a time you and I walked together along the Kurfürststrasse. You talked to me about everything. That's how I remember you. How long ago all that was!

My address: Irpen, Kievsky district, Southwestern railway, Pushkinskaya 13, to me.

---

15. Translated as *Within a Budding Grove*; *Remembrance of Things Past*; *Swann's Way*; *The Guermantes Way*.

Boris Pasternak to his parents

26 July 1930. Irpen.

Dear Mama and Papa,

I've only just received your and Lidochka's letters this week—they were brought by Shura, having waited about a month at his home. That's why I'm so terribly late thanking you for them. I had hoped that my reply to Zhonia would have come to your eyes, one way or another, so that you would know in good time that I was at Irpen with my family, and that we're all having a good and comfortable time here, particularly myself. Naturally, when I wrote to you from town I was under the influence of my mood—but don't exaggerate my neurasthenia. How far my fear of Moscow is more than subjective, you can judge from the following. No sooner had I reached the countryside, with its 'forest choir', its well, and its dark evenings, completely unlit for lack of kerosene, I felt well within a day, not because of the proximity of the wonderful garden, but primarily and most dramatically because of the greater comfort here compared to our living conditions in Moscow. Here we have three rooms with real walls, and there are only two families living in the house—we ourselves and the landlords. You can't imagine what that means. The thought of returning to town appals me. I should like to enjoy in full not only the river, forest, sun and air here, but also the real apartment, which merits the name of a human habitation. So—not everything here is my neurosis.

As regards G[orky]'s reply, I think I told Lida. We'll have to postpone our dreams of a meeting for a time. As soon as I get back to town, I may start applying on behalf of the two Zhenias. But for the moment I'm not thinking about that. I even have to be economical with my idle thoughts: I'm working a great deal—that's essential from every point of view, and work demands the strictest discipline, down to the finest detail. Allow the slightest deviation, and not only work comes to an end, but my health too: today it'll be insomnia, tomorrow my stomach, the next day something else. This requirement for pedantic egoism when I'm working is very hard to bear.

It's quite wonderful here. As soon as I arrived, I immersed myself in Rolland's epic, about which I wrote to Zhonia. It's a work of astonishing, Tolstoyan breadth of vision, poured out in a flood of genius mingled with verbosity. But it's so real, you forget that it's literature and has an author. Rolland knows of my existence, and if I yielded to my wish not to think about the author, and confined my discussions of what I had read to the circle of local orchards in whose company I enjoyed reading him, my striving to be unnoticed would itself be noticed. So I've been obliged to conquer something more than mere bashfulness, and write to him: there was something artificial in the whole situation, something that didn't match up to my own lively impulses, and it was with some revulsion that I conquered my constraint. As one grows older one becomes accommodating and indifferent; my letter to him was an extreme example of jejune obtuseness, further complicated by its impossible language. It's been sent, and that doesn't worry or frighten me in the least. I've begun to notice that I live and act as if both I and everyone around me had become dolls. Without troubling anyone's imagination or threatening to introduce anything new, the clockwork motor of correct behaviour and common sense does its work, and everything happens of its own accord.

I kiss you warmly. Enormous thanks to Lida for her letter. Zhenia's family also thank Lida for the medicine she sent.

It was Zinaida Nikolaevna, the wife of the great pianist Heinrich Neuhaus, who had rented the dachas in Irpen. Four family groups—Heinrich and Zinaida Neuhaus and their two sons; Boris's brother Alexander (Shura) with his wife Irina and their son Fedia; Boris with his wife and son; and the family of Valentin Ferdinandovich Asmus, a professor of the history of philosophy, all spent the summer here together. The pleasant company, the music and companionship of Neuhaus, and the success of his own work, helped Boris recover from the winter's depression and anxiety. His meetings with Zinaida Nikolaevna Neuhaus had a profound effect on him.

Boris Pasternak to his parents and sisters

11 September 1930. Irpen.

My dears,

This is a letter to all of you, otherwise it won't happen at all. Here's an indirect reason for my silence. Your last letter contained a number of pages for Zhenionok, as you call him. Contrary to his usual habit, he immediately dictated a long letter with answers to all his grandmother's questions—it was a good letter. I noted it down on one of my rough sheets, which are half written in ink and half in pencil, so that I could transmit it accurately, and put it aside until the next time I wrote to you. Seemingly I must have forgotten about it, which I can't forgive myself for. And when the time came to make fair copies of my work, and I was destroying reams of these rough drafts on which a mixture of pencil and ink was the signal for immediate destruction, I accidentally tore up Zhenechka's letter too. If that isn't what happened, it'll turn up very soon when we start preparing for our return home, and I'll reconstitute it.

But naturally this isn't why I haven't written for a long time. Shameful as it is to confess it, the interruption in our correspondence came about because I haven't had such a good time for ages as I did this summer at Irpen. Supplies were much better here than around Moscow, I worked a great deal and with some success, we were surrounded by wonderful people, close friends, we listened to a great deal of music—and I was miserly and held on to every moment of this golden time, which had suddenly begun pampering me as never before. What I'd like best of all is never to have to leave. However, everyone is gradually starting to disperse, and we'll go too, on the twentieth, if we can get tickets.

Incidentally, about the money for Zhenichka's birthday: of course, please add it to what's been saved, and I'll pay it over to him, thanks a lot.

Big Zhenia initially felt very well here, we had a love-affair together, and she was working just as successfully as I was. She did a number of pencil portraits, very good and technically fresh likenesses, and a beautiful oil study of an oak tree with a sunlit foreground and a deep, wild and shadowy background, a very good still-life, and a lot more.

You may be seeing her and Zhenichka. As soon as I get back to Moscow I want to put in applications for them. That's essential for many reasons. But I'll probably stay behind; I want to stay here—it would be difficult to explain why, but it's all tied up with my most fundamental approach to life—in other words, as ever, with work.

Dear Zhoniurochka, enormous thanks for Proust, what an astonishing writer he is! Rolland was much more forthcoming than G[orky] about my springtime dream of meeting you—although I never even mentioned it to R.—and he even recruited . . . Tagore to help me. Rolland wrote me a wonderful letter in the summer, and recently another short one, in which, if there's any solution to the riddle, it's only in the hope that T[agore] might constitute a sort of . . . protection—he advises me to go to Moscow, where T[agore] is expected—Rolland had spoken with him in Geneva. The only reason I'm writing this, of course, is to please Papa and Mama, but the only pleasant thing about it is the chance fact that R[olland] believed I was worthy of his trust and goodwill. And all that's in the spirit of Irpen too.

How wonderful Beethoven's late sonatas are, especially the *Hammerklavier*, which we listened to here!

I embrace you all very, very warmly, don't be cross.

Your B.

Shura was very sweet here in all that company, and probably left with his heart full of sadness, something which is extraordinarily dear to me.

Anxious about Boris's long silence, Leonid wrote.

Leonid Pasternak to Boris and Alexander Pasternak

8 November 1930. Berlin.

My dear, beloved ones,

We hope and pray to Vishnu that you're all well and happy. But sometimes we can't help wondering—amongst all your everyday domestic concerns, do you have any interest at all in two old people? [...]

How are you, Borya? It's just 20 years ago today that we set out together—do you remember?

Last week I stayed with Hauptmann[16] and sketched his portrait. I'll make a big painting of it at home—for myself. He lives in the mountains. [...]

Leonid here reminds Boris of how they had travelled together to Astapovo on 8 November 1910, where Leonid had been asked by Tolstoy's widow to make a pastel of Tolstoy on his death-bed.

Boris's next letter crossed with his father's, but echoes the same mood of distant recollection, harking back to childhood memories of his mother playing Schumann's piano quintet (Op.44) with the Conservatoire professors Anatoli Brandukov and Ivan Grzhimali, in October 1895, in the Small Hall of the Moscow Conservatoire. This scene's indistinct details appear also to recall the funeral of Anton Rubinstein, in November 1894, when Boris was four years old.

He too was anxious about a month's silence from his parents. Meanwhile, living conditions in Moscow had become much worse. There was famine in the countryside,

16. Gerhart Hauptmann (1862–1946), a prolific German dramatist who received the Nobel Prize for Literature in 1912. The portrait in question is in the Schiller-Nationalmuseum in Marbach.

private trade in foodstuffs was forbidden, and rationing had been introduced. He opens with reference to photographs of Josephine's new son.

Boris Pasternak to his parents

5 November 1930. Moscow.

My dears,

The last news I had from you was a postcard offering to send us gifts of food. Then, at Stella's, I saw some beautiful snapshots of the children. How the little boy reminds me of his grandfather and namesake! A lovely boy. And seeing something of Uncle Karl alive once more was strangely exciting. Something of old Moscow appeared before my eyes. When and where did all that happen?

But here's an even greater distance. Yesterday we listened to the Schumann quintet in the Small Hall. That was almost the first music that I ever heard in my remotest infancy. And immediately, there were the hyacinths done up with wire, and the plump rose-buds, and the pistachio-green silk ribbon printed with gold lettering—probably gifts for Mama. Or am I mixing all this up, and was there perhaps a wreath for Rubinstein's coffin in the corner? And there was an ashtray with an old man (Lear) on it, in oils, painted by Papa. Anyway, the quintet. Incidentally, the late Brandukov, just before his death, gave two concerts with Neuhaus, and talked a lot about Mama, respectfully, as he ought.

Neuhaus played splendidly, masterfully, *brillante* (*Allegro brillante*), and led the whole string section just right.

But what do today's performers do after a concert—where do they go? Just as if they had been suspected of theft, they were detained, they hung about (well, they played a little), the situation was explained and they were allowed to go. Cold, abstract streets; cold, tired people, tired trams and evenings. The *Allegro brillante* was over, so that was Robert Schumann, and then the performer walks away thinking—thanks for not beating me up. They wanted us to go round to their place, a student had brought them a whitefish from Tashkent and a big watermelon. But Zhenia had to get up early next day, and we all resisted, so on leaving the *brillante* they walked us round to our door, it was very boring and insulting—and we hospitably warned them that we would have invited them in, but Zhenia had to get up, and we had a bit of a drought, there was nothing to offer them to drink. And suddenly I remembered that they'd been selling Siberian salmon that morning (another memory from the distant past for you— like the quintet, or Grzhimali!)—we'd forgotten about it. And I'd forgotten that three days ago someone had rushed in and yelled 'They're queuing for vodka!', and I had run out and stood in the queue. So there was even vodka to drink. And we talked them round, and they stayed—(his wife is a beauty, just the kind that—judging by the accounts of her, and by her fate—Mary Stuart must have been)—they stayed and drank, and I was calling them both the Schumanns, and then I proposed a toast to him, simply—the late Robert.—So much for our everyday life and our graveyard merriment.

My dears. I'm doing all I can here, privately, through contacts, to get Zhenia and Zhenichka permission to come to you. I had no intention of bothering you about their entry visa; once permission was granted, I wanted to try the consulate here. But they're prevaricating about the permission—they don't grant it, nor refuse it, they just put it off again and again. If I had a German visa in my hands, I could hurry the decision one way or the other. Forgive me—here I am once again, unable to take a single step without you. You could rescue me here. I can't explain to you why I need this so much, but what blessings and happiness it would give me! It's difficult for me to explain to you at a distance how my position has recently become different from everybody else's general difficulties. It's not harder, but its distinguishing feature lies elsewhere. Believe me without any explanations—I won't deceive you. And don't worry. I want everything for the best. My rights are more limited than most people's, I don't always belong to myself, nor belong so completely, as other people do. But don't try to guess anything. Just forgive me for my requests and for the temporary burden that will fall on you if you're agreeable and we're successful. I'm more of a fool than most. I'm writing to you in a way that'll destroy me. Is this a way to write to parents like you? Am I not sure of your hearts and your imagination?

Zhenia is 30 years old, and Zhenichka 7. That's for the visa.

If you didn't make a mistake on your postcard, the money for Sonia has been requested for November 15th. I'll send her 100, if you agree, but I can't guarantee the date. All payments here are getting delayed. The publishers owe me over 1,000 roubles, but I simply can't get them, or rather—I won't get them before the 15th. But we too have got to find a way out of this situation, so it's most likely that I'll manage it with Sonia too.

It's very strange to end a letter without filling the page, particularly in these days of paper shortage. But it's very difficult to write about myself.

Warmest kisses to every single one of you, there and in Munich.

Your B.

This strange letter filled Lydia and her parents with anxiety—and with good reason. It heralded the crisis that was taking shape in Boris's family life. Leonid underlined in pencil Boris's words about the 'rescue' and 'happiness' which his wife's departure from Russia could give him.

Leonid Pasternak to Boris Pasternak

26 November 1930. Berlin.

Dear Boryusha,

I hasten to inform you that as from tomorrow you can go to the embassy and ask about the visa (or preferably go in a few days—perhaps it won't be ready so quickly). In short, everything on my side has been settled today, and Zhenichka will be able to come here and look after herself and little Zhenionok, as soon as you manage to get a Russian exit visa.

I'm terribly glad that I've been able to carry out your request so quickly (and so successfully), and to let you know about it. Of course you have to find out whether a visa has been received in the name of your wife Zhenia and Zhenionok, from the Ministry of Foreign Affairs, which will probably send off the papers tomorrow if they haven't already.

Well, Allah grant you success in obtaining the rest of the permissions.

I kiss you warmly, and all our dear ones.

Your Papa

PS. When I was asked for Zhenichka's maiden name, I racked my brains and simply couldn't recall it (but they said it didn't matter and they could make do with the maiden name 'so-and-so'); then, as soon as I got out into the street, I remembered it—Lourié. That's right, isn't it? But never mind, it's of no importance, there's no harm done.

Boris Pasternak to Leonid Pasternak

3 December 1930. Moscow.

My dear, beloved Papa!

Please forgive me for not acknowledging your gift (your letter about the visa) straight away, but actually allowing four days to pass. What an exceptionally noble and speedy piece of work! I kiss you endlessly. You can't begin to imagine how unexpected it was for me. You probably know that your letter followed one from Lida. I'm ashamed to confess that it aroused inexcusable suspicions in me. I didn't understand her concern for me, should Zhenia's trip take place and I remain here alone. And I interpreted her willingness to come here and join me as suggesting the undesirability of my appearing at your home—I imagined you didn't want me to come. Don't laugh at me and don't be upset. I myself am now ashamed of this momentary delusion. But Lida's anxieties strangely echoed the arguments of the Jesuit college on which everything depends.[17] They, too, don't wish to see me in solitude—they value me too highly. Now, of course, I don't need to be persuaded of my mistake. Your letter and the lightning speed of your results have shamed and annihilated me. I abjectly apologise to you and Lidochka for my unjustified suspicions, and please accept this confession on my part.

But as for myself, I haven't taken a single step in that direction. You're entitled to be indignant. Oh, Papa, I could write whole volumes and still not manage to explain our life to you, and principally—mine, it's all so unstable and shaky, and strange, and one doesn't know what to hold on to. I earn enough—my old stuff gets recycled and feeds us. But my new work creeps along wearyingly slowly, maintaining me in permanent slavery. And it contains sections and subdivisions which I approach with tense superstition. One can only love and meet with those whom *they* want; one can only do what *they* desire. But above all, until I've completed this work and got it behind me, I can't take up anything—least of all anything of practical importance.—Yet I have to waste half the day on feeding these plans, while constantly looking over my shoulder, away from what is intimate, from what life and fate have placed squarely in front of me, from my family which then meets me with a broad innocent gaze and a silent question— how has my home failed to please me, in what way is it too small and bad, what has it done wrong? Zhenia is a saint, given the life that she has with me! And it isn't she who's yearning to get away from here—it's I who am insisting on it. And while she accepts this, it's only on condition that I'll follow her soon after. Which remains a possibility.

Don't be cross with me—my dear, dear, dear Papa, and you, my equally dear Mama!

Together with your letter, I received an equally speedy one (in response to mine) from R. R[olland], almost in your tone of voice.

17. An oblique reference to the Soviet authorities.

'Cher ami. Je sens la douleur de votre lettre; et j'en suis pénétré. Ce que je pourrai pour l'atténuer, je le ferai. Mais dominez vos sentiments! Même votre art y gagnera.'[18]

Then he offers to hunt out his old 1916 article 'On Truth in Shakespearean Theatre' (it was the tricentenary, do you remember?) and adds *'D'une façon générale, prenez un bain dans Shakespeare! On en ressort plus fort et plus sage'.*[19]

I haven't quoted his summer letters, which are more specifically directed to me; I've quoted the above lines because I could hear Papa's voice in them. Just these lines, in which he addresses me like a boy. And what solicitude!—this letter was preceded by a postcard:

'Cher ami, je suis souffrant ces jours-ci. Je vous écrirai prochainement. Pour aujourd'hui, seulement un mot, afin que vous n'interprétiez pas mal mon silence. Je sympathise pleinement avec vous'.[20] —

I embrace you all very, very warmly and endlessly, my darlings, and thank you for everything. When I was sending the money to Sonia, I suddenly wondered whether Aunt Rosa was alive. My generation will never live to that age. As for Sonia's children—they are daughters, after all, and we don't know their husbands. I doubt they are Leonid Pasternaks or Romain Rollands. If it's not too difficult for Zhonia, ask her to send the English journal.

Yes—and I'd forgotten to thank you for the parcel! You should have seen us unpacking it—what a celebration that was! I went to the post office to collect it, and we opened it on Shura's dining table in the front hall. And some of the cheese and sausage did honourable duty on the spot.

That evening, Maria Yudina, a magnificent pianist from Leningrad, played two concertos (by Mozart and Beethoven) in the Great (Symphony) Hall, with completely unknown cadenzas by Beethoven in the former concerto and by Brahms in the latter. (The Beethoven cadenzas to Mozart are so bold, so inspiringly improvisational, that some listeners suspected Yudina herself of composing them—written on Mozartian themes, they emerge from such a modern, intricately modulated distance—and yet it turns out they're by Beethoven!) The dressing-room was besieged by: the Gnesins, Igumnov, Meyerhold, etc. etc. Old A.S. Shor came to kiss her hand, with the words 'How can I thank you?

18. 'Dear friend, I sense the pain in your letter, and am filled with it. Whatever I can do to relieve it, I will. But control your emotions! Even your art will gain by that'.

19. 'As a general rule, immerse yourself in Shakespeare! You'll emerge stronger and wiser'.

20. 'Dear friend, I'm unwell at present. I'll write to you soon. For today, just a word so that you don't misinterpret my silence. I totally feel for you'.

Permit me to love you'. And it seemed to me that I was hearing the words from a great distance, addressed to Mama. (Everyone always asks about her.) And we took Yudina off to our home, with Neuhaus. And this time it wasn't like after the quintet—there was no funereal mood—your parcel went the rounds. After that she played for us until about three in the morning—a lot of Schubert, and the *Kreisleriana*. The children woke up. Zhenichka cried quietly, and when asked why, explained that 'his eyes were weak'. And Fedia said she was playing so loud that his cold had got better.

Tear off this postscript and pin it to your old papers as evidence that I've carried out Zhonia's request on Stella's behalf to the tune of 50 roubles.

Boris sent regular remittances to his cousin Sofia Iosifovna Genikes in Odessa, because she and her mother, Leonid's sister Rosalia Osipovna Shapiro, lived in extreme poverty. Leonid was indignant that not one of Sofia's three daughters had helped their mother during their grandmother's last illness, nor paid the expenses of the funeral soon after.

On 26 December Josephine sent Boris the English journal *Experiment*, No. 6 (1930), containing an article on him by George Reavey, with four of his poems in Reavey's translation.

CHAPTER SEVEN
1931–1932

Boris Pasternak to his parents and sisters

8 March 1931. Moscow.

My dears!

I haven't written to you for ages. You've probably had some news about me—but what exactly? And in what form?—Well, for God's sake don't worry, and don't judge me harshly. I'll tell you about it as well as I can.

In mid-January I left home. To start with I stayed with the Asmuses, and since the beginning of February I've been at Pilnyak's. I've fallen in love with Z[inaida] N[ikolaevna], the wife of my best friend N[euhaus]. I've written you a lot about him recently. On January 1st he left for a concert tour of Siberia. I had feared this trip and tried to talk him out of it. In his absence, the thing which was inevitable, and would have come about in any event, has acquired the stain of dishonesty.

I've shown myself unworthy of N[euhaus], whom I still love and always will; I've caused prolonged, terrible, and as yet undiminished suffering to Zhenia—and yet I'm purer and more innocent than before I entered this life.

But first of all, first of all—don't have any fears for Zhenia. I'm not divorcing her; the words 'for ever' aren't in my vocabulary. Does humanity exist on this earth in order to add, to doom-laden things like death and disease, other fatalities of its own creation? I have always seen humanity's vocation as being to soften fate as far as it can, to liberate whatever can be liberated. And this isn't an opinion, a conviction of mine. It's me myself. That's how I've lived through these two months. That's how I once encountered her, and loved her, and thought to build our lives together, and taught her nothing. She loves me without sparing herself, suicidally, despotically and jealously. It's frightening to look at her—over these two months her face has sunk, and all this is telling on her as much as it did on the first day. Loving me like that means not understanding anything about me. But I don't reproach her—is she alone in this?

She doesn't understand that I'm not a man with precious qualities, not a character in a solid state, but—a living pointer, a fingerpost with the inscription 'Turn left for the shoemaker's'. She doesn't know that in order to love me, you must first love the shoemaker—the simple, ubiquitous, open, ever-renewed spirit of life which draws me to itself with all the meaning that is in me, because for me, 'living' means not 'existing' but 'signifying'; but you can only signify outwardly, for someone else, outside your own corner, while merely existing is something you can do for yourself, for your family.

23 March. I've written you more than one letter, but never sent them. And now this one has been lying around for over two weeks. It's out of date already.

It looks as if Zhenia will get permission to travel—I've managed to arrange it.

[...]

I'm still at Pilnyak's house as I write. In a few days, at the end of the month, I'll probably move back to Volkhonka. I'd like to spend the final weeks with Zhenia and Zhenichka, before our long separation. And how do I see things after that? Freedom, freedom, complete freedom for Zhenia; freedom which will be the first true, great bond between me and her. I shall be sad without them both. Although I've just spent two months apart from them, they're still in the same city as me, I've been ringing Shura to find out about them. But I'll cope with the sadness of our separation. Particularly as both my head and heart will have much to do in the immediate future—there are no holidays ahead for them.

So—they are my wife and son; nothing has changed there. After an interval, probably a long one, we'll meet again, and—God willing—we'll start a full life together in a new way. In recent years I've frequently been unfaithful to Zhenia in spirit. She's worn out with anguish. This final, full and open betrayal has felled her to the ground. She needs to rest.

My instinct tells me that you'll like Zhenichka and find him touching. And you'll feel close ties of kinship with Zhenia, with her high moral stature and the seriousness of all she has lived through and experienced with me, both joyful and bitter. I'm confident that they'll feel at home with you, and you'll give them the repose they need. Zhenia has become a good artist. I'll keep supporting them, there'll always be money, all I have to do is find a way to get it to them, and I will. Need I say that everything we've saved is for her now? This comment is prompted by my fear of your parental jealousy on my behalf. That would be absurdly inappropriate. But I don't need that money now. Not because I don't plan to visit you, but because new money will be coming in. They're going to translate me. The first thing—the first that I won't be ashamed to see in translation, that is—will be *Safe Conduct*. It's already been sold in a French version. And now I'm going to start working much more deeply and seriously. There is much that I only learned last winter.

I'll probably have time to write to you once or twice before Zhenia and Zhenichka arrive. At the moment I have two requests. 1) Please know and remember that they are closer and dearer to me than I am myself; and objectively, with no admixture of sentiment or pity, by virtue of their innate qualities and those acquired in their terrible, difficult life with me, they can and should also be closer to you than I am. And—I swear on my fate—they are twenty times more worthy of such closeness than me.

2) Don't answer this letter with frightened and astonished letters begging me to listen to reason. Any such replies would be wide of the mark. With all my heart, I fervently wish for a good outcome, and with all my soul I believe that it can come about.

I said that my spirit would have no leisure in the time ahead. Yesterday N[euhaus] returned to Moscow. It would be unchaste to tell you about our first talk with each other. I don't know how everything will work out. He's a great man with wide horizons, and a real musician of outstanding stature, almost a genius. I love him so much that when I heard of his arrival (and when we first met face to face) the joy of meeting him outweighed everything else for me.

I haven't sent birthday greetings to any of you. Forgive me, don't be angry. I embrace you all warmly. Write to me.

Borya

Zhenia and Zhenichka left for Germany on 5 May, 1931. There are long gaps in Boris's correspondence at this time, particularly in the letters he wrote after his wife's and son's departure. At the end of June he joined Zinaida [Zina] Neuhaus in Kiev, and then travelled to Georgia with her. He heard nothing from Zhenia, and worried about her health. She was at a TB sanatorium in the Black Forest, while Zhenichka spent the summer with Leonid, Rosalia, Josephine and her family at a pension on the Starnbergersee, near Munich. The letter that follows was passed on to Zhenia and later found among her papers.

Boris Pasternak to Josephine Pasternak

30 July 1931. Kodzhory.

My beloved Zhonichka,

What joy your letter brought me, and how I needed it!

It feels as if I were writing to you for the first time in my life, so much has changed in and around me. However tender my letters to you both may have been, however respectful those to our parents, I always wrote them with the lofty condescension of a good conscience, like an older person to his juniors.

But now I'm addressing you in the absolute embarrassment of perfect happiness. In a certain sense it turns me into a child; never in my life have I been so simple and clear.

The place we are staying at is supposed to be a children's holiday resort. There are lots of children about. Zina's elder son is with us.[1] I've been thinking about little Zhenichka countless times every day. During the long period of uncertainty before your letter came, I appreciated with all my heart's blood how ingenuous and gentle he is, how unchildishly unselfish and responsive, and how deservedly (so it seems, however much it torments me) I don't know anything about him. How can I thank you for your letter? And how, by what words or deeds, can I thank you for all your care?

You know, Zhonichka, I've only just appreciated that however quiet and modest a person may be, one's modesty is never sufficient in the face of life. One pretends to know life, in order to avoid embarrassment and preserve one's dignity in unfamiliar surroundings. The decisive factor here remains one's self-respect. But when you love someone unrestrainedly and naturally, without effort or doubt, then truth becomes dearer than anything else, and it gives you so much that self-respect would become an intrusive obstacle. And then, while remaining life's guest, you feel such a warm and brotherly welcome that you forget all about your protective camouflage, and become a guest of life without disguising your ignorance. Yet this delight has its reverse side too.

When I'm overwhelmed, ten times a day, by how beautiful Zina is, how close to me in her hard-working cast of mind—hard-working in music, in passion, in pride, in how she spends her time, in scrubbing the floor, in receiving friends from Tiflis; how simple and unpretentious she is despite all her beauty and success, and so on and so forth—I can never yield to such delight without a shadow falling on it. If she is so beautiful, does that mean that Zhenia is ugly? No, never, never! How immeasurably happy I should be if most human minds weren't composed like textbooks of formal logic, with every proposition forming the basis for a deduction that excludes the contrary assertion.

No, no, I'm so scared of this spirit of ratiocination that hovers round me everywhere like a phantom, sucking syllogisms from every living thing, that whenever I'm alone and Z. has gone downstairs with her son for half a day to make it easier for me to work, and I reflect on her charms with astonishment, I always pause in

1. Heinrich Neuhaus and Zinaida had two sons: Adrian (Adik), aged six at this time, and Stanislav (Lyalya, Stasik), aged five. Zhenichka was now eight years old.

sadness at this terrible boundary, obligatory for coarse fools, and turn with guilty tenderness to think of Zhenia, and study her whole being all over again from the first day I knew her. I swear on the life of that same Zina, on all that is highest and dearest to me in the world—I have nothing to reproach Zhenia with. I love her with all my soul, she is entirely guiltless. But, with my hand on my heart—I'm not guilty either for our failure to order our lives. In other words—and there's no need to be afraid of these words—we didn't *love* one another, in the sense of the love needed to enable us to share our existence. And that probably was my fault; on the other hand, why should I ever have incurred this guilt if it hadn't all happened spontaneously? Anyhow, we loved one another in some different way—in a way, I mean, that's only become feasible now that we live apart, in open and easy friendship, without either of us ever feeling that one of us has made a gratuitous sacrifice that the other has failed to appreciate.

I'm saying this to you for a purpose. To reconcile myself to Zhenia's wordless absence, which makes it seem as if I'd struck her out of my life altogether, banished her from the earth, cut her off from the air, and personally sentenced her to exile in non-existence—and that's more than I can bear. Even if I know that all that isn't true, I still can't bear the untruth. If my happiness were smaller and shallower, it would arm me against this unjust accusation. I'd be puffed up with my happiness, in a cheap and all-too-masculine way; flushed with delight, I'd be beyond the reach of that accusing spectre. But my very starting-point was that my happiness is so great that it disarms me and sets me on a level with Nature—it makes me as sensitive as a blade of grass.

I want you to know that Zhenia's power over me has grown, not diminished, and that it's in her power to make both herself and me unhappy again. I can't guess at the new form of this unhappiness, because the old one—life together—has already been tried out, and can't be repeated. But I want to say that I won't be able to resist being ground down by another's suffering; I'll lie to myself, but I'll give in to it. And this is all the more conceivable because the person to whom I am bound[2] is inwardly like me and spiritually free, that is—capable of self-sacrifice; like me, she's not demeaned by any apparent 'disgrace'. And yet, and yet . . . Maybe she too can be enslaved by pity. And yet, I say—however much I should like to share nothing but happiness with her, she'll be the only person with whom I'll share my suffering, if I must.

And now about my dreams, which I would call plans if I were more self-assured. I'll definitely come to visit you next summer with Zina, if she agrees, if we're allowed, if we're alive. One way or another, I'll turn up. Before that, during

2. Zina.

the winter, I'll try to take up, for the first time, the opportunities offered by the West. What a joy it would be if Zhenia could get over her pain by then, and forgive me. If she could only—not regain, but simply acquire, an entirely new and enviable world, in warm friendship with me, in that astounding, heaven-sent human intimacy of '*ty*'.[3] Only then, in pure and enthusiastic mutual trust, could we at last begin to see and decide how we are to live and continue to grow, and to bring up our children, and what to tell them.

1. VIII. 1931.

I shan't start tearing up what I've written above, but I'm worn out with it. I keep seeing Zhenia looking at me from the side and thinking: 'And these cold words— is that all he has left for me? from our life, from all those ten years?' If possible, don't show this to her. Let yourself be the only one to know that all this suffering is temporary, and that given time I'll put it right, all, all, all of it. I mean it. Imagine that I haven't written you anything, and will not, and that I'm permitting myself this imaginary silence not for safety's sake, but for two reasons. Firstly, because words are terrible in such situations. If I say that I'm grieving for Zhenia and love her (which is very close to the truth), the implications are nonsensical; conclusions would force themselves upon us which would bring unhappiness to us all, and me above all, and therefore they are unrealisable; on the other hand, if I say what I have said, and—truer still—if I live as I do live, then my words appear cold and heartless towards Zhenia, who is terribly dear to me.

Secondly, I can allow myself this sort of silence because you are all human too, and know me to some extent, and must have some idea of who I am and how I live and how things are with me. And that's probably closest to the truth.

It's a terrible pity that Shura, and particularly Irina, haven't written to tell you anything. They have seen a lot, and know a lot, and are impartial judges. And most importantly of all, they love Zhenia. But I know that I've imposed on you in a terrible, godless, unheard-of way, and—and.

Oh, what can one say!

Don't tell Zhenionochek anything about this letter either.

I had gone on communicating with him and Zhenia, in my own way (some might say in a horrible way). Then Papa's letter, and particularly his request for me not to write to Zhenia, frightened me. I believed him, and our correspondence stopped; and now I haven't the courage to write to them again. Previously it used to be a natural, family thing, and I didn't realise that it was shameless of me. But now . . .

---

3. 'Ty', the Russian singular pronoun for 'you', implies closeness and intimacy.

One outcome that would be hard for a while, but eventually a happy solution for everybody, would be my death. But at the moment I can't do that.

How different my letter to you would have been, 1) if it hadn't been for Papa's letter; 2) if your own letter hadn't been written in such a reticently anguished, latently stand-offish tone; 3) if we didn't have Zina's older son with us—a hot-headed, selfish boy and a brutal tyrant towards his mother. It's an extraneous patina on a basically wonderful child—but a patina acquired in his family, and from a distance it evokes a picture of a life that's unfamiliarly alien to our own, that of the three of us together. Each new outburst of his intolerable caprices conjures up its diametrical opposite, the image of Zhenichka, and again and again forces me to love, at a distance, all the three of us together—Zhenia, Zhenichka and me; our life.

And how different this letter would have been if Zina had been alone with me—her face, her character, her portion and her destiny, so powerfully uniting within themselves all that is feminine, as they did in Mary Magdalen; if I only had with me that which I have loved all my life, and have suddenly found. Then this letter would truly be a letter from here, from Georgia, with all its beauties and its rare, incredible attitude to us both, sparing neither strength nor time nor great resources.

My address is: Tiflis, Kodzhory, Kurort Hotel, room 8.

Leonid Pasternak to Boris Pasternak

18 December 1931. Berlin.

Dear Borya!

What a lot I ought to write to you on all sorts of subjects,—the terrible thing is that I know in advance that it's a pointless waste of time, because you, and all of you, act without thinking out the consequences in advance; you're irresponsible. And of course one's sorry for you as well, we are especially so—what a mess you've got yourself into, you poor boy! And instead of doing all you can to disentangle everything and as far as possible reduce the suffering on both sides, you're dragging it out even more and making it worse! Why do you write Zhenia such letters, which she doesn't interpret as you'd like her to but as she herself wants—in other words, your letters seem to be written by someone truly in love with her, whereas the actual facts say the opposite.

What did you imagine, and what do you imagine, will happen to—never mind Zhenia, but poor little Zhenionok, who will end up not on Volkhonka but in some chance home? And how will she answer his intelligent, adult questions?—after all, he's astonishingly sensitive and perceptive. That's why Mama and I again say to you, and earnestly beg you and Zina, to take this request and advice with all seriousness—it's the only way now to relieve, for a time at least, the general unhappiness.

You absolutely must, both of you, immediately go away to Leningrad or somewhere, and free up your room. If Zhenia and the boy can go straight from the station to their own little corner, that will at least give them some spiritual relief (and justify what you said in your last letter about 'her rights' etc.). If for some reason you can't go to Leningrad, then at least go to a hotel, or stay with a friend, or go anywhere! By doing that, you'll improve your own situation, and at the same time eliminate any new weapons against you in the hands of Zhenia and other people.

And then: have the courage not to be duplicitous towards her—that's deathly for her. Oh, one ought to write volumes—I've no strength left! It's clear that you're offering her friendship; well then, speak and act more decisively, because everything in your letters is indecisive and foggy, and she—yet again—interprets it all in her own favour.

She's leaving with the Levins on 22 December. We think it would be awkward for you to meet them, if the boy isn't going to be able to go to Volkhonka—anyway, it's up to Zhenia, whatever she thinks best.

I embrace you.

Your Papa.

The rooms on Volkhonka could not be freed in time for the arrival of Zhenia and their son. The two of them stayed for some time with her brother S.V. Lourié. Boris could not hope to explain to his father how totally inconceivable it would be to go and live in Leningrad, or even rent a hotel room for a time.

On 10 January, Leonid wrote about the preparations for his second one-man exhibition, which—as five years earlier—was to be held in the Hartberg Gallery, in celebration of his 70th birthday. It was to open on 6 March. The occasion was also to be marked by an enlarged second edition of Leonid's monograph with some new autobiographical reminiscences and a major essay by Max Osborn. It was to be published, as before, by the house of A. Stybel, an old friend of Leonid's.

Boris Pasternak to Josephine Pasternak

11 February 1932. Moscow.

Dear Zhonia,

Today is my birthday, and therefore exactly the right time—taking the post into account—to wish *you* many happy returns, and it's an opportunity to thank you and Fedya very warmly for looking after Zhenia and Zhenichka.

I showed everyone the photographs of Alyonushka and Charlie. What marvellous children you have. Everyone who saw the photos was enchanted.

It's very difficult for me to write to Papa and Mama. Or you. Or [Romain] Rolland, or [Raisa] Lomonosova. Or Marina [Tsvetaeva]. In fact, to anyone far away. Why? Because our correspondence has been interrupted. Because you all might have been perplexed by my silence and misinterpreted it as something deliberate.

It's impossible to tell the whole story. But unless you hear the whole thing, you can't possibly understand it. And I can't let mistakes and misinterpretations creep in. It isn't just about me, after all. It's also about two women who are dear to me. If they were misunderstood, it would be agony for me.

Sometimes I think you—all of you, all the family—almost regret that I didn't explain everything more explicitly before now. You all think that if I had explained it last spring, everything would have been different. Zhenia wouldn't have been banished to suffer so painfully—as if there were only two homes in the whole world, one on Motzstrasse and one on Volkhonka. You think that to protect myself from the—truly impossible—task of looking after a child, I was persuaded to take a misguided decision. In Moscow, everyone is amazed by this version of events—Pavel Davidovich [Ettinger], Bari, Aunt Asya, Shura and others. If it were true, your reproaches to me would be completely justified: if I'd spoken out more clearly right away, none of this would have happened.

The picture you've gradually painted for yourselves is complex and contradictory, yet it's fairly close to my own simple experience of it all. There were other considerations, too, that stopped me speaking candidly to you. I *couldn't*— knowing how my words might be misinterpreted to Zhenia's disadvantage. After all, I was going against our family's principles. I dreaded the coldness that Zhenia might encounter as a divorced person.

In this respect, Mama is astonishing. She had come to terms with what had happened. She'd heard good things about Zina from someone. So then she starts searching for explanations for everything—as if it were all the result of some impartial and sober decision. And what explanation does she come up with? The notion that Zhenia had somehow displeased me—by not loving me enough, by being a bad housewife and mother. By being *bad*. But she's not only not bad, her open-hearted character is too good for our family. Everything 'bad' is caused by the clash between her pure directness and the covert cruelty of our family's 'Tolstoyan' kindheartedness. I was the logical embodiment of these principles, elevated to an absurd degree. And Zhenia was their living and everlasting sacrificial victim. Zhenia herself—not our little Zhenichka over whom you and our parents are all breaking your hearts. Because he is going to have quite a different upbringing. Whatever happens to me will be an integral, uncensored part of that upbringing, which will be more honest than it would be if I viewed my duty in the family style. He'll be brought up a thousand times better than we all were ('a tactical error . . .' and all that).[4] He's wonderful. I love him very much and look forward to his future with joy. I don't understand how Papa, great man though he is, could have lived like that—with all those moral lectures on his lips—unless he was lying and acting a part for our benefit.

Now I want to say something briefly about all of us and what's going on. I need Zhenia to calm down. Until that happens, I shall have no peace myself. Last summer, I was under an intolerable strain. She couldn't write to me and I didn't have any news of her and Zhenichka. I wasn't in any doubt about how much you would help them in terms of time, nerves, material things and money. I was certain of the tender welcome you had ready for them. I was only afraid that Zhenia would encounter an authoritarian kind of warmth—weighted with admonitions—instead of that heartfelt kindness which makes its recipient carefree and full of faith in life, the best medicine against all kinds of suffering. I was afraid she would be bound to our parents' home by the terrible assumption that, beyond its threshold, gentleness or truth do not exist. I was tormented by uncertainty and by the weakness of my faith in you.

When Zina and I moved back to Moscow we settled in Volkhonka. Zina was violently against this, and so was I. But in Moscow there are no apartments to be had—there aren't even any *rooms* (more about that below). All my feelings for Zhenia—do I have to persuade you that I love her with all my soul, or explain in detail why, and what that means?—were intensified. There I was, living with Zina in the same place where every little thing summoned up memories of Zhenia—as if these things were learning from me how to betray her. What were my motives

---

4. Leonid frequently referred in conversation to 'the tactical error of the 14ᵗʰ February', the day of his marriage in 1889, which prevented him from going to Paris and—in his view—compromised his artistic development.

when Zhenia and our son arrived? I was desperate to see them. I had so many accumulated fears for her—so many cares and so much suffering—it was like having a second life that wanted to become my only life again. I'm probably very bad at understanding myself. As soon as I do, I'm unhappy. Because 'self-awareness' always brings with it a severe, judgmental quality—all that censure and rebuke!—like the pernicious notion of Destiny. Frightening. I always have trouble understanding what it is that I need—and this time I was completely off my head. I stopped thinking. I started looking for signs. I was ready to act according to whether a matchbox fell top or bottom upwards. Since I didn't disguise any of this, Zina was tormented as well. The matchboxes said I ought to go back to the past, to my family—no, to the victim and martyr, Zhenia. And my resolve was made all the easier because I was out of my mind—taking two contradictory decisions every minute. I forgot that Zina—a source of joy for me in all my suffering—was still with me. I probably imagined she wouldn't abandon me even if I left her and went back to my old life—in some inscrutable way, like an unexpressed thought or an unrealised dream, she'd transfer herself into all my new situations, she'd share my life with Zhenia. And how much I longed for that!

By that time they were already on their way. Mama and Papa telephoned me. What a nightmare! Nine years since I had seen them, and suddenly that conversation in the night, devoted to a single topic—that Zina and I should vacate the apartment. Like some hypnotic incantation. (From their point of view, it was saintly. I appreciated that: here they were, talking to their very own son, and for six minutes they talked about nothing but arrangements, nothing but their grandson. Just their grandson. Nothing else.) It wasn't possible to do what they wanted. Moscow hangs on to the status quo for years on end. It takes years to prepare a move—a change of address, any sort of change—which you need to schedule for a precise moment, if you want to live rather than vegetating.

So they arrived, these beautiful, young, elegant creatures. I was beside myself with joy. They found a home in the outskirts, beyond the Moskva river, in a working-class district. A cramped, uncomfortable flat. I often went to visit them. Sometimes I felt that if I were to go back to my old family, my feelings of serenity and tenderness towards Zhenia would be diminished. We would lose something of our open-heartedness. Things would be less good for her and our son if we lived together, instead of as we were—apart, with me going to visit them, and all that.

I wasn't thinking about myself. I wasn't clear enough in my mind. At the same time, other people saw me vacillating and realised I was in danger of making insane and unjust decisions. They started showering advice on me. Neighbours,

Shura and Irina, my Georgian friends—all the people close to me and who had devoted a lot of time and effort to this story of mine. Even earlier, in Petersburg, Aunt Asya had spoken of my returning to Zhenia as something 'inconceivable, a fairy-tale'. She said it would be unforgivable—just because I wanted a reconciliation, I couldn't blithely assume that somehow the other family, which I had also destroyed, would have reconstituted itself by the time Zhenia arrived, and that Zina would have returned to her husband—flying in the face of her feelings and of common-sense. Yet the more sound and self-evident all this advice was, the more it drove me back to Zhenia—because its message was directed against her, and I wanted to go to her side and defend her.

So, they were living with Zhenia's brother. There was a hunt on for a room—sometimes for them, sometimes for us. It depended on what was going to happen to the Volkhonka flat. But no room could be found. Week after week went by. Sometimes I made promises to Zhenia in all sincerity. Other times I felt that the fulfilment of those promises would bring us misfortune. Finally, with total justification, at one point her brother lost his temper over what was happening to her. He demanded that I vacate her living-space on the spot.[5] That was on the telephone. I had a dental abscess and wasn't going out. Zina's children were hurriedly taken to stay with their father. Zina and I moved in with Shura in his new flat—where they still had the painters in. We moved in to share their room, sleeping on the floor. Zina spent every day with her children, wearing herself down by sorting out that household—and returning here exhausted, just to spend the night. I was in such a state that, even if circumstances had allowed it, I couldn't have done any work.

The flat was free now for Zhenia. But her move was delayed until the place was cleared. I understood her reluctance—the prospect of loneliness in a deserted flat which she remembered as crowded and noisy. I knew what she was going through. Half of what Zhenia goes through, I go through as well, only with unbearable intensity. We experience the very same things, in different places and playing different roles—she cast on her own resources, I under the sway of an amazing, but terrible, terrible destiny.

I couldn't stand it. It was torture. One morning I said a few words to Zina. She collected her things together. She wanted to go downstairs herself, to find a sleigh. I went to get one, we quietly said goodbye, the sleigh disappeared round the corner, and she returned to her husband's flat, the husband she had left—but not back to him. Aunt Asya's 'inconceivable' event had come to pass. Zina had

5. At the Volkhonka flat.

been sacrificed. There was nobody in Shura's flat at the time. Everything happened without witnesses. I went back upstairs. I didn't cry. I was happy thinking
that perhaps a return to old times might give me peace—my poor, humble, but
absolute peace, which I had so completely forgotten!

Over at Volkhonka, they were still clearing out. Zhenia was due to move in
the following day. I was standing by Shura's window. Suddenly I was seized by a
terrible anxiety, as spontaneous as a sudden gust of wind. I rushed headlong to
Volkhonka. All our supplies had been left there. I had to do something. I knew
Zhenia shouldn't be there. Bursting into the house, I ran straight into her. I was
completely overcome and dissolved in tears. I started kissing her hands as though
she were my saviour. I begged her to understand—that I worship Zina, that it
would be despicable to fight against this feeling. Even if it were conceivable that
I could overcome it, this wouldn't bring us happiness. She began to comfort me.
She reminded me that she was making no demands. She even asked me not to
move in with her straight away. I went back to Shura's. But I couldn't stand being
there alone while they were at work. I moved in with Zhenia, and stayed there a
night and a day.

I admit that my decision was carried out somewhat dishonestly—but I felt a
constant, pressing need to comfort her, to spend time with her in a nice way.

At some point, naturalness deserted me. Instead of relaxing into the flow of
events, I interfered with them. I was frightened Zhenia would be hurt—particularly after the past year—by the discrepancy between our best intentions now
and the reality we had already once lived through. This consideration wouldn't
have occurred to me if I'd been on a desert island, or even in Papa's situation.
That was a dreadful night for Zhenia. We didn't sleep at all. We might as well
not have gone to bed. By morning we were discussing divorce. I went back to
stay with Shura.

Meanwhile I couldn't see Zina. I had let her go away for ever. She was visited
by Shura, Irina, and Irina's brother Nikolai. She made them all promise not to
report anything bad, so I wouldn't be influenced by the picture of her un-familial
life in her family. After my recent behaviour, I had to do something new to earn
the right to see her. On one occasion I asked Zhenia for a power of attorney—to
apply for a divorce. We were at Shura's. I wrote the text of the document myself
and gave it to her to sign. She signed it, put on her coat and left, leaving me all her
papers that I needed for the application. You can imagine what happened after
she'd gone. I didn't carry the thing through. I'll never be able to do it. All this is
hateful and doesn't in the least correspond to my past or my future—what has
happened to me, or what I want from myself and everybody else.

Then I asked Ina to ask Zina if we could meet somewhere, in some street—well, where else could we see each other? The next evening she came round: happy, lovable, gentle, not saying a word about what had happened. Everyone was so exhausted and aged by the events of the past month that we all needed to calm down—to spend some time living on our own. The only question was—where was everybody to find room for all this solitude? No need to ask. One knew in advance that in Moscow it was insoluble. I'd already made strenuous efforts, in many different directions at once, to try to find a room. They'd all failed. Meanwhile it had become dangerous for Zina to go on living in her old flat. It was intolerable, too, for her husband. Heinrich Gustavovich was an irascible man at the end of his tether. He'd taken on the impossible role of being a friend to her and he couldn't cope with it any longer.

Meanwhile the painters and carpenters had finished their work at Shura's and Irina's. Their three-room flat was looking habitable. I asked Irina if she would take Zina in—always supposing Zina would agree to return. This was the building at whose doors I had summoned the sleigh for her. Irina was embarrassed. Her position vis-à-vis Zhenia was difficult. She held Zhenia in high esteem and thought her in the right—despite her warm friendship for Zina, as I knew well. So I was left with no way out. Incidentally, during these days I hurriedly finished off a deeply heartfelt and powerful lyrical piece. Work always increases my sense of self-worth. It reminds me of what has happened, and why, and for the sake of what.

Now I want to tell you something. I want you to know this. In the afternoon I went to Zina's. Neuhaus, who has suffered so much because of me, said he wanted some sort of solid security for the future. Any sort of security—a room of his own, his children nearby, a piano to practise on, even a marriage with two divorces, one on each side, rather than uncertainty about my continued visits to her. I left feeling upset. At home I started writing a letter of farewell to Zina—telling her I'd decided to live by myself, while remaining ever faithful to her in my thoughts. I started the letter five times. I couldn't bear it, so I went to the Writers' Union to demand they find me a second flat, even if they had to dig one up from underground.

By then it was late. Ten in the evening. I found sensible and rational people there, good colleagues of mine, some of whom had a high opinion of me. They spoke a language I couldn't share, the language of peaceful sleep and an ordered life. Sympathetically, wanting to help, they mooted various possibilities like exchanging Zhenia's superfluous(!) living-space. Things of that kind which, to my way of thinking, were as inconceivable as divorce papers. I left them in a state of deep misery.

It was around midnight—and freezing. A terrible, accelerating conviction of hopelessness tightened like a spring inside me. I suddenly saw the bankruptcy of my whole life. No one understood me. And now, in my mortal alarm, I was incomprehensible to myself. My mind turned to Zhenia and Zhenichka. In my thoughts, I pressed him to my breast. I was running along the street. I was running because it was already after midnight. Telephoning Neuhaus would be insane, impertinent, close to thick-skinned insolence, given that I was running to Zina. But why to her?

Now I'm going to explain this to you. While I was still living with Zhenia, the winter before last, I was totally devoted to my wife and child and immersed in domestic concerns. (I never saw family life as a burden, the way Papa did.) When I was attacked by melancholy, a kind of *Todesahnung*[6] passed through my spirit. But I always thought that my last day—the day of reckoning, farewell and gratitude—the whole day from morning to night, would be spent with Zina. (This would have been during the March thaw.) She was then still Zinaida Nikolaevna to me, the wife of the wonderful Neuhaus. From our first meeting, that was the effect of her special beauty, her blood, her mystery, her past. I'd spend that day with her, and say goodbye to the world she personified for me. I wanted to place my affairs in her hands, to tell her how much, from childhood onwards, I had wanted to do for her—for woman, the friend of mankind. The friend of every one of us—most of us healthy and stupid, a few others intelligent and therefore half-sickly and exhausted. That was what I wanted to do, but I didn't do it. Everything I did, though, was done for her. And I wanted to tell her her own story, to delight her by showing that, without knowing her, I still knew her. That's who she is, and that's how I love her.

I was hurrying to her because I was afraid I wouldn't live till morning. I whispered her name. I thought of you and Mama and Papa, somewhere out there. You could have helped me, helped me a thousandfold—but it would have been in your own way. (How many other grandmothers and grandfathers there are, poor and humble, loving—without Tolstoyism!) Here I am, dying emotionally, handicapped by my heredity and my upbringing—just as you are—but I don't consult a doctor. Because I have no time, because I have to earn. What? Money? No: the right to look the air in the face.—And when, finally, after a whole lifetime, I experience a year of perfect happiness—of health, of natural warmheartedness, of reaching out to other people—Papa writes to me 'how does it come about...'—that his son can turn his lamed spirit into rude health? Papa weighs it up and waxes indignant. Judgment is passed. And this year plunges into a nervous

---

6. 'Presentiment of death'.

fever like nothing even I have ever known. Even if anything is salvageable, I'm still trapped in the circles of intersecting sufferings. Suffering would have occurred in any case, but it would be a million times easier for everybody if only Papa weren't so judgmental, if he didn't restrict himself to being right.

H.G. [Neuhaus] opened the door to me. '*Der spät kommende Gast?*,'[7] I think he said. I didn't hear him properly. I went through to Zina. She asked me what was wrong and why I'd come. I had trouble saying anything coherent. 'Why don't you say something?' she said. She went to lock the door after H.G.: he had gone out to a concert. I noticed a bottle of iodine on the medicine shelf and drank it off in one go. My gullet burned, and I started making involuntary chewing movements, provoked by the astringent sensations on my vocal cords. 'What are you chewing? Why does it smell so strongly of iodine?' asked Zina, coming back into the room. 'Where's the iodine?' She screamed and started to cry, busying herself about me. What saved me was that she had been a nurse in wartime. She gave me first aid, then ran to fetch the doctor. For an hour and a half they made me vomit, twelve times in succession. They rinsed out my insides, then took precautions against internal burns. I can't go through all they did. There are two kinds of danger in cases like this: the immediate effects (on the oesophagus and so forth), and the more delayed ones caused by the poison entering the bloodstream (on the heart, kidneys, etc.). All this, on top of my running through the streets, had exhausted me. The doctor said I must spend two days of complete rest in bed. And this first night, it would be better if I didn't move. I knew I'd stay there. I was in a state of utter bliss: I was lying down, Zina was moving noiselessly about me, making me swallow something. I was talking in a whisper: it was easier that way. I felt as though I were at home with her: it was like the beginning of winter again. At the same time, the thought of home brought back everything I'd been through—all the mathematical constants which had left me no way out and would leave me none. I was bound to encounter them again tomorrow and on all the succeeding days and years. Now, in this state of bliss, my pulse almost gone, I felt a wave of pure, virginal, totally untrammelled freedom. I actively, almost languidly, desired death—as you might want a cake. If there'd been a revolver by my side, I would have reached out my hand like reaching for a sweet. After what had happened, that would have been terribly easy for me. Somehow I knew without thinking what would happen after the shot was fired. I wanted to shoot myself because I was torn between my calm euphoria and my sense of the insoluble complexities which had produced this happiness. At 2 a.m. Neuhaus returned.

---

7. 'The belated guest?'

When Z told him what had happened, he ran in to my room. 'No, really, did you do that? Boris, you? I would never have believed it. Have I really overestimated you?' And so on. Before that, he said curtly to Zina, as if she were guilty in some way, 'Well, are you satisfied? Has he proved his love for you?'

At three o'clock, a female relative of his arrived with camphor and a syringe. (Her housemaid had been in the kitchen during the commotion: when she got home, she trumpeted it all around.) Finally, everybody left. Zina spread herself a bed on the floor next to my couch so that she could keep an eye on my heart. I don't know why I should confide this utterly incomprehensible fact to a woman and my sister—but if I have a daughter, then that will happen because of those minutes on the threshold of death. These great fundamental acts of passion are so pure and strong it's a pity they can't speak or answer questions. We should listen to them. Not to Papa's quarrels with Indidia.[8] Nor all the advice everyone here gave me. Nor, of course, to everything I write to you so helplessly. But I'm slandering Nature. Her answers take the form of absolute decisions: those answers are—births.

I wanted to keep my failed suicide attempt an absolute secret, and I've almost succeeded. Two or three people very close to the events found out about them the following day, to my regret; but I've sworn them to total secrecy, and over the past two weeks (since the 3rd, the day I poisoned myself), I've satisfied myself that they're keeping their word. There were only two people I wanted to tell about it—to share this brief experience of a precious situation, and one which ultimately showed no-one up in a false light (how passionately I longed for that!). Shura's Irinushka and Zhenia were the only ones to whom I wanted to confide these moments of solace. I didn't even want to tell Shura. Although he's helped me in infinite ways (he and Irina voluntarily spent the whole of two months sorting out us and our affairs)—still, a bit of the dispassionate estrangement which I've been feeling towards you all has rubbed off on him too. But when I went to see Irina, I found it so gratuitously offensive to be trying to have a confidential talk with her and without him, that I stopped trying to divide them. Shura burst into tears, hugged and kissed me for a long time. But I avoided telling Zhenia, for reasons of prudence. She knows nothing about it, and I don't want her to. Should our parents be told? I swear to God I don't know. I don't have a view on this. The picture they have of me may be an enviably flattering one. I should love to be the person they write their letters to, the person they think about, and if I were, I should be better, happier, and above all immeasurably freer and less weighed

---

8. Leonid's elder brother Alexander.

down by responsibilities. But these ideas of theirs are wide of the truth. When I actually see Mama before me, or—separately—Papa, I feel an aching tenderness towards each of them. But their actions are beyond my comprehension.

But don't say anything to Fedia. I know how he would react to all this. Pretty much like Papa. Papa always sees things as if someone else were doing just what he himself might have done—if only he, Papa, had not nobly chosen a more difficult path. All that is left to me in the way of family feeling—in a stable form, without pain or astonishment—is your intellect and understanding, and Lydia's healthy talents. Does this mean that I don't love our parents? On the contrary. Because this is an *old* wound, which has opened up again and which I now understand with absolute clarity.

Aunt Asya, for instance, is much closer to understanding my situation. This isn't meant as a reproach to all of you. You are far away, while she is in Petersburg. No great merit in that, for all her sensitivity. As a matter of fact, I don't know whether she liked Zina. I think she probably didn't—Zina always comes back from the hairdresser looking terrible, like a freshly-polished boot. And she always has her hair permed before any festive occasion—which, for her, includes visiting my aunt. All the same, Asya and Olya have been touched by Zina's fate and mine, and by its likely outcome. They were in tears when they said goodbye. Olya actually howled out loud. Without any correspondence between us, they always know everything about me. Olya has been listening to the accounts of me that she heard from her colleagues at the Institute—bottling it up for years. I was one of their special subjects of study. Quite recently, she couldn't hold out any longer and confessed I was her cousin. And Aunt Asya intuitively understands how this fate—of being common property, imprisoned by warmth on all sides—transforms one, how it makes one a prisoner of time. This is also an example of poor Russia's primordial cruelty: when she bestows her love on someone, the chosen object can never again escape her scrutiny. As if he were in a Roman arena, obliged to provide her with a spectacle in return for her love. If no one has escaped this fate, then how could I? Russia's love for me is as problematic as Germany's for Heine. But I'm afraid you won't understand me. You'll think I'm boasting. Oh, no. It's not my ambition I've described to you, but my actuality, my aimless, ongoing existence. I've described to you my duty towards Fate, a duty which Aunt Asya intuitively guesses at—that this existence of mine should take its course, unrelieved, while destiny watches.

Look at Papa, who has been and still is a great, great artist—far greater than I am. He will say, yet again, that he chose the hardest path—the heroic task of being a family man. And that's a lie. It's a lie because his heroic task is a heavenly refuge compared to what I have to do, and cannot. All comparisons aside, the domestic hearth requires no sacrifice. It's a place of rest and peace. Papa always felt the need to quote Tolstoy's praise of him, as if it could ennoble his peaceful, enviable and happy destiny, or somehow make it special. (That's what makes him a genuine artist.) Yet its virtue lay precisely in its peacefulness. It needed none of Papa's supplementary arguments.

It's a lie—what has happened to me would show him that. He stuck to his old words and reopened my old wounds. But perhaps one really needs to live here to understand all this.

In the world there is a greater warm-heartedness than our family's ethos. And it's simpler—not perpetually litigating and dividing right from wrong. Neuhaus's 80-year-old parents worship him. They were appalled and scandalised by what happened in the springtime. For decades, they ran a music school in Elizavetgrad. Now they are living out their lives almost destitute. For old times' sake, they still love Zina as much as ever. In summer, Garry's (that is, Heinrich Gustavovich's) mother wrote long letters to Zina in Kodzhory, giving her reassuring accounts of her son, who was staying with his parents at the time. You ought to read those letters, which were sent to my address. All the old lady's ideas came true, because they were inspired by an all-forgiving tenderness. All her news had a good effect. Zina was spared my torments. And every time my own grief about my family broke out, it frightened Zina so much, she only asked one thing of me—to let her and her son go, not to her husband, who'd left by then, but to his parents in Elizavetgrad.

I don't know whether you'll have the time and patience to read this letter to the end. Zhenia and Zhenichka's fate is something that haunts me—not their external fate, but their spiritual fate because of me. That will never end. I love them and could return to them, if I were able to perform great feats. But I love Zina with an even greater love. And I can't explain the difference between these feelings—either to her or to anyone else. Or their unhappy coexistence. The noose of these sufferings is drawing ever tighter, and I charge you not to turn your warm-heartedness away from them (you have it in overabundance), in the event that I can't hold out and all this consumes me, spontaneously, without my committing suicide.

Now—about my health, in case you get any wrong ideas. All is well, but my spiritual strength is over-strained. Once again, I don't know why I'm telling you this. The first week of absolute happiness, immediately after I drank the poison, was followed by unpleasant mysteries, unheard-of and unthinkable mysteries, I don't know whether caused by nervous exhaustion or by the iodine beginning to tell on me. But that's not important.

I started writing this letter on the 11th, but I put it aside and only took it up again yesterday, on your birthday. Zhenia sometimes makes an effort: she takes herself in hand, comes to life and goes out visiting. Then all that suddenly stops. She is suffering terribly and says that she can't live without me. The worst is that, when she's in that state, she can't be there for little Zhenichka. It isn't him who weighs her down. But she's so broken she's helpless to do anything for him. And she infects him with her own mood. She's suggested I should take him, but at the moment I have nowhere to put him. Zina and I can live in a phantasmagoric world—everywhere and nowhere—but one can't put little Zhenichka into such conditions. A new flat is out of the question before the autumn. A further complication: the authorities are asking me where my living-space is. In other words, where I have been living until now, if I haven't just arrived in Moscow? I ought to be handing over my share of the Volkhonka flat in exchange for a new one. But that would mean confining Zhenia and Zhenichka to a single room from now on. Under any circumstances, it would be insuperably difficult now for me to take away from them anything at all of my own—which once used to be theirs and ours in common. But in my present situation, it would be simply murderous, because abstracting my own rights from the common pool—which once used to keep all three of us fed and warm—would worsen Zhenia's position and make it as bad as it could possibly be. So I am registered as living with her. I've handed over my personal ration of food and commodities to her. And I'm living unregistered—inconceivable, given our registration system. There are so many drawbacks that only the confusion and contradictions of places, purposes, etc. prevents me from ever remembering or knowing what drawbacks there are.

And all this comes at a time when my work has been declared to be the spontaneous outpourings of a class enemy, and I'm accused of regarding art as inconceivable in a socialist society, that is, in the absence of individualism. Verdicts like these are quite dangerous, when my books are banned from libraries—when a newspaper has published people's replies to a questionnaire that was formulated with a degree of caution and indulgence rare in our times, but still acknowledged the verdict quoted above. I catalogue all this here, only because I feel like being communicative, in response to your news about the unimaginable crisis. I know it's no exaggeration. People round here read newspapers, and Zhenia described life in Germany to me. But you would be wrong to think that I mention this public side of my life because I have some hidden agenda here. That isn't the reason. I don't have the serene joy of caring about such things—unlike all of you, and Papa. Under the open sky one cares about them less than under one's own roof. This isn't irony but a letter from your brother. It is a sheer, unadorned platitude. It is the truth of a hackneyed phrase. It is—a cry from the soul.

Recently, it was Zhenia's maid's day off. In the absence of her next-door neighbour, Zhenia had a hysterical fit while I was there. Little Zhenichka witnessed it. Taking advantage of a moment when she went to the bathroom, he hurriedly said to me: 'You must understand, it's a nervous attack. But you keep on talking and making things worse.' Then he suddenly straightened up, his eyes filled with tears, and he said 'Anyway, when are you finally going to come back to us?' He went on and on, giving free rein to something that had accumulated inside him and tormented him for a long time. All his questions and reproaches were charged with incredible power. I turned away, crushed. He brushed my answers aside with the passion of a grown-up person, finally exploding with the forthright language of a will worn out with suffering. I replied vaguely: 'I can't . . .' and so forth.—'Well, just can then!'—'Zhenichka, one day you'll understand . . .'—'I understand everything already!'—'Who taught you to talk like this?'—'Nature teaches you.'

When Zhenia came back, he was running excitedly back and forth. He was talking about me in the third person, and appeared to be issuing orders. 'We simply won't let him go. I know him. "Some day" indeed! That means never. We just have to lock the doors. I won't let him go. Ring up Uncle Shura and tell him to bring his suitcase!'

This whole letter has one enormous omission—it's been apparent from the very second page, and repeated throughout the letter. I should have emphasised, more roundly than I did, that all my feelings towards all of you are long-held and independently arrived at. I haven't been persuaded by Shura—or anyone else. Least of all by Zhenia. In conversations with her, if ever I allowed myself to criticise you, it was precisely from her that I received the most brutal rebuttal. She says that in her situation—a woman crushed by misfortune, when even her own family found her a burden—you did more for her than anyone else in the world. She knows how this must have exhausted Papa and Mama. And as far as their way of life goes, she very understandably held it up as an example to me—in angry indignation. She wished for nothing better than that I should be like Papa. She says (and rightly) that I am not fit to lick his boots as an artist either. She thinks that all my attempts to call in question the rightness of our upbringing are blasphemy, blasphemy and blasphemy.

I've written this letter piecemeal. While I've been writing it, Shura's birthday has passed too. Recently I've become calmer, and in the last few days I have really felt well. If Zhenia could get over her sufferings, I should be perfectly happy—my own life has been going so well recently. But she really doesn't have the strength to live alone on Volkhonka. And when her inner emptiness gets worse, she feels—undemonstratively, but with full and menacing rightness—that she wants to die.

Forgive me all the unfairnesses in this letter. I'm probably going mad. I embrace you.

Your Borya

Josephine replied to this letter, urging her brother to break out of the closed circle of his misery and get urgent permission for a trip abroad.

Boris Pasternak to Josephine Pasternak

10 April 1932. Moscow.

Dear Zhonia,

It's very bad of me not to have answered you before. I did write some three replies, but once again they were very detailed accounts which it was difficult to finish. And so you were left without news of me.

[...]

In a word. I'm with Zina. She's very beautiful and I love her very much.—But little Zhenionok still hasn't calmed down, he misses me a lot and is visibly fading. That's terrible. It's killing me; and if only for his sake, all the arrangements ought to be changed. But the only solution, and the one which he himself voices as a childish dream—that is, for me to return—is unthinkable for the time being. I wouldn't cope with it, I wouldn't be able to stand it, I'd fail, and then everything would be even worse. Fate is in some way mixed up in all this; one day it'll all sort itself out, but not now and not in this way.

Next. I've no reason to travel at the moment, it's quite unnecessary and absolutely impossible. If I needed to, I'd take the matter up myself. Maybe they wouldn't turn me down now.

Evidently Papa has the same thing in mind when he writes a postcard to warn me that he intends to take up in more detail something I said in my postscript to Irina's letter. There I said 'May you, at least, be happy', etc. etc. In reply to this, he apparently means to give me some sort of advice. I have no confidence whatever that his advice will make me happy, and that line of thought won't bring him a single step closer to any real participation in my life, if he's genuinely interested in it. Anyway, there's nothing to be remedied here. I have come to know one particular side of Papa and Mama—one that I've long been aware of—in circumstances which I can't ever forget. I should be a villain to sustain and nourish this bitterness, and I don't. But the spontaneity of my relationship with them, which until quite recently remained as alive as it had been in my childhood, is now lost for ever. I love them, as one loves one's parents; but the feeling that my life is passing before their eyes, that it's close to them and can in some way gladden them—that feeling has gone. And once again, and again: Zhenia and Zhenichka worship them and hold them up as an example to me. But I have learned a lot from certain facts that seemed natural to my parents, and not to me.

[. . .]

You may not believe me, but Papa's exhibition, his 70th birthday, his success, his healthy creative interest in his artistic destiny, and the way that Mama shares it all—I see all this as entirely separate. I am sincerely, freely and uncomplicatedly delighted by it all.

I kiss you and Lida warmly, and thank you for everything. I embrace Fedia and your wonderful children, really wonderful—did I write and tell you how I've been showing everyone their latest photographs?

Do me a favour, please, and write to Zhenia. Love her as a member of the family. She's acutely sensitive about this, and is sad that her letter went unanswered. I'll write to our parents sometime, together with Shura; please give them my renewed greetings and congratulations.

Your Borya

I simply can't write Papa and Mama any more of my long letters. When I start writing, I burst into tears. I find them incomprehensible. And I probably overestimate the sadness of this discovery: they probably don't need, and never did need, all the feelings for them that I used to have and no longer do. When that's confirmed, things will get easier. We'll get through this somehow.

On 4 April 1932 Alexander (Shura) sent a telegram in the name of all the children to congratulate Leonid on his 70th birthday. Boris, still smarting, responded by explicitly dissociating himself from the general family celebrations.

Boris Pasternak to his parents

Early April 1932. Moscow.

Dear Papa and Mama!

With all my soul, I join in your celebration and share the general rejoicing. I'm terribly glad for Papa: he must have experienced real satisfaction, untainted by any incidental feelings of resentment.

Now I can easily understand the bitterness and awkwardness that always accompanied his success. Wherever such ambivalent feelings may come from, they are always vexatious, whether you feel you are overrated or underrated. I myself am valued immeasurably higher than I deserve, and I know this sense of disparity just as well as Papa, who has ultimately been sorely undervalued. It's good that this note has long ceased to resonate in his life, and what a splendid testimony to that is his exhibition and the way it was received! So—congratulations.

Mama, you ask what address it would be best to send the monograph to. If all you mean is the postal address, then any one will do—best of all, to Shura. But if you have any other considerations in mind, then without knowing them it's hard for me to answer you, and you'd best be guided by them yourself.[9] Everything in the USSR is nowadays rated only from the political viewpoint. In particular, An[atoly] Vas[ilyevich] now carries very little weight here. If you two want to give the monograph to him, as your friend, that's very kind of you, and I don't know how to advise you. I'm not clear about your and Papa's interests as regards the reactions and possibilities here. And even if I were clear about them, I have no experience whatever in this area myself: everything that has happened with me in this respect has always been done more or less without my involvement. I don't know what Pavetti wrote you, and I'm not sure whether he thought of telling you that for the last two or three years the press has stopped writing about art altogether—that custom has sunk into oblivion.

Please reply to little Zhenichka and write to big Zhenia. Keep up your contacts with them, I beg you. I'm very glad about your celebration—but the signature 'Fünf Kinder'[10] was—of course—not written by me; I was at Shura's at the time, and merely submitted to the family tradition of celebrations which he

---

9.   Rosalia Pasternak evidently feared that the album would be found in some way objectionable by the Soviet censors and the book would not be delivered. Anatoly Vasilyevich Lunacharsky, previously the People's Commissar of Education and a friend of the Pasternaks, had by this time lost his post.

10.   'Five Children'—a signature intended by Shura to refer to himself and his wife Irina, and Boris with both Zhenia and Zina.

inherited as a child. I don't like it, and recently I've had proof of how right I am to feel that way.

I embrace you all.

Your Borya

When Zhenichka developed severe scarlet fever, Boris temporarily rejoined his family in the apartment on Volkhonka. This letter goes on to recount details of Zina's past, which were later attributed to Lara, the heroine of *Doctor Zhivago*. The novel's first draft was begun in the summer of this year. In this letter's hypothetical transference of Zina's experiences to his sister Josephine, Boris also refers to the summer of 1913, when—as a schoolgirl aged thirteen—she fell in love with Nikolai Scriabin.[11]

Boris Pasternak to Josephine Pasternak

24 May 1932. Moscow.

Dear Zhonichka!

I'm not writing from Zhenia's flat. I haven't got an infection and I'm out of quarantine. So don't worry.

When I was writing *Spektorsky* in 1925, I planned the second half in the form of notes written by the hero. He was supposed to write them in town, in the summer. In my mind, I had him living on the bottom floor of a little detached two-storey house on Tverskoy Boulevard, which I think once housed the Danish consulate.

It's summer now; through my window I can see the Tverskoy, and I'm writing to you from that very same house. That's how life has turned out—a half-imaginary setting of half-imaginary events, and I've ended up there myself.

I moved here the day before yesterday. It's got two rooms; the bathroom isn't yet done up and the wiring hasn't been installed. It's a temporary flat made available to me, Zina and her children by the All-Russian Union of Writers.

Last winter, when you (like so many others) were reflecting on the trials and vicissitudes affecting me and my nearest and dearest, you confessed that what you cared most about was what would happen to me, and how I was feeling. You

---

11. The cousin of the composer, described as 'an undistinguished "old" man of twenty-seven or eight', in Josephine's autobiography, *Tightrope Walking: A Memoir by Josephine Pasternak* (Indiana: Slavica, 2005), pp. 6–7. She also confided this experience to Boris in a letter written soon after her marriage, in the summer of 1924 (see above, p. 13).

know me, and you'll believe me when I say that this sort of sympathy only added to my sadness, because I myself was full of contrary worries, not about myself. To be reminded that if all of you were to worry about anyone, it would only have been about me and not the others, aggravated my own anxiety and confirmed me in my fears.

But I'll answer you now.

I'm happy, Zhonichka. But I love Zina too much, and she loves me too much as well. One could live like this for a month or two, but we're in our second year of it.

In order to exist, to work, to build something, you have to be able to subordinate your feelings to some sense of calm and order, no matter what it rests on— whether it's the coolness of self-love or the coolness of a deliberately undertaken obligation. If Papa or Fedia were to take a look at the way I've been living these past few years, they'd go out of their minds with shock.

For Zina, this last year and a half (particularly this last winter) has been impossibly difficult, four times more complicated than before, endlessly rushing from one home to another, brought down first by pneumonia, then by operations, and she's still working non-stop. I have to earn an impossible amount of money. If I'm to succeed, I need a chance to concentrate. Instead of which we continuously bury this ordinary prose under a fog of happiness, as though we were in a smoke-filled shack with no chimney, till you can't make anything out any more. It'll probably be the end of us—living like this is impossible, and we won't cope.

She's very beautiful—she was one of the few noted beauties here. I've already told you how we live. We're ageing one another remarkably quickly; and it particularly affects her. For over a year now (partly through my fault), she's had to wash clothes, scrub floors, and so forth, and she has two children to look after. This is all very well so long as the children are with her, so that everything is within reach and she doesn't have to tear herself apart between two households.

I'll tell you who she is. It's as if Papa, at the age of fifty, had got married for the second time, to an eighteen-year-old girl, and you were the third daughter of that marriage, and Papa died when you were ten, and you suddenly turned out to be poor because a general's pension wasn't enough to maintain a large family from two marriages; and you lived in a noisy dacha at Sablino, with endless relations, cadets and schoolboys; and you fell in love with N. Scriabin at the age of 15, and gave yourself to him, and he was your cousin, aged 45 and married with children. And he had begun by meeting you, a schoolgirl, in private rooms, and then rented a secret apartment for your encounters, and you, still almost a child, had been his mistress for three years, dividing those three years between this secret life and preparing your lessons. And then the Revolution came, and life after it, this life that had started so mercilessly early for a woman. And that everlasting beauty of yours, and people constantly hanging round you and making passes at you. If everything had happened like that, she'd probably be closer to you than I can make her by writing letters and telling you about her. For me, she's a kindred soul, she's terribly, terribly close to me. Not close to me in the way that Papa, for instance, would probably think. Not through the effect of some Maupassant tale, the jealous pity of a great creative soul for the destiny of a young girl fated to become a beauty—that's a complex law which would need a lot of exposition, and naturally I'm subject to it too. But it's impossible to be a great and memorable symbol of your times, impossible to be a great poet, merely by having the luck to be born with talent and the ability to express it; and by having gained experience from your life. It's absolutely essential for this whole logical structure to be completely violated, almost by some disaster, so that the street and the unknown can burst in on it all.

Zina is vitally close to me because she has paid the full price, as a woman and a human being, for her right—a right granted to others free of charge, and one that she almost never exploits, unlike most cultured women—the right to pass judgment on life, on the soul, on her own story and her sufferings. And the fact that she doesn't use this right brings her close to me. She's just as silly, absurd and elemental as I am. Just as pure and holy, despite being completely depraved. Just as joyous and gloomy.

I sent Lida *Safe Conduct*: did she get it? Thank her for her money transfer to Zina.

Much love to you and all yours.

Your Borya

Boris Pasternak to Lydia Pasternak

1 June 1932. Moscow.

Dear Lidochka!

[. . .] It's been ten days or so since I left Volkhonka, Zina left Trubnikovsky Lane, and we both moved into two rooms in Herzen's house (the Writers' Union) on Tverskoy Boulevard. Almost at the same time, her children's nurse left them and the children were moved here too. The Regional Party Committee of the Urals has invited me to the Urals for the summer under very good conditions; we knew that we'd be going there at the beginning of June, so there was no point in hiring someone just for 10 days.

As a result, Zina has been rushed off her feet, the children are short of laundry and clothing, there are building works all around us, you walk straight into our rooms off the courtyard (they're almost level with it, on the ground floor), and no matter how much she washes the clothes and scrubs the floor (no exaggeration, she does it every day), it's only ever clean in the evenings, when she collapses exhausted on the bed without undressing, and falls asleep on the spot like a corpse. I'm very sorry for her, but all this side of her is very close to me, as is her whole attitude to life which has always been a difficult one for her. She was born into a milieu that didn't know the hidey-holes offered by literature, so all her life's experiences have been real rather than imaginary.

———

This letter has been lying around a very long time. I'm finishing it in Sverdlovsk (previously Ekaterinburg). As always happens with us, any talk about invitations summons up a picture which, far from corresponding to the actual reality, never bears the remotest vestige, the faintest shadow of a resemblance to it. We had three telegrams one after another assuring us that our dacha was ready and we should come out at once. Now we're here, temporarily lodged in a hotel in town, because the dacha isn't ready at all. The hotel, erected on a semi-Asiatic patch of waste ground, is the last word in American technology, our two-room suite has its own lavatory and bathroom, but they don't work and you have to go to the communal lavatories. That wouldn't be a problem if only this nine-storey American hotel hadn't adopted the army barracks approach. The communal lavatories don't have latches on the doors, the seats run side by side with no partitions, you invariably have to sit in company with someone else, and when the washroom doors are open you can be seen by passing hotel guests of both sexes.

11 June 1932. Matters are developing. The dacha now appears to be a myth. Not only are they refusing to make it available, they're even refusing to show it to us; evidently it simply doesn't exist at all. There's no point going on with this letter. Carrying on a conversation of a few words per day from the depths of uncertainty and chaos is a senseless activity. So forgive me if I send it off without a conclusion. Incidentally, Borovsky[12] is giving concerts here; he's staying in a

---

12.   Alexander Borovsky, a well-known Russian pianist who taught at the Moscow Conservatoire from 1915 to 1920, when he emigrated.

neighbouring hotel, and I'll probably meet him; Papa wrote something to Shura about how we ought to see him.

When leaving Moscow, I arranged for Zhenia with Zhenichka and Elizaveta Mikhailovna to spend two months in one of the rest homes near Moscow.[13] I hope that the promises I made to them will turn out more reliable than my Urals experience.

I've recently been reading the newspapers and following all that's happening in Germany. I'm well aware of the significance of it all; of all the international developments, this is the most important and ominous. And on the way here I was re-reading Remarque's *Im Westen nichts Neues*.[14]

I embrace you

Your Borya

Pasternak's journey to the Urals on a so-called 'creative mission' was an excruciatingly painful experience for him. First in Sverdlovsk and then at the Regional Committee's dacha on Lake Shartash, he was confronted by the unbelievable calamity of the mass famines of 1932. The horrific sight of endless lines of exiled, starving peasants and devastated villages contrasted painfully with his own lavish reception amidst the privileged lifestyle of the local Party officials, who allowed themselves every luxury and entertained Boris and his family as guests of honour in their restaurant. Unable to bear this, he returned to Moscow. Zhenia's trip with Zhenichka to a rest home in Kislovodsk was also a failure. They too found themselves surrounded by epidemics and starvation.

13. A 'rest home' (*dom otdykha*) in Soviet Russia was a centre for rest and relaxation for working people during their vacation (several weeks). Such centres usually belonged to professional organizations or big factories. The Union of Soviet Writers also owned a number of such centres in various health resort areas of the country.

14. *All Quiet on the Western Front.*

Boris reading Rilke's *Neue Gedichte,* 1933.

ndré Malraux, Vsevolod Meyerhold, and Boris Pasternak (left to right) in Moscow, 1936.

Zhenichka with pigeons on street in Germany, 1926.

Zhenichka (right) and his cousin Fedia (Alexander Pasternak's son), 1929.

Pasternak family group in Berlin: (standing) Frederick, Leonid, and Lydia; (seated) Josephine and Rosalia, 1927.

Frederick, Zhenichka, Zhenia, and Josephine (left to right), on a lake near Munich, 1931.

Leonid Pasternak with
Zhenichka, 1931.

Leonid and Rosalia with (left
to right) Charles and Helen
Pasternak and Zhenichka,
at a picnic in the German
countryside, 1931.

Helen and Charles Pasternak, 1935.

ichael Slater (Mikey) in his playpen, 1937.

Gilbert and Violet Slater, Lydia, Leonid, and Rosalia at the Slaters' home in Oxford, 1936.

Boris's dacha at Peredelkino, where he lived from the late 1930s until his death.

oris Pasternak and Kornei Chukovsky at the Komsomol Tenth Congress, Moscow, 1936.

natoli Lunacharsky addressing the Union of Soviet Writers in Moscow
(Boris Pasternak is in the third row), 1933.

Maxim Gorky.

Boris Pasternak and Maxim Gorky at the Presidium of the First Congress
of Soviet Writers, August 1934.

For information about illustration sources, please refer to pages 421–42

CHAPTER EIGHT
1932–1933

Boris's former regular and cordial correspondence with his father was only resumed in the autumn, after Boris's return from a short trip to Leningrad where he gave a public reading and visited his relatives.

Boris Pasternak to Leonid Pasternak

18 October 1932. Moscow.

Dear Papa,

Not a word about the past—here's my forgiveness to you, and you please forgive me too.

A few days ago I saw Aunt Asya, Aunt Klara and her husband. Their lives are harder and worse than last year, but with a few exceptions that's the same for everybody.

We've only just finished all sorts of house-moves and transfers of belongings. Zhenia has moved to Tverskoy Boulevard (her address is No. 25, apartment 7), to the rooms which we had been allocated earlier, while we ourselves have moved to Volkhonka. The old apartment was in a state of terminal dilapidation, and I'm glad that we managed to move Zhenia to somewhere better. They are better off for accommodation, but worse off for food: she eats in the Writers' Union canteen, which is in the same block as her flat, and of course that's worse than the home cooking she enjoyed when she had my pass-book to the reserved food store; meanwhile we were eating in the same canteen where she now goes with Zhenichka—we were expecting to go on eating there for ever. It was her own choice to move to Tverskoy Boulevard, and I had no alternative but a complete exchange: I had to put her in exactly the same position that we—Zina and I and her boys—had previously been in, as far as food was concerned. If I had cancelled my canteen rights on her behalf, and left her my ration book instead of taking it myself, we should have had no way of getting food at all.

Last year, when Zhenia was at her most miserable, she sometimes used to implore me to take Zhenichka to live with me. Then Zina and I went off to the Urals while they went to Kislovodsk, and for the whole summer Zina and I nursed the fond hope that when we returned to Moscow, Zhenichka would come to live with us. The first time I saw him there, I took him off for a walk; we went from Volkhonka to Tverskoy Boulevard to visit our home and the boys. On the way he talked to me like a grown-up, and tears were running down my face at the tragically mature, reticent tactfulness with which he alluded to anything that seemed to him to be 'my business', while trying to match it up with his own feelings, wishes and suppositions. He's been initiated into everything, he knows and understands it all, and the outcome of that walk and his visit to Zina, Adik and Lyalya was that he had no objection to coming to live with us (only so as to be living with me, as he later felt it necessary to explain to me). The boys (the older one is 7 and the younger 6) hadn't seen him since they were all at Irpen, and greeted him noisily and joyfully. For them, he's part of myself, and they love me. We all agreed that until any decision was made, he would come and visit us from time to time.

Later it turned out that I had misunderstood Zhenia: that had been a hysterical outburst on her part, and she wouldn't and couldn't be parted from Zhenichka.

In her new apartment (on the ground floor, with an entrance off the courtyard), Zhenichka has made great friends with Dima, the nephew of Kostia Bolshakov,[1] and spends every day out in the yard; he has joined the Union library, and is very jolly. The school to which Zhenia has decided to send him still won't give a definite reply about whether or not they'll take him, everywhere is so full.

Zhenia is working very successfully; she has done a beautiful drawing of Elizaveta Mikhailovna,[2] a good likeness with good technique—and it's only my constant fear of the future that stops me from saying that everything seems to have turned out all right, in the sense that the morbid madness of last year's experiences has been overcome and dealt with, and become a memory.

When we moved in to the Volkhonka, there wasn't a single whole pane of glass in the windows,[3] the rats had not only gnawed through the skirting-boards but actually torn them away, one of the rooms (under a faulty roof) had water leaking through the ceiling, and when it rained you had to put a tub underneath.

---

1. Konstantin Bolshakov was a friend of Boris's in his youth, when he was a Futurist poet. After the Revolution he changed to prose writing. He was arrested in 1937 and shot in 1938.

2. Elizaveta Stetsenko, Zhenichka's home tutor in French, and a much loved and revered friend. There is a vivid portrait of her in the adult Evgeny Pasternak's biography of his father, *Boris Pasternak: The Tragic Years 1930–60* (London: Collins Harvill, 1991), pp. 14–15.

3. The damage was caused by the demolition of the nearby Cathedral of Christ the Saviour, detonated and razed to the ground by the authorities in December 1931 (and rebuilt in the 1990s).

During the whole time I spent there before going to spend three days in Leningrad, it was impossible to get anything from the house committee, since neither window-glass nor any of the other necessary materials were available anywhere. Besides that, Zhenia needed to take all the furniture with her (except the Rosenfelds' cupboard) when she moved house. It was difficult to furnish this enormous area with the pathetic little items we had hurriedly got hold of for the tiny apartment on Tverskoy Boulevard. I'm telling you this so that you can understand my bewilderment when, on my return home four days later, I found the place unrecognisable, and in particular the room that Zina had set aside for my work. All this she had done on her own, with the single exception that the windows had been put in by a glazier. Everything else she had done with her own hands—the sliding doors on cords, the repairs to the mattresses which had completely fallen to pieces with collapsed or missing springs (one of the mattresses she turned into a divan). She had polished the floors of the rooms herself, and cleaned and sealed the windows for the winter—herself. Furnishing the apartment was made easier because the Neuhaus parents (both of them about 85 years old) had left Zinovyevsk (Elizavetgrad) because of the famine, and arrived with all their belongings. They gave us two cupboards, a number of carpets, and an upright piano for Zina (the grand piano that used to live in the Volkhonka apartment was a present to Zhenia from Mama long ago, and has gone to Tverskoy Boulevard).

I only learned that you had sent the monograph when I saw your letter. I checked with Irina who confirmed it. Don't be cross with her or Shura, that's what our life here is like now—and everywhere else too, for that matter. After all, you yourselves merely mention that somewhere or other you've read something or other relating to me, without thinking to send me the newspaper cutting itself. Anyway, the monograph is in my hands, and thank you very much for giving it to me.

Firstly, you write amazingly well. I read your autobiographical fragments without putting the book down; I only didn't like the fourth one, about Lovis Corinth, because of the review you quote. It's the same with your reminiscences about Rilke—you shouldn't have quoted what he said about me in his last letter (*Commerce*, etc.). His remark about the ten-year-old schoolboy at the station is worth including, because that's life and fate, it's a general remark which touches the reader. The same goes for Tolstoy's first reactions quoted in your memoirs. They aren't praise, but words spoken at Khamovniki, the unselected, living, randomly reported sounds of a very distant recollection. But as regards the same things in your chapter on Corinth and at the end of the Rilke chapter, they're an entirely different matter, they are close in time and begin to look like a testimonial to yourself based on other people's letters of recommendation. There was no need to do that; it's all somehow rather petty.

Among your paintings that I didn't know, I liked the portrait of Einstein best (your best work, I think), followed by Liebermann and Hauptmann. Besides those, the portrait of Rilke is particularly important to me. Wonderful works. It was also pleasant to remember a number of pictures, like the dray-driver on the frozen road, 'By the Samovar', and others—and all the Tolstoy pictures. But the monograph, like the autobiographical memoir, is spoiled by one unexpected feature which I'm at a loss to explain. This isn't a particularly nationalistic collection of sketches and portraits—why did you include so many portraits of Jewish men and women, who as models are not special in any way? Some of them are ugly, others grotesque, and the choice of them is so incomprehensible that it begins to look like some hidden thesis. As if you wanted to prove something.

Of course, it's no business of art to limit itself to depicting what is 'beautiful'—that's the fate of people like Bodarevsky.[4] You can, and you must, depict everything. But in that case, you have to present all these things somehow differently: more personally, penetrating further in some sense into the depths and distances of art itself, with more technique, more freedom, and more eternal significance; whereas in your case, they are often the most banal and superficial of your works, in other words the least creative part of the range of what you have thought through and achieved. I repeat—I know why you drew them, but I don't know why you put them in the monograph. It would have been more complete if it hadn't been so comprehensive; and the fact that you failed to understand this, again distressed me. You should have confined yourself to what you liked and had depicted energetically and with sympathy (such as all the Tolstoy pictures), without including all the rest which you had depended on to support yourself. Perhaps there was some pressure here—but at your age and in your position you could and should have ignored it, even if you had once profited by it.

The composition of the book, which anyone would suppose had been your own responsibility, is a puzzle. It's impossible to work out how you view yourself, and where you see yourself. This absence of any firm viewpoint wouldn't damage you in any way, on the contrary, it would elevate you, and I know that in actual fact you don't have any such fixed viewpoint. But then this feeling is contradicted by the sumptuousness and elegance of the edition, which gives an impression of certainty rather than doubt.

---

4. N.K. Bodarevsky (1850–1921), a mediocre painter and member of the Wanderers (Peredvizhniki) group of artists.

If I thought for a moment that any of these considerations had anything what-ever to do with your own essential quality as an artist, I shouldn't be voicing them for fear of upsetting you. But all this is something we can talk about calmly and almost joyfully, because our talk boils down to those childlike qualities of yours that have always rejuvenated you, and still do.

One of these qualities is your everlasting habit of talking about your 'tacti-cal error', exaggerating the burden of family cares, the machinations of envious rivals, etc. Even if such talk were well-founded, in other words if it were true, I still believe that adverse circumstances, persecutions, lack of recognition, and the like, would only hone a sharper and smoother edge to the unity and form of one's talent, which is in some sense homogeneous and integral from birth onwards. Whereas in your own case, the lack of consistency in your taste is so marked that it could only have been preserved and developed by great happiness in your life, and personal success that lulled caution to sleep.

Don't answer me at length, it would waste your time and strength, while a brief answer would be painful. Don't look for any 'secret and noble' reasons for the rarity and laconic brevity of my letters: such reasons did once operate, but now they no longer apply. The only real reason is the ever-growing difficulty of conversing with anyone whatever, on any topic whatever. That's also the reason why I haven't done anything for over a year now; I must get down to work.

I sent you the telegram because I had a frightening nightmare. Everything is much livelier and more expansive, and I'm much less dominated by family mat-ters, than you think.

I kiss you and Mama warmly. Thanks for your letter.

The next letter was delivered by hand, by Boris Zbarsky.

Boris Pasternak to his parents and sisters

24 November 1932. Moscow.

My dears,

Tomorrow Boris Ilyich is leaving, and I've sent my greetings and kisses with him. When I saw him after he had just come from seeing you, he told me what you had said: 'If they would only send us a photograph . . .'

I'm sending you three photographs of Zina, not one of which has come out well. The closest is the small cut-out from a large group picture at the dacha, with the head of her younger son just included in the picture. It was taken five years ago, while the big photographs are from the summer of 1930. Zina is very good-looking, but her outward appearance is very vulgarised on both pictures. It's how chambermaids get themselves photographed, and I didn't want to send you these pictures, particularly the smiling one. She's very well built, with good features, her best ones being her lively (black) eyes and her teeth. With some idealisation towards a classical type, one could build up her likeness from Aunt Klara, or one of those two sisters (the dark-skinned one) who lived below us at Molodi—I've forgotten their surname, but one of them had a boy with a face like that family friend who used to visit on festival days.

Of course, if Zina had been unattractive then nothing would have happened. But if she had merely been beautiful, everything would have ended as it had begun, relatively quickly and abruptly. Or—if you were to doubt (quite fairly) that break-ups can happen quickly (however desirable that may sometimes be)—I'll put it differently.

If Zina had merely been beautiful, and if now, after the end of the first fever of passion (which has already lasted two years) I had wanted to part from her, and for some reason wasn't able to do what I wanted, I should feel unhappy, secretly irritated, and so forth. Yet I have never been so calm and happy as during the last few weeks. I feel so good, simple and natural with Zina—as if I'd been living with her since my childhood, had been born and grown up with her. She has many things in common with me, she even bears a certain resemblance to me. While being entirely a product of the (military) bourgeoisie of petty-gentry origin, she has also been proletarianised by the extraordinary events of her life, her musicality, and the hard-working, industrious core of her strong (but quiet and wordless) temperament—in the same way that all this happened, for other reasons and on different foundations (a bourgeois background and art), in you, Mama and me. And so I encountered in her a lot of things which in us were regarded as specifically Pasternakian, but in essence were much more widespread and socially explicable. The only difference is that words and moods play almost no part in her make-up, being replaced by actions and real situations. I fuss over her much less than I did with Zhenia, not only because I love her perhaps more than I did Zhenia (a thought I don't want to admit), but also because I always treated Zhenia almost like a daughter, and always felt sorry for her. I can't conceive of a situation where I would feel sorry for Zina, she's so much my equal in emotional experience, the age of her blood, or whatever.

Zhenia is much cleverer and more mature than she is, and perhaps better educated too. Zhenia is purer and weaker, and more childlike, but better armed with the noisy weapons of her quick temper, demanding stubbornness and insubstantial theorizing. I have to confess that many of Zhenia's bad qualities come from me. But, carrying on the comparison, I'd say that while family life was a school for both of them, raw as they were in different ways, life with me not only brought Zhenia some undeniable benefit but also did her a lot of harm, while life with Garrik[5] only educated Zina and spiritually enriched her. (Although these two schools were astonishingly alike, in spite of the difference between Garrik's character and mine.) Their closeness is evident from my continuing friendship with Heinrich Gustavovich, however hard it may sometimes be for him.

He's a very contradictory person, and although everything settled down last autumn he still has moods in which he tells Zina that one day in an attack of misery he'll kill her and me. And yet he continues to meet us almost every other day, not only because he can't forget her, but because he can't part from me either. This creates some touching and curious situations.

Garrik's elderly parents have come to Moscow and are living with him. Both of them, particularly his father, are very fond of me (as I am of them, of course). This goes so far that when they want to influence their son (he never practises at all, because his talent ought to have earned him a world-wide reputation, and since this hasn't happened, he more or less doesn't care about anything), this 85-year-old man comes on foot to my flat, only to ask me to exert my influence on Garrik (if I agree with his arguments). And here, in conversation with this wonderful old man, I discover how completely I've forgotten my German and how such an earnest conversation in German exhausts me.

What an extraordinary family! The father is German, the mother Polish (she's Szymanowski's[6] aunt), and the two of them talk French together. Pavetti, who made their acquaintance at my flat, recently began going round regularly to see them. Zina and I dropped in once and found the conversation going on in four languages, because Pavetti was talking with Garrik in Polish.

I think it's the first time that I've written to you in this tone about all these things. Please congratulate me on this and let me congratulate you too. I'm afraid of tempting fate, but it looks as if everything has calmed down, and I should be happy if things could always stay the same for me and my nearest and dearest; there's no need for anything better.

The only thing that still remains a problem for me is little Zhenionok. Although one can't compare his present state with last year's horrors (he lives with his mother in a cosy little apartment, and I always find him full of mischief and even just a bit too depressingly silly; what's more, he loves his school, where I had

<hr>

5. Heinrich (Genrikh) Gustavovich Neuhaus, Zina's first husband.
6. Karol Szymanowski (1882–1937), a noted Polish composer.

some trouble getting him a place in mid-year). But it isn't only his moods I'm interested in. He's a child, and no judge of the resources available to him, which are only being half-used. We could be doing a lot more for him, if only Zhenia didn't set herself against it—pardonably, because of her odd sense of pride. It's not enough for him to be brought up by her alone. He ought to get in the way of spending more time with me. I often go there, but when I'm there, as ever, I become too diluted by the atmosphere of Zhenia's demanding and inflexible world, which little Zhenichka breathes the whole time anyway. Being with me would mean coming to see us on Volkhonka, because that's the only place where I'm entirely myself, natural and real.

I understand the painful complications that the boy would have to encounter in the person of Zina, as a fact of life. But he's already once succeeded in overcoming this same trauma, when I first met the two of them on their return and took Zhenichka to visit us, still on Tverskoy Boulevard, and he met Zina and the boys. Not only was he longing to see them again the next day (granted, he mainly wanted to see me)—he was even ready to discuss the idea of coming to live with us, and look on it positively.

But although Zhenichka coped with this visit and all its ramifications at once, in a very healthy way, Zhenia roundly condemned it and forbade all such visits in future. Since then there have been no more, and major benefits for Zhenichka's emotional stability have now been lost.

He hasn't got depressed as he did last year, and, I repeat, his mood is perfectly cheerful; but when, for the twentieth time and in his presence (technically unavoidable), I repeated my request to Zhenia to let him come and see us and visit the boys, I realised to my sorrow that he separates out Zina (who is completely innocent, incidentally) and views her, or tries to view her, with Zhenia's eyes, as the woman who has injured his Mama. This is a backward step from last autumn, and although it's a painless one for him at the moment, it may leave a needlessly bitter mark on him in the future.

When I press Zhenia to overcome her views and remove this obstacle for the boy—in other words, to let him come and visit me—she refuses, saying that this is madness and that no-one in his senses would support me. The very things that seem to me pedagogically beneficial and necessary, she believes will damage his development.

And when I appeal to the example of the Neuhaus family (the older boy Adik—Adrian—without asking anybody, dragged his nanny off to visit Zhenichka on their way back from play-group, and then came with her to visit him a second time)—the father visits his children, the children visit their father, they see both of us, the tragedies lived by the adults aren't carried over to the children—when I raise all this, she says these aren't human beings at all, it's a madhouse, Zina's not a mother, we must wait and see how the children turn out when they grow up (it's true they're less pampered than Zhenichka), and so on and on.

She's absolutely unfair as regards the Neuhauses (what sort of a thieves' den they live in is apparent from the way that Pavetti and Olga Alexandrovna are drawn to their circle); but she may be right—in the sense that she knows something better which she is actively providing for Zhenionok. It's precisely because I admit this possibility that I haven't turned my requests into demands, so as not to disrupt Zhenia's plans. But, as I say, it's only this that continues to upset and worry me.

If you have any thoughts on the subject, that are not on the side of Zhenia's opinions, and if you would like to write something to her about them, please do it in the kindest and least upsetting way for her, and make it look like a chance comment, not inspired by me. Do it in the same heartfelt way that you have always talked with her. I don't know what she's afraid of, the silly thing.

As for Zina, you'll grow closer to her spontaneously, because she's a plain, warm-hearted, guileless person, and no matter how you choose to approach her, it has to be done in an upright way, without any tension or over-familiarity, and also without any sort of formality.

I embrace you warmly.

Your Borya

Actually, you don't have to do anything about Zina. The only right approach is a free, honourable and natural one. She was deeply hurt by last year's dramas, and wanted to write to Papa then, but I wouldn't let her. That would have harmed Zhenia.

I've no time to read over what I've written. You can see how much I'm risking. It sometimes seems to me quite likely that one day, someone will have a use for my letters, and to my shame, my sloppy verbosity will be exposed.

[...]

In response to the enclosed photographs of Zina, Leonid wrote:

She is certainly very good-looking, and even more beautiful in real life, because she is simple and natural [...] I just imagined her as rather larger—judging by the photograph, it seems to me that her physical type is not large, but rather elegant [...].

About Boris's last three letters, he commented:

[...] they are so full of substance, so crammed with the burning questions of your life and fate (and my own too—for example, where you criticise my monograph, and talk about my destiny etc.) [...].

He summarized the content of each letter in succinct 'epigraphs'. For the letter analyzing the monograph, he suggested '*Who then, O Lord, if not I; and when, if not now?*' His implication seems to be that the Jewish content of his monograph was not dictated by the publisher Stybel, but was his own response to Hitler's antisemitic propaganda.

For the letter describing life with Zina:

I would place as an epigraph the following thought, from a letter of Boris Pasternak's to me: '... because I regard life as such an immeasurably subtle creation of chance and grace, that bursting into this complex construction with words of advice is simply dangerous.'

He regrets that Boris has too little sense of humour, which would have helped in family situations.

Pavel Ettinger's descriptions of Boris's public readings, which are frequently sold out, prompt him to

... congratulate you on this; but, as I've said, I'm not in favour of this kind of success. A writer, a poet, ought to be—like Jehovah—invisible and legendary, both to his *valet de chambre* and to the crowd, the mob, which can often applaud or boo him for a few kopeks. In a word, be very sparing of how you display yourself, and don't be carried away by this sort of material gain: only your literary, artistic work is valuable and meaningful. [...]

Finally, he agrees that Boris needs to be more involved in Zhenichka's upbringing, and says he has written this to Zhenia himself, more than once.

Boris's reply (below) is central to an understanding of his attitude to contemporary life at the time when his collection of poems, *Second Birth*, was being published. The generally accepted critical misconception is that the collection was a 'full acceptance' of socialist actuality ('You are nearby, you distant lands of socialism'). However, under this letter's cover of irony and barely opaque circumlocution, Boris roundly discredits the prosperity described by the Soviet press and professionals travelling abroad (not excluding family friends like Zbarsky and Levin). It is all a lie, a 'non-existent actuality'; 'the Apocalypse that you escaped from long ago has only become more complex and hopeless'. Boris clearly senses immediate danger to himself, and the possibility of a violent death.

Unfortunately two pages from his letter were lost (or intentionally destroyed by the Pasternaks in Germany). The unexpected transition of the concluding sentences, referring to the consequences of the First World War which determined the political situation in Germany and Russia, suggest that the lost pages referred to Hitler's success in the July and November elections.

Boris Pasternak to Leonid Pasternak

27 December 1932. Moscow.

Dear Papa,

I'm worn out by the burden of my 'authority'—false, evil and mythical: it makes my life impossible. That's the only reason I've taken so long to reply.

Thank you very much for your letter. What a pity if the cut-out from the group photograph has been lost. I'll ask Boris Ilyich too. You ask me what sort of a woman Zina is, small or elegant or something different? She's my height, and I'd describe her as rather tall. You see how misleading the smiling photograph is—her playful, sly look very naturally led you astray. Anyway, thanks for your letter.

But I should have started by thanking you much more for the Westermann offprint.⁷ First of all, I kiss you and congratulate you for the mere fact that so many pages of the monthly magazine are devoted to you and your work. The reproductions seem to be very good ones—aren't they? I get a very instinctive, direct impression of your happy and harmonious use of colour, as one usually only can by looking at the original canvases; and I'm delighted by it.

But I didn't like the article, of which (having seen the reproductions) I had expected so much. It's not sufficiently sober or objective, it doesn't have that

---

7. Carl Meissner, 'Leonid Pasternak', *Westermanns Monatshefte*, 1 (September 1932), pp. 213–220.

respectful austerity that you deserve. It's dominated by a kind of un-authoritative familiar chattiness; being written about an artist, it talks of art as if it were some kind of birthday party. The writer was a fool, and there's nothing you can do about that. It's all the more gratifying that despite all his celebratory outpourings, the works reproduced rise above his congratulations.

Apart from the neckties, for which of course I thank you very much, Lydia Alexeyevna[8] told me that you are still carrying on working, with ever-increasing boldness and success. What a wonderful man you are, and how I envy you! What a joy it must be to be near you and see all this. It's probably a great support to Mama, and perhaps Lida and Zhonia too, and Fedia. And I envy them too. Yes, I know, I know it all, I can imagine it all—(I do read the newspapers—I started reading them recently).

But do you have any conception, far away out there, about what's going on here? I don't think so. By the tone of your letters, it seems to me that you imagine things to be incomparably more normal than they are. Inspired and incorruptible newspaper correspondents probably reinforce your view, together with such brilliant, responsible, immortal and independent eyewitnesses as B.I. [Zbarsky] or L.G. [Levin]. But that Apocalypse which you long ago escaped from has only become more complex and hopeless.

I can guess what led you to give me and Zhenia the advice you did about little Zhenichka's upbringing: partly my complaints that he doesn't come to see me, and perhaps partly the unsatisfactory nature of his letters. Your admonitions to me are all meant half-seriously. In other words, if the situation were not to change (and one shouldn't in any circumstances insist on that), I would have to spend more time at Zheniochek's than my life allows me to. That would be absolutely impossible.

Perhaps naïve Soviet philistines like B.I. or L.G. live like that, are able to live like that; their belief in rationality safeguards them against posthumous responsibility and the presentiment of great catastrophes. You should ask them a bit more about that. They know a lot, and will tell you a lot. As for me, there's one thing I long for in relation to Zhenichka: that he should one day find out, and as soon as possible, how much I have loved him and still do. And with time I'll have a chance to achieve that. There's bound to be some random event which I'll have to seize on and make use of. Meanwhile there's no possibility of forcing anything. When I tried to send him to visit you, in the face of all your crises, I wanted to make life easier for him. I wanted to preserve him from those strange possibilities which I invariably accept when they relate to me, and which I'm trying to teach

8. Lydia Alexeyevna Bakh, a family friend and historian of the labour movement.

myself to regard as acceptable, if I haven't already succeeded. I failed to do that for him. What do I have left now, but to wish that he was with me, so that I could press him to my heart and bring home to him the living strength of my anguish, which has no faith in any sort of safeguards for the future, is not offended by anything, and blames nobody?

I am going to work—it's through work that I obtain forgiveness from the gods, influence my destiny and foster my own fearlessness. Work brings me closer to the absolute, the only solid ground in the groundless universe; it's through work that I fix my boy firmly in space, and incline certain forces in his favour.

Ah, you really can't imagine what my existence is like. You warn me against becoming overgrown by family life, and you miss the mark, no matter how subtly I understand you (even as regards a new baby). It's as if you were warning me against catching a cold—as if that were the gravest risk I ran. You lucky, lucky man. That's why you have humour, and I don't. It was probably Aunt Asya who wrote to you that I was humourless and over-serious.

But to come back to facts. Zina guards me jealously from contact with family routine—she won't allow a breath to touch me that might interfere with my solitude in my room, which she personally polishes with a foot-cloth every morning, and she grieves as though I were unfaithful to her when I'm obliged to listen to hundreds of people and read dozens of manuscripts, in our terrible famished time, when another person's misery deprives you of all your rights and turns you into an enslaved listener, until—driven mad by the constant repetition of these sacrifices—you become convinced that this compassion can do no good, nor bear any fruit beyond making you yourself barren. And then you refuse to take notice of anyone or anything, until that leads to some crass mistake which frightens you.

But it wasn't those obstacles that prevented me from working; I accepted them precisely because I couldn't work. I couldn't—despite the fact that my circumstances are unusually propitious, I'm reasonably well-off, have a good understanding with Zina, and the two boys live here almost noiselessly, having been taught by their mother not to disturb me, without violence to their will, gently, without ice and darkness, without mutual bitterness. I couldn't—despite having the strongest of urges to work. I couldn't—because that conditional reality which people like B.I. imagine and discuss, doesn't exist in the world, and art can't occupy itself with what doesn't exist, even though at present that's what it pretends to be doing.

Finally, I myself should have realised that I'm blind or superficial and inexperienced, when not only the critics and B.I., but Irina and Shura and Garrik and people close to me have all started telling me that I'm narrow-minded, out-of-date and short-sighted. And the thousands of roubles I've been paid oppress me, and the terrible forbearance of the authorities, and the evidence that I'm recognised—oh, yet again you've got a wrong idea of me if you think that I walk onto the stage like a conqueror, like some Mogilevsky or Sobinov[9]—no, I would go on stage as if I were Zhonia appearing before a fifteen-hundred-strong State Choir, all made up of familiar faces (this reminded Aunt Asya of Rasputin)—and if they had started attacking me, I wouldn't have defended myself. There wasn't any money at the time, and I had to get to Leningrad. And when they paid me there for Leningrad and Moscow, I suddenly discovered that Anna Akhmatova was dangerously ill and had absolutely no money, and I had difficulty persuading her family to accept the 500 roubles that I should have brought home (but there was a little more left over).[10] But your advice is right, it remains true even outside the context of artistic careerism which is foreign to me, and I hasten to assure you that I follow it; I am exceptionally—indeed unacceptably—natural, and that itself strikes weak people with no moral imagination as some special kind of play-acting. All that is so depr[essing . . .]

[. . .] [Two pages missing]

With those words to Zhonia, I should like to kiss her and Lida and Mama and all of you goodbye, and end this letter. But since Shura will probably not write to you for some time, I'll tell you about him. They've returned from the Crimea, Irina is better, but Shura hasn't put on any weight. Little Fedyushka is coughing again and keeping to his cot (little Zhenichka, too, is almost transparent and very skinny; his pleasure at starting school is over now, and he's lonely there, though they've treated him kindly).

More about Shura. They're working a lot. He's morose and bored, and although he hasn't aged, as you wrote somewhere, he's thin and rather unsociable, because even he is your son too, not somebody else's, so the general hopelessness and joylessness and all the rest can't fail to leave their mark on him—after all, he's not a rhinoceros.

And how about me, perhaps you'll ask? Well, where did that explosion come from, which changed us and hurled us about so? In the summer of 1930, when we no longer had any strength to go on living, and I succumbed to that temptation,

9. Alexander Mogilevsky (1885–1955) was a well-known violinist who had played with Rosalia Pasternak; he emigrated in 1922. Leonid Sobinov (1872–1934) was a distinguished opera singer.
10. For details about Anna Akhmatova's life, see p. 43, n. 1.

I thought that we wouldn't see 1931 or 1932, we'd die in the winter, and then if little Zhenichka had survived alone with Zhenia, you would have taken him in and they would have been spared.

But we all stayed alive, and Zina and I are happy, and no fears frighten us, but my heart often aches for Zhenichka (and would ache even if he were with me). But this, it seems, is all just my raving.

Oh, unhappy life! But something causes me to be like this, something without which I wouldn't have anything else, neither eyes nor hearing. Look at what that mad 1914–1918 war did! And now it'll soon be 1933 (I can't bring myself to wish you a happy New Year)—and mopping up will take such a long, long time yet, that one day, some time around 2014 perhaps, people will realise that the war, despite its four-year root, was really a hundred years' war.

But I know, I know how terrible things are with you too, and my heart bleeds: poor, poor, utterly innocent German children, poor German *Mittelstand*,[11] honest, upright and brilliant! I weep and bid you goodbye.

Your Borya

In an attempt to dissipate the dark impression cast by the last letter, Boris wrote to apologise for his 'excessive emotionality', drawing an idyllic picture of Zhenia's life with Zhenichka—an idyll immediately undercut by his request for money to spend at Torgsin, the chain of state shops selling scarce goods for foreign currency. Zhenichka was suffering from malnutrition, vitamin deficiency and boils. Fresh fruit and other essential foods could only be bought for him at Torgsin.

Boris Pasternak to his parents and sisters

4 January 1933. Moscow.

My dears,

Forgive me the somewhat excessive emotionality of my last letter—I touched on too many topics—I'm afraid it may have upset you. My Zhonia, how I long to see you! But one can't say anything with words, not because they are powerless (—if not in words, how could one say anything?), but because there's too much of everything, you can't encompass the whole, yet only the whole is alive and astonishing.

11. 'Middle class'.

When everything in the world is made clear, and people rediscover how to live, and they calm down, and there are artists again, then it'll be possible to write letters; but at the moment, tasks and destinies aren't allocated, or facilitated, or delimited. Nothing can be carried through, and the last wafting of something resembling life is still to some extent preserved in an absolutely unattainable whole, which one can't even make use of, it's so generalised and distant; in that whole, over which world politics is cudgelling its brains. Details died long ago. Details lie, and amaze us with their anachronism. And yet the whole of life is in its details. That's the sort of time we live in!

I've just been to see Zhenia. Their place is bright and clean. Two tiny, tiny rooms. How wonderful they both are, to live and survive!! Zhenichka read aloud to me from *The Mysterious Island*,[12] holding his chin in his hands. He read about the pirate ship flying up into the air, and how the people on the shore fished out the broken fragments; and he was reading this prose like lyric poetry, solemnly, in a mournful sing-song voice; and his profile was very beautiful, with a trans-figured kind of beauty, almost capriciously refined. And Zhenia sat opposite him, cleaning her palette—clever, sad, friendly and understanding. And when I went home (well, how could I have been remotely humorous?), I thought, here they are, just as I had always wanted them to be—no, a thousand times more wonderful, but precisely in the direction that I wanted; and it's sorrow that has made them so, my sorrow and theirs, and the fact that I'm not preventing them from being natural, as I always used to prevent them with my constant jealous criticism, always fearing that they might displease someone or other.

[…]

Has any more money come in for me apart from Zhenia's sum which isn't being touched? If so, get it transferred to Torgsin—Zhenichka has boils again, but it's not serious, this request is just by way of a luxury.

Leonid Pasternak to Boris Pasternak

11 January 1933. Berlin.

Dear Boryusha!

[…]

In a few days, Anatoly Vasilyevich [Lunacharsky] will be returning home; I've met him frequently during this visit. And Natalia Alexandrovna,[13] whom

---

12. By Jules Verne.
13. The actress and theatre director Natalia Alexandrovna Sats.

I met at a soirée; I've started painting her portrait (she's very beautiful!) [...]
They're very fond of you and said a lot of nice things about you, which always
makes us very happy. Incidentally, they say that a five-volume edition (?!) of your
collected poems is being planned. [...] I laughed at this in all sincerity: 'What
do you mean, five volumes?', I said in surprise—'as far as I know, he's only produced a few slim booklets?!' [...] But we think it's true, and so we congratulate
you and wish you the very best of luck. [...] I showed him (and lent him) my
monograph. [...] He thought it would be highly desirable and very possible
for the People's Commissariat for Education to acquire a certain number of
copies (at least a hundred, I should think). [...] He asked me to note down
for him the essential details about the price etc. I wanted to give him the book
[...], but it turns out he has masses of books he's sending off separately, and I
(knowing how books get sent and how they arrive [...]), decided on what he
also thought was the best course: for you to lend him your copy for a couple of
days. [...] So—this is my request (and I don't expect it'll be very difficult)—
when he rings you up. [...]

Of course I'm sure—I know—that nothing will come of this, but it's my duty
to try everything—after all, it's disappointing that the book isn't available in my
homeland, but only abroad where I'm a stranger . . .

I wrote to Shura a few days ago, and now I'll say it to you too—we know very
well, we understand more than you think about the wonderful tales that the
Pepas and Lyovushkas[14] tell us about how you live, and it's all the more depressing for us since our position, like yours, is—temporarily, I hope—a desperate
one, but I can say definitely and with assurance that we have to be cheerful and
confident that things will certainly get better. [...] We have to devote ourselves
resolutely to our work—you in particular mustn't let your creative power and
drive weaken. [...]

In your last letter you ask us not to be upset, and apologise for upsetting us
[...], and you end your letter with a description of how you visited Zhenia, and
how Zhenichka read *The Mysterious Island* to you [...]—in short, you wallow
in your soul's torment over pictures like this. [...] So here's our advice and our
plea to you (after all, it's not hard to imagine how your own home surroundings,
Zina, etc., appeared to you when you returned home from Zhenia)—don't perform this kind of vivisection on yourself and others! For God's sake avoid such
scenes, don't return to your old life, fly high above everything, be strong, so that
you can steer your ship along a true course, after all the grief and misfortune
you've lived through!

14. Another reference to B.I. Zbarsky and L.G. Levin (see above, p. 13, n. 22; p. 140, n. 30).

[…] Have you really not had enough—your lives are already so full that in order to work, to be creative—you have to tear everything up, or preferably—free yourself. […] I know, I know how difficult that is. […] But you must, with gritted teeth—you must! […] Forgive me for writing to you about this, you understand everything perfectly well yourself—but that's what a father's heart does to one! […]

Boris did not reply to his father's request. In some alarm, Leonid wrote to enquire, and Boris—still hoping for a friendly meeting with Lunacharsky—reassured his father with a telegram:

4 MARCH 1933. MOSCOW.

GESUND DANKE TEILNAHME BORIS
[HEALTHY THANKS SYMPATHY BORIS]

But on the very next day, unwilling to prevaricate any longer, he wrote openly to his father to explain why Leonid's desire for an official purchase of his monograph was out of the question. He begins by describing Lunacharsky's recent vitriolic speech to the Union of Soviet Writers, and refers explicitly to some aspects of the Soviet apocalypse, the introduction of bread rationing and of passports tying people to their place of residence. His father's congratulations on the publication of his collected works, originally planned in Leningrad, are brusquely negated—the edition has been censored, and *Safe Conduct* attacked for 'idealism' (an accusation tantamount to branding him a counter-revolutionary) and cut from his volume of collected prose. *Safe Conduct* remained banned in the USSR for the rest of Boris's life, and when he asked Gorky to defend the publication of his collected works, Gorky's refusal deprived Boris of the opportunity to complete the prose novel he had begun.

Boris's insight into the kinship between German Nazism and Russian Socialism is remarkable for its time.

Boris Pasternak to his parents
[Original in French and German]

5 March 1933. Moscow.

My dear Papa and Mama!

Forgive me for not writing for so long—somehow I couldn't manage it. I don't know how I can speak to Lunacharsky as you ask—it's fearfully difficult, and I can't bring myself to do it. A man who's had a stroke and is half-condemned to death, grown old and changed, who makes a public speech about playwriting in front of an audience of writers—a speech full of hatred and menace, a blood-thirsty revolutionary speech, when he's practically at death's door. I listened with horror, and with inexpressible pity for him. It would be difficult for me to go to him—besides, they say he's ill again. Perhaps you might ask Shura.

You were too quick to rejoice about my collected works—they've been banned. What's more, a few days ago they prohibited the second edition of *Safe Conduct*, dedicated to Rilke's memory. Although all these unpleasantnesses are trivial compared to the way people live here, I'm still going to write to Gorky, however difficult that too will be.

[...]

As I've often written to you, I sometimes feel as if I'd gone mad or was having a bad dream. The imposition of passports is going to hit me too, bringing the two women into collision—so far they've both been my dependants, and I've been supporting them equally. What's more, Zina's aunt is living with her; she'll probably be evicted, and has nowhere else to go. Garrik is already in trouble. And our neighbours—the Frishmans and Praskovya Petrovna—are living in fear as well. There have already been a lot of agonizing problems with bread coupons. And yet writers are made much of. How do ordinary people manage?

Soon it will probably become impossible for us to correspond, with growing suspicion on both sides. That's why I'm writing more openly than ever before, saying exactly what I mean—so that in future, if this letter reaches you and nothing happens to me, we can confine ourselves to mutual enquiries about our health. More wholeheartedly than most, I welcome any attempt to allow people to live like human beings at last—here most of all, since all the tribulations we've endured were inflicted in the name of that very aim. And however strange it may seem to you, what oppresses me here and in your society there is one and the same thing. It's the fact that this movement is not Christian but nationalist, carrying the same danger of degenerating into the bestiality of fact; it's lost touch with that age-old gentle tradition that breathes transformations and premonitions, rather than mere observations of blind emotion. These are twin movements, on the same level, one provoked by the other, and that's what makes it all the sadder. They are the right and left wings of the same dark night of materialism.

When you answer this letter, just let me know that you received it and tell me about your health. And let me know whether I should go on writing to you in Russian, or whether German would be better. If it became difficult for us to correspond as we have done so far, I should start writing to you in bad broken French, for practice.

Have you read the biography of Wagner by Guy de Pourtalès? Do.
I have lots of plans, I'm desperate to work, but all this is no use to them—it's
'idealism'.

I kiss you warmly.

Your Borya

Thanks for the press cutting. They always get through.

Hitler's election as Chancellor in March 1933, and Stalin's escalating reign of terror,
made correspondence between Germany and Russia very dangerous. Accordingly,
Boris's next letter is written in French, except for the last paragraph (in German) and
the valedictory wishes (in Russian), to smooth its passage past the censors. Boris
was surrounded by instances of political persecution, and frequently he had to intercede on behalf of one friend or another. In the spring of 1933 he was trying to help
the wife of Neuhaus's cousin Viktor Blumenfeld, who had been arrested and imprisoned. Blumenfeld's wife was denied a passport, and she and her little daughter were
threatened with eviction from their Moscow apartment. Through Yakov Agranov, a
high NKVD[15] official whom Boris had met at Mayakovsky's house in the 1920s, he
managed to get them permission to remain in Moscow.

Boris Pasternak to Leonid Pasternak

[Original in French and German]

22 April 1933. Moscow.

Dear Papa,

Thank you very much for your postcard of today and the previous one. [...]
Don't be cross with Shura and Zhenia for their perpetual silence: their absti-
nence at present is more pardonable than it used to be. They're perfectly well, as
are Zina and I and all of us.

Little Zhenichka adores you. 'Dedushka'[16] is almost God for him—a higher,
inaccessible authority. He never comes to see me. So far, nothing has changed
with the women, and the two of them ignore one another.

I embrace Mama, and you, and all of you, and poor Fedia, with all my heart,
as tenderly as may be. I have no fears for you; it's only our separation that makes
me suffer.

15. The People's Commissariat for Internal Affairs—the State security ministry.
16. 'Grandpapa'.

Human fate gets no easier, and there's no decrease in the number of misfortunes. There are always occasions for me to put myself out to help one unfortunate or another. I waste my time interceding for them, and do almost no work.

The ridiculous fact of my writing to you in such bad, even faulty, French is not only due to my having thoroughly forgotten my German, but also for another reason. During these times of enhanced presumption, it is the language of Rilke's last book (*The Orchard*) that arouses in me the memory of his great discretion, the modesty of his genius. I'm saddened at having unlearned the language that I loved so much, but don't be upset by that.

Write and tell me whether I may write to you in Russian; in German I'd be ashamed for every mistake. Forgive me this letter, stupid and vacuous.

I embrace you warmly

Borya

Hitler's election victory and the anti-Jewish decrees that followed it—particularly those forbidding Jews to work—called into question the Pasternaks' plans to continue living in Germany. Leonid's reply (now lost) evidently raised his and Rosalia's concern not to be a burden on their son-in-law Frederick, who had his own family to care for, as well as other dependants. This accounts for Leonid's cautious allusion to his being 'attracted' by an exhibition in Paris. The family were in fact considering emigrating to France. The reader has to become increasingly alert to covert messages blandly implied in these and subsequent letters. The French part of Boris's reply below attempts to warn his father against the kind of severely negative reception his return to Russia might provoke.

Boris Pasternak to Leonid Pasternak

[Original in French]

8 May 1933. Moscow.

Dear Papa,

I'm waiting impatiently for the sealed letter[17] you promised me.

Obey your own laws, my dear ones, don't accommodate yourselves to your fears about our laws:—write openly all that you want to say about your moods, your opinions, your affairs, your health, and Fedia's too. Has he still got his job?

Aunt Asya is worried about your silence, I'll reassure her for you.

17. As opposed to a postcard.

Our wish for you to visit us goes along with the hope that your presence might smooth my family problems and reconcile the opposing parties. You will certainly guess at the magnificent reception (rather more disagreeable than pleasant) that the government here would prepare for you.[18]

In any event, before taking any decision, think well about the increased difficulties which would complicate your life here; being unused to them, you would feel their strangeness twice as strongly.

[Original in Russian]

14.V. This letter has been lying around for a week, and now I've received the sealed letter I was waiting for. And since you've written in Russian, I'll answer you the same way. Yes, our arrangements!

If you were to come here for the summer, then obviously not one of the questions you raise in relation to Fedia could arise in connection with me. Not only because I'm your son, but because, although I'm responsible for a total of 7 dependants, that doesn't weigh on me morally in the slightest. It would be all the more natural and joyful for me to have to look after you as well. And of course, if you're having second thoughts, that's probably not because you are unsure about me—it's more to do with the end of the French part of this letter.

I can easily imagine how you must be drawn to the portrait exhibition in Paris. I have long been attracted—and I say this without any sort of diplomacy—by the highly talented humanity and courage of French culture, striding like air and light through all the endless petty discomforts of our actual lives, and I'm very sorry that I not only don't know French as well as I'd like to—I almost don't know it at all. Yes, all this is extremely stupid, and perhaps the only way for everything to come right eventually is through some kind of mechanical resolution.

We're staying in town for the summer—though it would be far more interesting to know how you yourselves will arrange to spend it. I can imagine the cyclopean difficulties of all this.

Thank you very much for your letter. I'm sorry for this hurried and incomplete one. In future I'd like to be guided by your instructions on what I should write, what's interesting for you and what you ask me about.

Your Borya

---

18. The implication is that the reception would be hostile; a point cryptically repeated in the next paragraph.

Boris Pasternak to Rosalia Pasternak

4 August 1933. Moscow.

Dear Mama,

From your letter of today to Elizaveta Mikhailovna, I conclude that the long letter I recently wrote to you all hasn't reached you.

What a pity. One thing you might have gathered from it is how, year by year, it's growing more and more difficult to correspond with the West—not because of any external obstacles, but for the most immediate and innocent of reasons.

The children are growing up, my separation from you is entering its tenth year, topics arise that you don't know the first thing about, people and circumstances change, and even before they changed you didn't know about them.

In the letter that went astray, I also told you something about little Zhenia. And big Zhenia too. It's a pity, too, because the letter was less gloomy than usual.

And now I have another long letter to you in front of me, which I started a week ago. Instead of finishing it, I'm sending you a shortened one in its place.

On the 30th I visited Zhenichka at the children's camp. They only let parents visit once a month, for educational reasons. On the day I arrived, visiting wasn't allowed, it was against the rules, and I just wanted to have a talk with the teacher, but Zhenichka (whom I had recognised from a distance in the woods, and had been watching for some time) suddenly saw me. So we did see one another. But more about that later. He had been missing his mother badly all this time. A friend of hers who had sent her daughter to the same camp had visited the girl illicitly in the middle of July, and when she came she saw Zhenichka too. She found him so desperately homesick that she herself insisted that his mother must visit him, and she came the very next day.

But the female teacher who met her persuaded her not to let her boy see her, on the grounds that he had made a sudden breakthrough and it would be a bad idea to upset his calm mood at its very outset.

So I did see Zhenichka, but only spent a very short time with him, just an hour and a half, since it wasn't a visiting day. That will be the day after tomorrow, on the 6th, when Zhenia is going to see him.

His freckles are always like a knife in my heart. Where does he get them from, and why has it all turned out like this? There is, in all this, an extraordinary and utterly inexpressible sense of 'what for?', which torments me constantly, making me lose all sense of reality and suffer what one might call spiritual vertigo. All right, I grant it, I have sinned greatly—towards Zhenia, say, or God, or Fate perhaps (I can't say more precisely what exactly my sin has been—it's not the present one, not the sin of rupture, but an earlier one—that our marriage was too superficial, too randomly decided on). But in that case, I ought to be the one expiating all this. Why does my child have to? If you only knew how acute and perceptive he is, how much better (inwardly) than many others! But there's no question that his little face, splattered with spots—so splattered that the film of them obscures the expressiveness of his eyes, such deep and speaking eyes—no question that this is already weighing on his destiny, and will do so even more heavily in future. No question that the dingy cobweb spreading over his well-cut face is already tangling up his relations with other children, his situation in school, and so forth.

Perhaps all this is just my imagination—anxious and pathologically jealous for his welfare. To me it seems to be objective. But whenever this sort of feeling has prompted me to take any kind of action (treating his freckles, say, or giving him a tougher and more manly upbringing, not so isolated from other children), Zhenia would always interpret it as a sign of morbid imaginings, which for some reason hurt and exasperated her.

It was, after all, partly our disagreement on these points that brought about our separation, by making it completely futile for me to take any interest in Zhenichka and his upbringing. But maybe I'm wrong about that too; maybe all I used to do was panic and make despondent comments, without giving any positive directions or genuine advice, and that would inevitably irritate her. Perhaps Zhenia was right—perhaps she still is right, if we look at everything in a cheerful and optimistic light.

But it seems to me that he never really gets on with other children, and that's not good for him. It's nothing to do with the things that people in your country are so concerned about,[19] because there are more than enough boys and girls of his blood everywhere—at his school, and even at the camp. Rather, it's a question of the contradictoriness of his own qualities, enhanced and complicated by fate, example and circumstance, in other words by his upbringing. And here again, there's no point in criticizing anything; his mother Zhenia is made of unbending stuff. So it might have been possible to change something, if little Zhenichka were living with me. I won't list the advantages that that would bring him, because if you added them all together they would probably still not outweigh the fact that a bad mother is better than a good stepmother.

19. This refers to Zhenichka's Jewish origins.

So—I saw him, and without letting him see it, I wept inwardly. There's no doubt that he is a piece of something that is terribly strongly mine; fearfully, indescribably dear to me; yet within him and around him, everything is so alien to me!

That was how I returned home from seeing him. And on the way I imagined myself talking to you, and I asked myself where I had found all those illusory good things that had filled my last letter to you—the letter that now seems to have been lost. Where did I find it all, how did I dream it?

And, of course, in this state of mind I tumbled down to the lowest abyss of hypochondria, particularly since Zina, with her salutary effect on me, wasn't near me (that day she was on duty at the children's camp at the dacha, where Fedia was among the boys she was looking after). By the way: he's feeling very well, he's got better, although at the beginning he was far more homesick than anyone else, just as Zhenichka was.

Mama, your tone is unfair when you insist that no-one ever writes to you both. People are very busy, and writing properly would take volumes.

6. VIII. 33.

Yesterday I saw Irina and Shura. It seems that they also wrote you a long letter about three weeks ago. So it's clear that letters are getting lost. Like me, they addressed their letter to Lida. I'm sending this with no hope that it'll reach you.

In the lost letter I wrote a lot about myself, not about personal matters but in wider terms. I also wrote about Zhenia.

I'll repeat the most important things. Zhenia has coped well with her grief of last year. She's succeeded in setting herself up really cosily on Tverskoy Boulevard, and has collected a large group of friends and acquaintances, interesting and worthy people from various social circles. Once that had happened, her relationship with me also moved to that cordial and friendly footing that I had dreamed of during the worst days of our separation. At that time, through the dark shroud of last year, I could see nothing good in the future. Now it has all happened, in the best way possible. Zhenia's present life is better than anything I could have expected. (Have I written to you about this already?)

She has made palpable progress in her drawing. Only now has she learned to convey a living likeness in a drawing, in a very special and dignified (if timid) manner. She has done portraits of a lot of army officers in the high command (the whole academy). She also did such good portraits of Pilnyak and Vera Inber that I myself offered to sit for her for one of her commissions. Her picture of me was not only better than the one by another engraver whom you know, Pavel Davidovich,[20] who worked on me at the same sittings: it was better than anyone's who has ever drawn me, excepting of course you alone, Papa.

She's very friendly with Pilnyak and the composer L. Knipper (a nephew of O.L. Knipper-Chekhova, the actress at the Moscow Art Theatre).

During the winter my concerns were inevitably of a financial kind, and understandably focused on Tverskoy Boulevard; and that sometimes hurt Zina's feelings. There were actually some very nasty moments to do with sharing out our ration coupons, and that sort of thing. Last winter, with the famine and the housing shortage, you can imagine how hampered I was at every step relating to the issue of passports, the tightening of the rationing system, reviews of family numbers and dependants, norms for housing, and other aspects of everyday life. One after another, every new decree filled me with fears for Zhenia's tenure of her flat, the security of her rights, etc. We've only recently become officially divorced.

Our frequent disagreements (and I'm intolerably brusque and rude on such occasions) upset Zina and made her feel insecure.

Now I'm alone in the flat with her (the children are at summer camp, and she has sent her aunt away), and once again, as at the very beginning, I have seen the measure of her exceptional genuineness, as a human being, a woman, an unfulfilled artist, a worker and an ally. It would be stupid to write about my feelings for her or hers for me; let me just say that they are appropriate and natural, in other words justified and understandable.

Recently, without any adverse effects for Zhenia, we officially got divorced, and in a few days I shall register my marriage to Zina.

Not long ago, her first husband Hein[rich] Gust[avovich], the boys' father, developed a sore throat, and the side-effects and complications showed it was diphtheria. The complications were acute and developed into polyneuritis: he developed an ulcer of the larynx which made him start to lose his voice, and then his limbs became half-paralysed. Yesterday he was taken by ambulance to the physiotherapy institute for long-term treatment. These cases are always protracted and difficult to cure. This is particularly frightening for a pianist, and we're very worried about him.

At the end of August I shall almost certainly leave for the Azerbaijan region of the Caucasus for two or three months. I don't want to go at all, since I've finally managed, with great difficulty, to get down to work, and have only just acquired

20. Ettinger, i.e. 'Pavetti'.

a taste for it. What's more, it wouldn't be friendly towards Zina, who purposely shared my summer in town with me (otherwise she might perhaps have joined her children at the dacha) so as to make it easier for me to work. But I'm telling no-one but you about this—the subject hasn't been raised between us, and she hasn't made me any reproaches of this kind. On the other hand, the arrangements are very tempting, both financially and in many other ways. Furthermore, the Caucasus is the Caucasus, and this would be a Caucasus that I don't know, not the Georgian part but the land of Shamil[21] and other places (Shemakha, Gori, Karabakh, Gandisa, etc.). I'll probably go.

From the point of view of Zhenia's opportunities, her acquaintances and connections, you'll be intrigued to know that her interests coincided with mine as far as this expedition was concerned. I was the only one to regard them as mutually incompatible; she, with her adherence to principle and rejection of convention, saw nothing inconvenient in our joint presence in a single team, as 'mere acquaintances'. The point was that before approaching me, the organisers of the expedition included her in the party, as an artist, at the suggestion of Pilnyak who was a member of the team. It goes without saying that travelling like that would be absurd—no kind of explanation could smooth over the gratuitous offence to Zina, and any explanation would be indecent when real life hasn't stepped in to replace it. For instance, my friendship with Garrik, our visits to each other, and my closeness to his old parents, all seem perfectly natural, needing no explanation, because that's the way things have been from the start, having been (as it were) wrested from life with our own hearts' blood. It hasn't worked out that way with Zhenia—she's too direct and rigorous for that. Little Zhenichka, for instance, not only doesn't come to see me on Volkhonka; over the winter he has become frozen into a rigid denial of Volkhonka—an embittered feeling which isn't his fault, but which will cause him quite unnecessary suffering in the future (in his conception of my life, and his distorted view of his own place in it). But I've stopped interfering in this; I don't criticise Zhenia's independent world, and maybe she's wiser than I am.

I should like her to make the trip. It would do her a lot of good. But it looks as if I will be the one who goes, not her.

One could go on like this for ever. I embrace you all.

Your Borya

---

21. Shamil was a nineteenth-century leader of Chechen resistance to the Tsar.

The girls might write to Zina while I'm away. She'll be lonely, and she's a wonderful person.

Zhenia's portrait of Boris has survived. Although it was done in unfixed charcoal and has deteriorated over time, it still remains one of Boris's best likenesses, and has been frequently reproduced.

Boris did not travel to Azerbaijan, but Zhenia joined the expedition to the tea plantations of the Caucasus.

Shortly after this letter, two postcards sent by Boris reached Munich but were subsequently lost. In the letter that follows, Leonid Pasternak discusses them in detail, making plans to return to Moscow or Leningrad, where they had been invited by Leonid's sister Asya Freidenberg and her daughter Olga. As a precaution, 'Dresden' is used to denote 'Leningrad', to avoid arousing the German censors' suspicions.

Leonid Pasternak to Boris Pasternak

8 September 1933. Munich.

My dear Borya,

I have before me your last three letters: a postcard of August 9th, another one of the 18th, and your very long (15-page) letter of the 4th, re-dated 6.VIII two pages later. I'll start with your last postcard of the 18th (you got an immediate reply to your telegram, and one long letter, you say, has gone astray. That's very, very vexatious and sad. Particularly for us, since we find your letters so precious and interesting!).

[...] So now, despite my inappropriate mood, I don't want to put off my letter to you any longer, otherwise you'll worry needlessly about our health etc. Since we're on the subject of health, we're all, all, as well as we could possibly be, thank God. In Berlin, when two people meet and one of them asks: '*Wie geht es Ihnen?*', the other replies '*Gesundheitlich—Gott sei Dank*',[22] presuming that the accompanying sour smile speaks for itself.

So I'm starting with your latest postcards. I confess I had been sorely missing your letters, and wondering why you had stopped writing. (It turns out that you had written, and the letter seems to have got lost; but why should letters of a family kind go missing?) At the end of the postcard, you write that you have received

---

22. 'How are you?' 'As far as my health goes—fine, thank God'.

a letter from Olya, 'and when I had read it I began to fear that you have too little confidence in us'. [...]

I don't know what Olya wrote to you, but it's not difficult to guess from that sentence of yours. The fact is that I had been writing to her about the 'cyclopean' tasks and problems (as you characterised them!) which have beset us old people at this inappropriate time of our lives, forcing us to make all sorts of different plans against all kinds of eventualities, in view of the unexpected and ominously unpleasant turn of 'fate' [...]—in short, it was along those lines that I was writing, and also mentioned the steps we had taken towards travelling to Paris, etc.

In reply I recently received a letter from her [...] in which she earnestly begs me, with the most moving arguments, to abandon all our plans for setting out on our travels again, at our advanced age, and going to Paris, wandering around, beginning a new life, and instead says we must come and visit her. The Dresden Academy, she says, will appoint me a professor, and we'll have an apartment, a home of our own ('since you won't want to be a burden to other people'), that we'll 'have a pension', that times are getting better; in a word, it was such a touching invitation from her—and of course, from your aunt—that it moved me to tears. I answered her a few days ago [...], saying that if the worst came to the worst and I wanted to take up her suggestion (having, as I do, little confidence in her optimistic notions), I could only consider it if I got an official invitation of some kind, and that, of course, takes time. [...]

I wrote that we had not, and could not ever conceive of, any doubts about your and Shura's filial willingness to help us in our old age. But as regards your phrase, Boryusha, about 'confidence', I said to her, as I say to you now—how can we have any confidence, when you—especially now—are burdened with the cares and anxieties of two families, while Shura's situation is even worse and he must be having difficulty making ends meet ... Anyway, let me respond to the sentence you dropped into your last postcard about our doubts or our 'lack of confidence' [...]—you'll understand, of course, that in such an important question one can't base oneself (in my art too, after all, I'm a 'realist') on one sentence on a postcard, or the words of your first telegram: '*kehrt zurück*.'[23]

To finish with your last postcard [...], while your news about Zhenia's artistic journey to the Georgian tobacco plantations, and about her success as an artist, made me very happy, your final factual sentence: 'I probably won't go to Azerbaijan' saddened me. You know how much I'm in favour of every trip you make to new places, and how I want you to travel. See how good your Caucasian

23. 'Come back'.

poems are! One can't help feeling refreshed. But you can't suck material out of your fingers.

Also on that postcard, before the sentence about our 'lack of confidence' in you, you wrote: 'Are you sufficiently aware what precious and welcome guests you would be—in my home, or Shura's, or Zhenia's, or Olya's, wherever you want'. Of course—we're quite aware of that! The opposite would be sad, and unmerited. […]

But this last long letter of yours, I'm afraid, is full—if not of moping, then of invented, silly and pointless worries and self-torment—all about Zhenichka's freckles and such fanciful nonsense. Of course, as a poet you're entitled to talk like that, and you're very good at it too. And you're absolutely right to say that it's getting more and more difficult to correspond with the West as the years go by, and not just for external reasons but for the most 'innocent' and immediate ones; 'the children are growing up, and our separation is running into decades'. Thank God—on September 18th it'll be exactly 12 years. […]

Boris Pasternak to Leonid Pasternak

[Early October 1933. Moscow.]

Dear Papa,

[…] The girls and Mama are right in their suspicions: life is still hard for most people here. Even if that didn't affect your own lifestyle, you couldn't escape observing things, even at home. On the other hand, Olya is right too, thinking as she does mainly of the moral atmosphere. The wrongness of your ideas about life here even reflects on what you say about your pre-conditions. Arranging your departure may involve you in lengthy preparations, but I don't know what there would be to prepare at our end. What you say about an official invitation, I think I've understood. As soon as your wishes are clear and to some extent settled, let me know and I'll arrange for you to be officially invited.

Warm thanks to all of you for the presents, letters and cards for Zhenichka's birthday. He had a very jolly day. Apart from Fedia, he invited a school-friend called Strelkov, a very nice, bright boy.

A few days ago I had to go to the offices of the Chief Public Prosecutor of the Soviet Union, to make representations on behalf of a relative of Neuhaus's. It was during the hours when Zhenichka attends school, and in the same district. Nowadays he goes to school alone, and I walked him there for the pleasure of it. His school is at Patriarch's Ponds, at the corner of one of the most prostitute-ridden alleys, with cellars, potholes in the road, cockroach-infested bakers' shops, tumbledown courtyards, hooligans, street musicians and cut-throat knives. He's in the afternoon group, meaning that he goes to school after one o'clock and returns home at six. His school premises horrified me, but I was very, very pleased with Zhenichka himself, and untroubled about him. He was a bit reminiscent of Sashka Freidenberg as a high-school boy—the imperious rapidity with which he hailed boys on their way to school, often even boys he didn't know at all—'allies', he explained to me, that is children from his own district, as opposed to boys from the neighbouring area beyond Sadovaya who might beat them up.

It's also very nice in our apartment. All this is thanks to Zina's labours. We don't have a maid, and Zina has sent her old aunt off to Tula, so our living-space (the old studio and drawing-room) is very un-Muscovite, spacious and empty. In view of its size and cleanliness, and also of the fact that Zina is responsible for two boys aged six and eight, it's simply amazing how she copes with everything—housework, travelling to the store on Myasnitskaya, cooking, looking after the children, and sewing for the whole family. In addition, she takes the younger boy (Lyalik) to kindergarten every day, and fetches him again at six o'clock. Her boys are getting an enviable upbringing. They not only spend time with her in the evenings (over games or lessons), but help her around the house too—sweeping, washing up, and so on. Naturally, she never finds time to play the piano. She gets very upset when she hears about my delight in this domestic aspect of her life, commenting that such cook-housemaid's laurels aren't flattering to her and she's not trying to earn them; on the other hand, she doesn't make a tragedy out of our present way of life either. Financially speaking, we wouldn't have any difficulty taking on a maid, but in summer we were forcibly struck by how much pleasanter and healthier it was to live on our own without any domestics—not that they pilfer from one, but even if they just help themselves as much as they please to butter and oil and other good things . . . Besides, it would be a shame to give up the peace and quiet we have here now.

If I were writing you a postcard, I should confine myself to the statement that all's well with us, and thank you on Zhenionok's behalf and thank you, Papa, for your letter to me.

So regard this letter of mine as a postcard, and keep well.

I embrace you warmly.

CHAPTER NINE
1933–1935

In late November 1933, Boris went to Georgia, as part of a writers' delegation, to obtain linear glosses for a selection of Georgian poetry in translation that he was preparing with Nikolai Tikhonov. The following letter refers to untraceable news reports, which Boris also describes in a letter to his friend, the Georgian poet Titsian Tabidze, as follows:

'On the basis of some telegraphic reports in the English and Scandinavian press, my father has written to me of his happiness at my trip and . . . congratulates me (!) on it. You see, it seems that he read that I had headed (!!) a writers' delegation, which then continued its journey to the Crimea (!!!), and Papa was particularly pleased with my speech (!!!!) which I had given in Tiflis (!!!!!). My dear friends, is there any point after this in our doing any work, when each one of us, without affording the least pretext, can suddenly become the victim of some mysterious speculation, not only unreal as regards ourselves, but unreal in the light of its own aims?'

There is also no record of the account of an episode at the excavations of Pompeii, described by Olga Freidenberg in a letter to Leonid and retailed with relish by him.

Boris Pasternak to Leonid Pasternak

8 December 1933. Moscow.

Dear Papa,

I'm answering your letter, and also, through you, the separate letters I've had from Zhonia and Lida. Congratulations to Lida on her bold and unexpected début, and my thanks to Zhonia and Fedia for this new proof of their invaluable solicitude (which hasn't yet reached me but which you mentioned in your letter); and thanks to Mama for her touching message to Zina. Zina wants to answer her, but I don't know whether she'll find the time. Although she has recently enlisted the help of Praskovya Petrovna (Pasha that was), who's now working for us, she still has both her boys ill with measles, and what little leisure time she has left I take up with my chatter and foolishness. The reason that I squashed my congratulations and thanks into such an ugly mess in one sentence at the start of this letter is that you and Mama are under something of a misapprehension, which I'd like to put right as quickly as I can.

Probably every person is like a motif or melody, which habitually suffers distortion over the course of one's life, being put out of tune by one's idleness or forgetfulness, or cut short by circumstances; only in rare cases does one suddenly come to hear oneself again, and take possession of oneself. It looks as if I'm a tune to be whistled, a trivial tune in a major key, because my essence—throughout all that has happened and has yet to happen—is happiness, the fact of happiness, with its lack of content and lack of reason, and often contrary to reason. All this I experienced once again, in a new form, in Georgia, a wonderful country to which I'm linked by the literary traditions of the last century and by personal friendship with two or three people in the present one. On my way there, I was conscious not only of my own age but also of that of my travelling-companion and later my hotel room-mate—Nikolai Tikhonov. But I'd shed all such feelings by the time I left Georgia, having wallowed in bottomless baths of wine daily for two weeks on end.

Do you know what a litre is? It's two ordinary-sized bottles. Well, at one dinner near Kutaisi (geographically just above it), over the course of 10–12 hours, 30 of us drank up one hundred and ten litres of red wine. It's excellent, it can make you unconscious but you never feel sick from it, and the only problem with that kind of intake is that you have to keep running *pour le petit*.[1]

That was at the end of November. I left Moscow covered in snow, but in a garden on a mountainside above the Rion (where the vino-electric power-station I've just described was set up and cleared away in a single night), the last roses were still in bloom. That was in the centre of ancient Colchis, on the ruins of the ancient Mount Ea, the goal of the Argonauts' expedition, where archaeologists locate Medea's palace, near the newly-constructed Rion hydroelectric power-station (a real one this time).

All that happened on one evening, but there were 14 evenings like that, in various places. You'll get an idea of them if I tell you that for these excursions, my best friends Paolo Yashvili and Titsian Tabidze used to get hold of a separate railway-carriage with a conductor, who uncoupled and coupled it up en route according to Paolo's instructions—the only added complication to these manoeuvres being that he used to sleep through the night-time stops and leave

---

1. i.e., to relieve yourself.

us at the wrong places, so it was an absolute miracle we never crashed or got run into by a long-distance express.[2] Needless to add it was (to paraphrase Rimbaud) a *wagon ivre*[3]; in the morning, on our way back to Tiflis, I was so light-headed I wanted to strip off and chuck all my clothes out of the window, replacing them with new ones. Only the knowledge that you can't buy anything in Tiflis confined me to throwing out my cap, and then buying a replacement. All my other exploits were similar—except that I was the only non-speaking member of our delegation—I not only didn't make a single speech anywhere, I didn't even take part in a single official meeting or 'working reunion'.

And so you'll understand how I was reduced to embarrassed laughter by your congratulations, and what a thunderbolt it was to hear that all this had appeared, as you tell me, in the English press. Are you really not teasing me, did you honestly read something somewhere? No, truly, aren't you making fun of me? If so, then it's even worse than you think, and it's only the light-heartedness I brought with me from Georgia that can help me to skate over and forget this shameful misunderstanding.

You probably don't realize how awful it is. If I'd invented some kind of Chlorodont, say, which was advertised everywhere, or if I were trading in contraceptives or stockings, then I could understand it: my situation would be one of exalted chivalry and nobility compared to what it is now. Or I could have understood it if rumours were being spawned about Gorky or Gladkov, Fedin or Pilnyak—even Ehrenburg.[4] There are some grounds for invention there, those people have done something, and whatever it is they've done, all the tales would have had something to attach themselves to. But I myself am nothing more than a myth and a tale (against my will and with no help from me); I've been invented by my well-wishers so that they can go on inventing things about me. I'm far from overestimating what you tell me, I understand how tiny this mythical observation was: it's the Chekhovian fame of the man knocked down by a cab who finds his way into the daily chronicles. But all the same, why does the X or Y who's the subject of this sort of fantasies have to be me, rather than some other member of that crowd who do nothing and say little—surely there's no lack of them? So there's my first refutation.

2. Titsian Tabidze was a Georgian poet and friend of Boris Pasternak, who translated his poetry into Russian. Arrested during the Great Terror, he was executed in prison.

Paolo Yashvili was a Georgian poet and co-founder with Tabidze of the 'Blue Horns' group of Symbolist poets. He welcomed the Revolution and wrote celebratory poetry, as well as translations into Georgian of Pushkin, Lermontov and Mayakovsky. In 1937 he went to the headquarters of the Union of Georgian Writers and blew out his brains.

3. A 'drunken carriage'.

4. All were prominent Soviet writers who enjoyed official recognition.

Secondly: I wasn't too pleased (to be honest) (and incidentally, I haven't told Zina what I think) at Mama's comment that she doesn't know whether Zina too, like Mama, had enjoyed public success (those aren't Mama's actual words, I'm using my own for conciseness, but that was the sense of them), and that although Mama's tragedy was the greater, she still understands Zina, and let Mama's example, incommensurable though it is, serve as a support and reassurance for Zina.[5]

Comrade parents, I recognise this tone, and I've never liked it. It's a completely trivial point, but it used to irritate me in the past, with Zhenia and Zhenichka, in other words whenever I wanted my nearest and dearest to see you, great and wonderful people that you are, in your true light, without those commentaries which you employ to recommend yourselves to their attention and emulation. Because—however great you are in your own essence, which is self-evident to anyone, beyond any need for words—your personal philosophy of life can sometimes be quite petty.

Hence our frequent misunderstandings, for which I myself may sometimes be responsible. I don't remember what I wrote to Lidochka, but it's most unlikely that I was complaining about the difficulties of my life or Zina's. I may have simply described them—not only without sighing about them but without claiming any merit for overcoming them, since it isn't I who overcome them—they somehow overcome themselves. And Zina copes with real life without any feelings of tragedy or exaltation, though it sometimes leaves her exhausted. She manages to do this partly because she's very light-hearted and young in spirit, and partly because she's lived through so many experiences of all kinds since the age of 14, not imaginary but real ones, one hundredth part of which would have sufficed for some women and given them enough to remember and talk about for their whole lives—so many experiences that she simply lives, if I can put it that way, rather than having an attitude to life, whether tragic or otherwise. That's utterly characteristic of her, but that same lack of ponderousness is there in Zhenia too. Even little Zhenichka knows life better and more deeply than we used to when we were children.

Was ist der langen Rede kurzer Sinn?[6] I always find it unpleasant when you try to express an emotion or thought of yours, in itself perfectly valid, by choosing some absolutely unsuitable, extraneous kind of petty-bourgeois sermonizing,

---

5. Rosalia will have been referring to her own musical career, as a solo pianist with an international reputation, which she gave up on her marriage. Zina was originally a pianist-pupil of Heinrich Neuhaus.

6. 'What is the point that I'm making at such length?'

inevitably false and always hypocritical. This is an arbitrary form which has nothing to do with you, and it's all the easier for me to say this because it sometimes puts me in an embarrassing position, not before Zina or anyone else, but before the truth.

Now the episode at Pompeii (which Olya wrote about)—I like that, that's quite a different matter! Because that's a part of reality, with all the air and the ruins and confusion of epochs, far and near; because it's a fortuitous event, a fresh and fleeting one, which appeared in order to disappear again.

Don't be angry with me. If I've allowed myself this mild criticism, it was only in order to gladden you, because through it you'll see and remember what you already know quite well—that despite all we've suffered and will suffer in the future, we are freer, happier and more independent than you, because we are half-savages and our history has allowed us to be that, without sacrificing our dignity. And to know that about your children and grandchildren will give you pleasure.

I embrace you warmly.

Your B.

[...]

Boris Pasternak to his parents

[17 December 1933. Moscow.]

My dears,

In my usual stupid manner, I said things to you in my last letter that I shouldn't have said, and now I don't know where to hide my head for shame and regret. You'll not only be far from the truth—you'll simply kill me, if you take my trivial and utterly unfounded complaint seriously. For God's sake forgive me. Starting from the ridiculous assumption that one is only impertinent in one's youth, I allowed myself to be impertinent in order to make myself out to be youthful. I love you terribly much, as you are, and wouldn't wish to see you any different.
[...]

I've imported into my life: table wine, walks and a light-hearted attitude to everything. All that's lacking is work. That'll find its way in too, and then everything will be wonderful.

I kiss you hard. Best wishes for the approaching Christmas.

B.

His father replied:

Leonid Pasternak to Boris Pasternak

22 December 1933. Berlin.

Our dear Boryusha!

Today, hot on the heels of your letter of the day before yesterday, we received your postcard, and laughed heartily at it—we were sure that your beautiful (and, of course, interesting) letter would be followed by a message of penitence, as it has been. So now we both swear to you that it didn't offend or upset us in the least. On the contrary, it made us both laugh. [. . .]

So, dear boy, calm yourself and forget it, it's not worth talking about. [. . .]

From 1933 to1936 Boris played an increasingly active part in public life. After Maya-kovsky's suicide it was explicitly hinted that Boris was duty-bound to take on the role of the representative Soviet poet of the time—a prospect which both repelled him and was, he knew, fraught with danger.

His Soviet experiences made him anxious that any anti-Nazi activities of his might endanger his family in Germany. He was particularly anxious about signing an article in support of the Austrian rebels of the uprising of 12–15 February (*Literaturnaya Gazeta*, 23 February 1934), and an open letter welcoming the arrival in Moscow of the Bulgarian communists Dimitrov, Popov and Tanev, who had been accused of instigating the Reichstag fire. Brought to trial in Leipzig, they were acquitted after a brilliant defence by Georgy Dimitrov, which aroused worldwide admiration. André Gide and André Malraux played an active part in their release, travelling to Berlin in January 1934. Boris saw this event as evidence of a real victory of the individual over organised tyranny. The letter appeared in *Literaturnaya Gazeta* on 28 February 1934, signed by Boris Pasternak, Paolo Yashvili, Titsian Tabidze and Nicolo Mitsishvili, who were in Moscow at the time.

Boris Pasternak to his parents

27 February 1934. Moscow.

My dears,

Today is your wedding anniversary. How I should have loved to be with you on this day. And once more, how many years is it that we've been apart! I congratu-late you and wish you good health and a long, long life.

And Fate has decreed that on this very day, Dim[itrov] arrived in Moscow on an aeroplane after his release. How often in recent years I've been restrained in certain of my impulses by thoughts of you. There was a collection for the Austrian workers, I gave 500 roubles and wondered—do I dare, won't that indirectly affect you somehow?

Here I'm being spoiled beyond my deserts. It's just like in my childhood, when I lived in a home created by you and your merits, and through the house, like a draught of fresh air, there wafted everything that was great and significant; when day after day, I saw so many great men coming as everyday visitors; when I could enjoy the company of Scriabin and others as though it were something self-evident; all this, which fate had granted to you, I swallowed down gratis, like some feature of my nursery that I was entitled to.

I don't have any revolutionary merit whatever, nor any social merit either; despite all my admiration of certain aspects of our life today, what I should like would be simply to write good things, quietly and inconspicuously. But that same expansive style of my childhood now permeates my life today—this time with no explanation at all, because it can't any longer be explained away by you, as it once could be. There's the same closeness to everything that's going on in the world; to the best ideas, which everybody is busy thinking through right now, and which for some reason have to be thought through with my participation; the same intimacy with great events, intimacy that I haven't earned but which has simply dropped freely, passively, into my lap. Somehow or other it's become accepted these days that if people want to make the proper arrangements for some event, then I have to be there, or send my regrets, or else somehow my absence has to be explained away.

So when I was telephoned to be told about this man's arrival, and asked if I wouldn't like to have my personal message of welcome printed in the next day's papers alongside Gorky, Vsevolod Ivanov and a few others, I'm afraid I couldn't help yielding to the pent-up excitement with which I'd been following his story. I dictated my message by telephone, simply feeling how utterly inappropriate it was for me, a mere pawn on the moral scale, to be sending my own personal message to such a moral hero. And I addressed it from myself and my friends. Tomorrow I'll regret my hasty action for another reason too: it was written too briefly and not well. I think it was something like this: 'Welcome. In addition to the messages you will receive from all corners of the world, please accept my own and my friends' expressions of delight. The past year has been illuminated day by day by your courage. Thank you for your example, your living proof of the miracles that can be wrought by a sense of duty. You have placed us under a lifelong obligation, because you have beautified a part of our memories.' And then my signature and those of three Georgian poets. Reassure me that this is all right, and not unpleasant for you. But don't be afraid that I'll let myself go even more, and forget myself. I am always constrained by you, and I honour and love this constraint, but in this case I couldn't help myself, my feelings were so strong.

Here everyone is more or less well, in other words everybody in my household or Shura's who had been ill with flu has gradually recovered. Only Zina, who got straight up out of bed to start an impossible spring-cleaning job in what is still a whole third of the old Volkhonka apartment, sweeping the dust off the ceilings, washing the floors and windows, and so on and on, is feeling very ill again. I'm trying to persuade her to see the doctors, and I hope everything will be all right.

On my income tax form for the past year, I declared an income of 29,000 roubles, every last kopek of which I spent during the year. Even if there were some possibility of saving, I wouldn't—perhaps—because I'm utterly incapable of it. But there was no such possibility, and the only thing I'm glad of is that, despite my relatively modest lifestyle (apart from good food), I still manage to cope with quite a range of personal responsibilities.

These days I often receive proposals (from the world of publishing, or out of the blue from the Party headquarters in Georgia, or some other place—but with our centralised structure all of this originates from a single top initiative of the State) suggesting that I should radically reorganize my life, simplify it, double or even triple my earnings, shut myself safely away on my own in some ravine on a river bank, free myself from dependence on contracts, print the same stuff again and again as often as I want, etc. etc. To all this I invariably reply that it would be hypocritical of me to pretend that I'm a poor man, and that compared to the average earnings not only of the workers, but even of the most well-to-do sections of the intelligentsia, my earnings are unreasonably and immorally high. And that this income, hard though it may be to get, is enough for me. That I love life and art too much, in all their prosaic reality, and I should feel miserable and empty without them, out there beyond the golden frontier of buying gramophones, American wardrobes, rare libraries, and all that. And I refuse. To be honest, I do it to some extent at your expense, and particularly at Zina's, since she even turns my garments (coats and the like) with her own hands, not to mention her own clothes and the children's; but of course there's a cost to me too. But that's what has to be done, I think; otherwise it would be unscrupulous from all points of view.

It's also true that in avoiding all these temptations there isn't a drop of self-sacrifice, because when I ask for a thousand roubles and they offer me five, and I turn down four, I am giving up the lesser part. The main thing that I live on, the mysterious and undeserved goodwill which still continues to flow down to us from some unknown source, remains with me.

But I've gone on too long, it's bedtime. I embrace you very, very hard, and congratulate you again. Thanks for the postcard. Best wishes to everyone. Reassure me about what's worrying me. Kiss Fedia, Zhonia, Lida, Alyonushka and Charlik.

I'm already getting autograph requests from . . . Argentina, enclosing a photograph of me with the caption in Spanish: *El poeta*. I'm ending this letter on a scrap of my reply in French.

In August Boris participated in the Writers' Congress in Moscow. His speech at the evening session on 29 August was greeted with an ovation. Many speakers mentioned his name and praised his work. By the time of the Congress, the leaders of the Union of Writers and senior figures in the Soviet government had come to regard Boris as the central figure in Russian poetry, representing the highest cultural achievements under Socialism—a view promulgated by Nikolai Bukharin in his official report to the Congress. Boris himself was oppressed by all this attention and saddened by the false atmosphere of the Congress, which he felt had betrayed his hopes.

The next letter covertly refers to Boris's telephone call from Stalin, which related to the noted poet Osip Mandelstam's arrest in May 1934 for his clandestine verses satirising Stalin. Boris appealed, through Bukharin, for Mandelstam's release. Stalin, with typical suspicion, wanted to probe Boris's motives for his intercession. The three-minute conversation was in the nature of a concealed interrogation. A few days after Stalin's telephone call, Mandelstam's sentence of exile at Cherdyn, near Perm, was commuted to residence under supervision at Voronezh. (Some years later he suffered renewed persecution and was interned in a labour camp where he died.)

When Pasternak calls his first translations of Georgian poetry 'sh..', he principally has in mind two recently published poems by Nicolo Mitsishvili and Paolo Yashvili, in honour of Stalin. Boris made the translations in order to help his friends, who were suffering from hostile criticism which was soon to escalate into serious political persecution.

The end of the letter expresses a timid hope of some liberalisation in Germany. Boris uses his father's personal code, 'Auntie', for the German government.

Boris Pasternak to his parents and sisters

Moscow, 23 June 1934.

My dears!

[...]

Today I found [at Zhenia's] these three photographs of Zhenichka. They were taken outdoors somewhere near the Petrovsky Gates (near the Ekaterininsky Hospital, do you remember), by a theatre director called Polyakov, a friend of Zhenia's. Zhenichka is wearing his Pioneer's necktie, in celebration of May 2nd. You can see how covered in freckles he is—they're swarming all over his face like bees on some sticky-faced urchin in a French children's book, disfiguring his otherwise very sweet features. All the same, I'm sending you the pictures. [...]

The one thing that saves me is that everybody treats me very well—people from the most diverse and diametrically opposed sections of society. Last week I even received a telephone call (for the first time in my life) from St[alin] himself. You can have no conception what that means. I didn't even tell Zheniochek about it. One could so easily be tempted to flaunt the fact, without meaning to. If one didn't conceal it, it could give one an unrealistic sense of euphoria.[7]

The most upsetting thing is that I'm simply not managing to do any serious work. I've been translating Georgian poets, but that's not work, though these little odd jobs (pure sh . . !) have kept me in food. When the book is printed—incomplete and rushed though it is—I'll send it to you if that's allowed. But that won't be before the autumn.

I kiss and embrace you all, Dedushka, Babushka, Fedia, my sisters and nephew and niece. I'll write from the country to let you know my summer address.

In some strange way, some sixth sense tells me things may be getting better for you, and the family atmosphere getting more relaxed. I'm alluding to your Auntie.

Boris Pasternak to his parents

2 October 1934. Moscow.

My dear Papa and Mama!

Yesterday we arrived back in Moscow, and I discovered your postcard which had been waiting for me here since mid-September. And how I was worrying about

---

7. A rumour of direct contact with Stalin would strike literary bureaucrats as proof of the poet's special status in Soviet literature. Such calls from the Leader were very rare.

you in Odoevo! What ideas were coming into my head! Anyway, thank God, life and I have so arranged our respective roles, touch wood, that I am constantly prepared for the worst, and claim no right to anything different, while instead Life guides me through an unbroken sequence of happy surprises.

I'll write more about you later on (I was very frightened by Mama's complaints of frequent dizziness, in her letter to Zhenionok). As for me, I repeat—I have nothing to complain of; on the contrary—everything is unexpectedly good.

Travelling was very difficult, as it always has been in Russia, out in the wilds away from the straight highways.

It's been a beautiful summer. I was in the Tula region, not somewhere in the Crimea, yet I was bathing in the river until the end of September. Then, suddenly, we started having morning frosts, and day-long rain turned the roads to mud.

The day before yesterday, at 8 in the morning, we each of us pulled on some 40 pieces of clothing—padded jackets, coats, then great peasant overcoats with huge collars and long sleeves (I myself had nothing warm with me, not even a coat). We travelled in a horse-drawn cart for about 5 hours, then in a train until 8 at night. We were supposed to change at Suchinichi onto a fast train for Moscow on the Bryansk line. Naturally, our train was 20 minutes late, and from the end of our carriage we could see our fast train pulling out, and on it the three 'soft class' seats (equivalent to the old 2nd Class) that we had telegraphed to Bryansk to reserve.

Night fell on that station in the wilderness, and night trains passed with no possibility of our getting aboard, and the stationmaster gently uttered some promise or other that he couldn't keep, and the signalman brought him pillows and blankets to his office, and we dreaded what would happen to us when he went to sleep and we'd be too embarrassed to wake him, when even with his help nothing was working out!

It was the purest socialist Chekhov. You, Papa, probably remember that sort of thing very well from the years when you used to carry Markov's[8] (I think) visiting card to just that sort of office, on the Kursk railway (I expect you'll be surprised at my remembering such things—I was younger than Zhenichka is now). That night on the journey, with the children and our baggage—baggage that we had pared down to only three pieces, in the expectation of difficulties of this kind, but it had proliferated again from three pieces to nine, huge ones too, because of our companion on the trip, the housekeeper at the Odoevo house, with her little girl. Nodding off to sleep, washing in the buffet before dawn, behaving respectfully towards the people there; being forced to make polite, helpless requests to them,

---

8. The first husband of Rosalia Pasternak's sister Klara. He was a prominent railroad engineer.

just like everybody else; the consciousness that despite all your connections and opportunities, anyone else would have been in Moscow long ago—and finally, a sudden explosion under pressure from Zina. A visit to the main-line signal box at the station (you can guess what that would have equated to in your day). Threats of telegrams to the People's Commissar of Internal Affairs if we weren't allowed to proceed straight away; and a train just drawing into the station—eight minutes of chaos with suitcases and bags—the miracle of our departure despite everyone's disappearing in different directions, with me, the porters and the ladies losing each other and all hunting for one another. Since the train guards didn't know what the answer was going to be, they refused to let them board the train, while I was getting place-cards and racing back across the track just before the whistle went. And yet, and yet, all this is wonderful.

But of course, I didn't mean to entertain you with this tale of a night on the road; I wanted to tell you about our easy arrival, I mean the pleasure of the fact that after absence and uncertainty, we found everything at home in better order than we could have dared hope.

Yesterday evening, as soon as I had eaten, I set off for Tverskoy Boulevard. Zheniok had telephoned the day before to ask whether I was back, and to say that they were going to have a bath-day, that is, they were going to heat water for the bath, and I was to come and wash after my journey. When I arrived, Zheniok was in the courtyard in front of the apartment, chopping birch logs (sawn in half) for the bath. He didn't know I was there, and to begin with he didn't see me in the darkness of the courtyard—it was so full of people that he didn't notice the indistinct figure standing not far away. So I was able to watch him splitting the wood. And he wasn't doing badly, the clever boy! When the chopper got wedged in a knotty bit of log, he turned it upside down just as you're supposed to, and hit the back of the chopper against a stone. Wasn't he glad to recognise me!

His Mama wasn't at home—she'd gone to a parents' meeting at his school. He and I spent a wonderful three hours together. They have the same woman who used to work for them on Volkhonka after their trip abroad, and then left—a plump, elderly, tranquil lady called Elena Petrovna; she had come back to them in summer. So Zhenia and Lena treated me to tea, heated the bath for me, and so forth. He talked a great deal and very well about his summer; apparently he'd been fishing, with some success. Once he even caught a big chub and a gudgeon, and they grilled them. Next year he wants to buy a fish-trap.

They've had their apartment whitewashed, and now it's even lighter and cosier. For his birthday, Zhenia gave him (besides books and so forth), her drawing of me, framed and glazed (you haven't seen it). It's full-face, and very good—the best portrait that's been done of me, apart from yours. Incidentally, I came out very well on a picture done in Odoevo by a provincial photographer (an ex-schoolteacher), using what was practically a home-made camera, knocked together out of tattered wooden boards like a street-organ. Or was that just a case made to hold it? Anyway, he used to travel round the villages with it as though it was a performing parrot. Well, that photograph (done in mid-September) and Zhenia's portrait of me are the only worthwhile ones that I know of. I never come out properly, and horrible ugly pictures of me get passed around.

Zhenichka was telling me about you, and your present to him—many, many thanks to all of you. And he showed me your letter, we read it together, and were sorry for his grandmother and Lidok. I was terribly pleased with him and cheered by him this time. There's just one bad thing—the absolutely unbounded adoration with which he envelops me. I mean, the fact that it's excessive. But it's a good, manly, joyful love. Unforced.

Lena (the maid) told me that every evening when Zhenichka goes to bed, he says goodnight to my portrait (the one by his mother) as though it were me, calling across the room 'Goodnight, Papochka'. He knows every detail about the Writers' Congress—he was reading it up in the newspapers (as was Zina at Odoevo), and collecting the cuttings together with Elizaveta Mikhailovna. And suddenly he astounded me by saying 'Oh thou, my Mindiya, Mindiya mine!'—naming the hero of a Khevsur poem (that's a mountainous region in Georgia) that I had been translating in the winter, and hadn't shown anyone. It turns out that it had just been published in Tiflis, and since nobody knew where to find me, they had sent a copy to Zhenia's address. You can imagine how astonished I was, until he explained it all to me. All this happened after he had gone to bed. I looked for the book where he told me—first on the table in the next-door room, then on the sideboard there—but couldn't find it; so up he jumped, and rushed around barefoot from one corner to another, and eventually found it. It turned out that he already knew the poem. It would make the letter too long if I were to quote his thoughts about it. He asked me whom I was more sorry for, the hero or his wife. I answered honestly (that's what I really think) that I was more sorry for his wife. That surprised him. He's on the hero's side.[9]

But I'll go on about this another time, when you've read the poem yourselves. My son's a good boy, it seems to me, and he's growing into my great friend. That's a joy. And he's healthier, stronger, and has put on some weight.

9. The poem relates how the hero, Mindiya, chops down a tree for firewood at his wife's insistence, and thereby loses his supernatural understanding of the forces of Nature.

But we have to transfer him from his present school to a better one. At this one (Patriarch's Ponds and the alleys round Bronnaya, the worst area, full of thieves and prostitutes), older louts from all the blocks around start pitched battles with the schoolboys on their way home—and he's in the evening group, and after all he's only eleven, too young to get into fights like that.

As regards the steel horse, there was a misunderstanding. Papa, you must have seen the photograph and decided that he has a bicycle? No, that bicycle belonged to the amateur photographer who took the picture, an acquaintance of Zhenia, and as far as Zhenionok is concerned it's nothing but a decorative prop.

To round off my account of the boy, I want to praise his mother Zhenia. She's clever and wonderful, she's seen it all through, do you know what I mean? Both she and he. Good for them. But how much that cost us, through all those years! How much more than any normal family! And yet, isn't this the solution to that eternal problem: in order to purify the air in a family, and elevate it to the heights of true Platonic chivalry—one has to introduce a second family beneath it? No, I'm joking, I'm writing nonsense, but I just can't calm down, I got so beautifully, blissfully excited yesterday!

What misfortunes are falling upon poor little Lidok! Why did that happen? She should eat more butter. Meanwhile Zina is now (following Zhenia's example) dissatisfied with me for walking about like a tattered tramp, denying myself comforts and furnishings and so forth; but where nutrition is concerned, I insist on spending all the money we have. You mustn't believe that Zina and I really quarrel—no, I'm only talking about a difference in style. But all I know is this: food and work. I don't need anything else.

And you know what's up with Shura, poor soul? I myself only found out yesterday. He caught some sort of infectious eczema, and suffered with it for a whole month on end. He brought it with him to the Crimea, and it spoiled his whole holiday. Well, he's getting better now—we spoke on the telephone. And Irina can't get rid of her boils.

But Shura's apartment is so smart, you could photograph it for the magazines. And the way he dresses—compared to me, he's just like a foreign aristocrat. Irina too. They should eat more, instead of polishing their floors.

I wanted to write about a lot of things, but I've got carried away by details and haven't told you anything. Write and tell me clearly what's up with Mama. In detail. And—are you all still in your old homes? So the moves never happened?

I'm sending you *The Snake-Eater*—read it. At the moment it's the only copy— a proof. Later on, if my sisters want, I'll send each of them a copy. Share out my photographs between you—there should have been three prints of each, but at the moment I haven't any.

I embrace you. B.

At the same time as this letter, Pasternak sent some photographs, with comments written on the back. One of them reads as follows:

Anton the coachman, Zina with Stasik, and I. 1934. A wonderfully colourful peasant. On the other photograph, the group, he's next to me. He kept asking me to give him a written certificate, believing that Maxim Gorky would then stamp it for him in the office. A certificate to say he's an excellent driver. I totally failed to convince him that no such stamp exists in the office or anywhere else. But you can follow his reasoning: a house of writers, so the head of it must be Maxim Gorky, and I'm one of his subordinates—a departmental head.

Boris also sent his translation of the Khevsur poem 'The Snake-Eater' by Vazha Pshavela, with the inscription: 'To Papa and Mama from the translator. Moscow, 2.X.34. I haven't checked it all, but on a superficial reading I've corrected whatever caught my eye. Please send me Zhonichka's and Lidochka's poems. Are they in German? I'm very impatient to see them.'

Boris Pasternak to Josephine Pasternak

7 November 1934. Moscow.

Zhonichka

[...] I recently received a letter from the family, in which our parents voiced the thought, and sorrowfully accepted it, that we might never meet again. We and they, in particular.

I myself had also started to think this way, and maybe I even wrote to them about it. But recently my mood has been completely different. If they look after themselves, and if, God willing, they remain in good health, I'm certain that I'll soon see them.

If I belonged to myself alone, in other words if I were an entirely private person, I would, even now, set off for somewhere in Switzerland to visit Rolland, and try to invite them there. Or else I'd go to France, and visit them on the way.

But in my position, taking a trip somewhere or other like that means making some sort of a statement, or committing myself to saying something about it on my return. That's why I haven't been able to come to you straight away. Personally speaking, nothing would have held me back, because there wouldn't be any risk or unpleasantness. But indirectly, you would have put me under a constraint, to keep silent about my trip, and that would be an unnatural and impossible task for me in the life that I live.

If I can overcome the obstacles—that is, all the joyful, unexpected and exciting circumstances that surround me every day—and if I can write what I have planned to, in peace and quiet, then next year, if I'm alive, I shall definitely go abroad.

[...]

Boris Pasternak to Josephine Pasternak

27 November 1934. Moscow.

Dear Zhonia,

I'm sorry my last letter was such a placid and vacuous one. But we've lived through such a lot here, and—more to the point—I come to hear about so many mishaps and misfortunes, there's so much I have to sort out, making representations and interceding for people, that some unavoidable curtness on my part is pardonable.

Zhenia told me, to my surprise, that Stella has some of the things you've written. I've just asked to see them, and read them through. Do you remember what you sent her? It was 'So slowly . . .', 'I cannot compose songs', 'Are you waiting?', 'Night Violet', 'Air', '1934', 'Autumn', and 'Cinerarias'.

I found all these poems astonishing. I had expected something more disorganised, spiritual immaturity, a lack of universality in your language, without specific relevance to anyone; some helplessness of taste. Apart from the rare, self-evident triumph, art without mastery of the craft is always displeasing. One is embarrassed for a writer who has ventured into a sphere where more is demanded of him than he has to offer; so that he uses the language of poetry to convey no more than a part of himself, and that a small and insignificant one.

That is not a shadow you have cast on yourself. On the contrary—I am simply amazed by this aspect of your writing. You have a sureness of touch with your themes, a natural turn of phrase that says all that needs to be said; you move within that space between tension and transparency which is the only place where one can say what one wants, in the way one wants to say it. I found all these qualities in you, to a degree that is rare even among fully-fledged creative writers.

If a part of a work of art always bears witness to its creator, you can be congratulated on what it says about you. Behind your words there stands the image of a very serious, noble life. However well I knew you (or thought I did), I have never known you like this.

You simply have to come and see us. When you speculate about possible publication, you're indulging in irrelevant illusions. Firstly, illusions in the sense of false hopes; and secondly, unnecessary ones—in other words, what you're hoping for is not what I think you need.

There's no sense in explaining the first point after the second. But if you want me to, let me just say this. When a person gains a reputation in any area, he acquires authority. His authority is based on the power of hypnosis. As an authority, he is granted the right to pronounce elementary truths. And people listen to them. But it isn't just a matter of hypnosis. People don't resist an authority, because in secret they regard him as toothless. As for his bread, he's won it off everyone else in the battle for survival. That was something he had to worry about in times gone by; it's too late for that now.

All this shouldn't be taken too literally. I mean to say that it's not until we reach the end of the road that we're allowed to talk in a human way. When we start out, we have to fight for that right and win it bit by bit. I wouldn't want to call this a fight—what I really mean is that it's only truly a fight when the fighter doesn't know he's fighting.

That makes the fight what it really is—something challenging in the total originality of its form, not relying on generally accepted forms and therefore initially utterly defenceless. Its contents are reduced to irreconcilable details; its universal thesis amazes one with its naked weaponlessness. With time, this itself becomes a weapon.

What has all this to do with you? Here's what. There's no way that you can force people to listen to your voice, true though it is in spirit and tone, merely because it is true. For you, it's too early for that—you're not an authority.

So, if you want—I won't say, to be published, but simply to be yourself for a certain number of people, never mind how many—then you will have to fight: fight for some truth out of which there flows the truth of your individual poems.

When I ask myself where your chief poetic strength lies, I see once again that it's in your sincerity, the depth and genuineness of the music of your life, its uninvented reality—it's in your life itself. And it's so deep that it forces me to read you like the pronouncements of an authority, obediently catching the nobility and sureness of your style, for all its lack of originality. This is where you do have to fight.

Even before this, when I thought about you, I used to believe that you could and should, without forcing yourself in any way, be inwardly and perhaps outwardly more free. After reading these poems, I'm ten times more convinced of this. Just by listening to them, you can hear the poems themselves tell you where and how you ought to be bolder and more active. Oh, not in literature, not in your artistic manner, and no, no, not in poetry—but in your own personal life, in your relations with other people, behind the double meshwork of habits—those you have acquired yourself, and those you have imparted to other people. That's why, you real poet and real person, I call your literary illusions unnecessary. People for whom literary success can make up for an unsatisfactory life go about these things in a different way. Your own case is much closer and dearer to me: for you, literary success doesn't play this role. So there's no point in seeking it.

12.xii.34

It's excruciating, writing about all this. I almost stopped loving you while writing this letter—I mean, for as long as I was writing it. I don't have time, people prevent me from working. Ultimately, I so need and want to work just now that in all honesty I don't care a scrap about anything else in the world.

And suddenly, in the middle of all this pandemonium, I'm obliged to take up, on your behalf, questions that are more difficult than anything outside of childbirth; and knowing practically nothing about you, basing myself on what may be your exaggerations, I have to pick them painstakingly apart for you, knowing that it's all pointless because it's inconceivable to do it at a distance.

Stella told me you liked my letter and sent me love. That made me very happy, and absolves me from the need to complete this excruciatingly theoretical analysis. This sort of thing makes me inwardly ill. The moral of all I wanted to say boils down to this: You are far richer than your self-imposed limitations allow you to be. You ought to let yourself be bolder, more active, more inwardly expansive in your relations with other people: you would harm nobody by doing so, would cause nobody to suffer, and you'd enable yourself to give those close to you something healthier and more exalted than they are used to from you. I can't be more specific about this, because I don't know anything about you. But in my view, this is the only topic that I can properly discuss with you.

There's one thing I envy you, every day. And Lida. The fact that you can see Papa and Mama whenever you like. As far as this concerns the sort of feelings

I'm writing about in this letter, it relates particularly to Papa. How I miss him—miss the chance of being with this great man, and sometimes reassuring him and reminding him that there's no need for death to frighten him, because everything he used to dream about as a young man has come true, and more; because this remarkable life has happened; all this has been, and now is. What a happiness it is for me now, knowing all this, to have such a man for my father—such a real man, for whom one need feel neither fear nor pity in his old age, as one pities someone who is weak or weakening. For he never has been weak, and never could be.

How I envy you the fact that it's you who tell him all this, and not me. And how you probably underestimate the joyfulness of this opportunity, failing to realize its importance and necessity, both for him and you; unaware of the pain you would suffer if you were parted from him at this time. It's right here, in the midst of this sort of conversation, that you should be learning fearlessness—learning not to be afraid of anything. And after all, what is there to be afraid of, Zhonia, what is there for him or you to be afraid of, when in our case and his—such a man and such an artist as he is—even the inevitable is not frightening? Once again, one can't touch on this sort of thing in a letter. But I do envy you.

Give them a big kiss, Mama and Papa.

Your B.

Boris's painful sense of the constraints hampering the professional poet, as contrasted with the amateur's freedom, in part explains why the hero of *Doctor Zhivago* is not himself depicted as a professional poet.

Josephine's poems were published in Berlin in 1938 as a collection titled 'Koordinaty' ('Coordinates') under the pen-name Anna Ney.

Boris Pasternak to his parents and Lydia

25 December 1934. Moscow.

My dears!

I must write to you at last. Why do I do it so rarely? I'm writing a big prose thing, which is growing in breadth and becoming denser and deeper, and I can't drop it for a single day. Besides, I don't work every hour of the day, I only manage to devote a small part of each day to writing.

And then, after my rest and recuperation at Odoevo, I've become so taken up with my health that I've started taking a siesta in the afternoons, going for walks, trying to get all the sleep I need, and so forth.

Soon it'll be New Year. I don't care whether I celebrate it or not, or how or where. Never have I had less need for distractions, never such a strong wish for concentration and tranquillity.

I'm now the same age as you were in 1906, Papa, when we were in Berlin. You were painting Bebe and Rachel[10] at the time, I think. Just remembering you then strikes me dumb with shock at the comparison. You were a real person, a father of four children, all of them already taking off in different directions. You were the Papa I remember so well, there was no overtaking you on your path. Faced with your image, tall and broad as the world itself, I'm an utter nonentity, nothing but a little boy. I'm the same as I was then, except that I have a broader chest and not a single tooth left. [...]

I'm afraid you may have unsealed and read the letter I wrote to Zhonia at your address. I started writing it when she was staying with you, and didn't know she had left. Who could blame you for reading it? You had every right to. But a lot of things I had written to her alone, in that letter—some of them about you—may have seemed outrageous and upsetting to you. If I had meant to say those things to you, I should have said them all differently. If things have happened as I suspect, then I'm very sad about it, and I won't be at peace until Zhonia or Lida reassure me. And it's all Zhonia's fault! It was thanks to her that I had to descend to such profundities—and that's something I do professionally, elsewhere, as part of my work, and I do it in a different way. And repeating the same sort of analysis in real life, because somebody needs me to, is something I can't stand.

What can I tell you? Why am I writing to you? To say that Seriozha told me about Maliutin, who's 76 years old and working tirelessly and with great vigour? And about Nesterov, who's become a portrait-painter?[11]—Or that we're all well, me in particular? And that we'll certainly meet again, and that I couldn't live if I didn't believe in that?

Here's what I'll tell you, Papa. I wouldn't be bothering you about your pictures of Astapovo or Aldridge,[12] if they were reproduced in your monograph. But they're not.

10. The sisters of Boris's friend Ida Vysotskaya.

11. Sergei (Seriozha) Durylin was an author, art and theatre critic, and a close friend of Boris's during his literary début. Sergei Maliutin was a Russian artist, a colleague of Leonid Pasternak's at the Moscow School of Painting, Sculpture and Architecture. Mikhail Nesterov (1862–1942) was a Russian artist known for the religious themes of his paintings; in the early 1930s he switched to portrait-painting in the officially approved style of Socialist Realism.

12. Astapovo was the railway station where Leo Tolstoy died. Tolstoy's widow Sofia Andreyevna summoned Leonid to draw Tolstoy on his death-bed there, and Leonid took the young Boris with him. Ira Aldridge (1807–1867) was a black American actor who emigrated to Britain and achieved success and fame; he visited and performed in Russia in 1857.

Yet what a delight I felt on looking through it in my search for them! I hadn't leafed through it for some time, and suddenly I received a full broadside from you, straight in my face. What a marvellous artist you are! How much temperament in your realism—that's what art should be, it's like the *Allegro vivace* from Tchaikovsky's 6th Symphony (ask Mama to remind you of it)—everything from start to finish in a single burst of movement.

To compress my judgement into the compass of an exclamation—it seems to me that your most successful subjects have been Tolstoy and Zhonia. And how you drew them! You drew Zhonia in such a way that she gradually grew up according to your drawings of her, she followed them in her life, her upbringing relied more on them than on anything else. Do you feel this too? What is your opinion of yourself, how do you feel about all this? If I were in your place, with such a life behind me, I'd be in the seventh heaven. What a life, what mastery, what meetings and memories!

While as for me, I've realised something—rather late in the day. Nothing that I've written about exists any more. That world has gone, and I have nothing to show this new one. It would be bad if I didn't understand this. But thankfully, I'm alive, my eyes are open, and here I am, hurriedly reinventing myself as a prose writer in the Dickensian mould. Later on, if I still have the strength, I'll become a poet along the lines of Pushkin. Don't imagine that I want to compare myself with them. I'm just naming them to give you an idea of my inner change.

I could say the same thing in a different way. I've become a particle of my time and my nation, and its interests have become mine.

So—I wish you a happy New Year, happiness and health; let's think of each other on that night.

Since one of the girls will probably be visiting you around this time, and Zhonia has just been, that means it must be Lida. If my deduction's right, then— I kiss you, Lidok.

Forgive my hurried letter; they'll be even more hurried in future.

Your Borya

The prose writings mentioned in this letter were not completed and have not survived. They probably represented a continuation of the ideas embodied in 'Luvers's Childhood' and 'A Tale'.

Leonid answered Boris's letter at once. Everyone including Josephine was very pleased with his analysis of her poems. Her writing was in full flow at the time; since the spring, she had written 80 poems. 'And such beautiful poems!'—Everyone

laughed as they remembered the oft-repeated family saying: 'And it's all Zhonia's
fault!'

Leonid Pasternak to Boris Pasternak

8 January 1935. Berlin.

[...]

Let me pass on to—what I could call your very special letter, a wonderful
one full of profound meaning. In it you first tell us that you're very busy with a
new prose work [...], and in this context you write: 'I've realised something—
rather late in the day. Nothing that I've written about exists any more', etc.—you
probably remember those brief and pregnant lines of your new 'credo'. But as I
believe that you'll remain yourself, as before, and will still be honest and sincere,
which has always been your most attractive quality and the essential source of
your strength, besides all the other qualities of your talent and creativity—I was
particularly happy to read what you said about 'hurriedly reinventing yourself as
a prose writer in the Dickensian mould'. God grant you may! Your prose writing
has always been particularly interesting and dear to us; your tastes and ours long
ago came together in Dickens's *Tale of Two Cities*, to say nothing of Pushkin. So
you have our blessing on your new prose work!

[...]

Boris Pasternak to his parents

Moscow, 14 March 1935.

My dears!

Yesterday Shura brought me one of the photographs you sent. What a splendid
drawing! How little Mama has changed. Just a little nicer-looking and her hair
a trifle greyer.

I haven't written to you for a long time—please don't be offended. This
month has been like that. The Georgian poets arrived, and we went to Leningrad together—I've already written to you about that. Then the Board of the
Writers' Union opened its plenary session, with morning and evening meetings
and all sorts of encounters and banquets. Even I found these nocturnal carous-
ings and homecomings at six in the morning a strain on my heart. And above
all, there were interesting people there—people like K[onstantin] Fedin, and my
dearest friends after Zhenionok: Titsian Tabidze and Paolo Yashvili. Soon my

translations will come out and you'll see what sort of poets they are. So we had gatherings at my home too. And once again I got out of the way of working.

As you know, Pavetti has been dangerously ill. But it's all right, he got through it safely—he's a marvel. I went to see him and he showed me your postcard. And told me about the Dominican.[13] He's lost a bit of weight, but he doesn't let things get him down. At my age, I'm more careful than him in many ways.

[...]

I'm depressed by the progress of my work (the novel). It's moving forward terribly slowly, and as it progresses it gets more and more uninspired. The worst thing is that I'm frightened of working as assiduously as I used to. I've become a timorous pedant, avoiding even mild signs of fatigue.

As ever, my chief consolation is little Zheniok. We've transferred him to a model school. He finds that it's not so much ideal as showy; his previous, ordinary school had more discipline, and the boys—children of poorer and more average parents—were cleverer than they are in this one, which is harder to get into. He's working well and takes an interest in absolutely everything. He's top in Russian and literature, but he's also good at mending his friends' radio sets, goes to a physics group, and so forth.

The international chess tournament ended here yesterday (they played at the Museum next door). Lasker, Capablanca, Flohr and others were here. Once I found Zhenichka at a chessboard with newspaper cuttings beside him, re-playing the competitors' games. Paolo Yashvili attended the tournament, with a pass to get to the tables themselves. On one free day I took Zhenichka to visit him and Tabidze at the Metropole, and left him with them. That day was a real treat for him. He had lunch in their room, with all the delicacies from the restaurant. Then Paolo took him to the tournament, and he ended up just behind the barrier, next to all the stars. Paolo took him down to the café set up in the Museum for the week of the tournament, and they drank tea and Narzan water. Then P[aolo] bought him a chess book, and in it he got the personal autographs of the main contenders in the tournament. In the evening they telephoned me from the Museum, Paolo went back to the tournament, and I went to pick up Zhenichka and take him home. He had so many things stuffed in his pockets and under his arms that he couldn't manage them all—oranges, the chess book, signed photographs of the celebrities. He was skipping along behind me, chewing something that he kept taking out of his coat-pocket and hiding in his fist. It turned out to

13. In 1935 Leonid Pasternak painted a portrait of the Dominican monk Prior Menn.

be the remains of a bun that he had started eating in the café and then hidden. A sweet boy.

But Fedia is lovely too.[14] On one occasion there was a knock at our door when nobody else was at home. On her days off, Zina stays with the children all day at the Soviet Writers' House, where they spend the mornings learning sculpture with Pozniakov (Serov drew his portrait),[15] doing French, and so forth. So— there was a knock at the door, and I opened it. There was Fedia, in a long-sleeved, over-long overcoat made for him to grow into, and a fur hat—a proper little Tom Thumb. He'd come on his own, to visit us—it turned out that Zina's elder son had rung up to invite him that morning, without telling his mother, and then had gone out with her and his brother. We both stood there nonplussed, and I was struck by the grown-up way he reacted to this childish mix-up; he went straight to the telephone and called his home. He's grown up extraordinarily over the past year.—Later on I told Zhenia about this, and Zheniok in the next-door room called out 'What's so surprising? He's a Pasternak!'

Once again, as so often, I've written you something quite different from what I wanted to—nothing but trivia. But you'll gather the main thing you need to know—we're alive and well. Missing everyone's birthdays has become a bad habit with me; forgive me, Mama and Papa, please don't be cross.

I kiss you all, and send a big hug to Zhonia's children. Keep well.

PS. Time is passing, and while this letter has been lying around, a lot has happened in the world. Things may change, and please remember how many difficulties we've already surmounted, guided by a belief that all our trials will end well. Don't be downhearted, and don't worry about us; remember that you're always with us in all our thoughts. I don't know what to say or how to advise you. When I look for comfort, I think of Fedia,[16] and rely on him to look after you. Let me know how you are. I kiss you warmly, endlessly. And yet—you'd be better here with me.

Boris's letters at this time testify to his profound tenderness towards his family and his anxiety about the worsening persecution in Germany. From 1933 onwards, lead-ing members of the German intelligentsia began to leave; they included Thomas Mann and the Pasternaks' friend Albert Einstein. By March 1935 Leonid had become

14. The son of Boris's brother Alexander (Shura).

15. Nikolai Pozniakov (1879–1941), dancer, ballet director, and pianist, was Professor of Piano at the Moscow Conservatoire. Valentin Serov's portrait of him, made in 1908, is in the Tretyakov Gallery.

16. This refers to Josephine's husband Frederick.

anxious about the safety of his works in Germany, and deeply concerned about the uncertainties now threatening the previously secure lives of Josephine and her family. Boris placed his trust in the connections and pragmatic personality of her husband Frederick, by this time Director of the Bayerische Vereinsbank in Munich.

Boris Pasternak to his parents

12 April 1935. Moscow.

My dears, why haven't you written for so long? How are you, and what's new? We're all right here, and everyone is well. Papa, Gordon Craig[17] asked me to send you his greetings. Do you remember him? He certainly remembers you perfectly, and asked a lot of questions about you. I thought your only connection to him was your portrait of him, but he told me that he's also got your picture of Scriabin in his collection.

He recently arrived in Moscow, and I met him at an afternoon première at Meyerhold's. After the show Zhenia and I went to dine with the Meyerholds; he himself turned up later, as did Sergei Prokofiev.

In the newspaper photographs Craig looks ancient, but when he talks, his characteristic youthful exuberance and the breadth of his artistic talent burst through the wrinkled grey exterior and make him as young as ever. But what a lot of water has flowed away since then, and how everything has changed!

We were talking three languages at once—French, German and English. The only ones who knew English were Prokofiev, who speaks it well, I myself (very poorly), and—particularly well—that same [Sviatopolk-]Mirsky whom you know through *The London Mercury*. He has been here for over two years, and now rejects me with just as much fervour as he once valued me. He does so by right, and from the purest of motives. He's a member of the English Communist Party, and I must appear to them quite justly as a betrayer of their hopes, an uninteresting and trivial individual. With all his complex, morally strained biography, he's an absolute Nekhlyudov,[18] straight out of Tolstoy.

Craig is planning to stage *Macbeth* in English here, using Russian actors, and then to take his production on tour in Europe. He hasn't chosen his theatre

17. Edward Gordon Craig (1872–1966), British actor and theatre director, and first husband of Isadora Duncan. Leonid's two portraits of him, made during Craig's visit to Moscow in 1912, are still extant. Leonid's letters to him were destroyed by Craig's daughter after her father's death. Nothing is known of the fate of the Pasternak art works once owned by Craig.

18. The dissipated and anguished protagonist of Tolstoy's novel *Resurrection* (originally published with illustrations by Leonid Pasternak).

yet—I believe he's settled on the Maly.[19] Of all the productions currently open in Moscow, he liked *King Lear* at the Jewish Theatre best.

I'm writing you this letter instead of a postcard, and you shouldn't expect too much from it. If I get carried away with writing, it'll lie around and who knows when it'll reach you. Let me know whether things are all right with you—a postcard will do. Everybody sends you greetings and kisses.

May I send you my Georgian translations when they come out? The publishers want to produce a high-quality volume, but probably they'll try too hard and it'll turn out tasteless and pretentious.

I kiss you very, very, very warmly.

Your Borya

After his return to the USSR, Dmitry Sviatopolk-Mirsky came to a tragic end. With the support of Maxim Gorky, he became a leading Soviet literary critic, but in 1937, soon after Gorky's death, he was arrested, and soon afterwards perished in the Kolyma labour camp.

19. The plan to stage *Macbeth* at the Maly Theatre came to nothing.

CHAPTER TEN

1935–1936

In the spring of 1935, while Boris was suffering from severe depression and insomnia, he received a call from Stalin's staff ordering him to attend the Antifascist Congress for the Defence of Culture, in Paris. André Gide and André Malraux had requested the addition of Pasternak and Isaak Babel as delegates, to give the Congress greater authority.

The day before he left Moscow Boris telegraphed his parents to say he would be stopping in Berlin for some hours and would like to see them. His parents, alas, were in Munich, and only Josephine and Frederick were able to meet him. Josephine describes the occasion in detail in her essay 'Patior'. Boris still assumed he would be able to meet his parents on his return journey. However, in order to avoid possible 'provocations' in Germany, the Soviet participants were ordered to return from Paris via London and a sea passage to Leningrad. Their chance of meeting was lost.

Writing to his parents (on hotel notepaper) from the Palace Hotel in Paris, where the Soviet delegation was staying, Boris alludes to Frederick's fears that his speech at the Antifascist Congress might compromise his parents' safety in Berlin and Frederick's own position at the bank.

Boris Pasternak to his parents

3 July 1935. Paris.

My dears!

I must write to you, despite everything. I find it difficult—it makes my head spin. We won't meet this time. In any case I won't be travelling through Germany, but by sea via London. No-one on the delegation is travelling via Munich, and I haven't the courage or strength to make the trip on my own. Of course one couldn't imagine anything stupider or sadder—but what can I do, when my health has suddenly been so strangely sapped, and then instead of letting me recover, fate subjects me to surprises like this trip. Needless to say, Paris didn't help me sleep. Papa can't have any idea of how I'm feeling, writing as he does to tell me what I'm to see here. One day they took us to Versailles, and after seeing one or two halls I had to drop out of the palace tour. I'm incapable of doing anything whatever on my own, and if you imagine that a week's stay near Munich is going to put right what's been wrong for two months (progressive loss of strength, sleeplessness every night, and growing neurasthenia), you're expecting too much. I don't know how it all came about. Perhaps it's all a punishment to me for Zhenia and the suffering I caused her at the time. I don't know how things will turn out, and I don't want to think about it. But if ever I am well again, then we'll meet properly. As for now—whatever, whatever am I to do? V.P. Potemkin[1] remembers you well and himself started talking about you. He thanks you very much for your greetings.

The French literary world welcomed me very warmly and kindly, but I wasn't able to be particularly active, firstly because I was ill, and secondly at Fedia's request. Don't expect any extensive letters from me on my journey, either from here or from England. It may be that even when I get home, I'll continue my silence for a long time, until I'm properly on my feet again—if that's granted me. Shura also exists. Let him replace me temporarily, as far as our correspondence goes. And don't be cross. Just supposing I had set off through Munich or even Berlin, on my own, and on the way I had gone mad with misery? No, I don't have the courage for that. Oh, if only you knew how weak and miserable I feel. God grant this all leads somewhere—it can't go on like this. So don't be surprised, or upset, or angry, at how stupidly this has all turned out. I explained some things to Zhonia, the story of my condition and how they forced me to make the journey—there's nothing to add. Once more—forget about me for a while, let Shura stand in for me. Do you remember how recently I was congratulating myself on my good health, and inviting you and the girls to stay with me,—well, that chance has gone (I mean, the chance for me to take part in such things). I end in haste: it appears that we're setting off via London tomorrow, we leave at 7 a.m.

Boris spent three days in London, where he met Raisa Lomonosova, and (at her recommendation) saw John Rickman, a well-known Freudian psychiatrist. After his sea passage to Leningrad, he stayed a week with the Freidenbergs there, too worn out to return to Moscow.

On 14 July 1935, he sent his father a telegram (in German):

SAFELY ARRIVED LENINGRAD FOUND AUNT ASYA WELL AND HAPPY KISSES EMBRACES—BORIS

1. Soviet Ambassador to France.

Boris Pasternak to his parents

16 July 1935. Leningrad. Hotel Evropeyskaya.

My dears,

I expect Aunt Asya is already writing to you, and I don't know what she's writing. But she's very anxious that you're worrying about my health, and at her insistence I sent you a telegram from here yesterday.

All that's wrong with me is insomnia, or rather insufficient sleep; I started sleeping much less in April, and now it's become a habit, I get 5 to 6 hours a night. This drains me, distresses me, infuriates and torments me. I don't seem able to get myself better, or rather I'm not fated to—no matter how often I've made the effort over the past 3–4 months, somehow or other it all turns out to be impossible.

I probably should have gone to the first convalescent home (at the end of May) by myself; but I went with Zina. There I only got worse. Then, when I went to a different one in mid-June, on my own this time, I was suddenly sent abroad, with no chance to refuse. Fedia and Zhonia saw me. After that my health just gradually broke down. I won't go on, but let me quote one last instance to prove that I was clearly not fated to recover normally.

I arrived in Leningrad (I love the sea and don't get the least bit seasick) in a state of complete hysteria—because of insomnia and the constant subconscious fear that it was making me unfit for normal life. As soon as I got to the hotel, I rang Olya and asked her to come over. I burst into tears in front of her, just as shamefully as I had in front of Zhonechka. Aunt Asya and Olya invited me to spend another week with them for a rest. Not only did I accept their invitation—I found to my joy that in the absolute darkness and peace of Olya's room, I passed my first normal night for three months. I rejoiced in sleep as if it were something unheard-of, and was ready to boast of those seven hours of repose. The same thing happened the following night. I was overjoyed to find that while the Russian, French and English sedatives I'd had to poison myself with during my journey, night after night for over a month, had failed to bring me any rest, I found it in the quiet, the cold, the cleanliness and moral decency of Aunt Asya's and Olya's home. Well, then—it looked as if I'd discovered the road to health, and I'd be able to profit from my aunt's invitation and stay with her for 20 days or so, sleep my fill, calm my nerves, and recover from my impressions and other people.

But it wasn't to be. From the very first day, I could see how I was imposing on them. The first night, they both had to share a bed, and didn't get enough sleep, because Olya had given me her own. I bought myself a new bed. But then it turned out that that wasn't any help either, because Olya's room where I was sleeping had thick curtains, while my aunt's room, which she had moved into, had light ones, and Olya wasn't sleeping so well there. I was so selfishly keen to go on staying with them, despite the obvious inconvenience I was causing them, that I was going to buy dark curtains for Aunt Asya's room.

But that morning, Zina rang up from Moscow, full of anxiety about my failure to arrive, and the rumours of my illness, and the lack of any news from me, and announced that she was coming to Leningrad to fetch me.

But I'd agreed with my aunt that I'd be hiding away from all my family and friends for the time I'd originally planned to stay—and she'd even wanted to write to Zhenia to tell her not to come, supposing she had wished to; so when I agreed to let Zina come, Asya and Olya got very indignant and said that the whole plan was spoiled now, and I should leave with Zina, and so on.

All this is too profound and subtle for me to understand. In my view, their proposal was simply impracticable, more than they could manage; but if it had been technically feasible, then for me to see Zina for one or two days wouldn't have made it in the least impossible for me to carry on staying with them after Zina had left. It all looked as if they had been wanting to lay down their lives for me, and I had trampled their noble impulse underfoot.

Was ist der langen Rede kurzer Sinn?[2] The thing that's tormenting me and making me suffer isn't an organic illness—it's not something people die of—so calm down, everything will come right somehow. But don't be surprised, upset or shattered by the fact that we didn't meet. In Paris, I was in a state of semi-insanity; during that delirium, I couldn't have undertaken any voluntary or rational activity. All that time, I was looking at this mass of people, the financial expense, and all the rest, as though it wasn't my own journey, as though it wasn't really happening. I know that we will meet again. It's quite possible that it may now become easier for me to travel abroad. But to all this flood of possibilities, feelings, opportunities, smiles, and so forth, I feel like saying: not yet, not yet, some other time. What can I do?—somehow or other I've lost my way, and I have to get back on the rails again.

Zina's arrival in Leningrad instantly liberated me from half the panic-stricken fantasies that had haunted me through my sleepless period. But that very same joy that had once knocked me off my feet, now merely exacerbated my insomnia.

2. 'What is the point that I'm making at such length?'

So, don't worry, keep calm. Write to the Volkhonka address—there'll be a delay, but your letters will reach me. I shall be somewhere on the outskirts of Moscow, and your letters will be forwarded.

I kiss you all endlessly. My warm, warm thanks to you, Fedia and Zhonia, for all that you have done. Don't be surprised. When I calm down and am more or less myself again, I'll write and tell you about my trip, instead of talking of nothing but my stubborn desire to regain my lost record of eight hours' sleep a night.

Your Borya

Boris Pasternak to his parents

[End of September 1935. Moscow.]

My dears!

Congratulate Lidochka from me on her and all our happiness, and accept my warm congratulations for yourselves on this occasion.[3]

How wonderful this all is! I read her letter to little Zhenionok, and am burning with impatience to meet her husband. How splendid it would be if she were really to come and see us! It was only very recently that I visited London, in such a strange, abrupt way, as though in a dream. So it's easy for me to imagine her future life, at least in a territorial, external way.

Now, a few words about me. When I was in Leningrad, I wrote to you at Aunt Asya's insistence. I was far from being as well then as I told you I was—but I had to say so to reassure you.

Do I have to talk about the things that surprised and saddened you so? I was so hopeful then, and am even more so now—hopeful that we'll meet again soon, under different and better circumstances; so it's better not to go on about all this. In any case, the unheard-of absurdity of the fact that I didn't come to see you speaks for itself. Could anything explain it, if the thing didn't explain itself by its own unexampled uniqueness? Judge from that, what a condition I was in at the time. Life had stopped for me, and for four months on end, all that terrible summer, I was waiting for it to return. Over more than four months, there wasn't one night when I slept longer than 5–6 hours. That only ended recently, a month ago, when I moved back to town.

3. Lydia had got engaged to Eliot Slater, an English psychiatrist working at the Kaiser Wilhelm Institute of Psychiatry where she was also employed.

Naturally the consequences of such a long period of sleeplessness, and the spiritual depression that provoked and maintained it, were bound to become apparent. On September 1st, when that dreadful summer ended, with its travels and moves hither and thither, and with my stay in the crowded 'rest home' which did nothing for me save give me a painful awareness of separation from Zina—when I finally regained my peace of mind, after the fog of my morbid imagination had dispersed, I could distinguish a number of objective, easily comprehended problems, which stood out against the clear background of my restored spiritual equilibrium. I had long been suffering from pains in my heart and my hands, lasting days on end; I developed headaches, and suffered a general decline in my strength. All these things are gradually passing off on their own, but in addition I myself have started soberly and calmly putting my health right again. I've obtained a pass allowing me to use the Kremlin hospital, and the first thing I'll do is get myself some false teeth.

In the spring, when all this started and I stopped sleeping, I gave up my work, and all summer I made no attempt to take it up again. And it may be nothing more than the recovery of my normal manner of working that has begun to restore my mental balance.

Still, something has happened to me, some screw or other has come loose. But it can probably be put right again, otherwise there wouldn't have been this improvement—for in many ways I've got much better.

Exactly a year ago, when you were pleased about some success of mine, and you wrote to ask exactly what it was about—that was when my moral misfortunes were already beginning. In all honesty, I don't know why, any more than you do. Unfortunately all this fuss to do with the Writers' Congress, first here and then in Paris, happened at a time when I was temporarily unproductive. Papa, you've worked successfully all your life; perhaps you don't know the sense of shame and discontent that affects one at such times.

It's no good writing poetry all my life. From time to time there have been periods when I've been drawn to prose. Sometimes it was successful ('Luvers's Childhood', *Safe Conduct*). But compared with the technique of writing poetry, it comes so hard to me that I expect my attraction to it is some sort of pernicious aberration, which does nothing for me but make me stagnate, mark time on one spot, and copy out the same thing fifty times over, casting me into despair every time I do. What I want from it, and from myself, is probably unattainable; perhaps I don't even know what it is I want. No, that's not the way that prose-writers work—never mind the Tolstoys and Prousts, just ordinary writers, even talentless ones—who are happier than me and infinitely exalted above me simply because they can churn out volumes and volumes, rather than single pages chiselled out mind-numbingly one by one.

It's also true that my last attempt at finishing 'Luvers's Childhood', at giving it an ending, in simple prose relevant to the present time, was constantly hampered by the requirement to see our present reality from one particular, ready-made, universally compulsory viewpoint. The compulsion was particularly severe three years ago when I first took up this work, and the relentless obligation to write something other than what I was thinking made me give up the task. That was when I took up translating from Georgian. Since then the pressure has eased a bit, and it's become possible to take up the work again—but this is a second attempt, without the freshness and joy of a first beginning. That was how I spent last year, working at this stuff; but I lacked the directness of approach of an artist responsible only to himself, making his own way along his chosen path. Because that was after the Congress,[4] which left me with the bitter dregs of a terrible, inflated self-importance, ludicrous over-estimation and embarrassment, and— worst of all—a sort of gilded captivity, a feeling of obligation towards I knew not whom, imposed on me by I knew not whom, by way of advances paid to me that I had no need of and never asked for.

All of this was, in part, responsible for my illness too. In other words, if I'd had anything fresh and recent to look back on during my first attacks of insomnia, anything I'd just done and was satisfied with, I should have had some sort of moral prop which would have helped me get better more quickly. But here I not only had nothing of the kind—worse still, some fiendish prompting led fate to saddle me with a second congress, an international one, on top of the first. This time I felt it even more acutely—with morbid acuteness at the end, like a person in a mortal quarrel with his own self—as I was forced to witness, instead of real work, real achievements, nothing but other people's opinions, baseless fairy-tales hashed up all over again, applause, ovations, and a lot of fuss being made of my own sick self, I don't know why or for whose benefit. I almost wept—I often did literally weep—as I fought off these attentions, while being force-fed with a nau- seating stew of morally excruciating approbation. Have you ever heard anything like it? I don't know why I'm writing about this; let me leave it all aside and try to finish.

I shall need a great deal of strength to repair my reputation, so disgracefully inflated, so divorced from the truth, against my will and without my knowledge. I shall need a great deal of strength to stick calmly and courageously to the modest

4. The first Congress of Soviet Writers, in August 1934.

task of doing my real work. It's hard for me to take it up again, because I've not quite recovered yet, and I need to give up a number of bad habits (chiefly smoking). But that's what is going to be difficult—not earning money, or sorting out my family life, or anything else. What I mean is that while I may have nothing to make you (or my friends and family) happy at present, there's no reason for you to be distressed on my account either. Forgive me for not writing to you for so long—forgive me for everything. I'm longing to get better, to write something new, and to go abroad, perhaps, with Zina.

I kiss you all warmly, Fedia, Zhonia, the children, and Lida, and I congratulate Lida again and again with all my heart.

B.

You needn't write to me—I'll get news from Shura.

Leonid Pasternak to Boris Pasternak

21 November 1935. Berlin.

My dear Borya!

I haven't written to you for a very long time. I've meant to write to you on many occasions, but it didn't work out—I couldn't write, I didn't know what to write about after our 'disappointment' in connection with your 'non-visit' . . . but as in the Swedish legend about the mother's heart (and probably the father's too, though it didn't get into the legend), we were very anxious about your ill-health, your nervous breakdown, insomnia and so forth. Your letter when you were staying with Aunt Asya, and her own letter, and Olya's, reassured us a bit. But as for writing to you . . . somehow I couldn't do it—what would have been the point of writing, giving you advice on how to act and how to organise your life . . . I'd written the same thing so many times, to no purpose whatsoever.

I have one deep-rooted conviction and certainty about you—that your constitution is fundamentally a healthy one. Of course there are plenty of ways of wrecking it. You yourself wrote in your last letter that 'the first thing I have to give up is smoking!' What's the point of writing you elementary truths about how to safeguard your health, and how you ought to live so as to be able to work as well . . .

But then there came a letter from you that required me, forced me to write to you. You were complaining that you could no longer work as you used to, that you couldn't 'rise to those previous heights' (an expression of Leo Tolstoy's, when he was finding it difficult to work after his illness); that you were 'impossibly overestimated' (at the [Writers'] Congress, 'all that pomposity', and 'worst of all, that gilded captivity')—you've probably forgotten that letter. Anyway, Lidochka wrote a very good reply to it, just what I would have wanted to write, all about how success had spoiled you, and about your fears and glances over your shoulder, and about how you have to work for yourself alone, and remember those brilliant, vital words 'Poet, don't cherish . . .'[5]—the only thing I would have added (for Mama and I know how much you are suffering, particularly now, and blaming yourself for not coming here)—stop making promises and reassuring us that 'we'll definitely meet soon', that 'you'll definitely come here in the spring'; and in your last letter [. . .] you were understandably thrilled about 'Papa's plans', which meant that in one way or another we'd see each other soon, and 'if Papa doesn't manage it, let him write, and then I'll arrange to come in spring'.

My darling, darling Borya, don't you yourself feel what all this sounds like— don't people say just this sort of thing to calm a crying child . . . so stop writing about this, stop blaming and tormenting yourself, my dear boy! Never mind how painful it was for us—when you were only a few hours away from us, a step or two, and unwell, suffering, and upset—you must have been longing to see us, and we'd certainly have comforted you, you'd have got some rest (what could be better than having your parents near you?) and would have gone back in a completely different frame of mind. That's what I think—I'm certain of it: after all, it was at Aunt Asya's that you said you had your first night's sleep without a sedative.

Anyway, I want to finish with this question once and for all. So that was what fate decreed, something prevented you, something stronger than you and outside your will, if one can speak of the will here at all. I was talking to Pepa once— 'I can't understand Boris' . . . 'With his fame and importance . . . he could have anything he wanted' (we were saying that you ought to have your own little house with a garden, outside town, many people nowadays are doing this—even your namesake the writer[6] had been telling me about his 'hut' with Karelian birchwood furniture).

22.XI.35.

What a notable day in our lives and the lives of all the family! We've just been with Zhonia and Fedia, seeing our dear Lida and her fiancé Eliot off to England. What an enormous amount is contained in these half-dozen words!

5. The opening words of a sonnet by Pushkin, exhorting the poet to ignore the public's opinion of his art, and trust only to his own judgment.
6. Boris Pilnyak. He was arrested in 1937 and executed soon after.

Our parental parting words, all the blessings, tears of joy and grief, the inexpressible anxiety that has been constantly with us over these last few weeks—and then today, and today's parting, have all filled the cup to overflowing! What a fairy-tale!! What a miracle! A gift from the heavens, from destiny—from the Lord God, and just when everything seemed so hopeless. [. . .]

Lydia's marriage to Eliot Slater ultimately cleared the way for all her family in Germany to make their way to safety in England. At this point, however, the family were still considering moving to Paris, or—their preference—to Moscow, to which they had always intended to return.

The following letter deals with the plenary meeting of the Union of Soviet Writers in Minsk, which was devoted to poetry. Boris's speech, warning against what he saw as ominous signs of a shift in Soviet cultural politics, towards an increasingly prescriptive and intolerant approach, aroused marked official displeasure.

Boris Pasternak to his father

2 March 1936. Moscow.

Dear Papa,

I'm sorry I haven't written before. I've been out of Moscow. It's very difficult to explain at a distance why the whole month of February dropped out of my life, wasted on empty talk. It's to do with the activities of the Union of Soviet Writers, which periodically organises plenary meetings in different cities—this time it was Minsk. To give you an uncritical account of all this would be dishonest, but analysing these aspects of our life in such a way as to prevent you from drawing false conclusions is very difficult. People here love to make great promises, they exaggerate and poeticise. The only true and indisputable facts are the foundations of our existence and its historic trends. And they are the main thing.
[. . .]

Boris goes on to discuss his parents' projected move back to Moscow, explaining that renting a flat or even hotel rooms would be very difficult, but they would be accommodated somehow or other—'Don't I, and Shura, and Olya and everyone else, get by somehow? Well, you'll live with us and do the same.'

The next letter follows a telephone conversation between Boris and his father, in which Leonid mentioned having met Nikolai Bukharin, editor-in-chief of *Izvestia*, during his visit to Berlin. Boris was excited by the possibility that Bukharin might have explained aspects of Soviet life that Boris could not raise in his own letters. His mention of recent attacks on Bukharin relate to a hostile article published in *Pravda* on 10 February 1936. The stand-off developing between *Izvestia* and *Pravda* also affected the reporting of Pasternak's speech to the Writers' Congress. A highly abridged and amended version, entitled 'On Modesty and Boldness', was published in *Literaturnaya Gazeta* on 24 February. Bukharin's fall from grace led to his arrest in 1937. He was tried at the last show trial of 1938, and sentenced to be shot.

Boris Pasternak to his parents

6 March 1936. Moscow.

My dears!

I've just spoken to you on the telephone. Soon I'll repeat this pleasure, from Shura's flat.

I've forgotten what we talked about, but it was a great joy to hear your voices. What a lot they gave me. Last summer, when we spoke between Berlin and Munich, I didn't feel it so strongly. It makes me so happy to find that your voices (as people say about one's pulse) are so strong, even and full. They give an impression of youthfulness and confidence in the future. And also (something of a rarity nowadays)—what purity of language! So when you arrive, we'll still be able to be proud of you.

N.I. [Bukharin] must have explained to you all that he could and wanted to about matters that are so vast they can't be described. He's a wonderful, historically extraordinary man, but fate hasn't been kind to him. I'm very fond of him. He's been subjected to attacks recently from people who aren't worth his little finger. But one can't explain all this. I was completely unaware that you knew him. I've been thinking about him all day.

This is one of those topics that I had in mind in my last letter when I said that they're difficult to discuss at a distance.

Incidentally, when I was out there in Minsk people were constantly trying to undermine me, so as to blow me up on social issues—but suddenly all that turned out for my benefit. Don't look for any echoes of it in *Literaturnaya Gazeta*, which is edited by someone from the same clique. It's not a question of personalities, but something very different. But the newspaper won't give you any idea either of my speech or my role in the whole affair. And my speech, which was conversational, simple and delivered impromptu (saying whatever came into my head), was much bolder and more comprehensive than what I subsequently made of it, and then there was the editor's censorship on top of it all. And then, when I deleted the beginning of the speech, I couldn't allow my own hands to leave in place the stenographer's note about the prolonged ovation (the whole audience rose to their feet and applauded me) when I appeared on the stage. So, that didn't get into print. (I'm writing this just for you—the rest of the speakers, when they proofread the shorthand notes, inserted applause for themselves.) And another thing: if you're planning to read that issue, read the next one as well, with the conclusion of the plenary meeting and the remaining speeches.

And it's all pointless. (1) These reports won't give you any idea of what really went on, and (2) none of it all is worth your notice, it's nothing but provincial trivia.

When you come, you'll see everything for yourselves. I can't wait for you to arrive. I kiss you warmly.

B.

I'll telephone you, if fate allows, on the 12th towards evening.

Boris Pasternak to his parents

19 March 1936. Moscow.

My dear ones,

What a delight to hear your voices on the telephone! How I treasure this feeling—a pleasure too simple to need any explanation. But time and again, it seems such a miracle to hear your hesitations, your unhurried gentle tone, all the mannerisms of your speech, and to realise how alike they are to the same things that I sometimes encounter here, as more or less close approximations—either in someone else, or perhaps in myself as the inner voice of duty, or as the dreams that direct my work, or elsewhere. There is a range of inexplicable affinities that make one more attracted to one person than another, and the same sort of range of ideals, impossible to formulate, to which one unconsciously subordinates one's life. Well, your voice, Papa, is terribly reminiscent of both these things, and the reasons are obvious: partly heredity, partly the effect of the upbringing I received even before I was old enough to remember it, and which I now continue to obey by myself; in a word, it's life.

There's no getting away from the disturbing fascination of these feelings. When I put down the telephone, I told Shura about it. Now I understand why

I love Meyerhold so much.[7] He has something that reminds me of the qualities in you which I can perceive even over the telephone. Even when he's talking about matters of which he has more experience than anyone else in the world—even when he's absolutely convinced of what he's saying—even when talking about his immediate plans for the theatre—he still speaks with a gentle lack of compulsion, a half-perplexed preoccupation, and invariably with a look over his shoulder—at his wife, or the Arts Committee's policies for the theatre, or our critics, or the West. The image of this ageing artist is inseparable from that of the child with seven nursemaids:[8] they include his family, English and Chinese theatrical traditions, the USSR, his ailing liver, and life. All of them are his nursemaids, and each one of them is precious in her own way, and they all have to be reconciled. It was just the same when you mentioned Mama and Zhonia and Nikolai Ivanovich during our conversation. I probably live the same way too.

It was only after our conversation that I remembered a photograph taken this winter, and I enclose it just as an illustration. One picture shows him and me with André Malraux (the French writer), and the other one has me and Malraux on our own. Neither has come out well.

How I long to see you both, on an evening like this, after six minutes on Barbarossa![9] What a shadow this deprivation has cast over our lives, though we're too used to it to notice; and how it has probably shortened our lives too! Do you remember the summer? No, the healthier I am now, the better and happier I am, the more firmly I justify my summer episode of hide-and-seek. It would have been dreadful if you had seen me like that—worse than a separation. But as the delirium passed, little by little, step by step, and I became myself again, became the person I have always been when my life goes as it should—then, how much I need you, what a joy it would be if you could live with me a little bit too. There's probably no-one else with whom I could talk better or more deeply about the most important things—life, human experience, history, art. And these precious people still aren't here to talk with me. And the years are passing!

I sometimes think that if I have made any choices or laboured over anything in my life, if I have achieved anything, then somewhere, in the depths of my soul, I did it for you. And now you aren't here—and whom was it all for? The one thing I understand, out of everything you'll be discussing with Boris Ilyich [Zbarsky],

7. For details of Meyerhold's life, see above, p. 150, n. 39.
8. 'A child with seven nursemaids has no-one to look after it'—a Russian proverb.
9. Barbarossa was the name of the Berlin telephone exchange for the Pasternaks' apartment.

is this: I am simply famished for you. And if, for good reasons of your own, you prefer to do something else rather than come here now—never mind, things can't go on like this, I'll come to England or France to spend a little while with you and see you. The only question is—when.

Now, so as not to hold up this letter, let me mention a few things. Don't inadvertently let on to Boris Ilyich that I sometimes allow myself some friendly criticism at his expense. He would find it unpleasant, and he is showing such energetic concern about your future that I simply don't know how to thank him.

I was most reassured by my conversation with you on the 12th. I was talking from Shura's flat, and the time before it was from Boris Ilyich's. And on that occasion the Zhenia I mentioned was Zhenia Zbarskaya,[10] not our Zhenia as you inferred. The misunderstanding was easily cleared up.

You can congratulate Shura on his successes. He's planning to send you some newspaper cuttings praising his projects. All in all, his work is falling into shape. Things are good for me too, despite all the inevitable difficulties of our time. That's one of those topics that are hard to explain at a distance. The official requirements relating to art that get voiced here from time to time are sometimes expressed in rather brusque, military-like language. People's ideas about these things sometimes progress from the primitive to the downright false.[11] But you have to take a broad view of everything, and find a grain of truth in any situation, no matter how unexpected; that's what I always do, as far as I can.

I haven't been able to tell you anything to the point, but never mind—now we have the telephone in reserve. If I need anything, I may give Boris Ilyich a verbal message.

I may ring you on the 23rd or 24th, but don't expect a call, so as not to be disappointed if anything prevents it.

I kiss you all warmly—Zhonia, Fedia, Alyonushka, Charlik.

Your Borya.

Perhaps next time I'll just talk to Mama alone, otherwise we always seem to leave her till last. I give you a big hug, Mamochka.

---

10. The wife of Boris Ilyich Zbarsky.

11. Boris is referring to the Soviet campaign against 'formalism' in art, which was being carried on in *Pravda* and other newspapers (reminiscent of Hitler's contemporaneous campaign against 'degenerate art' in Germany). Boris was a leading figure opposing the official campaign.

Boris Pasternak to Lydia Pasternak Slater

25 April 1936. Moscow.

Dear Lida,

Here's the beginning of a letter from Lomonosova to Zhenia; it relates to you.

'Today I was at our consulate, and they asked me to find out the address of B.P.'s sister Lydia Leonidovna. They said that she had recently got married here, and gone up to the consulate, but they had forgotten to make a note of her new surname, and now they don't have either her name or her address. I'd like to know her address myself too. After all, we have to meet.'

Zhenia, in her simplicity of heart, asked Stella, and was ready to carry out Lomonosova's request—she would have told her your address, without asking you. But I myself, not knowing what your plans and feelings are, would leave all this up to you. If you like, you can satisfy the consulate's curiosity, and if not, you needn't. And the same goes for Raisa Nikolaevna [Lomonosova]. But if you'd agree to meet her, I'd be very glad, and if so, let me know as quickly as you can. I haven't written to Lomonosova all winter, though she's a delightful person, very interesting and straightforward.

[...]

Of course, I'd already been thinking along these lines earlier on, when you first went to Oxford—my hands were constantly itching to write to Raisa Nikolaevna and let her loose on you—or perhaps puzzle you in some way, by getting her to send you flowers or something. But if I'd said a word about you, that would have violated your privacy, and I didn't know how you'd feel about that. Sometimes it's actually pleasant not to have anyone home-grown around, when you're in a new country, as fresh as an unread book. Of course it would have been very simple to ask you. But I kept putting it off, as I put off so many things, and particularly the most important things, in my fiendish life. You can imagine how I kept wanting to write to you: you, married, and in England, the land of my dreams from 1913 onwards, when I first started tackling Keats and Coleridge, Swinburne, Poe and others, on my own. And now all this has happened to you! How strange it all is!

Today, while I was getting your address from our neighbours, I discovered by chance that you're about to be a mother. And I hadn't known anything about it, and probably that's all my fault again. I'm with you in spirit, with all my heart, at this time.

Oh, this incredible life! The absurdities of life here, the obstacles they create for writers and artists, are beyond belief. But that's how a revolution has to be, as it grows and grows to become the event of the century, advancing to become ever more visibly the centre of the world. What can individual destinies and biographical justifications mean in the midst of all this? History has here created something intractably huge, and that fact elevates one. So long as we remember it, we can stop looking over our shoulders and drawing sad conclusions. (I remember your wonderful letter. I was deeply grateful to you for it. I don't remember whether I said that to you, i.e. whether I replied to it?)

Oh, how I long to do some proper work! And I'm not the only one. So what's wrong? That's hard to explain. But a lot of the obstacles are our own fault.

Two of the most important things about this winter are: 1) that something is going to change with Papa and Mama (that his presence here took on a potential reality, that his voice was heard on Prechistensky Boulevard, in Shura's telephone receiver, that he's magnificent, and that I spoke with him twice); 2) that I'm well—well in the same sense that I was impossibly, unthinkably ill so recently—not ill in the sense that Zhonia or you, or anyone else, might be, not in any way that one could even dream of—and that for six months on end!

Now, somehow or other I have to stand up for myself. I've set myself a harsh programme—to listen to nobody but myself!

I don't know what Papa will decide on—I mean where they will go. At his age, all this worries me. I miss them terribly (with all the meaning in my life, with all the power of my past experience). There's both filial love here, and something else. After all, Papa is an artist—with even more meaning in his life, and more power in his own past experience.

Alongside this uncertainty, I have a different feeling, which has unexpectedly come to life again since my recovery, after having gradually faded over the past five years—a feeling of my links with the West, with the world of history, the world's face—an irresistible feeling of my need for it, and a feeling of separation that nothing can make good.

It's a sad comedy when people translate me, or try to. The attempts don't justify the interest that provokes them, in fact they rather compromise it. And then I look round and realise that there actually wasn't anything to translate—there was just some kind of activity, significant in terms of a process, but there aren't any individual books about this or that, nothing like *Bovary* or *The Idiot* or *Dombey and Son*. But quite apart from the stupidity and immodesty of such comparisons, the fault isn't mine. That's what the times were like. Rilke and Blok didn't have Dombeys or Bovarys either, none of the people I idolised had them. And once again, the Revolution was responsible. But let me come back to the translations.

What is it that makes them get published? Is there any place for these irrelevancies, can one make any sense of this senselessness? Yes one can: the only sense they have for me is the way they reflect my yearning for Europe, my constant life there in spirit. The sense of these translations lies in the fact that we ourselves exist in just the same way as them: because you are all abroad, and indeed in different countries; that this is how life has translated the apartment on Volkhonka. And finally, the sense of these shamefully irrelevant translations is the fact that Bovarys and Dombeys in some form or other will undoubtedly come into existence, because that's all there is left to write, there's nothing else to do: because the Revolution has happened, and as soon as people acquire the freedom to detach themselves from it just a little bit, so as to recall it as a whole and think about it—what could possibly appear then, if not great realist art? And if I live to see it, I shall be living within it myself.

I'm sorry—I'm writing in haste, and I got carried away. [...]

Your B.

The following letter to Leonid and Rosalia was prompted by a conversation with Boris Zbarsky, who had returned from Berlin and told Boris how anxious his parents were about their future.

Boris refers to an article on art by Paul Valéry, sent by Leonid, which reminds Boris of the artistic dogmatism of the Peredvizhniki (Wanderers), the school of painters against whom the Group of 36, with Leonid Pasternak as a founder member, had rebelled in 1902. These reflections are provoked by the recent 'Discussion on Formalism' taken up by the Soviet Writers' Union and all the Soviet press. It was a condemnation of the best and most promising elements in contemporary Soviet culture, including the works of Shostakovich, Meyerhold and others.

Boris Pasternak to his parents

18 May 1936. Moscow.

My dears!

[...]

Thank you very much indeed for the presents. *Vater und Sohn*[12] is a book of such profound tenderness that I was afraid to show it to Zheniochek, seeing how sensitive he always is to the peculiarities of his life away from me. But we found ourselves looking at it together, so much '*en père et fils*', and he was so moved by it, and laughed so much, that as it turned out you couldn't have chosen a better book. The way we looked at it should have been a picture on its own pages, a scene from the same moving story.

The Volkhonka apartment doesn't have a bath, while the one on Tverskoy Boulevard does. Zhenia is in the Crimea. Zheniok is staying with Eliz[aveta] Mikhailovna, as master of her bright and quiet little apartment. While the bath-water was heating, we looked through the book and Zhenichka explained the meaning of the almost wordless pictures to E.M. and me. He's very sharp and perceptive.

Thank you very much for the Valéry article. Please thank the translator too, and congratulate him on his outstanding success. I know Valéry's articles, and how difficult it is to translate their language—and meaning. In this case, every-thing has come across, almost including his very voice. But I didn't know the ar-ticle. It opens another old wound. What can one do about all this—just imagine if, in the days of the Group of 36, the Wanderers in the person of the feeblest of them had been the law, and any mention of Manet would have got you ... locked up.

B.I. [Zbarsky] talked most enthusiastically about you all, and thought you looked splendid. I recently met the American journalist Louis Fischer[13] in the street and he said the same.

But there was one thing that upset me. B.I. said that Fedia was indignant at our (my and Shura's) behaviour and attitude towards you, and it sounds as if B.I. himself agreed. This is all very simple to explain, so please take it calmly.

Can you or Mama ever have really imagined that you could, in any way what-ever, be 'an inconvenience' to me or Shura, as sometimes does occur in life, for

12. *Vater und Sohn* was a strip cartoon recounting a boy's activities with his father.
13. An American journalist who lived for many years in Soviet Russia, and was married to a Russian.

financial or other considerations? Can't you see that even if, say, Shura got the Nobel prize, and I married the Princess of Wales, our relative status in terms of power and importance would stay the same till the end of time? Can't you see that for us to live together with you is something one can only dream about and long for, that closeness to you is something one can only be proud of? Is that really not clear?

I'm purposely not talking about emotions and feelings here, and I'll willingly concede that we're unfeeling and selfish. All I mean is that if this favourite theme of filial ingratitude were to have the slightest resemblance to reality, we should have had to be even more arrant, tasteless fools than we actually appear to be.

I had the impression that Olya and I together had been inviting you here ever since the year before last. And I've always repeated that you would be sharing my life without entering into all its details—I mean, you would live exactly as you wished.

I can understand Shura when he describes present-day life in less shallow and idyllic terms than B[oris] I[lyich]; he's just more honest about it. Does that imply that he'd prefer to see you permanently far away from us? As for me, I don't touch on present-day life at all. First of all, I think (exactly as he does) about the constant happiness that your presence would give us. Secondly, I simply need you: your presence would give meaning to a whole range of material improvements I'm expecting but which I haven't made proper sense of yet. It appears that this summer I'll be given a dacha of my own in the writers' village, and in the autumn I'll get an apartment (in exchange for the Volkhonka one). I hadn't mentioned this before, because I've spent the last four years hearing promises of this kind, and no longer believe in anything. But it's precisely in line with this spiritual tradition that I've kept on repeating: come and be with us. And then we'll see—together. What more should I have said or done? What more has been done so far by other people—not ungrateful people, but the only people who count in our system, i.e. by the State? So what's up? If the only obstacle is that we seem inhospitable, then let me reassure you: it's nothing but a myth, there are no obstacles of that kind, so come as soon as you can and see how wrong you were.

It's really odd. As though you and Fedia and Zhonia had never met me! You see, I'm such a lover of objects and money, greedily accumulating both around me, with a well-ordered household and family, and 'personal considerations' of my own . . . an enemy to all forms of sentimentality and emotional excess, and so on and on . . . ! Just remember: once upon a time Zhonia mentioned that she'd like to come to spend the summer with us, and at once everything was ready at the embassy on Unter den Linden.[14] And don't think that I'm justifying myself, or trying to give Shura credit for not being anything like the monster that he must have been, if his gloom had arisen from the myth that I've just exploded. I repeat: in our case there's no merit in our being in love with you, since all the conditions for it are there, and it would be simply stupid and obtuse not to be in love.

Or perhaps all this is the result of my troubles abroad last summer? But didn't Zhonia and Fedia see me—or were they blind? Was it really not clear to them that they were faced with a man whose existence had been temporarily prorogued, someone temporarily suspended from being, *ein Nichts*,[15] shattered, tormented and worn out by that diabolical interlude which was fated to coincide with my journey, the journey I had been longing for, for so many years, and which had now turned out so hellishly? Couldn't they see that? And anyway—didn't I travel through Berlin, didn't I send you a telegram to Berlin, wasn't it you that I wanted to see in Berlin?

I wouldn't have fought shy of that, because it would all have happened of its own accord—the rails would have brought me there, as they carried me on to Paris and Tsvetaeva, and then to Lomonosova in London. Because those places were on my way. But carrying all this to you in Munich for you to see—that was beyond me. It was just as impossible as it was for me to take up the priceless opportunities I had in Paris, opportunities that simply thrust themselves at me. Malraux asked me whom I would like to meet—or, to quote a name you know well, there was talk about Valéry too. 'He'll be delighted to meet you', they said. But I turned everything down. André Gide said to me: 'I'd like you to know how fond of you we all are here. Doesn't that give you some sense of support?' And I was running away from them. A few steps from me, at the same Presidium table, was Heinrich Mann.[16] Regler, Weinert and Klaus Mann[17] (son of Thomas) came up and asked me if I wouldn't join them in a visit to him (H.M.), but I didn't even get myself introduced to him, though he was just one seat away from me. That's the measure of the rift between what I was at the time, and what I felt for those two great novelists.

14. The Soviet embassy in Berlin.
15. 'A nothing'.
16. The elder brother of Thomas Mann the novelist, he was also a novelist who wrote on social themes.
17. Gustav Regler, Erich Weinert and Klaus Mann were German left-wing writers, all then in exile from Nazi Germany.

And finally—I don't know if I told you: When I got back, Rolland was staying here with Gorky. Twice I was summoned to town, at his insistence. But I crept away to be with Zina in the country—a decrepit railway halt just short of Shchelkovo, which the post scarcely gets to—the sort of place where you kill a whole day just to drop in on somebody for a minute; a place of puddles, with a wild tangle of forest paths, and several different, mutually incompatible house-numbering systems; a deathly, addressless place. And then, on the eve of Rolland's departure from Russia, there suddenly appeared, in this rectangular plot of stinging-nettles, a grey-haired woman (a lecturer in French literature, as it later turned out—a Russian), whom he had specially sent for me, with instructions to bring me back dead or alive. And I spent two hours explaining to her how impossible this was, citing my precedent with you; and she went away unconvinced. And that was how I failed to come to see you in Munich, do you understand? My God, my God, how many times am I going to have to explain it to you?

So what is Fedia getting indignant over? Fischer's words also gave me the impression that you don't know how I feel about you. Once when I was approached for some biographical details, I just gave them information about you two. Isn't that axiomatic?

I'm not the least bit offended, and please don't tell me I'm wrong. But I'm sorry that you are inventing yourselves sources of non-existent injuries—particularly such incredible ones. And all these dialogues are so demeaning! Shura said to me: it was probably Fedia who started all this off, just to keep B.I. amused—like discussing the weather.

I embrace you heartily.

Your B.

Boris's fears that Pepa Zbarsky's idle gossip would mislead his parents were unfounded. Leonid quickly replied, reassuring him that neither Fedia nor Pepa Zbarsky would ever alter his feelings towards his son.

ris writing, at Chistopol, 1943.

Boris at the front as a war correspondent, with the journalist Semyon Tregub, 1943.

Anna Akhmatova and Boris Pasternak, 1946.

Boris, his wife Zinaida (Zina), and their son Lyonia, at Peredelkino, 1946.

Boris gardening at Peredelkino, 1946.

Above, left: Evgeni Pasternak in army officer's uniform, 1946.

Above, right: Boris's second son Leonid (Lyonia) with his nurse, 1940.

Left: Lydia Pasternak Slater with her children (left to right) Michael, Catherine (in front), Ann, and Nicolas in Oxford, 1945.

ɔris, Lyonia (on left), and the Georgian poet Georgi Leonidze, 1957.

ɔris with Olga Ivinskaya, 1957.

Boris with his wife Zinaida (right) and Nina Tabidze,
reading the telegram announcing his Nobel Prize, October 1958.

The writer Kornei Chukovsky, with Boris and Zinaida (right)
celebrating the Nobel Prize, October 1958.

ris with Olga Ivinskaya and her daughter,
na Emelianova, 1958.

Irina Emelianova, daughter of
Olga Ivinskaya, 1959.

ris after a performance in Moscow of Goethe's *Faust* by Deutsches Schauspielhaus Hamburg,
:h Gustaf Gründgens, who played Mephistopheles, 1959.

Boris Pasternak in Peredelkino, 1959.

For information about illustration sources, please refer to pages 421–42

CHAPTER ELEVEN
1936–1939

Boris was well aware that no matter what promises might be made, there was no serious prospect of an apartment or work being found for his father either in Moscow or Leningrad. He used the earnings from his Georgian translations to buy one of the first houses built at Peredelkino, so that there could be no further grounds for complaint, and realistic plans could be made for his parents' return. There was no doubt that they had to leave Nazi Germany, 'because of your landlady's sickness', as Boris wrote to his father. Now they could come to stay with him at any time.

Boris Pasternak to his parents

[July 1936. Peredelkino.]

My dears!

It's been a long time since I wrote to you. I've often meant to, and even started a letter, but abandoned it because I found myself analysing or describing things that are difficult to understand at a distance. I have to give that up, or I'll never get anywhere.

To start with the most important thing: I won't attempt to discuss the practical details of how you should organize your lives from now on, since I don't believe in the idea of any official intervention, or the possibility of any common language between an artist (as pure and as talented as Papa) and the present time. But I've never put the question in those terms.

You must come to us because of your landlady's sickness—come on a visit to me and Shura; and we'll see what happens after that. You know, in your heart of hearts, what B.I. [Zbarsky]'s schoolboyish pronouncements are worth; you've known them all your lives, not in his person but as a generalised typical abstraction, and thank God you've followed a different and loftier path, your own one. All that rubbish has nothing to do with you, it's all stale lies, fairy-tales for children. All I can write about is what I really know and can vouch for. So: if you came, you would live with me, and while I'm not in a position to give you any more than I live on myself, I could free you from any worries here in my own home. That's something I know for certain, with no mistake. It wouldn't change my daily life much, I mean it wouldn't cause me any extra trouble; on the contrary, as I've already told you, the joy of having you here would give meaning to my existence, strengthen me and lighten my life.

I live in a dacha here, a very large and spacious one (two floors, six rooms, with two verandas and a balcony). The room I'm writing to you from is as big as your studio on Volkhonka, with light from two sides. It's made for winter living, and if you came I would live in it with you the whole year round. My heart would be lighter, I would be aware that the purpose of my life was near at hand, and I would start investing money and energy in my (as yet incomplete) household, and my work, and my vocation, and so forth.

I'll probably give up the idea of a new apartment in town, and just keep the old Volkhonka apartment as my *pied-à-terre* there. That proposed new apartment, in addition to the dacha, turns out to be more than I really need. What's more, as you've surely guessed, I'm afraid of any sudden change for the better in my living conditions, since I can't share them with little Zhenichka. I'm afraid, too, that if I had to maintain all this on a much larger scale, it would divert my finances in one direction to such an extent that I wouldn't be able to support Zhenia in a way that balanced my own lifestyle. In short, I probably won't take the new apartment.

I don't really know how to write about things like this, I don't have the words for it, and I'm not sure whether you'll understand anything I'm saying.

If you came to live with me, it would be a happiness and a help for me, a new stimulus to my work, a source of warmth and light. I can't imagine you existing here under any other conditions, even if you were given your own apartment. Could one leave you out there on your own, without an interpreter and comforter? Don't blame me—just as I can see everything clearly from a personal, heartfelt viewpoint, in the context of my invitation for you to stay with me (and then everything is clear to me, in all its practical reality: you will be happy with me), so too I'm incapable of imagining you coming under any other circumstances. I don't know if I like everything, if I'm really happy. I don't know if you'll like everything, or if you'll be happy. But you are the people I love most in the world, except for Zhenichka, from whom I'm separated; that's beyond doubt, and I should like to seize hold of that indubitable fact with all my strength. That's all. That's something one can live by, and build on. All the rest—isn't my specialty.

So—what am I trying to say? If you're seriously contemplating coming here, come and stay with me. I can't give you any other advice, and I can't imagine anything different.

Zhenia, Zhenichka and El[izaveta] Mikh[ailovna] are at Odoevo, that same place where I spent the summer with Zina and her boys two years ago.

How is your health?

I kiss and embrace you heartily.

Your Borya

Write to the town address: the post doesn't work here yet. It's on the Bryansk line, three stops beyond the Ochakovo halt[1]—do you remember?

Leonid replied on 7 August, welcoming Boris's invitation but suggesting that he would first like to visit Lydia in London—she was expecting her first child in November. He also wanted to visit Paris to investigate the possibility of living there. Boris's irritable response was prompted above all by recent political events in Russia, which made him increasingly doubtful of the wisdom of his parents' return. He had been encouraged by Bukharin's draft of a new constitution enshrining the triumph of 'Socialist humanism'; but the Moscow trial of Kamenev and Zinoviev in August 1936 put an end to any hopes of liberalisation.

Boris Pasternak to his parents

[September 1936. Peredelkino.]

My dears,

I still haven't answered your letter. But I finally saw B.I. [Zbarsky] a few days ago.

Papa, you greatly exaggerate the importance of my feelings towards you both. Or rather—you see it all in the wrong light.

What do I keep trying to say in all my successive explanations? Nothing but this: that I can't undertake to make an independent judgement on how you're to live or what you're to do; but I'm ready, in an absolutely fateful way, to seize on your arrival as something settled and decided upon by yourselves, and to welcome it joyfully, as an opportunity for us to be together.

---

1. Ochakovo was the stop on the railway line close to the Karzinkino estate, where the family had spent the summer together in 1918.

At the beginning of summer, when I invited you to stay here at the dacha, that was done purely selfishly. In that huge landscape composed of money-spending, anxieties, new rooms, and contradictory and muddled emotions, which my own circumstances made ever more complicated and unmanageable, something indisputable and definite would have appeared, in the shape of yourselves. That would have made things easier for me, not harder.

But the summer has passed, and you aren't here, and that complacent fool B.I. tells me in superior tones that all he needs is to know whether the apartment on Lavrushinsky Lane[2] will be available or not (nothing else matters); because if it is, then perhaps you may arrive in March. But how do I know what'll have happened to me by next March?

Oh, how difficult all this is to explain! And everyone around is so kind, and everything I have to say about myself, to make myself understood, is so unpleasant.

So far, I've been able to cope with my spiritual difficulties (both of a family and social kind) because, as it were, they determined my lifestyle. The modesty and inconvenience of my outward circumstances (the apartment, the domestic to-ing and fro-ing, the shortage of money, and all that) matched what was going on inside me. Until now, my inner discord hadn't been aggravated by any excruciatingly painful awareness of external discord—between an outwardly luxurious environment, and feelings of loneliness, death and treachery in my soul.

And now that has been added to me. I've moved from the cramped quarters on Volkhonka into a two-storey house, half of which I don't need, and not only has it quadrupled my monthly outgoings by thousands of roubles—more fundamentally, it requires me to feel unbounded, heartfelt joy and optimism about the future, to echo the beauty of the stretch of woodland running alongside the house. On the other hand there's no point in my waxing poetic over the village customs—with the life that we all live, these are far from being harmless and innocent. Even if my heart were filled with joy, I might still be offended by the atmosphere of greed and philistinism here.

What has my life been about for the past three months? Missing Zhenichka. Not because I regret that 'all this' won't be his—but because I'm longing for him, and for myself, and for my life—and for poverty (and I shall regain it!). This is the first time during these years that I've found myself in such a situation, I mean

2. This was the new Moscow apartment. It replaced the one on Volkhonka, and became Boris's Moscow home until his death.

with such an arrangement of pressures and meanings. But I'm repeating myself, I've already said all that.

The point is that even if I wanted to, I can't assimilate everything of Zina's and make it my own. Unlike Zhenia, she's so hard-working she forgets everything else, she never spares herself, she knows life in the very same colours that are so near to me, and this—together with her appearance—is what attracted me to her. But—as often happens with characters like hers—when it's a question of her children, she'll bare her teeth like a she-wolf even when there's no need. I remember I used to have disagreements with Zhenia about Zhenichka's upbringing, and they poisoned my relations with her. Here it's even more complicated. But I can't narrow down my own life, or even a small part of it, to make myself a mere wordless presence when she's around; that's too difficult, and it would do no good. Sooner or later, somehow, this will end. This very summer, it all hung by a thread.

I should simply love to be alone. Somehow, I have to simplify my life to suit my tastes and convictions. For a long time, it's been a mess—it's impossible to exist and work with hell in one's soul. The only way I could part from Z[ina] would be if I could leave her properly set up, without needing to worry about her. I hate going into these details—at one time you might have got to know her at her best, and you didn't, and now I seem to be betraying her when, through no fault of her own, she appears at a disadvantage—and behind her back, too. I'm forced to make this admission to you, so that you understand how difficult it is for me, in ignorance of your final decisions, to enlarge in advance on my requirements and possibilities and appetites, in preparation for your hypothetical arrival, and to present my everyday way of life as something permanent, when its transient nature becomes clearer to me every day.

And once again, I repeat: there's no contradiction between the new facts I've just told you and what I wrote to you in the spring.

It's absolutely clear that your presence does mean something to me. And consequently, if you were here, neither my home nor my soul would be so empty, and some of the details of my daily life which I find at times so painfully obtrusive that they prevent me from seeing anything else, would dissolve to nothing—if you were near me. And that's what you're extolling me and thanking me for!

As a matter of fact, it's dishonourable of me to talk of the secrets and interests of wholly innocent third parties, even to you. As for B.I., there's no question of my mentioning any of this to him. Perhaps I can hang on till next March in the situation you would have found me in last spring; perhaps not. You don't need to worry about me on that account; in other words, you mustn't make indirect inferences about 'So that's what Boris's life is like'. I live as many people do, as most people do, because the times we live in affect us, never mind where or how. In my case, they have produced failure and confusion in my family life. So I naturally can't guarantee that I'll be able to delay any unexpected or urgent developments until next March—developments that might turn out to affect you in the most immediate way, i.e. in your accommodation.

And once again, don't misunderstand me: no matter when you come, I'll be inexpressibly glad to see you, and somewhere, somehow, you'll be accommodated, better than me. But I'll arrange that in March, or shortly before. Arranging it in September with a view to next March is harder than you can imagine at your distance.

I don't mean to discourage you. Carry on as you had planned; that fits in with my wishes. There's one thing that you yourselves need to know, and no-one else does, and that's precisely what I've told you in this letter.

B.I. thinks (and imagines that the comparison is flattering to me) that everything in my life is sorted, as it is in his, that I'm happy with my paunch, my lot, my situation. And that to crown my long-lasting and secure state of wellbeing, I'm inviting you over, a year in advance, in the firm knowledge of where I'll be then and what will have become of me.

In contrast to that, I desire two things, almost equally:

1) your arrival, and 2) a change in my life that would allow me to live with peace in my heart, i.e. productively. And maybe, given their remoteness in time, the second aim will be achieved before the first.

The government treats me just as you and Fedia once used to: it trusts me, forgives me and supports me. But what I got from you was tens or hundreds, while the government pays me tens of thousands, without getting any benefit from me. Things can't go on like this, and that weighs on me. I've occasionally thought that I'd fallen behind the times, that I didn't understand something about the present, or had some fateful disagreements with it. Nowadays I usually attribute such feelings to my own mood, to personal considerations for which history bears no blame. But don't imagine that I'm condemned to grieve for days on end, or spend hours in floods of tears tearing my hair. No, no, fortunately I'm well, I'm treated wonderfully—much better than I deserve, and all the disorder in my life boils down to the fact that with circumstances as they are, it could and should be incomparably better and happier than I've so far managed to make it.

It would be a good idea not only to avoid showing this letter to my sisters, but to destroy it. And as always, I haven't written anything that I ought to have. And what I ought to have written, I've forgotten, and I'll remember it when it's too late. Oh well, never mind.

I embrace you warmly.

Your B.

Leonid and Rosalia spent some seven weeks in Oxford with Lydia, her husband Eliot, and his parents. They were enchanted by Oxford's libraries and ancient buildings, and by Eliot's charismatic father, Professor Gilbert Slater, an economist and Shakespeare scholar. But their trip to France and England brought no solid comfort. The economic crisis meant there was little interest in art, and artists suffered.

In Russia, the situation had deteriorated further. Evidence extorted from Kamenev and Zinoviev implicated Bukharin, and he too fell under suspicion. The following letter is the most urgently minatory, and the most obliquely coded, that Boris was driven to write to his parents. He had to get his message past both the Soviet and German censors.

Despite his arrangements to house his parents, he now had to make it clear to them that they should on no account return to Moscow. A month and a half had passed with no reply from Moscow about an exhibition of Leonid's paintings; this was because Juvenal Mitrofanovich Slavinsky, who was responsible for arranging the despatch of pictures to Moscow and for the exhibition itself, had been arrested. The letter attempts to convey a coded explanation of this, immediately following the sentence openly warning his parents not to be surprised if there is official silence about 'this summer's ongoing correspondence about an exhibition'. Boris's abrupt transition to the trial and execution of Joan of Arc, and the specific reference, by name, to the mediaeval chronicler Juvenal des Ursins, who had written his history in prison, should have alerted Leonid to the association of Juvenal and incarceration. Boris further attempts to reinforce his subtext by a loaded literary reference to a 'naïve little Mitrofanushka', and in the original Russian by an additional (untranslatable) word-play on the surname Slavinsky.

Boris's warnings against Zbarsky's unreliability are now expressed forcefully and directly. He further, intentionally and frankly, advises his father to consult Yakov Zakharovich Surits, the Russian Ambassador in Berlin, 'as a great art expert' (which he was not), because Leonid had met Bukharin at the Embassy, and Surits might also have been able to warn him of the situation that was developing.

Significantly, at this time there was a hiatus in Zbarsky's contacts with the Pasternaks in Germany, which Leonid complained of in a later letter to his son. But it is not
at all clear that Boris's warnings were understood by his family in Germany.

Boris Pasternak to his parents

24 November 1936. Peredelkino.

My dears,

Papa's letter from London has been waiting here for around a month and a half
(since October 14th), alongside two incomplete answers from me. The main
thing that needed a reply, which I could have sent you straight away, relates to
the new apartment. I've paid for it, and it's there for you.

But however nice that may be, it's not in the least binding on you, and it
shouldn't in any way influence your decision. These discussions have dragged on
so long that you may be feeling differently now. Don't regard yourselves as committed, to me or anyone else.

Amongst all the things that are changing or have changed over these past
months, what remains unalterable? The fact that your arrival would be the greatest happiness for me. But neither my desire to be with you, nor the availability
of the apartment, nor anything else whatever, should influence your plans, Papa.
You can make use of all this, if you've made your decision; but you have to decide
on the basis that you haven't committed yourself to anyone in any way, and that
in your time you have worked so hard, so honestly and so magnificently, in a
field of distinction and honour, that you have earned the right to a proper and
untroubled rest, wherever you find it and in whatever way you wish it. If it's to be
with me, I've done everything necessary; if it's with Olya in Leningrad, that can
be arranged too, and so forth—you can even go to Lida or Zhonia.

After all, you haven't sold yourself to Pepa or become the slave of his empty
talk. The apartment mustn't be a pretext for tying you down, nor the opposite—
your excuse for not coming. If you're fed up with Pepa, you can tell him to go to
hell without further ado.

This isn't the first time I've delayed answering your letter. There can be no
excuse for this disgraceful behaviour. But unlike previous years, there are reasons
for it now, although of course they can't justify it.

The point is that I'm still at the dacha, and indeed I'll probably spend the
winter here. I very rarely come to town, not more than twice a month, and the
mail piles up there. In addition, I'm still intending to meet with Pepa before sending off this letter, but he can only be got hold of in the evenings, and next time

I go to town (on the 26th–27th) I'll definitely arrange a meeting. So I'll finish this letter in town. Perhaps the accumulated pile of letters at Volkhonka includes news from you too, which will also need answering.

Your news, particularly about Lida, makes me very anxious. But God willing, the opposite may happen and there may be news of a great joy for me.

How difficult it is to understand someone. Each time I'm due to visit town, my anxiety reaches a peak. What will be the latest news from you? Is Zhenia all right? You might think that would make me go there more often, and mail wouldn't accumulate for as long as it does now (I sometimes don't pick it up for almost a month). But you and Mama probably felt something similar, so closely is this self-torture bound up with the world I inherited from you, and with your creative work. How difficult that has always been, and how immeasurably more difficult it has become in our day, all the world over. So don't be surprised if you don't get a reply to this summer's ongoing correspondence about an exhibition.

Oh, what a powerful thing history is. Here I am, reading Michelet's 20-volume *Histoire de France*. At present I'm on Volume 6, covering the terrible period of Charles VI and Charles VII, with Joan of Arc and her trial and burning at the stake. Michelet quotes page after page from the original sources, the *Chronique de Charles VI*, by the contemporary politician and '*prévôt des marchands*' Juvenal des Ursins. Where is that Juvenal now, who can say?—yet here I am reading his chronicle, half a thousand years old, and my hair stands on end with horror. That contemporary gained fame[3] by writing down what he lived through, despite spending an age imprisoned in the Tour de Nesle, which might have led cynics to regard him as a naïve little Mitrofanushka.[4] And the Roman Juvenal has gone, too . . . why am I going on about them?

This is where my letter stopped, uncompleted, when Shura, Irina and little Fedia arrived at my dacha, bringing a postcard from you. Hurrah, congratulations on your new grandson, and above all congratulations to Lida, her husband and his parents. What a great, great joy—it seems miraculous to me, accustomed as I am to living in a constant state of alarm and tension.

Well, well, so a new life is starting, in a new place, while I have never even seen Munich, and fifteen whole years of your lives have passed that I know nothing about. Oh, how I long to see you all! If you could find somewhere to stay out

---

3. 'Gained fame' in Boris's Russian is '*slaven*', echoing Juvenal Mitrofanovich's surname Slavinsky, whom Leonid had nicknamed 'Slavushka'.

4. Mitrofan is a character in the play *The Ignoramus* by the eighteenth-century author Fonvizin. Again, this echoes the name of Juvenal Mitrofanovich Slavinsky.

there, I might fly off over the sea in summer and stay with you;—that's probably nothing but an idle dream.

Have Olya and Aunt Asya written to you yet? Aunt Asya has had pneumonia; she's better now. But Olya has had very serious unpleasantnesses in connection with a book she's published, she had to come to Moscow about it and I saw her.[5] What a humorist she is, she never loses her presence of mind—she's a wonder! Now, after the news that Shura has brought me, I'll send this letter off without waiting for Pepa. He can write to you himself.

I embrace you tightly.

Your B.

I don't even know whether you ought to hurry up and send off the pictures. But what can I know about it? Even Ya[kov] Z[akharovich],[6] as a great art expert, is a better judge of that. I'll write about that separately some time.

The anniversary of Pushkin's death on 29 January (old style), 10 February (new style), coincided with Boris's birthday. The centenary of Pushkin's death in 1937 was ceremonially commemorated by a Plenum of the governing council of the Writers' Union. Boris was unwilling to speak at this meeting because of the conflict provoked by his refusal to sign a petition calling for the execution of Kamenev and Zinoviev, his unwillingness to endorse the public condemnation of André Gide's book *Return to the USSR*, and the distorted interpretation of his poem 'Summer Notes' (which V.P. Stavsky, Secretary of the Writers' Union, had denounced as a 'slander against the Soviet people'). Boris was forced to explain himself in print, and ultimately also obliged to speak at the final session of the Pushkin Plenum, where he had to defend himself against political accusations.

Boris Pasternak to his parents

12 February 1937. Peredelkino.

My dear, beloved Papa and Mama!

Don't be surprised either at my silence or at my unproductiveness, so conspicuous over the last few years, or at anything, anything at all. All this is due to the

---

5. She had just published her doctoral thesis entitled *The Poetics of Subject and Genre in Ancient Literature*, but after being savagely criticised on ideological grounds in *Izvestia*, the book was withdrawn from sale. Boris interceded with Bukharin on her behalf, but to no avail.

6. Ya.Z. Surits, the Soviet ambassador in Berlin.

peculiar nature of our life, which is impossible to describe at such a distance. Oh, these distances!

[...]

Thanks for your congratulations. I always remember the 29th, because that (the 29/I) is the date of Pushkin's death, and this year is the centenary of his death. That has been the occasion for great and very noisy celebrations here, and it's shameful that I'm not playing any part in them. But recently I've suffered a number of misunderstandings—that is, the things I say and think aren't always understood correctly. I'm physically unable to tolerate banal commonplaces, while saying something of one's own is only possible in periods of calm. If it hadn't been for Pushkin, I wouldn't have been put off by the risk of misinterpretation. But when it's a matter of his name, I should regard any slip or awkwardness as an intolerably crass, indecent insult to his memory.

[...]

Zhenia has been ill for over a month with pleurisy, but it wasn't purulent, which would have been simply terrible. She's very emaciated. Zheniok is ill too, with flu. Both of them are a constant reproach to me, I'm always thinking and grieving about them; being without Zheniochek is particularly hard for me, but even if Zhenia's return weren't beset by other difficulties, our characters are such that I don't think we could live together. Poor her—such a wonderful, acute person, but with a challenging and inflexible personality, which has been the cause of all that has happened. Papa, Papa, there isn't a single undamaged place in my life, yet I live and will go on living. And think what still lies ahead!

One thing is good—winter in the midst of Nature in the countryside. What a fount of health and repose! I've taken up writing prose again; once again I want to write a novel, and am gradually writing it. But in poetry I'm always master of the situation, more or less knowing in advance what's going to come of it and when it will come. Here, on the contrary, I can't predict anything; with prose, I never believe it'll turn out well. It's my curse, and that makes me all the more powerfully drawn to it. But what I love most of all is lopping branches off the fir-trees for firewood, and collecting brushwood. If only I could give up smoking altogether—though at present I'm not smoking more than six cigarettes a day.

So how is everything going to turn out? Where will we finally meet, and when? You can feel how powerless and insubstantial those words are; I mean they're worthless, one can't believe in them.

Perhaps, if I finish the novel, that'll untie my hands. Perhaps that'll awake a will for action, and I'll start to make plans and be successful.

But meanwhile I'm like someone bewitched, as if I'd cast a spell on myself. I've destroyed the lives of my family on the Tverskoy;[7] and with this feeling and awareness within me, what can I say about my own life? Even in social matters, things aren't as clear to me as they used to be; I'm more inactive, because I have less confidence in myself. Actually, if you look at me, the only healthy things within me or close to me at the moment are Nature and work. Both of them absorb me completely. Is my devotion to them really such a sin and a crime that I have to be ambushed by some catastrophe, so that I never see you again, never see Zhenia living a different life, nor anything, anything at all of the things that worry and goad me? But there's no choice, and I live, in faith and sadness, faith and fear, faith and work. Isn't that what's called hope? Please don't be cross with me.

22 February 1937

This letter has again hung around (10 days). Zhonia's celebration is already past, and now it's time to congratulate you on your 48th wedding anniversary. Soon it'll be your golden wedding!

Live on in all your vigour and health, and bring us joy, my dear ones.

I kiss you both, and embrace you endlessly.

Your Boris

Leonid met Sergei Prokofiev and his wife Lina Ivanovna at a concert given by Prokofiev at the Soviet embassy in Berlin, and made a drawing of this occasion. The Prokofievs then visited him at his home and looked at his work. But by this time, Soviet citizens had learned not to raise political topics in conversation.

The rapidly darkening atmosphere of terror, and even the cryptic allusions in the following letter, continued to escape Boris's parents. The final sentence 'Doesn't your Yasha ever read the newspapers?' is a vain attempt to direct Leonid's attention to the recent trials of Radek and Pyatakov, the arrests of Bukharin and Rykov, and other ominous events widely reported in the Soviet press.

Pepa Zbarsky, who had previously given much valuable help to the family, now appears in a more ambivalent role. He was able to travel between Moscow and Berlin, and to transmit messages between Boris and his parents; but Boris now felt that he was being duplicitous, undermining Boris's attempts to warn his parents about the dangerous state of affairs in Russia, and instead encouraging them to suppose that his advice against returning there was motivated by idle indifference to their concerns.

7. That is, his ex-wife Zhenia and son Zhenichka.

Boris Pasternak to his father

6 April 1937. Peredelkino.

Recently I was in town and read your letter to Shura. I also read him the beginning of my own letter to you; he can confirm what I say.

It was a business letter, which I had intended to finish and send off. But meanwhile the circumstances that led me to write it have changed, and now I have to write a different one. It was about the apartment, but since that option has failed, there's no point in repeating what I had been planning.

I also met Prokofiev in town. He and his wife are both absolutely enchanted by you. I wouldn't bother to say so if it wasn't significant, a living truth. But that's just how it was—the youthful radiance of their expressions when he and she talked about you, in great detail—about Papa's Bach and other pictures, accompanying their accounts with exclamations of 'What wonderful parents you have', as if they weren't talking about old people but contemporaries of their own. All this was a huge comfort to me after the depression and anxiety I had fallen into when I read the passages in your letter relating to Pepa.

[...]

I honestly don't understand. Don't you know how glad we'll be to have you here? Then what's the problem? On the other hand, is it in my power to re-make the whole of my previous life in time for your arrival, i.e. to become richer, more influential, younger and happier by that time than—inevitably, and not entirely fortuitously—I actually am? Come and share my life with me, I keep repeating. What more can I say?

For the rest, let Shura write to you. You can't imagine how difficult it is to write. My hands fail me, and I'm almost reduced to abandoning the attempt. My troubles are far from over, and probably never will be. I repeat, all this is very hard to explain.

But I'm working, that's the good thing, and if nothing prevents me, maybe I'll have finished the first part of the novel by the autumn. Oh, if only someone could talk to you about me the way the Prokofievs talked about you!

Well, I've covered four little pages without saying anything, so I'll take my leave and embrace you. Doesn't your Yasha ever read the newspapers?

Your Borya

Leonid Pasternak to Boris Pasternak

25 April 1937. Berlin.

Dear Borya,

I wanted to write you a detailed letter in response to your last, where you write about the Prokofievs' enthusiastic accounts of us, but I haven't been able to get down to it—I've had to write endless letters of thanks for the congratulations and good wishes I was sent for my 75th birthday. But I mainly wanted to tell you not to get depressed about me and Mama, nor about Pepa from whom I haven't heard for over two months, since there's actually nothing he can do for me at the moment. And the only piece of good news in your letter was that you're working, writing a novel, etc. So the purpose of these lines is to tell you to stick to doing the most important thing, i.e. writing, and keep your mind on this, because this work is more important than anything, anything else. And since you're hoping to complete the first part by the autumn, Mama and I wish you the very best of luck, and send you our blessings. Everything else is secondary, so don't think about anything but your creative work—it's more important than any transient things in life. And when I need to present you with a practical problem or a request, I'll make sure to write to you about it. So you needn't worry. Meanwhile we embrace you, and wish you health, strength and success in your work.

Everything here is as before. Somehow it'll all sort itself out.

Your Papa

Boris's next letter refers to a prose work, the manuscript of which was lost during the war. Individual chapters were published in 1937–1939 in *Literaturnaya Gazeta*, *Ogonyok*, and *Tridtsat Dney*. A more complete manuscript was sent to the journal *Znamya*, and survived in the editor-in-chief's archive. It was not until 1980 that this text was printed, under the title *Patrick's Notebook: The Beginning of a Prose Work*. In essence, it was a preliminary treatment of the idea that received its final expression in *Doctor Zhivago*. See also pages 315, 331, and 365.

Boris Pasternak to Leonid Pasternak

12 May 1937. Peredelkino.

My dear Papa!

What a wonderful postcard you sent me—I don't suppose you yourself realise how precious it was. What I'm going to say applies equally to Mama. I've got so used to addressing both of you through you, Papa, and pouring out my wonder and delight and gratitude to you both. How much you have both done for me during my life, and how much you continue to do even at a distance!

What a load of imaginary terrors you have lifted from my mind! What a host of unnecessary pangs of conscience you have dispelled! And all by means of a few lines on a postcard, through the magnanimity and youthfulness of your language. Whoever told you that this would be so timely, that this was exactly what I needed right now?

Work, work . . . Who hasn't declined and conjugated that word? Have I ever written a letter without talking about it? Work . . . There's even a special way of pronouncing the word—jutting out one's jaw and growling it through clenched teeth, 'wo-a-arrrrk'—which best expresses its essence, one that we're all fed up with and have no faith in, so that one wants to retort 'We know! It's an old story!'

So how did you know that this time it wasn't just talk? Who prompted you to encourage me?

Tomorrow I'll be in town, and I want to send off this letter. When I sat down to write it yesterday, I planned to tell you about many things. But among my own few remaining teeth, which are keeping the false ones in place, some are loose and painful, and recently they've been forming abscesses. Over the past month there have been three in the lower jaw, and now there's a fourth in the upper jaw which blew up yesterday evening. These teeth have to be removed, but the dentists in town are arguing and dithering, and meanwhile I can't get rid of the swellings.

I'm sorry, but this is a dreary affliction, and it's preventing me from finishing this letter. Even if the pain weren't wearing me out, it would conflict with the mood I was in when I began to write. Of course it's only a temporary unpleasantness, and maybe when it's past I'll come back to what I wanted to say—which is that even if my separation from Zhenia and from you, and Zhenia's stubborn nature, make it impossible for me ever to be happy, even so, I do now possess the nucleus, the dazzling nucleus of what one could call happiness. It lies in a manuscript, accumulating at an astonishingly slow pace—the manuscript which once again, after an interruption of many years, has placed me in possession of something voluminous that's expanding in an ordered way, living and growing, just as if my autonomic nervous system, so disordered two years ago, was now looking at me, full of health, from the pages of the manuscript, and returning to me from those pages.

Do you remember my little piece called 'A Tale'? That was merely a decadent fragment compared to the present work, which is expanding into a coherent whole, with far more modest but also more enduring material. I recalled the 'Tale', because even if it did have certain merits, they were only of an internal kind. The present work is full of the same sculptural conviction, but wholeheartedly so, and as I say, in a simple and more transparent form. I keep thinking of Chekhov, and the few people to whom I have shown parts of the manuscript have recalled Tolstoy. But I don't know when it'll be printed, and I'm not thinking about that. (Perhaps I'll write later about this.)

Now please let me stop—I can't take my mind off the pain.

I kiss you very, very warmly, and wish you good health with all my heart, and once again many, many heartfelt thanks for the card.

B.

The relief and joy Boris gained from the calm tones of his father's postcard primarily reflected his hope that Leonid had at last deciphered and taken to heart Boris's coded warnings, and given up any thought of returning to Moscow. But Leonid's next letter from Berlin (not included here) returned to the old theme.

Boris Pasternak to his parents

1 October 1937. Peredelkino.

My dears!

[...]

You must have realised that my prolonged silence, just when Mama had first injured her leg and then been in bed with a cold, must have had some other explanation than hard-heartedness or the blackest indifference towards you, the best and dearest beings I have in the world.

And indeed these are anxious times, not only as regards family events. The general tension creates so much suspicion on all sides that the mere fact of an entirely innocent correspondence with one's family abroad sometimes causes misunderstandings and forces one to abstain from it. But I can't entirely give up getting news from you, or giving you signs of my own existence.

When you console Zhenia about my feelings for her, you're not far from the truth. In the evenings, when I've been immersed in my work and then gone out for a walk, and come home with my thoughts elsewhere, it often seems unnatural and strange to me to come to a home without the two of them in it, and to hear other people's voices there instead.

That is a feeling I'll never lose, and I hope, just as you do—that is, just as vaguely and indefinitely—that one day it'll all change. I can't imagine this any more clearly, because that would mean having to hate or condemn Zina, and she gives me no cause for either—this woman with her seven-month belly, slaving over the most menial work from morning to night with no domestic help, tormented by the whole of her past life, and tormented by me too. On the contrary: of course I love her, in whatever sense the word 'love' can have for me personally, in my fifth decade, after all that my whole generation has been through. My love isn't as easy or smooth, or as primordial, as it could be if we weren't a divided family, lacerated by suffering and constantly looking over our shoulders at that other family, the first ones, with immeasurably more right on their side, who think they've been rejected, but haven't been . . . I don't love her like that, but differently; so in some way I do love her.

So, you know that she's pregnant. When they sent me to Paris and I was ill (oh, all that was quite, quite different from the way I described it then; the reasons were in the air, they were all-embracing: I was agonised by what people were turning me into—do you remember?—I was oppressed by my loss of selfhood, offended by the need to exist as an inflated, completely absurd legend. Now that's all over, and it's such a joy—I breathed such a sigh of relief, and stood so tall, and recognised myself again, when I joined the ranks of the persecuted!)—well, at that time I was very anxious to have a shared future with her, and to leave behind a living memory of us.

The reason was that then, in my despondency, I could feel the breath of death upon me—it's difficult to explain, but I could see that through no fault of mine, my own life, though brought into being by you and so imbued with your truth and modesty, had become nothing but a piece of theatre. Even my own life!— that realisation annihilated me. So, at that time I was bidding farewell to the world and to life, and all the immeasurable genuineness, truth and magic that is in them. And as a farewell gift, I wanted a child from her. But strange to say, it was she and not I who was prevented by physical causes. She consulted doctors, and was given various treatments, and gradually I got used to the idea that the thing wouldn't and couldn't happen. Perhaps I stopped understanding how and why I had wanted it. In other words, her present condition is entirely unexpected, and if abortion weren't illegal, we'd have been dismayed by our insufficiently joyful response to the event, and she'd have had the pregnancy terminated.

But now that there's something in preparation, a new and unknown being promising to enter the existing order of things, it would be unthinkably base to talk about it in the way I've just done. It's on its way, and good luck to it. It's better and stronger and higher than me or my feelings and calculations, and moreover it belongs to that same land of vague hopes in which I see Zhenia's future, when I think about life, and myself, and them, and everybody.

[…]

Leonid's plans for an exhibition in Moscow, and for moving there, encountered inevitable obstacles because, as Boris writes in the next letter, 'everything material is absolutely unfeasible here'. The Soviet ambassador Yakov Surits, who had been involved in the arrangements, had now left Berlin to take up his new post in Paris.

Boris Pasternak to Lydia Pasternak Slater

[December 1937. Moscow.]

Dear Lida,

What joy your letter gave me! I've been given the picture of Mikey standing in his playpen, looking round and laughing out loud. What a lovely boy!

[…]

During the time it takes for letters to arrive, circumstances change. Clouds gather, and difficulties accumulate. Then the horizon clears, and once again things get easier. One must either reply immediately, or after a double delay.

[…]

How much and how strangely things have become intertwined! When I first started reading in English, before the war, there was nothing in the world I longed for more than to visit England. That longing grew stronger when I encountered English poetry, personified in Keats, Coleridge and Swinburne. I discovered a new and unexpected understanding of the influence exerted by, say, Byron, on Pushkin, Lermontov and their time. As always when talking about creative writers, the physical influences of language, phonetics, the structure of speech and so forth, play an immeasurably greater part than ideas and world-views. These latter influences are always secondary, and it's mostly people of the second rank who are affected by them—society figures and critics who envelop art in their talk and writing about what's been said and written—rather than creative artists themselves. Real artists will always be affected by palpable things, peculiarities of people's condition and behaviour (that was true of Rilke, who was most profoundly influenced by France and the French)—and not by the latest commonplace ideas which could easily have been translated from one language to another, but which in the present instance happened to be worded in French.

And the fact that English poetry had exerted such an influence on our own classical poetry (and on recent German and French poetry, as I later discovered) was such a revelation to me that I decided that English poetry was poetry itself, occupying the same position in European history after the Renaissance as Greece did in the ancient world.

And then there followed the years of deprivation. With ever-growing willingness, we gave up our knowledge, habits and inclinations. Bit by bit everything was forgotten. I only had a little English left when I translated Swinburne—whom I had overrated; and by the time I translated Ben Jonson's *The Alchemist* I didn't know the language any more, and had to help out the original text by looking at a French translation.[8]

And then it had to happen that I arrived in London in a sort of dream, without knowing what I was doing, just at a time when I not only didn't remember anything of what I've been talking about, but in addition—unlike every other year and month of my existence—I no longer wanted, was no longer capable of wanting, anything—not life, nor a foreign country, nor poetry—and I spent three days in Russell Street without seeing it, though now I see it as if it were before my eyes.

I'll probably supplement the novel—which will take a long time to write and won't earn me a living—by taking up translation, particularly from English. If it's not difficult for you, and if the book isn't too expensive, could you please send me the English anthology *The Albatross Book of Living Verse*, edited by L. Untermeyer. But this isn't in any way essential, I can do without it. Or if you have a collection to hand with a better choice of poems, you can send that instead, just as you like.

I had wanted to tell you some interesting anecdotes about our life, and instead I've gone off on abstract topics. I'll do it next time, in a letter to you or Papa: I've received both his postcards, and send him and Mama many thanks from me and

8. Boris's interest in English literature dates from 1913–14. He translated Swinburne in 1916, and Ben Jonson's *The Alchemist* in 1919.

Zina. All is well with us. All is well with Zhenia too, but that can't be told in a few words, and we'll postpone it till my next letter.

I should very much like to say something to your husband, beyond mere greetings, and if I'm not doing that now, it's not that I'm prevented by our not knowing each other, but because I'm certain that we'll meet in the future and I don't want to anticipate a living joy by an indirect foretaste.

So there you are, Lidok.

The *Albatross Book of Living Verse* that Lydia sent to Boris remained in his possession till the end of his life; it was one of a small number of favourite books that he kept in his study at Peredelkino.

Boris Pasternak to his parents

6 January 1938. Moscow.

My dears, Happy New Year!

This is to wish you health and long life. Everything that happens, and everything I feel, makes it vital and essential that you live many more long years, so that after some few shorter years I may see you and tell you everything! This is my daily prayer to fate, my most timid, superstitious and heartfelt wish and vow.

I constantly want to write to you and talk with you. Recently many things have happened that have made this need of mine particularly pressing.

I have at last moved into Lavrushinsky Lane. This means that the remaining miscellaneous items that remained on Volkhonka after I had twice sold off my library, and handed over Shura's and Zhenia's shares, and after any number of moves and transfers—all this has been shifted, purged of extraneous rubbish, put in some sort of order, and divided, along with my own old stuff, between Peredelkino and my new apartment.

I have once again looked meticulously, down to the last scrap of paper, through the records covering almost sixty years of our existence, starting from the volumes of *Artist*[9] which passed in order before me. I read through everything, held every paper in my hands.

I spent almost ten days on my own preparing everything for the move. But I was constantly reminded of doing the same sort of thing together with Mama, on

9. An illustrated journal published in the 1890s in which some of Leonid's works were reproduced.

Myasnitskaya in 1911. The circumstances of the two occasions, and the objects of our concern in each case, can't be compared. It's as though they were two similar happenings in two different ages, centuries apart.

And at the same time I saw your lives pass before me—yours, Mama, and Papa's. What a sense of pride filled me then, over and again, at the realisation—with so little spoken—that these were your lives that had been lived, enviably worthy, honest and real, marked out to the uttermost pitch of spirituality by great gifts, success and happy creativity. That nothing had subsequently been added to these lives; that the greatest deed that I had achieved after that was to preserve your good name unsullied and to a certain degree exalted—that name which I received ready-made from you, with a broader, fresher, happier and more significant content than it has now.

Thank you, Papa, for your last letter. Please forgive me, both of you, for this belated reply. The joy that I wrote about in such vague and indistinct terms would have been too narrowly sentimental for a man of my age, if I attributed it merely to the imminent arrival of a baby. Rather, it was rooted in the certainty that some day everything will become easier and will sort itself out, and that certain dreams and requirements of mine (such as meeting with you), without which my life couldn't be called a life, will come to pass. And you were right in thinking that this line of thought, the only one that allows me to exist and work, is only conceivable in the countryside, where it's inspired and sustained day after day by Nature and the purity of its example.

But my baby is born, he's a sweet, healthy boy, and seems to be wonderful. He was clever enough to enter the world on New Year's night, on the twelfth and last stroke of the clock, so that the maternity home's records put him straight into print as 'the first boy of 1938, born at 0 hours on January 1st'. I've named him Leonid, after you.

I would have liked to write to you on the 31st, after taking Zina to hospital, but it's too late for that now, the moment is lost. I got up before 5 in the morning, in a hard Christmas frost, feeling rather unaccustomed to the Moscow of today, as if I were a stranger here, a new arrival. I hadn't got up so early for a long, long time, and I revelled in the walk home, from the old Nikolo-Yamskaya Street (behind Zemlyanka) to Lavrushinsky Lane, where the Tretyakov Gallery stands. I had no idea that so many people get up and switch on their lights at this hour, and I found much that was old, familiar and reassuring in my morning observations. People with an artistic temperament are always drawn to the poor, to those whose lot is humble and difficult; everything is warmer and more mature there,

there's more soul and colour than anywhere else in the world. On my way, I came across the settings of some old, forgotten memories. But all this is so impalpable, it's better not to talk about it.

Zhenia and Zhenichka are at Peredelkino now. I haven't seen how they've set themselves up for his holidays, and I'm afraid they'll be bored. I'll go to see them in a few days. I don't know whether Zhenia knows about the new baby yet, but probably the news has reached her. I expect it's all painful for her, awakening and stirring up old bitter feelings. But she'll have to come to terms with it—in the best sense, I mean without injury to her soul or any brutal pressure on her. I think that from my side, everything that's wanted is there. I've never had that carnivorous sort of family feeling, that power-hungry delight in one's own nest, and all that; and I have even less of it now, with the passing of years. They haven't changed for me, nor for you. You must keep up that gentle kindness with which you've surrounded Zhenia recently. So what has changed?

A child has been born (rather late, admittedly) to a man and a woman, according to the laws of Nature, on a frosty New Year's night; a dear, calm boy, dear and calm as the very fact of his arrival, not so much in a family as in Nature, almost not in a city, on a snowy night. And God grant him happiness and health, and Zhenia too. Everything is so simple and obvious. Zina had a difficult birth, but she seems to be made for difficulties, which she bears wordlessly and easily. She's a marvel, and if you want, and it comes naturally to you, without constraint, then write to her (or send her a telegram).

I embrace you warmly. I kiss each and every one in Zhonia's and Lida's families.

Your Borya

In the summer of 1938 the Pasternak parents left for London, anticipating the further deterioration of conditions for Jews and foreign nationals in Germany. Leonid's pictures were crated up and sent to the Soviet embassy in London. At almost the same time, Leonid and Rosalia received confirmation that an apartment awaited them in Moscow. Leonid recalls: 'I arrived in London absolutely shattered, scarcely able to cross the road. Undertaking a journey to Moscow at that point would have been madness.'

They were soon joined by Josephine and her family, who had fled from Munich, abandoning their home. With the German invasion of Austria and the Anschluss, their Austrian passports no longer protected them. They planned to travel on to the United States, where they hoped to be granted refugee status.

Boris Pasternak to Lydia Pasternak Slater

30 October 1938. Peredelkino.

Dear Lidochka!

Firstly, forgive me for my outrageous delay in congratulating you on your new-born baby Nicolas.

That almost sounds like society talk, as though I had been late in fulfilling some formal obligation and was apologising for it. So let's put it a different way: I myself have something indescribable crawling around here, known as Lenchik[10] or Lyonka, so it was my own life that reminded me, and I know what children are. As for the new events in your own life, I could and should have written something—I should have written whole volumes. So why didn't I?

Well, let's put it even more simply. On September 16th everyone here moved to town, and I remained alone (completely alone, without the housemaid or even our dog, which had to be taken to the vet in town because she was run over by a lorry and lost an eye); and the only reason was so that I could be here, in peace and quiet, amidst the beauty of autumn, and in solitude, in order to write to you. But a month and a half has passed, and I still haven't written. And finally and even more definitely: I continue to live here on my own, in this big two-storey jerrybuilt house (it was built three years ago and already it's rotting and sagging), in a damp forest where it gets dark by five, and it's not at all cheer-ful at night because all the unavoidable work (heating, tidying, cooking and the rest) reminds me of 1919 and 1920, which was the last time I was with you and our parents; and living even on this reminiscence of similarity, for lack of the opportunity to actually meet you, has become such an absolute requirement for me, displacing all else, that I'm prepared to make any sacrifice for it, and I become like an animal and am capable of forgetting myself in defending this need. Because, aside from everything else, it's a kind of happiness too.

Every week I go to town to work. I spend the night there, and see my little baby parrot (the way he wriggles about, shakes his head and coos—his favourite sound being a guttural 'ko-ko-ko'—reminds me of those little round dwarf par-rots), and then I come back here.

I arrived here today, between one and two o'clock, and immediately started working; I haven't stopped till just now, at 10. Over the past 24 hours the house has got cold. Opening up all the double-locked doors, carrying down from the

10. 'Lenchik' was also the nickname given by some family members to Boris's father Leonid.

attic everything hidden away there to keep it from thieves, and putting away everything I've brought here from town (because I keep things as tidy as Mama does)—all that takes a few quarter-hours and half-hours.

But that's not the main thing. What sort of a person would one have to be, to live in the middle of a wood and go shopping for firewood? I'm not allowed to chop down trees—this area is supervised by the forestry authorities—but that's not the point. These fir thickets need thinning out, which yields mountains of fir branches (the broad side-branches, thick as your arm)—all of it ready fuel for several years, for the kitchen stove at least. And that takes me at least half of each day. I've got huge reserves of neatly chopped and broken fir twigs, inside and outside the house. And what should I do in wintertime? I dislike going for pointless walks, and I'm no good at it. Hunting for mushrooms or berries is pretty difficult in November. So the brushwood serves as an excuse for disappearing outdoors for three or four hours at a time, in a forest cutting a long way from the road, among the tall pines; the rare glimpses of the sky, the silence, the falling dusk, here and there a whole tree starting to drop all its leaves, like the leaves falling on the miller in *Rusalka*,[11] because a crow has settled on a birch-tree or a squirrel has rocked it while leaping from one pine to another. And suddenly it grows quite dark, all at once, so that it's hard to find the bundles of brushwood you've piled up in different places. And once again, somehow this reminds me of Mama. (But why? The atmosphere of Ochakovo![12] And this is only two stops away from there! Or is it the kitchen on Volkhonka? Do you remember the special names we gave to the big chunks and little slivers of wood for the stove?)

And the mice! the mice! There are so many of them, and they run so wild, you have to yell 'Scram!', or 'How dare you!'—and even then they ponder whether to go away or not, while you're cooking scrambled eggs with sausage and they're climbing out of the brushwood on all sides to breathe the intoxicating smell of frying butter, and squeaking and singing out.

Well, that's enough of that. I've already said quite enough to convince you that I'm quietly going mad. But what do you expect? No matter how my life turns out, fate has made it impossible for us to meet, and that has torn the heart out of my life and made it forever pointless, and so a matter of indifference to me.

[...]

Now if I add something about myself, you're bound to misinterpret it and get an utterly distorted picture of the way I live. But I'm an incorrigible, inveterate

---

11. *The Water-Nymph*, a play by Alexander Pushkin.
12. The estate belonging to Stybel where the Pasternaks spent the summer of 1918.

bunk-dweller or attic-dweller, a student, a 'corner-lodger', as one friend very appropriately called me. My happiest memories are of the difficult, hard-up periods of my life—they have more earth, more colour, more of a Rembrandt character. I need life to subject me to hardship. One of the reasons why I broke up with Zhenia was that, although she didn't devote herself exclusively to Zheniochek, she still used to indulge him indirectly, she used Pasha's hands to bundle him up and fondle him, and spoiled him in other ways as if she was trying to redeem herself by pouring herself out for him and those attached to him. Of course you can't take all of this literally, it's a caricature and wildly unfair to her. But just the nuance is enough. And of course all the same things will happen with Zina and Lyonia, but firstly I'm going to be more determined and ruder, and secondly it'll all be more difficult for her. She's constantly wailing that I create artificial difficulties, and that if I didn't strive to make sure we had only a little money, we'd have a lot more.

Neuhaus's father has died—old Neuhaus, aged 92. He came from Kleve or Karkar am Rhein, spent over 50 years in Russia but never learned to speak Russian. He was a highly cultured musician (they used to run a music school in Elizavetgrad) and a very interesting old man—hard-working, with democratic leanings. He read something every day, in all manner of languages, until the end of his life (or until his last illness). He enjoyed talking with me, even more than with his own son (oh dear, once again—we've got to meet, you can't tell these things in a letter). In the spring he sent for me, and after complaining bitterly about how healthy and full of vigour he was, and how lonely, he asked me to help him end his life while he was still able to do so like a human being, before he became a burden to everyone. He wanted me to get him some sort of firearm. Of course I rebuked him and said that I didn't have anything of the kind, and it would be difficult to get hold of. When he caught pneumonia in the autumn he was so afraid he would recover, as he had done the previous year, that he crept into the kitchen and cut his throat with a big meat-knife. But that wasn't what killed him—he was so weak he fell down there, in the shared communal kitchen, and the noise of his falling brought people running to pick him up.

Now, why did I start writing about all this? Aha. Of course, he didn't go around naked, there had to be something left after he died. Zina used his vests and underpants to sew a whole wardrobe for Lyonichka (not a huge collection actually—for all his parroty-ness, he's quite large, built like a bear, like the late Yura Serov; people usually think he's one and a half years old or more). But that isn't the point. Zina is upset because I'm pleased that the boy is growing up in cramped surroundings and slightly, though only seemingly, straitened circumstances.

Our neighbours at Peredelkino used to have a playpen—I mean a little fence for babies learning to walk, like the one in the photograph of Mikey. I took it over for Lyonia, but while he was at Peredelkino he was still too young, and then there was no way of bringing it to town because the room Zina shares with him is no bigger than the playpen itself: it was difficult squeezing a bed and a table into it, and the space that's left is barely enough for his cot.

Chatter, chatter—why do I go on? How many days have you spent reading this letter, you poor thing?

What I probably wanted to say is that I'm attracted to this austere way of living. It's just as pleasant as swimming in the river in winter.

It's November 1st, and even today I've stayed faithful to this habit. There's a road that runs above the river on one side. Seeing a naked man in this landscape is something absolutely unheard-of, blasphemous and offensive. Passers-by scold me or whoop at me; they stop and don't dare come close, or else they do approach and endure the sight of me, and finally say 'Aren't you cold, dear sir?' or something of the sort. And I explain that I'm in training, or that it's a habit of mine. That satisfies them, and they go away reassured.

[...]

The following letter refers to the arrest in summer 1937 of Asya Freidenberg's son Sasha. Pasternak disguises the information by referring to him as 'Sashka Confined', which he transliterates into Russian as 'Sashka Konfaind'.

Boris Pasternak to Lydia Pasternak Slater

12 January 1939. Moscow.

Dear Lida,

Thank you for the wonderful photograph and your long letter. [...]

Everyone you ask about is alive and well, but communication with Aunt Asya has become difficult and I don't know anything about her. Let me explain at once. I'll write absolutely straight, so you needn't waste time looking for hidden meanings.

You know how proud, fiery and implacable she is. The last time I heard about her was through Olya, who had come to Moscow to sort out some unpleasantness with her book. Since then we hadn't heard anything from each other—everybody had quite enough to worry about. Then, last summer Irina (Shura's wife) visited Leningrad, and brought back the following story. Aunt Asya had refused to receive her, and got Olya to tell her that she had cursed me and Shura for our indifference and lack of interest in them, and asked us to forget them and stay away. All this to the accompaniment of sobbing behind the door, and signs of the most genuine, indescribable suffering. Irina discovered from Olya that their main affliction was *Sashka Confined*; furthermore, she was losing her sight. But which of us could have guessed all this on our own? When I found out about this anathema, I tried writing to Olya, but got no reply. Now you'll be wondering whether all this is fair. Of course it isn't, but is that the point? How painful it must be for Aunt Asya, if her suffering blinds her to such an extent that she judges me and Shura as if she and everyone else were living in the present time, while he and I were stuck in Turgenev's day.[13]

Maybe I'll go there one day, and get our banishment lifted. And I'll go to see Klavdinka[14] at the same time, and then I'll write to you about them in more detail. Meyerhold is enticing me to come and work at the Alexandrinsky theatre[15], and I think I'll accept his proposal, mainly so as to see the family there.

I'd like to give you an idea of the tone I wanted to use in my prose piece of the year before last, so I'm enclosing a passage from the beginning. Real grown-up people wouldn't be prevented from being themselves by any external circumstances—Papa is sufficient proof of that. I've never thought I was that kind of person, and if any proof was needed that I'm not, let me just say that the least trifle is sufficient to distract me and cool off my enthusiasm, and shake my self-confidence . . . Not that it's always just trifles either.

In short, the piece that I started writing with great enthusiasm at Peredelkino three years ago, in the winter, has been put off twice because of difficulties in my everyday life. The second time, I put it off so thoroughly that it'll be difficult for me to take it up again, even if things sort themselves out and it becomes conceivable to do so. Anyway, time will tell.

I've got 7–8 chapters finished in fair copy, 3–4 in rough and needing revision, and several in my head. I've thought through the whole story line, and although I can't even formulate the main difficulties, it's shameful that no novel exists—nothing but talk. Shameful that it hasn't been written in spite of everything. Could it be wrong of me to send you this fragment? But I'm sending it in the same spirit that Mama would have played a Gluck aria or the Rameau variations—for the sake of a pleasant two minutes, if it's pleasant for you; for calm and peace.

13. That is, as if Boris and Shura were living protected lives, as if it were a century ago.
14. Sasha Freidenberg's wife.
15. In Leningrad.

I kiss all your family, and ours, very very warmly. I repeat—everyone at Shura's, Zhenia's and Stella's is alive and well. I think the same is true for Petersburg and Kasimov,[16] but we need to find out. You're right to get their news through me, instead of personally writing letters to the back of beyond. I embrace you.

Your Borya

The trip to Leningrad that Boris dreamed of never took place. It had been planned so that he could take part in Meyerhold's production of *Hamlet* (translated by Boris), at the Alexandrinsky Theatre in Leningrad. Meyerhold's own theatre in Moscow had been closed down.

An extract from the novel *Patrick's Notebook*, entitled 'Departure to the Rear', was published in the magazine *Ogonyok*, No.1, 1939. Of the seven or eight finished chapters Boris mentions in this letter, six are now known.

February 27th, 1939, was the 50th wedding anniversary of Boris's parents. Their golden wedding celebrations were held very quietly in London, with only their immediate family present. In his letter to Lydia, Boris contrasts this with the grand occasion and the crowd of guests who attended their silver wedding celebrations in pre-war Moscow in 1914.

Boris Pasternak to Lydia Pasternak Slater

[March 1939. Moscow.]

Dear Lida,

I started a letter for our parents' wedding anniversary, but I felt I'd never finish it. I seemed to see before my eyes their twenty-fifth (14th February 1914), and that led me on to memories and reflections. So I intentionally just sent a telegram. But please, one of you (you or Zhonia), write and tell us what sort of a day it was, and how Papa and Mama spent it.

I shan't write much now either. Lyonia's nanny has left. She had some farewell pictures taken of the two of them (she's not much older than him herself, just 17), and gave one of them to us. I'm taking the opportunity to let you see it. I think he has our family mug. He often reminds me of either Papa or Zhonia, when she was his age. What's more, he has Mama's habit of twisting his ear; and he holds up three fingers of his right hand as if giving a blessing, which Papa told

16. The Freidenberg family in Leningrad, and Rosalia's brother Osip Kaufman in Kasimov.

me I did at his age as well. He's doing it in the photograph too. Everything he's wearing, apart from his shoes, was made by Zina.

This is the first time he's been photographed—we've never had time. Zhenia and Zhenichka will also be seeing him for the first time—I'll show them the picture before putting it in the letter. I love him not a bit less than Zhenichka, that's to say I simply adore him—he's got under my skin like a maggot in an apple. What a face he has! Poor boy, he's just gone down with whooping cough.

I kiss you all warmly. Write and tell me about Papa and Mama.

Boris Pasternak to his parents

29 April 1939. Moscow.

My dears,

One surprise after another. Yesterday, after two years' silence, there was a letter from Olya; then this morning there was yours to Zhenia and Shura, and this afternoon one for me too. So you liked Lyonia, did you? He started getting better from his whooping cough, but then got worse again. He ought to be sent to the country, but we've handed over our dacha at Peredelkino to some other people and rented a smaller one (in the same place) instead. This one is now being redecorated, they're sanding and painting the floors, so we can't go there yet. I took the other house, the huge one, because I was counting on your arrival; and then later on, when I'd forgotten the original reason, I kept wondering what on earth we had this monstrosity for—far too large and spacious for us to cope with. Now we've got something half the size, and instead of being in the woods it's next to a meadow, in the sunshine—that'll be better for our kitchen garden.

Our Lenchik has started walking—it's really comic. He's always been used to having his hand held; and when he discovered that it was possible to walk on his own, he still found it too frightening to give up his old habit, so he either presses his little fists to his chest, or he bunches up his trousers on his tummy (to have something to hold on to), and walks swaying from side to side and singing excitedly like a drunk. He's also started imitating grown-up talk, copying the squabbles he's overheard here. His fast, excited gabble, all in bird-like squeaks, is terribly funny. He loves me far too passionately, just as Zheniok did when he was small. That's a real tragedy. Whenever I come down from my study, I have to check whether he's out for a walk, otherwise I'm trapped and there'll be tears—and I'm not made of stone myself. But he's not unique, no doubt you have the same problem too.

At Olya's, so far as one can tell from her letter, everything goes on as before. But Aunt Asya, it turns out, had gone almost totally blind, and now she's had an operation and she's got her sight back! They took out the lens and put in an artificial one, just think of that! There's no point repeating what she says in her letter, but the whole tone of it speaks of a new springtime, a sort of lightening . . . She's had some other personal dramas too, these last two years. That was when they laid their curse on me. Now it turns out they never did. Or anyway, the curse is lifted. After two years of black, impenetrable darkness, there's a gleam of sunlight. Many people have felt the same. Apparently this doesn't apply to Sashka[17]—but Asya's letter is full of energy and drama, it breathes love and exaltation. And she's such a talented writer that I'm not able to respond in kind.

Yes, well—your letters . . . I spent two sleepless nights drawing parallels between that twenty-fifth anniversary of yours and the present fiftieth. And of course I deliberately sent nothing but a telegram, so as not to be overcome by my emotions. The whole subject is too enormous and upsetting.

Anyway, I don't know much about your life, and yet I seem to see it before me. I don't remember if I told you this last autumn, but—despite Lida's own independent household, and despite the fact that you're both equally and absolutely dear to me—even so, in my imagination you all revolve around Zhonia's and Fedia's two children, like a central point. I don't know why, but it feels to me as if this is their story; and the thought that they are the principal actors in it makes my heart ache with pain and pity, and makes them dearer to me than I can explain to myself, or to you. As though I myself were somehow part of it as well; as though, if I were to analyse my feelings towards them, and the way those feelings arose, I should somehow, somewhere, in the distant past when Zhonia herself was an Alionushka, or even a Lyonia—I should find Rilke, and my romance with Marburg, and all the rest. And of course, Papa's Munich Academy, and Mama's Leschetizky . . .[18]

Of course I terribly want to see you. But will I be allowed to? And then, what am I to do with my life? Admittedly, I've been doing nothing but translations over these past few years; but even translations can be little ones or great ones. At the beginning of the year I started work on *Hamlet*, and by early April I had translated two and a half acts—half the play. Then I had to do other things all

17. Sasha Freidenberg had in fact been shot the previous year.
18. Leonid studied at the Munich Academy in 1880, and Rosalia in Vienna under Theodor Leschetizky. Their correspondence from this period still survives. They married on their return to Russia.

through April. I ought to finish the play. I'm doing it for a theatre. But when will I manage to finish it? So far, I'm just doing the roughest of rough drafts. But we shall meet. Only we mustn't think about it, or chivvy and irritate one another.

Shakespeare—and *Hamlet* in particular—has probably been translated some fifteen times at least. Some of the translations are quite recent. I don't like being critical of work done in the past. And the Russian translations of Shakespeare—up to and including the most recent attempts by Radlova and Lozinsky, very good poets—have been so variable, with good parts making up for less good ones, that there's no need for a new translation, least of all one of *Hamlet*.

But if they approach me (out of snobbery or for any other reason) and press-ingly urge me to do a translation, then why shouldn't I take advantage of such a theatrical whim, even if I have no hope of standing comparison with my pre-decessors? It gives me an excuse to run away and hide myself in Shakespeare's depths. And a visit there (I mean, the chance to read him slowly) is an utterly incomparable treasure. Ah, Shakespeare, Shakespeare! Even in translation! And as for the original! But whom am I telling this to? You have always known this better than us. And the passages that have become familiar sayings that everyone has heard in their childhood, in the old translations—I heard them from Papa, and they still sound in my ears, resisting any substitution as unthinkable.

Your entrenched silence, particularly from you two girls, had begun to frighten me. And then, on the very day I was going to send a telegram to ask how you were, I met Pavel Davidovich Ettinger at the theatre where the new production of *Nora*[19] was on, with Giatsintova, and he told me his recent news of you.

So, Papa, you're still painting? What a wonder you are! And what regular handwriting you have!

Well, goodbye for now, my dears. Warmest kisses to Mama. If I tell you not to write so much to Zhenichka, or Shura, or me, you'll be bound to think I'm making some oblique reference to the censorship or something of the sort. But I swear to you on Lyonia's health that I'm saying it without any hidden mean-ing, just as I would have said it ten or fifteen years ago, and always have said. It simply makes me ill to think of the effort you put into writing, and how little we deserve it. I read and re-read what you write, and don't know how to respond to it all.

---

19. The Young Workers' Theatre (TRAM) put on Ibsen's *The Doll's House—Nora* with the fa-mous actress Sofia Giatsintova in the lead. Boris had known her from childhood, because her father had been the Inspector of the School of Painting where Leonid taught.

So—goodbye then, and mind: keep well, keep faith patiently, don't upset one another, and for the rest—we'll see, *Hamlet* or no *Hamlet*. Above all, keep calm. Oh, what a terrible thing it was that I was a bit crazy that time.

Your Borya

But don't stop writing to us.

Leonid Pasternak to Boris Pasternak

9 May 1939. London.

[...]

We're terribly glad, all of us (though the others don't really believe it—I do) that you have this entirely natural and praiseworthy desire to come and see your decrepit old parents, after 17 years' separation, while we're still alive (I was 78 on April 4th, and Mama is 73!!).

This last year has greatly aged us and aggravated our heart disease. We've had to live through so much, and still do—every day now—in complete ignorance of what lies ahead and what surprises are awaiting Europe tomorrow.

[...] Zhonichka and Fedia with their children are leaving for America soon. You can imagine all that lies behind those few words [...]

Your wish to visit us is all the more timely because you'll be able to say goodbye to them before they leave. [...] Since you've been commissioned to produce a new translation of Shakespeare, I think a visit to London and the British Museum library, and the Oxford library, could help you in your enormous task. Incidentally, last winter I sent Pavetti the book *Seven Shakespeares* by Eliot's late father—do you know it?

Fedia decided to move to America after flying over there from Munich in September, because foreigners here have no hope of finding employment in the foreseeable future. And there's no future for the children of 'refugees'; and they're afraid for them in case war breaks out. So not only he, but his friends who have fled Germany, robbed of all their possessions—they're all gradually moving to different parts of America, where they immediately get full citizens' rights. [...]

You're surprised that I'm still painting: well, to end this letter with less of a dirge, let me tell you that I've not only done a large portrait of our doctor's son, but I'm very eager to work—and if I can, that's the best answer to all life's adversities. [...]

Josephine and Frederick Pasternak's departure for the United States was delayed, and with the outbreak of war in September Frederick was interned for some time as an enemy alien. He and his family remained in England.

Boris Pasternak to Leonid Pasternak

21 May 1939. Moscow.

Dear Papa,

Forgive my delay in answering, and many thanks for your letter. I'll press on with my application, but don't hurry me. It's my own fault. People scold me for being such a chatterbox, and I have nothing to say in my defence.

Don't talk about doubting my devotion to you, or my wish to see you—I can't bear it. I can't produce a full and clever answer to such suspicions. If you don't know it yourself, ask the others and they'll tell you that it's not in my power to prove what I say.

Lyonia and his mother and brothers have been away at the dacha since the 15th, while I've stayed behind in town—partly to discover whether I'll be given permission to travel or not. One of these brothers, the youngest, is a very sweet and capable lad, although he's idle (like everyone nowadays, including Zhenichka). As far as the oldest is concerned, who's aged 13, he's an out-and-out tearaway along the lines of Sashka or Alyosha, but with no talent—dozy and spoiled, very good-looking and ominously well-developed physically before his time. My life is poisoned by Zina's protectiveness towards him—she won't let me give him a proper thrashing, which would do both me and him a lot of good.

During his last days in town, Lyonichka started walking (oh, I've already told you that), and got into the habit of coming up to the 9th floor in the afternoons to see me. His favourite activity here, which he repeated time and time again in identical detail, was looking through your German monograph. I love him terribly. When he catches sight of me, I become his prisoner for a long time, and when I escape I'm pursued by long and bitter tears. Under Lyonichka's influence, I've started re-reading fragments of your autobiography (from the monograph). How superbly they are written, and how interesting it all is! No, no—how unequivocally perfect, meaningful, significant and noble this all is!

Leo Tolstoy's granddaughter[20] came to see me with a friend of hers, and they talked a great deal about you. She had already spoken to me several times before

20. Sofia Andreyevna Tolstaya-Esenina, the director of the Tolstoy Museum in Moscow. She and Boris were good friends.

about how she loved your illustrations. 'Of all Tolstoy's illustrators, not one has come so close to him or embodied his ideas so faithfully as your father.'—'Yes, yes, the drawings for *Resurrection*, they're just brilliant', put in the other. 'And what about the ones for *War and Peace*, and the portraits, and the drawings for Lermontov?', Tolstaya interrupted her. And we all agreed that you have no equal.

Please don't get depressed if I'm refused permission to travel. It'll probably be a postponement rather than an outright refusal, and I won't renew my application. If my trip is postponed, then once I've finished *Hamlet* I'll start sorting out your sketches and studies—everything that's jammed into a few baskets and trunks here for lack of space.

But let's have faith that we'll meet. I'll do everything I can to make it happen; beyond that, it's in God's hands. I've taken in your news about Fedia and Zhonia, and am filled through and through with it. But don't fret, don't fall into despondency, don't grieve: you're a great man and a hugely great painter, you've lived a wonderful life—I could never have dreamed of even a tenth part of it; how could you be full of grief and gloom? Everything will be all right somehow, it'll be worthy and exalted, just you wait and see.

I embrace you and Mama warmly, and all Zhonia's and Lydia's people. Our own lot, of course, still haven't answered you, the villains!

Your Borya

Boris Pasternak to Leonid Pasternak

12 June 1939. Moscow.

Dear Papa,

Forgive me for not answering your postcard straight away, as I wanted to. I kept meaning to write to you, struggling with the difficulty of conveying certain feelings and facts, and suddenly your card arrived, and your all-seeing father's heart had already guessed half my thoughts. Thank you, thank you.

For the time being, I think it's out of the question for me to try to get permission to see you in the ordinary way, without making extraordinary efforts and submitting special requests. That's why the realisation of this dream will have to be postponed for a time, though I'm not giving it up and never could. Postponed for how long, you will naturally ask.

One might give a simple answer: until I make up my mind to make these extraordinary approaches to influential people. It's not possible to approach them whenever one feels like it, in all the chaos of everyday life. Don't be surprised if I raise the question of my work, specifically in this context. It's essential for *Hamlet* to be finished—until it is, my own conscience will lack the strength of conviction which alone gives one the right to make approaches of that sort. Anyway, it's all impossible to explain. So it'll have to wait till the autumn.

But let me tell you that I've never missed you so much, never been so keen to get up and go. So if some miracle were to fall from the skies—joining a literary delegation, say, or winning some prize or other—or if Fortune smiled on me in some even more insane way, then no *Hamlet* could stop me, and I'd be off in an instant. That's on the one hand.

On the other hand, if Fedia's and Zhonia's departure and the separation from them were to leave you very miserable and sad, and you wanted to come back to us again, you must know and remember that nothing could be simpler or easier, and it would be the greatest possible happiness for each one of us. It could be done without all the burden of irreversibility that goes with life-changing decisions. You wouldn't have to sort out everything at once: bringing over your baggage and the pictures, for instance, could be done later if it was holding you up.

The London-Leningrad route is ideal—trouble-free, with no changes. The sea is calm, and the boats comfortable.

So, barring any unexpected happy surprises, this hope will have to be deferred for a while, and we ought to keep each other calm and avoid needlessly raising this fraught topic.

Your card helped me reconcile myself to the bitterness of this temporary situation. This is how it found me. Zhenia's flat is being painted and whitewashed, and I'm in town on my own. She asked me to look after Zhenichka while the decoration was being done and he was sitting his school exams, and he's come to stay with me. I think the postcard came on the first morning of his stay, when I went downstairs with him to have breakfast and found the card stuffed into the crack of the door.

Zhenichka and I have been living apart for nine years now, and it feels just as strange and unreal as when our family lived on Myasnitskaya and I used to find my way into your separate studio, and felt that I was a guest in your place and that you yourself were different, and younger, than you were for me at the other end of the same building, in our own apartment. That was a very pleasant observation. He's a fine boy with a good heart, clever and gifted, but too childish for his years, both mentally and physically—I mean he could be more manly. He's still got the freckles that always upset me. If it weren't for them, he'd be very good-looking.

22 June 1939.

It's a barbarous habit, not finishing letters in time. Ten days have passed. Zhenichka has got through to the top class but one, the ninth (the combined lower
and middle schools now have ten classes), and my letter is still lying here, not
sent off. One of the most painful restrictions I suffer from is the fact that I'm
prevented from exchanging regular and meaningful letters with you. But we're
all terribly busy, no-one has any time, and probably I'm the only one of the whole
family to write to you sometimes, ignoring the lack of time—it's so vital and precious for me to hear your voices answering mine.

You're quite wrong to think that I exaggerated anything that Tolstaya or the
others said about you. What is surprising about the fact that they talk about you
like that? Isn't it natural to love you as an artist? Thank God—your career has
been one that anyone could envy.

Well, I must say goodbye, or I'll never finish. I'm still in town, which is very
stupid, because I could have been doing the same things in Peredelkino. But
that's the way it turned out—I got stuck here, partly in the hope that my travel
application would go through smoothly and quickly, which was evidently very
naïve on my part.

I haven't seen little Lyonichka for over a month—a piece of lunacy only I
would be capable of, since he's only twenty minutes away! This whole time has
also been an interruption of my work on *Hamlet*—I had to tear myself away
from it. I've been translating some poems by Sándor Petöfi, a Hungarian poet
of the 1840s (from German versions). At first I didn't like him much, but then
I discovered something close to me in him, and got carried away. There was a
time when I was attracted by Lenau and influenced by him, and this Hungarian
has something reminiscent of Lenau, Franz Liszt and others—common ground,
shared origins and so forth; so I'm not sorry to have spent some time on him.

I've collected the best of my translations of the past few years, and am going
to get them published.

I'm afraid it looks as if a hen has been walking over this letter—I don't know
whose fault it is, the pen's or the paper's, but it's one of them, not me, poor fellow.
Get one of the girls to read it aloud to you so you don't strain your eyes, and give
them all, and their husbands and children, a big kiss from me.

I embrace you endlessly, my darlings.

A tantôt.

Your Borya

Boris's application for leave to visit his parents 'on general grounds' was turned down, and his only remaining hope was to submit an 'extraordinary application', in other words a personal request to the government—probably to Stalin himself. He could not make up his mind to take such a step at this time. Meanwhile Yezhov had been replaced as head of the NKVD by Beria, who started by emptying a whole floor of the Butyrka prison, arousing misguided hopes of an end to the terror. Hence Boris raises once again the possibility of his parents coming to Moscow. But all such hopes were crushed when, a month later, on 19 June, Meyerhold was arrested. Boris was profoundly affected, since it was at Meyerhold's request that he was translating *Hamlet*. He could not mention any of this in his letters to his father.

Boris Pasternak to Leonid Pasternak

15 July 1939. Peredelkino.

Dear Papa,

Well, what about Zhonia and Fedia? Are they about to leave for America?

I've been at the dacha for two whole weeks now. I told you in an earlier letter that here at Peredelkino, a village of writers' dachas, I exchanged my previous house (too large, and in the middle of the forest) for another, smaller one which is sunny and looks out onto the fields.

I wasn't here for the move. For a month and a half, Zina lived in the house and arranged it single-handedly, as well as looking after the kitchen garden which is so big we can barely manage it.

It's lovely here. I've wanted to write to you from the first day I was here. It's very sad that you can't see it. I'm afraid that my enthusiastic tone may upset you: not that knowing I'm happy could make you sad, that would be too stupid for words; but perhaps you might think 'Now he's settled down. People don't yearn to travel long distances unless they're discontented. He doesn't really need us; what more could he ask for?' And you'll decide that I've gone off the idea of coming to see you.

But these two things have nothing to do with each other. Rather the reverse: the better my life is, the more I long to be with you and share it with you.

But seriously, I'm being completely honest when I tell you that this is just what I could have dreamed of all my life. The views, the open spaces, the comfort and peace of a well-ordered house, all these things used to put me in a poetic mood— even vicariously, when I saw other people enjoying them. Sloping hillsides like these, stretching out to fill the horizon along the course of some river, with birch-woods and gardens and wooden houses with attic storeys in the Swedish or Tyrolean style, seen at sunset on a journey, out of some railway carriage window, used to make me lean right out and gaze back at those hamlets, magical, unearthly, shrouded in beauty. And suddenly it turns out that, on the declining slope of my own life, I find myself surrounded by these soft colours, full of meaning, that I used to see only from afar.

It's a strange thing (and a great good fortune) that this isn't my own property. But my lease doesn't make me any more dependent on the organisation responsible for the dachas than you were dependent on the Society of Artists or the School of Painting. [...]

My present neighbours are actually my best friends. I'll give you their names, because they're known abroad, and even if you haven't heard of them, the girls might have done, if they keep up with Soviet literature, even in translation. They are Konstantin Fedin and Vsevolod Ivanov. Ivanov has a more elemental talent than most, while Fedin, also talented, is the most upright and cultured of them all. Incidentally, he's Director of the Literary Fund, the organisation that looks after writers' real-estate questions. He is, as it were, in charge of Peredelkino, the house on Lavrushinsky and a large number of sanatoria including one in the Crimea where Zhenia and Zhenichka are currently staying. But you don't feel his authority any more than you might have felt that of (say) S.N. Trubetskoy as Rector of the University. It's all very much in his personal, unaffected style. I thought of sending you (Zhonia, I mean) a story by him. During the war he found himself in Germany and was interned as a prisoner of war. Well, that's what the story's about.

What an endless letter. I'm just going off to town. A hurried goodbye to you. Soon I'll write you a proper, finished letter. I embrace you.

Borya

The dacha described in this letter, on the edge of a broad field, became Pasternak's refuge for the rest of his life. It was there that he died on 30 May 1960, and thirty years later, on 10 February 1990, the centenary of his birth, the house became a museum dedicated to his memory.

Leonid Pasternak to Boris Pasternak

14 August 1939. London.

[. . .] And another thing, just to finish. About a month ago, Mama played the Schumann quintet at the home of the Director of the British Museum, whom I recently met. (His family all play as a string quartet.) And he—as the chairman of the Contemporary Art Society—bought a number of my graphic works, which will go to a number of different museums, beginning with the British Museum.

CHAPTER TWELVE

1939–1941

On 22 August 1939, a week before the outbreak of war, Boris's mother Rosalia Pasternak died in London.

From Lydia Pasternak Slater to the Pasternaks in Moscow

25 August 1939. London.
Saturday

My dears!

Mamochka never woke again—on Wednesday night she had a haemorrhage in her brain, and simply stopped breathing, with no struggle or suffering. Fedia was with her, having replaced us for that night. Her funeral was yesterday, at the crematorium—my God, how can one be capable of writing this!—poor you, my dearest family too—but we here are penetrated through and through by her, as is every object and every minute of the day—poor, poor Papochka! He's bearing up amazingly well, but how he is suffering . . . Today we're all leaving for Oxford, to all the children—all our hopes are in them now.

Of course, she was lucky to die as she did—not from cancer, never having become crippled, and not having outlived any of her nearest and dearest—she often begged Papa to promise her not to die before her, and he did promise!

Please let all the family and friends know—I shan't write to anyone else. Papa also asks you to publish an announcement about her in the press. Write to us in Oxford, if you can: Slater, 20 Park Town. What a strange thing life is.

Lida

Boris only responded a month and a half later.

The terrible summer of 1939 was marked by the arrest of Meyerhold, of whom Pasternak was very fond, and the savage murder of his wife. During the same period, Marina Tsvetaeva and her son returned from abroad. Her daughter and husband, who had returned two years earlier, were arrested soon after her arrival. These were

foremost among the many 'strange and bitter events' that he could not describe in
his letter.

Boris Pasternak to the family in Oxford

[10 October 1939. Moscow.]

My dear, dear ones!

This is the first letter that I have been able to write you, for various reasons, after
Mama's death. It has turned my life upside down, devastated it and made it meaningless; and in an instant, as though drawing me after it, it has brought me closer
to my own grave. I can't tell you just now about the strange and bitter events that
have begun happening to me and around me, following on that blow.

It aged me in an hour. A cloud of unkindness and chaos has settled over my
whole existence; I'm permanently distracted, downcast and dazed from grief,
astonishment, tiredness and pain. This is my mourning—which isn't worn
here—and my news bulletin—such things aren't issued here. Everything falls to
pieces in my hands, and I catch myself forgetting who I am and imagining that
I'm Papa—I cry out and weep, and this feeling that I'm like him dulls the edge of
our intolerable, unbearable separation.

God grant you all peace and happiness, you and your children, your homes
and those who live there. I don't know how to thank you, I kiss your hands for
remembering us, my dear precious Lida, my wonderful sister—I know what it
must have cost you to remember us at that time, and write a letter through that
sea of tears.

One day, when we meet—(but what am I saying—Mama is no more, Mama
who was and is you all, and all of us?) . . .

Well, goodbye. Live and sustain each other's lives, look after Papa, my dear,
beloved, and wonderful father, my pride and envy forever, through the years
and years of this horrible bottomless separation, my everlasting model, creative,
inspired, indomitable . . .

Live, live, for who knows—perhaps we may still one day be granted the happiness of meeting again.

Your Borya

Naturally everyone around us, and particularly Shura and Zhenia, have asked
me to write from them as well, and to mingle their expressions of unconsolable
loss with yours and mine. They're silent only because it's so very difficult to correspond, even under such exceptional circumstances, even when we have lost

someone who is dearest to us. We ought now to be sitting together and remembering the most distant and precious details of Mamochka's life, and telling each other about them—instead of which one is reduced to the merest commonplaces, cold and insulting, obvious to all and needed by none.

Boris Pasternak to Leonid Pasternak

14 October 1939. Peredelkino.

Dear Papa!

I got your postcard yesterday, the day after I had sent you my letter. It's terrible to say so, but I went mad with joy on seeing it—I had never expected to hear from you so soon, and was feeling completely incapable of starting a new existence without Mama. I couldn't shake off a feeling of homelessness, of time stopping, of an end—as when the cold weather takes hold, on those impenetrably black autumn evenings; and into this atmosphere your letter came, reminding me that you're still there. And how direct, firm and courageous your handwriting is.

Of course, Mama's death alone would have been enough to knock me sideways—that goes without saying. But the news fell on prepared ground.

I am mortally tired of life, its bombastic triumphalist stupidity, its boastful parading of empty appearances which it proclaims to be self-evident truths, its insatiable greed.

I wrote in my letter of two days ago that some time would have to pass before I could come to terms with my terrible miscalculation (for I had always believed I would see Mama again), and start a new and sorrowful chapter in our history— the chapter without Mama. When I've got used to it, I'll be able to write more easily and at greater length.

I'm sending you a photograph of Lyonichka from this summer. When the sky grew grey over my head, and the emptiness and silence of non-existence spread out in all directions, he (together with Shura, Zhenia and the others, not to mention his own mother and all the members of our everyday domestic circle)—he was the only clear sound amidst the pandemonium, the only link with a holy and noble life, the only thing that I lifted up, and carried in my arms, and bathed with my tears. I've always thought he looks a little like you. Prokofieva, who saw him last summer and knows and remembers you, thought that the upper part of his face was from you, while the lower part was his mother's. The way he holds his head, I think, is completely yours.

He's very attached to me, loves order and quiet, and because of his attachment, the features of my old age involuntarily appear, stamped and carved onto his face—my contemplative, taciturn, gloomy side. On this photograph he's a year and a half old.

Thank you again for the healing that breathes from your postcard. I couldn't be writing in this way if I didn't have it on the table in front of me. That's enough for now.

I kiss you all very, very warmly. If Lydia has a spare copy of Prof. Slater's book (about Shakespeare), and if it isn't too much trouble, do ask her to send it—I'd be interested to see it. But that isn't in any way essential.

When I sat down to write to you, I meant to say something different, but forgot. This is something that happens more and more frequently.

Your Borya

Leonid had sent Gilbert Slater's book *Seven Shakespeares* to Ettinger, and was offering to send it to Boris too. In his next letter, Boris has to retract his acceptance, for fear of the new dangers of corresponding with a foreign country, following the pact of friendship just signed between Germany and the USSR.

Boris Pasternak to his father and sisters

4 November 1939. Peredelkino.

My dears!

Did you get my letters? Stupidly, I wrote something to Lydia about a booklet of Prof. Slater's about Shakespeare, but don't let her send anything. I swear I don't know how these things get done nowadays. You never know, it might cause problems.

[…]

I get a very strange feeling when I pick up my pen to write to you. I have trouble imagining that you exist in the world, and that I, your son and brother, exist, and that all this writing of letters into space is thinkable and somehow meaningful. Before this, quite recently, the feeling wasn't so extreme. Mama's death has carried away some last drop of reality. And apart from that, it's also a question of my own old age and tiredness. Probably I've been kept alive until very recently by a constant state of tension, and with Mama's death it has snapped.

But your letters bring me back to life; every line of your postcards (please keep to postcards for the time being) is a joy to me in our separation, a heartfelt luxury of almost forbidden intensity.

But why complain? The translation of *Hamlet*, which I finished in a rough draft in August and which I'm now copying out in its final version, is an astonishingly powerful, bottomless and inexhaustible source of comfort. It's as though, in my present orphan state, someone had installed a great conservatoire organ in my room, and I were living on nothing but Bach from morning to night. I think I've done a good translation. It's too early and pointless to talk of its outward fate. Obviously it won't perish. But working on Shakespeare is a joy beyond compare.

I kiss you all. If I've upset you by anything I've said, please forgive me.

Your Borya

Leonid Pasternak to Boris

18 November 1939. 20 Park Town, Oxford.
My dear son Borya, my dears every one!

Some two weeks ago I wrote a long letter with a detailed description of our dear Mama's and Babushka's death, and also of our move to Oxford. Unfortunately this letter (with a photograph of dear Mama in the garden) was returned with a note to say that letters addressed abroad have to be short and with no enclosures. That letter was a reply to yours to Lidochka, your first letter after Mama's death, and to your second one with the photograph of dear little Lyonia.

What can I say about the words in which you, her loving son, wrote about your so beloved mother (forgive me for stripping down any expression of my feelings here, to keep the letter short as I must). You found the right words, right for all of us, to express our immeasurable grief at the loss of our dear Mama. While I was writing you a reply, incidentally advising you to take yourself in hand in spite of everything, because you have young children and it's your duty to bring them up and set them on their feet—we got your second letter with the photograph of dear little Lyonia, almost as if you had sent it to reassure me, and saying that Lyonia (alone) had reminded you of the sacredness and nobility of life.

And then yesterday (tell Shura), we had his postcard with a postscript from Ina—how grateful we are to them and how we share their sorrow.

I'm living with Lidochka and her family, while Zhonichka and hers are not far away. Perhaps I'll tell you some more about this, piecemeal, next time, and meanwhile I embrace you all.

Papa

Lydia Pasternak Slater to Boris Pasternak

29 November 1939. Oxford.

My dear Boryusha,

How glad your last letter made us! We here have exactly the same feeling—I and Zhonechka in particular—that reality, warmth, and something 'living' is only to be found in contacts with Papochka, or you, or Shurochka—or with a few of Mamochka's former friends—while everything else—even people close to one, like Eliot or our personal friends—are in a different category, one doesn't want them, they don't matter. The children, of course, are a special case, but being so involved with Mamochka's perception of them, they belong to the first group. Write to us as often as you can, whenever you possibly can—and we'll do the same. Thank you, my darling, for everything!

Your Lida

[…]

Leonid Pasternak to Boris Pasternak

30 November 1939. Oxford. 20 Park Town.

My dear Borya!

A full three months have passed, and I'm still getting moving letters of sympathy for poor Mama's death—everyone loved and valued her so much. She died the death that she had wished for all her life—with no suffering, suddenly and while unconscious. Of course, the last winter with four attacks of influenza had weakened her health. But she had recovered, and a few days before her death, when she discovered that Zhonichka wasn't going to leave for America after all, she said she felt happy. On the day of her death, there was no warning of the catastrophe; she worked, made the lunch as usual, and so forth. After lunch we rested as we always did. Zhonichka and her children were at the seaside. There was nobody at home but the two of us and Fedia, who had to stay in town on business. Around 5 in the afternoon, I had to go out as well, to deal with my exhibition.[1] Mamochka insisted that we should both go out and not worry about leaving her alone. She sat on the bed to dress. I went into the next room for a

---

1. Leonid was still trying to arrange the despatch of many of his paintings to Moscow, both for an exhibition and for presentation or sale to Soviet museums.

minute. When I came back, she was sitting in just the same position, but I was struck by some movements as if she were trying to keep her trunk and head from falling backward. I even shouted to her not to fool around, and called her name loudly as I made my way to her through our narrow room, and shouted—what was wrong with her? Not a word in reply. When I reached her, I froze with fear, seized her with both hands, held her from falling backwards, and loudly called Fedia to come and help. I had to call him several times before he came running upstairs (supporting the weight of her body had started giving me terrible angina pains), and he helped me to lay her on the bed. She remained unconscious. Fedia ran for the doctor.

I'll finish next time.

Papa

Leonid Pasternak to Boris Pasternak

4 December 1939. Oxford.

My dear Borya!

I hope you got my last postcard describing dear Mama's death. I continue.

Fedia ran to phone the doctor. I was feeling her pulse and still calling her—but not a sound. She was profoundly unconscious. At the same time her pulse remained normal, which gave me some hope—although I was beset by the gloomiest thoughts. I realised that she had probably had a stroke, since there were signs of paralysis in the right half of her body. She began to vomit copiously. At last the doctor arrived and diagnosed a stroke (cerebral apoplexy and paralysis of the right side). He said she was not to be touched or woken, and was not to be given any medicine until she woke up. Then a second doctor arrived, and came to the same conclusion, and finally a third one—who said the same again, but she (this was the wife of our family doctor, and a doctor herself) advised that Mama should be transferred to a nursing home near their house, where she could be cared for better than at home (since 'her recovery could take 2–3 weeks'). So that evening she was transferred to the nursing home. She was still asleep. Next morning Zhonichka and Lidochka arrived. We took turns watching by her bed—but she continued deeply asleep without regaining consciousness, and on August 23rd, still without recovering consciousness, after 56 hours of profound sleep, at around 11 at night (Fedia was on watch), she quietly fell asleep for ever.

After the cremation (which was what she had always wanted—she was afraid of being buried alive in a state of lethargic sleep) and the funeral service (dear

Fedia of course arranged everything, since I wasn't capable of it), we all moved to Oxford. I am living with Lidochka and her family, while Zhonichka and Fedia with their children are not far away from us in an apartment they have rented. The urn with Mama's ashes has been brought to the local crematorium. There— I've told you all I can, in brief, so that you may all know how dear Mamochka died.

I embrace you all.

Papa

Boris Pasternak to Leonid Pasternak

14 February 1940. Moscow.

My dear Papa!

All your postcards, including the last one with birthday greetings, arrived with no delay. Although I had reasons, and very good ones too, for putting off my reply, it's still terribly mean of me not to have answered you before now.

Firstly, I thank you very warmly for your description of Mamochka's last day (the last day she was conscious). By the time I received it (all the postcards arrived more or less at the same time), my work had already helped me to overcome my initial annihilating sense of grief, and I read it with tears of sorrow but without any death-dealing sensation of emptiness. On your side too, there was so much concentrated observation, alongside the pain, in what you wrote that when I read it, I could see everything, and lived through that day together with you in my thoughts.

I have wanted to write to you for a long time, but I always had a sort of super-stitious fear (quite natural in our times) that some stroke of fate would prevent me from finishing my translation of *Hamlet*.

One day, if we survive and peacetime brings us together again, I'll tell you about the indescribable misfortunes that I witnessed at first hand while this work was in progress—worse than anything that ever happened before.

Leaving aside the original reason for my translation,[2] one could say that I was translating freely, not bound by any contracts, nor earmarking my translation for any particular theatre. In November, when the work was only half finished, the Moscow Art Theatre started showing an interest—they were already planning to produce it in a new translation, and had signed a contract with a lady translator.

2. That is, the commission from Meyerhold before his arrest.

I wanted to write and tell you about the day when I read my translation to the theatre board and Nemirovich-Danchenko.[3] First of all, he remembered every detail of your last meeting with him; but since, at his age, there's no great difference between your own age and mine, he promoted you from being my father to my brother, and kept talking about you, your pictures and the plans for an exhibition as though we were brothers until I told him that I was your son, not your brother, however old I might be in years and appearance.

But that's not the point. You ought to have seen that 84-year-old scamp in his boots and gaiters, with his oval-trimmed beard and not a single wrinkle on his face, running across and up the stairs to the rehearsal room where the reading was happening, sitting and listening from 2 in the afternoon to almost 7, with a break for lunch; eating lunch with practically no dietary restrictions, and apparently not needing a rest (which I have to have after lunch), and going on listening and discussing it all! Without flattering him in the least, I could wish that in five years' time I could be as he is now.

They liked my translation, but it was a long time before I knew what that would mean in practical terms, since I didn't ask any questions or drop any hints. Then they rang me to say that the theatre had accepted the play and wanted me to finish the translation in the same style by such and such a date. At first the play was to be directed by Leonidov, but Nemirovich-Danchenko outbid him and will be directing it himself.

This work has been an absolute salvation for me. Many things, particularly Mama's death (the other things you don't know about, and they would take too long to tell) would have driven me out of my mind. I achieved the aim I had set myself, translating the thoughts, situations, pages and scenes of the original, rather than the individual words and lines. The translation is utterly simple, smooth, understandable on a first hearing, and natural. In an age of false and high-flown rhetoric, there is a great need for a direct, ardent, independent voice, and I involuntarily submitted to this. At present people like the play, but later on they'll say—with some justification—that I've simplified the text, reducing its metaphorical and ceremonial aspects—the things that Tolstoy attacked.

Thank you for your birthday greetings. My birthday also caused me some trouble. I happened to discover that the Writers' Union was preparing some sort of celebration in my honour. I don't think I declined anything rivalling the splendour of the Triumphal Arch, and I doubt that I missed very much, but the fact

---

3. Vladimir Nemirovich-Danchenko, co-founder with Konstantin Stanislavsky of the Moscow Art Theatre. He died in 1943; his plans for directing *Hamlet* were never realised.

is that I was very much against the idea, and it was really quite difficult to get it called off.

That took time as well, just when my extended deadline for delivering *Hamlet* to the theatre was running out and my birthday was coming closer.

I celebrated my birthday in an unusual manner, away from home. I escaped to the theatre on Kamergersky[4] with my manuscripts, and spent the whole day in the director's office. By the evening I had finally finished what I had to do, actually in the theatre, and then went to a Chopin soirée given by the pianist Sofronitsky[5] who's married to that Lyalya Scriabina (Vera Ivanovna's daughter) who used to be one of the tiny children at the dacha at Obolenskoe,[6] etc. etc.

Zhonia's birthday is approaching; my best wishes to you, her, and all of you. Forgive me for writing you such nonsense, but there's no way that letters can replace a meeting.

Your B.

Boris Pasternak to Leonid Pasternak

[22 May 1940. Moscow.]

Dear Papa!

At the end of May, God willing, I'm going to Leningrad to give a reading of *Hamlet*, and after that and after I've seen Asya and Olya, I mean to write to you at greater length. I would be feeling perfectly well but for a rather unpleasant episode: yesterday when I was washing, I bent over awkwardly and then straightened up just as unsuccessfully; as a result, I've strained the muscles and ligaments of my sacrum. I'm worried this may mean I have to cancel my trip.

I wouldn't have sent you any cuttings, but Pavetti said that he had sent you a less substantial review;[7] if you're to be sent anything, of course, it has to be this one.

I've been having a lot of success reading my latest work here, to packed houses, and I hope to repeat this in Leningrad and Tiflis. How irritating that I've never in my life had any sustained practice in speaking English! Last year I used to go and

---

4. That is, the Moscow Art Theatre.
5. Vladimir Sofronitsky, a well-known Soviet pianist.
6. Boris described the summer of 1903, spent at this dacha, in both his autobiographies; it is also described in his brother Alexander's memoirs. The Scriabin family had rented the next-door dacha, and the families became friends.
7. That is, a review of Boris's newly published translation of *Hamlet*.

chat with a young lady for an hour a week; it was a real pleasure, but I soon had to give it up for lack of time. Otherwise I could have taken up an offer from our local radio committee and given you the chance to hear my voice live. I've been asked for the second time to write something about my *Hamlet* translation for a fifteen-minute broadcast on our foreign service (my thoughts about Shakespeare and so forth) and to broadcast it personally into the ether—in English. Naturally I refused, for fear of disgracing myself.

My only sorrow is that I'm an old man, and that most if not all of my life has passed in vain. Otherwise (though all this is probably false and illusory), I'm once again full of hopes and plans. Of course we're constantly worried about all of you, but I try not to think about what's happening—otherwise how could one live, and remain human, and do any work?

Your B.

CHAPTER THIRTEEN
1941–1948

Boris's letters reflect his growing anxiety over the start of the German campaign on the Western Front, the Battle of Britain, and the London Blitz. The gap of over a year in this correspondence is mainly due to the war; the few postcards and telegrams the family exchanged must have been lost in transit. The postcards and telegrams Boris sent to England during the war years were all written in English, and are reproduced unchanged below.

Boris Pasternak to Leonid Pasternak
[Original in English]

The 19th of June 1941. Moscow.

Dear papa!

I sufficiently imagine, how suspectable a letter, not to speak of a photograph or of a book in foreign language must be in such times as ours. Yet I try to send you the new-appeared Hamlet-*tragedy in my version, and the card here enclosed. Perhaps after the examinations it must necessarily undergo both on our and your side, it will happily reach your eyes.*

The represented is your grandson and namesake Leonid, the most coward, fantastical and sliest creature ever seen, whose chief passion is drawing, and who, being asked: 'Who is painting better than anybody' points at your admirable chalk-and-oil studies on the wall and replies 'My grandfather'.

I spent with him this winter in this postofficeless village, the very reason why I asked (and it remains for the future) to use for telegraphs and letters Shura's town-address. Our country house is my blessing. God helping I hope to dwell my lifetime not in the town. Last year we got our spacious kitchen garden,—the fruit of our own, esp. Zenaida's labours—half a cellar of potatoes, two casks of sauerkraut, 4000 tomatoes and a great deal of peas, french beans, carrots and other vegetables not to be consumed in a year.

Eugene has brilliantly made his school abiturium.1 After our new rules he must turn soldier this autumn. Eugénie was newly at Leningrad. All the people are living and at health. Mamma's death is kept secret from the aunts Anne and Claudie.[2]

On the contrary I esteem you strong enough as to learn without farther harm than the calm and inevitable sorrow, the late death of uncle Joseph and your niece Sophy.

After all you know of me it is needless to say what grief I have to suffer at the incessant events in the West. As it will seem the feelings are here generally for the English cause. Among other intentions I am occupied with Romeo and Juliet, *half of which I have already made in Russian.*

Judge my Hamlet *not too severely. Accustomed to good old translations you will never like it. Excuse the vignettes, which are partly tolerable but for the most helpless and childish. And the abominable paper!*

And now, farewell! Never make you torments with letter writing of today. We shall content ourselves with your telegraphs as before. Pardon me if my lines will bring you any annoyance.

Farewell once more. Except the war I might say myself overhappy with my life, save that I never understood nor will ever comprehend that I and you will die some day.

Commend me to your sons-in-law and their wives and children, my dear sisters and nephews and nieces. How are Lydia and her baby?[3,]

I embrace you endlessly.

Your Boris.

During four months in transit, the following letter and a separate parcel containing Boris's translation of *Hamlet* miraculously survived the hazards of war, and reached Oxford at the beginning of November. The envelope bears a note in Leonid's hand—much altered since his wife's death—'Rec[eived] 1 November 41, Oxford'. The English postmark on the parcel reads 29 October 1941—three days earlier than the letter. The photograph of Lyonia bears Boris's English inscription on the back: *'March 1941, when 3 years and 2 m. old. How he likes his aunt Joan!'*[4]

1. The school-leaving examination.
2. Rosalia Pasternak's sisters Anna (Asya) Freidenberg and Klavdia (Klara) Margulis, who both lived in Leningrad.
3. Lydia's daughter Catherine was born on 12 March 1941.
4. Josephine.

Boris followed his letter up with a telegram to announce it and (as it were) help it on its way:

[Original in English]

20 JUNE 1941. MOSCOW.

ALL WELL THANK GOOD NEWS EXCUSE LONG SILENCE

—BORIS PASTERNAK

Hearing nothing for a month, he telegraphed again. By this time, the German invasion of Russia ('Operation Barbarossa') had already begun.

[Original in English]

28 JULY 1941. MOSCOW.

ALL WELL LOVE HAPPY SHARE COMMON FEELINGS HOPES SACRIFICES

—BORIS PASTERNAK

A few months later, a reply arrived from England.

[END OF NOVEMBER 1941. OXFORD.]

BORIS PASTERNAK GOGOLEVSKY 8 MOSCOW

LETTERS BOOK WIRE JOYFULLY RECEIVED AWAITING PERSONAL GREETINGS

ALL WELL WRITING FORGIVE DELAY VERY BUSY LOVE TO ALL FROM ALL OF US

—LYDIA PASTERNAK SLATER

Leonid Pasternak to the family in Moscow

20 December 1941. Oxford.

My dears, happy New Year!

Health and happiness to you all! I'm sending this postcard on the off-chance—I wonder if it'll reach you?

We're all alive and well. If only we had a bit of news from you! We embrace and kiss you, and God preserve you. We're with you all, with all our hearts, the whole time!

Your Papa

The family in Oxford to Boris Pasternak

1 JANUARY 1942. OXFORD.
HAPPY NEW YEAR LIONIAS BIRTHDAY BEST WISHES LOVE
—PASTERNAKS SLATERS

Boris Pasternak to the family in Oxford

[Original in English]

4 November 1942. Moscow.

My dearest,

I will use my short stay in Moscow and write you some lines about myself and mine. I stay here at Shura's lodging, where everyone is at health. Before my depart from Tchistopol (near Kazan) where I spent last winter and am about to return for this following, I had a letter from Olga from Leningrad. I do not write you from such a dark and distant spot like Tchistopol because I fear it to be too complicated an enterprise. More than 14 months ago Zina is gone there with all writer-wives and children and got there a place of vice-directress of the writer-child-house, where Lionitchka is placed. Eugenia with Eugen are at Tashkent. Eugen is there student at the War-academy. My dream of me, of which little Leonid always takes part, is to go to meet you after the war to England. After Hamlet *I have translated* Romeo and Juliet *and will now begin* Antony and Cleopatra. *Telegraph me at Shura's address at Moscow papa's health.*

1000 kisses and greetings.

Your B.

Boris Pasternak to the family in Oxford

[Original in English]

8 NOVEMBER 1942. MOSCOW.
BRIEFLY DWELLING MOSCOW BEFORE RETURNING NEAR KAZAN EMBRACE ALL TELEGRAPH FATHERS HEALTH
—BORIS PASTERNAK

The family in Oxford to Boris Pasternak

10 NOVEMBER 1942. OXFORD.

OVERJOYED THANKFUL ALL WELL FATHER WORKING LONGING FOR NEWS ABOUT SHURA CHILDREN ALL RELATIVES LOVE BLESSINGS

Boris Pasternak to the family in Oxford
[Original in English]

24 November 1942. Moscow.

My dearest, my adored!

It will come time, I will relate you all we had to endure the last half of our separation. My work is undone through my forced futility. That is the worst in my steady embittering. But now we have to thank God. His grace is immeasurable. Papa is well and working according to your inestimable wire! What bliss! Two years of such a war and we are yet at life!! Its most terrible part is probably over. How many nights have I spent in my forest-trench past my late country-house!! How often observed the fires and bombardments during my night-fire-watches on the roof of our town-house!

Boris Pasternak to the family in Oxford
[Original in English]

25 November 1942. Moscow.

My dearest!

It is the sequel of card I wrote you yesterday. I resume. One night a year ago, when I was on guard on the roof of our house of 10 stories in the town, a fougas⁵ hit in some steps from me the building and demolished many lodgings. Another fell in the yard with the same results. Much earlier Zina is gone with the children in a retired spot past Kazan, destined for the evacuated children of the writer-organisation. She is there till now. I lived there a year with them. Now I am already 3 months in separation from Lionitchka, my little angel. I will visit the front and then return there. Eugen with Genia are in Tashkent. He is a student at the tank-faculty of a military academy. I embrace you endlessly.

Your B.

---

5. A fougasse is an improvised landmine, but Boris must here be describing incendiary bombs dropped from the air.

Boris Pasternak to the family in Oxford

[Original in English]

28 NOVEMBER 1942. MOSCOW.
WIRE RECEIVED UTMOST JOY ESPECIALLY ABOUT FATHER EMBRACE HOPING
FUTURE MEETING ALL WELL EVER USE SHURAS ADDRESS
—BORIS PASTERNAK

Boris devoted the second winter of the war in Russia to translating Shakespeare's *Antony and Cleopatra*. His whole family returned to Moscow in June 1943, but their Moscow apartment was occupied by an anti-aircraft battery and the dacha at Peredelkino had been ransacked. The most painful experience for Boris was the destruction of his father's archive of paintings and drawings; he could not bring himself to tell the Oxford family about this until after his father's death.

Leonid Pasternak to Boris Pasternak

22 August 1943. Oxford.

My dear son Boris,

How are you all? There hasn't been a letter from you all for a long time. We are all right here and all well, thank God.

My dear Borya, don't leave me without any news from you in my old age (I'm in my 82nd year)!

We embrace you all, wish you health, and kiss you warmly.

Loving you,

Your Papa

Before even receiving this postcard, Boris sent a telegram:
[Original in English]

27 AUGUST 1943. MOSCOW.
WIRE IMMEDIATELY PAPAS HEALTH BROUGHT FAMILY MOSCOW TEMPORARILY
ROOFLESS MUCH SATISFACTION SHAKESPEARE TRANSLATIONS THE REST
IMPOSSIBLE ENDLESS KISSES
—BORIS PASTERNAK

Two days later Boris joined the troops at the front near Orel, where there had recently been fighting. He returned convinced of an early victory, and sent an optimistic telegram to Oxford.

Between this time and the end of the war, no letters passed between Boris and his family in Oxford. He did send them copies of his new translations of Shakespeare, but these went astray and were never received. The only communication was by telegrams, exchanged at long intervals, those from Oxford reassuring Boris about his father's health and announcing the birth of Lydia's second daughter, Ann, on 3 August 1944. Boris always hoped his books would eventually arrive, and repeatedly enquired about them in his telegrams. But instead of the long-awaited confirmation of his parcel's arrival, he suddenly received news of his father's death.

Boris Pasternal to the family in Oxford

[Original in English]

9 JULY 1945. MOSCOW.

CRUSHED DOWN BY DREADFUL NEWS. HOW TO SURVIVE THE IRRECOVERABLE LOSS OF THE SAD DISCOLOURED LIFE WITHOUT THE ADMIRED GREAT MAN ARTIST LIFE EXAMPLE POOR POOR DEAR FATHER ADVICE MY HOPE OF OUR NEAR COMMON MEETING NEVERLESS LOVE DO NOT LOSE COURAGE HOLD. SHURA WIVES CHILDREN SUBSCRIBE. YOURS IN GRIEF AND COMMEMORATION MORE EVER

—BORIS PASTERNAK

In the summer of 1945, Isaiah Berlin, then a Fellow of All Souls' College, Oxford, and a good friend of Josephine and Lydia, was sent to Moscow to work at the British Embassy. He met Boris on several occasions, brought family photographs, and told him about the lives of Josephine's and Lydia's families in Oxford. (He later published a vivid record of these meetings.[6]) He gave Boris a copy of a recently published collection of English translations of his prose,[7] which delighted Boris—it was his first book in English. Lydia sent him various articles of clothing, including his father's shoes, and copies of her own poems in English, including 'I am allergic to the touch of spring' which Boris mentions in his reply. These poems were later published in book form.[8]

6. Isaiah Berlin, 'Meetings with Russian Writers in 1945 and 1956', in *Personal Impressions*, ed. Henry Hardy (London: Hogarth Press, 1980). See also p. 379.
7. *Boris Pasternak: The Collected Prose Works*, ed. Stefan Schimanski (London: Lindsay Drummond, 1945).
8. Lydia Pasternak Slater, *Before Sunrise* (London: Mitre Press, 1971).

To make up for the loss of his Shakespeare translations, he handed Isaiah Berlin several copies of his *Antony and Cleopatra* and *Romeo and Juliet* to bring back to Oxford. One copy is inscribed 'To my dear sisters and their families. Borya. How terrible that my letters and some 12 books have disappeared!'

He also inscribed a copy of *Zemnoy prostor* ('Earth's Vastness'), a little book of his war poems, published at the start of the year, with the words 'To the Pasternaks. My dears, when will I ever see you again? Your Borya'.

Together with other items, he attached the following letter to Lydia—in Russian, at last.

Boris Pasternak to Lydia Pasternak Slater

10 December 1945. Moscow.

To beloved Lidochka, in place of a real, long letter, which it still, still, isn't possible to write. But never mind, even if we never meet (how painful! how terrible!), never mind! Everything deserving of long survival is especially, fabulously alive. Nothing will perish. Thank God for everything!

[…]

Instead of a letter, here's an article about Chopin. It has a little of both Mamochka and Papa in it. […]

Why don't you write to me? You might send a letter some time, when someone comes here. O my dears!! If only you knew everything!!!! I can't go on, I begin to howl.

On the margin of the article is another note:

Lidochka, I wrote this last winter at the request of a newspaper (but they didn't print it). I wrote it around February 11th, as a birthday present to myself, in a dacha in the forest where I was spending the winter with Lyonichka, my younger son.

But within myself I am happy, undeservedly happy!! I haven't told you anything yet about the great thing that I want to tell, and shall tell, if I survive—and by now my destiny is such that it's as if it had all been told and was already known.

Isaiah Berlin's final departure from Moscow was delayed; meanwhile he had delivered this package to Oxford and returned with letters from the sisters. He now agreed to carry the following long letter (in Russian) from Boris, describing in detail the events of the past five years. It contains one of the first mentions of Boris's work on the planned novel *Doctor Zhivago*. Enclosed with the letter was an early draft of Boris's poem 'To Marina Tsvetaeva'.

Boris Pasternak to his sisters

[End of December 1945. Moscow.]

Dear Zhonia and Lida!

Why is there no word from you about Fedia, and about yourselves, your homes and children? Thank you for your 'Spring', Lida. Good for you! Do you do a lot of this? I've asked several times about Alyosha, Styopa and Ena[9]—are they alive? Don't be surprised at me fussing like this. I'm going to fire sentences at you, to keep things brief.

Actually, the main obstacles stopping me from writing are not the weakness of words, my own weakness, or the rigours of the censorship. All my life, I've felt as if I was living for our parents and you, as if I was on display to you, for your pleasure. And now it's too late for Papa and Mama. Coming to see you in England would be more than the summit of happiness for me: at our meeting, I think, my life would take those few final forward steps that it has always lacked. Only then would I understand what it is I have to say to you—the most alive, painful, important things: meeting you would make all that clear to me. The fact that I can't guess these things in advance, and don't want to fake them, is what makes our correspondence relatively worthless if not impossible.

Papa! But that's an ocean of tears, sleepless nights—and if one wrote it down, it would be volumes, volumes and volumes. It's bitterly disappointing that my letter sent to him via Maisky[10] never arrived. In it I had told him everything (as I once told Rilke), everything that I had stored up to tell him over my whole life, especially these last years. My astonishment at his perfect mastery and talent, the lightness and ease with which he worked (jesting and playful, like Mozart), the sheer quantity and importance of his works—my astonishment being all the more lively and intense because comparing him with me in all these respects disgraces and annihilates me. I told him not to be hurt at the fact that his huge talent hasn't gained a hundredth of the recognition it deserves, while I am obliged to burn with shame when my own role is so monstrously inflated and overrated—my

9. Members of the Austrian branch of the family, Frederick Pasternak's relatives. Frederick's brother Albert (Aliosha) perished in a Nazi camp. His daughter Ena came to England and then emigrated to Australia. Frederick's nephew Stephen (Styopa) emigrated to South America.

10. Ivan Maisky, the Soviet Ambassador in London.

half-mythical role, founded on a few (very few) fragmentary and formless trifles, most them worthless and rejected by me (this is my constant quarrel with audiences and young people, who defend *My Sister, Life* and *Themes* . . . , impervious to my arguments proving how bad they are).

I wrote to Papa that life has not treated us unfairly, fate has not undervalued or injured him, that in the last analysis he is still the winner—he, who lived such a genuine, authentic, interesting, rich and active life; part of it in the 19th century, so blessed for him, and part of it keeping faith with it—and not in the wild, devastated, unreal and fraudulent twentieth—where my own share, instead of everything real that surrounded him, instead of his freedom, his fruitful activity, his journeys, his sensible and beautiful existence—has been nothing but pleasant words which I sometimes hear, and never deserve.

Incidentally: in all these years there hasn't been a single mention of Papa, probably on the grounds that he was politically suspect. So the obituary by Grabar[11] came as a complete surprise (the stupid inaccuracies in his article are understandable and excusable). I enclose it. And another thing:—Shura has just given me his letter to you, and to avoid repetition, I won't touch on the questions he raises.

Don't be too worried about the collection of Papa's works that have remained with you. If you can arrange an exhibition in London in a style that befits you and humanity in general, in a tactful and honourable way, without selling your souls to the devil or signing your names in blood or any other threepenny fanfares— go ahead and arrange one. If not, don't worry and don't feel guilty towards other people or Papa's memory. All this won't go away, even if I'm wrong about my longevity or yours, or if my belief that I'll get to visit you is a delusion. Don't on any account send anything over here yet.

My experiences with Papa's possessions have been typical. For over ten years, because there was so little room in town, I kept his archive of rough sketches (charcoal drawings from school, rough drafts of sketches, oil studies from all through his life, ever since his earliest years, and a few finished works) in a trunk weighing 15 poods[12] and some portfolios, and was tormented by the thought that this was all hidden away, doing no good to me or anyone else. It wasn't till just before the war, in the spring of 1941, when things had got a bit easier at the dacha (I spent a few happy winters with Lyonichka there) that I sorted through the contents of the trunk, picked out a lot of wonderful works and with

---

11. Academician Igor Grabar, 'In Memory of Leonid Pasternak—Noted Russian Artist', *Moscow News*, July 18, 1945. This was a shortened translation of an obituary published in Russian in *Sovetskoe Iskusstvo* ('Soviet Art'), Moscow, on 13 June.

12. 246 kilos.

tremendous difficulty (any practical, material undertaking being almost impossible here) had them framed and put under glass, and covered the walls of my dacha and my apartment in town with these beautiful things. But that only lasted a few months.

When the air raids started, and Zina and the children moved to Chistopol (Kazan province), I was faced with the question of where to collect these pictures together to protect them from the bombs (in September Moscow was bombed every night). It would have been easy to carry the pictures across to the Tretyakov Gallery myself (I live opposite), but the gallery was being evacuated and they had refused to accept any outside works. The Tolstoy Museum offered to help, but in those October days when the front passed through the village where our dacha is, there was no hope of getting hold of a truck and no way of transporting the pictures. Despite all that, I divided up the pictures I had selected and hung in my home, and managed by hook or by crook to store them in three different places (to lessen the risk of their all being destroyed). In one place, Zhenia's empty and abandoned flat (she had gone to Tashkent), most of the pictures survived; but everything at the dacha and the town apartment was burned or destroyed.

All in all, everything here (particularly with me) seems to melt away, wear out and perish, rather than appearing and being within reach. My material baggage is very light, like a student's, despite my age and the presence of the children.

By the way—a month before Papa's death we buried Zina's eldest son Adrian, 20 years old. He died of tuberculosis of the bone, which had kept him in hospital all through the war. That's life: his mother, who adored him, knowing he was at death's door and that every minute counted, tore herself in half between Sokolniki (the hospital) and Peredelkino (us and the dacha), and on the day before he breathed his last, she came to us to dig up the potato beds, so as not to miss the harvesting season.

As I was saying, our circumstances here are very simple. I don't keep my rough drafts or letters, and have almost no library. When I went to visit Zina in Chistopol in the winter, I left some of our parents' letters in Zhenia's flat, and they survived; but the rest, the best of my correspondence, together with some letters from Gorky, Rolland and others, and all (about 100) of my letters from Marina Tsvetaeva (who hanged herself in Elabuga, where she had been evacuated—I wrote a poem to her, which I enclose)—this whole collection I handed over for safe-keeping to some student girls I knew at the Scriabin Museum. I recently heard that one of them, devoted to me and an admirer of Marina, used to carry them with her everywhere she went, never losing sight of them so that they shouldn't be lost; and three months ago, while returning from Moscow to her home at Bolshevo, completely exhausted, she absent-mindedly left them either in the railway carriage or under a fir-tree in the wood where she had sat down to rest.

There you have the fate of objects around me. (What a mechanical way of addressing you—I'm writing to you both, and keep on using 'you' in the singular, alternately imagining you, Lida, and Zhonia!)

Now a few words about something quite different. Of course it's more than a joy to me, it's a sort of divine happiness to have found my way—even accidentally or through a mistake by my well-wishers—into the company of names that I have always treasured above everything in my life—Rilke, Blok, Proust. To find myself surrounded by this atmosphere is natural and right. A great consolation for me, with my harsh fate, has been your Personalists involved in the journal *Transformation*.[13] I don't know them in detail and can't say anything about them individually, particularly not as artists, but the overall spiritual phenomenon of a sort of brotherhood, its ideological tendencies, its main features (Symbolism and Christianity?),*—all this coincides astonishingly well with what's happening to me; it's the thing closest to me, the warmest spot on the cold wall that separates me from you. I know that it isn't the English press or literature, nor anything noticeable in the area of English public opinion; I know that they (Bowra[14] with his splendid translations and his profound and fascinating books about the Symbolists and epic poetry, the magazine *Horizon*, and two or three people at the universities) don't mean anything, they're just a tiny corner. But it's just this corner, which for simplicity I call England, and then the young people in Russia, and thirdly Georgia—these are three points of a sort of miraculous, inexplicable contact between me and fate and time, a mystery or a romance, which might fuel a lot of superstition, because it's all like an unexpected fairy-tale.

You see it in the concert halls which sell out as soon as my name appears on a poster—and if I ever hesitate while reciting any of my poems, I'm prompted from three or four different directions. You see it in the meetings and the letters I've been getting all my life; and you see it with the Georgian intelligentsia and the art in the Caucasus, which I hadn't visited for twelve years. I flew back there

13. Pasternak derived great solace and support at this time from the interest and encouragement of a group of young English writers. They were the founders of the Escapist movement, which regarded war as an unconditional evil. They published the journal *Transformation*, devoting a great deal of space to the leaders of European Symbolism—Proust, Rilke, Blok. They counted Pasternak among their kindred spirits, and published translations of his prose and verse.

14. Maurice Bowra was an Oxford academic, Warden of Wadham College and Professor of Poetry. He was an admirer of Boris Pasternak, corresponded with him, included him in his anthology *A Book of Russian Verse* (London: Macmillan, 1943), and himself translated a number of Pasternak's poems.

for two weeks last October. It's a bit like your Scotland—mountains, ballads, chivalry and openness, drums and bagpipes, all-night feasts with speeches till morning, and every family with marvellous wine from their own vineyards, the way we have our own potato beds.

I'm 55 years old, we're living in a cold and sobering Soviet era, and I'm not a gushing young lady:—I never imagined all this was still possible. Of the 14 days I spent there, I only slept two nights. I don't understand how I survived this ecstatic dissolution of my whole self in others, and others in me, without becoming ill. It's interesting that this world of somewhat sacrificial, inexplicable success, the miracle of total mutual understanding and giving of oneself, constantly surrounds me, always watching me from somewhere nearby. You'd think there could be nothing better than to give oneself up to it uninterruptedly, for the whole of one's life. The surprising thing is that I very rarely allow myself to enjoy it, and I avoid performing for years if not decades on end. But I'm starting to rattle on—I must shorten this letter.

I'll probably write to Bowra and Schimanski.[15] I'm reluctant to write in Russian, but writing in English will take time.

Apart from liking Schimanski and wishing him well, because he expresses views that are close to mine and dear to me, I feel he's done an immeasurable amount for me, far more than I deserve (I'm afraid it may have been too much), and has placed me under an eternal obligation to him. I'm terribly pleased with the book of prose and his most interesting introduction, and only two things have cast a shadow on my pleasure (which is why I wondered whether he might have done too much). True, he says in his introduction that if I had been involved in the publication, I might have handled the material differently, etc.

Anyway: 1) I was upset that in addition to the worthwhile work *Safe Conduct* (though even here there are pretentious and incomprehensible passages which could have been thrown out) and 'Luvers's Childhood', they've also translated and printed the awful *Mark of Apelles, Letters from Tula* and *Aerial Ways*, which I dislike so much that I'm afraid of them and would like to forget about them. 2) It seems to me that the book will put people off by the immodesty of its outward appearance. How can the publishers not have felt it tactless to print a picture of a fine-looking eight-year-old barefooted boy,[16] or one of me and Mayakovsky that's been retouched over and over till it's unrecognisable,[17] or caricatures by

15. Stefan Schimanski was an English critic and translator. He edited a collection of Boris Pasternak's writings (*Boris Pasternak: The Collected Prose Works*, London: Lindsay Drummond, 1945).
16. A sketch of Boris as a child by his father. This is now in the Ashmolean Museum, Oxford.
17. Boris was rightly irritated by one of the illustrations in the English edition of his prose works

Kukriniksy?[18] Of course, in each case it's my fault for not being an Apollo—but that being so, was there any need to strip me bare to this extent? I think (and this would be so right and proper that it wouldn't shatter me or kill me)—I think that the immediate effect of this book, followed by Cohen's translation of the poems (or will there be a collection of different people's translations?—Bowra's are very good) will be to unmask and publicly disgrace me as a pretender despite myself (yes, the emperor has no clothes!).

But once again, this isn't the fault of literary critics or translators, nor is it purely my fault alone. It's an anomaly in the development of artistic life and work in our time, not only here but in the West as well. All the movements since the Symbolists have exploded, remaining in our consciousness as a bright and (perhaps) shallow and empty riddle. Even in the movements that followed, the only creative elements are still Rilkes and Prousts, as though those men were still alive, as though it were they who had sunk and been corrupted and fallen silent, but were yet going to recover and start writing. The merit of groups like the Personalists is that they're aware of this. I have the same awareness. Here's what I'm planning. I should like to act as the expression of everything within me that derives from that breed of people; to act as their continuation, filling out the twenty-year hiatus that formed after them, completing what was left half-said, and correcting misunderstandings. And most importantly, I should like to do what they would have done if they had been me—that is, to do it a little more realistically, but speaking in the persona that I share with them; to relate the main events, particularly in our country, in a prose that would be far simpler and more open than I have used so far. I have started on this, but it's all so remote from what's wanted from us here, and what people are used to seeing from us, that it's difficult to write regularly and assiduously.

I want you to be clear about one thing. Not only do I share the bewilderment that must be aroused in England by collections of writings like mine—I feel it more strongly than anyone. If I live and work a little longer, all that will be cleared up and the gaps filled in. At all events, if I don't write to these people personally and if you know them, please give my warm and heartfelt thanks to the editor and publisher and everyone who has done me the great honour of paying attention to me. And let them not be upset or depressed if people start slanging me.

---

edited by Schimanski, in which a blown-up detail from an old group photograph depicted Pasternak with Mayakovsky.

18. A friendly caricature by Kukriniksy, a famous team of three Soviet graphic artists, showing Boris on the podium at the first Congress of Soviet Writers (1934).

That chaotic writing of long ago, followed by a period of translating and a period of long and half-imposed silence—I have more than that to say. But of course, I shall come and see you.

Well, I have to stop. Please note that correspondence by telegram (ELT) is very convenient, if it's not too expensive for you. It's amazing how many pages I've covered in this letter to you without saying anything. You have no idea how much I would give to be able to embrace Fedia, sit with him a little and hear his short, abrupt laugh!

Ask Mr. Berlin about everything. He came to my dacha and saw me 2 or 3 times, Zina and Lyonichka too, and today he'll be seeing Ina and Shura.

My translations of Shakespeare have been very well received and reviewed, but while the Moscow Art Theatre was 'preparing' a production of *Hamlet*, all the guiding spirits in this project died one after another (Nemirovich-Danchenko, Sakhnovsky and others). It's the same everywhere. If my Shakespeare were staged, I should grow rich. But nothing is being staged anywhere now. Theatres are institutions that depend directly and to an extraordinary extent on the 'Court', and if I can say anything really definite about myself, it is this: no-one is more reticent about those in power than I am, and one more step in that direction would be fatal.[19] This is what has given rise to the ambivalence of my life here. But I can't do otherwise—that is my choice. All in all, I can't complain: the things that I have wanted to say have been heard more fully than I could have dreamed. In a certain sense, my life has been serene and happy.

How wonderful, expressive and beautiful the children are in the photographs! What splendid, laughing boys you have, Lida, and how the girls look like Mama and you! Papa on the bench in spring 1942 is still just the same as he was all his life, but in the last photograph he's quite laid low, poor man.

A few words about us in connection with the pictures, exhibitions, and transport. I think that our lives are going to pass through a completely different stage, when life will be easier, the simplest essentials of everyday life will be available, it will be possible to travel, official bodies will be more responsible, and their promises firmer and more reliable. Till then, we should avoid touching Papa's things. It's still too soon for that. People may assure you that this stage has already arrived, but that's as much a lie as ever.

Is Lomonosova alive? Why does no-one mention her? If anything interesting comes up that relates to me, let me know.

Thank you very much for the shoes (Papa's?). They came in very useful. Try

19. This rather cryptic language implies that Boris avoids sycophantic praise of the authorities.

answering me by post. I'll write too. Well, let's say goodbye. I'm certain we'll meet.

Your Borya.

*[Marginal note by Boris] What I like most is their articles: there have been a number of very good articles by Herbert Read and a good article by Stefan Schimanski called 'In the Bomb Shelter'.

The optimistic warmth Boris felt at this time encouraged him to start work on *Doctor Zhivago*, which he hoped would become a work of European significance.

Boris's post-war public poetry readings were a triumph, as he describes, and the authorities soon put a stop to them. Nevertheless, they showed him that he was in touch with his readers and listeners, and stimulated him to further creative activity in both prose and verse.

In the summer of 1946 a member of the British Embassy staff, Miss A. Holdcroft, arrived in Moscow with gifts and letters for the Pasternaks from Josephine and Lydia and from Raisa Lomonosova. Boris wrote back (in Russian) via Miss Holdcroft.

Boris Pasternak to Lydia Pasternak Slater

26 June 1946. Moscow.

Dear Lidochka!

Don't be surprised that I'm replying so late. Can you imagine—people thought it would be rude of me to thank you and Raisa Nikolaevna [Lomonosova] by telegram, as I meant to. And then it all took a long time to get done. [. . .]

What can I say? How can I thank you and Fedia and Raisa Nikolaevna? You've done more than clothe us—you've decked us out in finery! [. . .]

A lot of things went to Shura and Irina. That was thanks to Zina, who painstakingly distributed everything; when selecting garments for me, she went for quality. She took a brown knitted dress for herself (I think it came from Raisa Nikolaevna), and it's just right for her. The brightly-coloured red one (and I think the dark-brown one with a yellow pattern as well) I took to Zhenia. But she brought it back next day. She said (probably quite rightly) that Zina and I live on too grand a scale (that's her expression), that I've ceased to be aware of people and to feel things in a human way, that she couldn't sleep for thoughts and memories, that it's disgusting and extortionate of us to accept and use these things, that she's returning the dress because she didn't have any part in our division and wants nothing to do with it, and that you and Zhonia probably live much worse, I mean with many more difficulties, than I do. From one point of view all this is utter nonsense, from another I expect it's more than true. All I mean to say is that our delight and gratitude are tempered by some regrets and pangs of conscience.

Your English poems impressed me, and gave me something to think about, no less for their artistry than for what they tell one about your inner life—which is important to me and which seems to have been none too joyful.[20] And I was surprised to see that your memories of your early life in Moscow have remained so alive for you, despite all that you've seen and been through since then.

As poetry, I liked two passages best of all:

1) the stanzas: 'Some hundred years ago . . .', 'Alas I must . . .', 'At night, at times . . .'

2) 'O streets of Moscow'—both stanzas.[21]

I've had invitations to come to the West, I think to Prague and Paris. But I don't want to go without Zina and Lyonia. Perhaps next year I'll try to get permission to take them with me. There have been two soirées here—one in what they call the 'Hall of Columns' (where Koussevitzky and Nikisch gave their symphony concerts, which Papa painted)—that was a joint one with Akhmatova and the Leningrad poets—and then one on my own, in the Polytechnic Museum. Perhaps you heard about them, and how I was received—there were some foreigners in the audience, so the news might have reached you. Next year it'll probably happen even more. It's very difficult to describe how we live— ordinary life has nothing to compare it with. All the same, your people have understood it pretty well—the dim remoteness, the silence, the horrible, disgraceful thirteenth century we live in. In the midst of all this, I move around on a knife-edge—I no longer have any choice. Everything has become too fixed. It's interesting, exciting, and probably dangerous.

The *Iskusstvo* theatrical publishers have collected five of my Shakespeare translations and commissioned a preface from me. They asked me to write whatever I liked, freely and boldly, and swore that they'd print it. That kept me stuck in town for a whole month, holding up our removal (Zina and the children are in the country, without beds or crockery). Now it's written, and they're sighing and rolling their eyes at what I say—and of course there's no question of it being printed, it's so far removed from anything acceptable. I'm sending you four

20. Lydia's marriage was breaking down at this time.
21. The verses Boris quotes are the last three stanzas of 'Abandoned' and two of the middle stanzas of 'Cornflowers', in Lydia's collection, *Before Sunrise*.

copies of this preface. It's been handed in to VOKS,[22] and I'm told it'll be sent on from there to their London branch in early July.

Could you please keep one copy (the faintest one) for yourself and Raisa Nikolaevna, and give three to [Isaiah] Berlin, for himself, Bowra and Schimanski. I'm sorry to trouble you, but I don't know their addresses, and I'm so rushed I won't have time to write to them all.

You and Zhonia and Fedia may quite reasonably be surprised that my letters, with what they tell you about my interests, contain so little in the way of personal feelings towards you and your families—so little domestic warmth, and so much hasty, businesslike, self-absorbed egotism. That's absolutely true and it's precisely what Zhenia meant when she returned the dress. But here I am writing to you, and thinking about your children and your homes which I've never seen, and about Zina and Lyonia who've been away for a month in the country, and about Zhenichka who has just done brilliantly in his final exams—and I can't get away from the feeling that despite all this, the best letter I could send you all is my article on Shakespeare, and here is this letter of mine, it's finished, and I'm sending it. What more could I add?

If the article is to be translated, the translation must be in good, very simple language that sounds natural to an English ear and doesn't draw attention to itself; its laconicism must be inconspicuous, as it is in Russian, and the original thoughts in it mustn't seem original, but such as a child could understand.

I kiss you warmly, and your children, and Zhonia and Fedia, Alionushka and Charlik. You know better than me how I love you and everything of yours, and your way of living and loving, and how I miss you.

It's finally turned out that I have by my side a person who is terribly close to me, and terribly like me. Zina has passed some of life's examinations with outstanding success, the main ones being: the children's evacuation, and running the kitchen in a children's home in the provinces, and the death of her eldest son. She understands very well whose wife she is, and whose risks (and what risks) she is sharing. Tirelessly, like a labourer, she keeps our far from easy family life going, and forgives me many things. I scarcely talk to her either, because my conversation with her, too, is all in my article.

This summer I'm going to practise talking English with Afinogenov's widow, an American, so as to speak the language absolutely fluently.

I embrace you all endlessly.

Your Borya

22. The Soviet agency for cultural relations with foreign countries.

[...]

The dramatist Alexander Afinogenov's widow was an American who spent the summers in Peredelkino not far from Boris's dacha. English conversations with her improved his familiarity with the language. He also listened to British broadcasts for the same purpose (systematic jamming had not yet been introduced, though listening to foreign stations was suspect).

A message reached Boris from his sisters in Oxford in 1946, saying that they wanted to send Leonid's paintings back to Russia as their father had wished. Boris replied in a handwritten message in English (intended as a telegram) which was personally delivered to Oxford:

'Never think sent off fathers works pictures till definitive securing postwar ways and betterment our life conditions spare damages losses embrace heartily you all. Boris Pasternak.'

After November 1946, there was a ten-year gap in the correspondence, caused by Stalin's post-war reign of terror, the Cold War and the descent of the Iron Curtain. The silence was only broken by one telegram and one letter, both in 1948. On receipt of a letter and a family photograph delivered by hand, Pasternak telegraphed (in English):

17 JANUARY 1948. MOSCOW.
RAVISHED SPLENDID PHOTOGRAPH WILL WORK THE MORE BOLDLY HAVING
SUCH SUPERB NEPHEWS AND NIECES. PROUD OF THEM TENDERNESS LONGING
BEST WISHES CONGRATULATIONS TO ALL IN BOTH FAMILIES.
BORIS PASTERNAK.

Boris Pasternak to Frederick and Josephine Pasternak and Lydia Pasternak Slater

12 December 1948. Moscow.
My dear Fedia and girls!

It was an enormous joy to get your letters, photographs, the children's wonderful letters in Russian, and the live accounts of people who had seen you. But all that is always so little, I want to see you all with my own eyes. And what's more—I have another link to the world as well, and events like this open it up like a half-healed wound—it bleeds, and it's painful.

I'll do everything I can to ensure that you get a copy of the half of my novel that's already in manuscript. I want you to know my actual thoughts at the present time, or at least the most important ones. If you know of a good Russian copy-typist, and can get hold of a little of the money owed me anywhere over there to pay her with, please try to make another three copies and check them carefully, so that a narrow circle of interested persons can later read it—starting with Bowra, Schimanski and others.

My most cordial greetings to them and to [Isaiah] Berlin. 'London Calling Europe' has just (Friday December 11th) broadcast an article by Schimanski about a Finnish composer (could it have been Sibelius?—the name was hard to make out), but the article, from the *Manchester Guardian*, was splendid.

To come back to the novel. Printing it—I mean, publishing it in print—is absolutely out of the question, whether in the original or in translation—you must make this absolutely clear to the literary people whom I should like to show it to. Firstly, it isn't completed, this is only a half of it, needing a continuation. Secondly, publication abroad would expose me to the most catastrophic, not to say fatal, dangers. Both the spirit of the work itself, and my situation as it has developed here, mean that the novel can't appear in public; and the only Russian works allowed to circulate abroad are translations of those published here.

Last spring, a new edition of my selected lyric poetry (consisting almost entirely of 'The Year 1905'), 25,000 copies of which were printed and ready for distribution, was pulped on orders from above on the day before publication day. Public appearances by me are regarded as undesirable. The restrictions placed on me (I can only be conceived of as a translator) make my situation sombre and tense, yet internally more independent and clear than anyone else's could be.

You won't like the novel because it lacks cohesion, and was written in such haste. One reason is that I couldn't drag it out, I'm not young any more, and anyway, anything could happen from one day to the next, and there were a number of things I wanted to get written down. And I was writing it in my own time, unpaid, and in a hurry so as not to overstretch my budget, but to try and make time to get down to some paid work.

What can I tell you in conclusion, so that you know all about me? Even if you should hear one day that I've been hung, drawn and quartered, you must know that I've lived a most happy life, better than I could ever have imagined, and my most solid and stable state of happiness is right now, and in all the recent past, because I have finally learned the art of expressing my thoughts—I possess this skill to the degree that I need it, which was never the case before.

We live well, and everyone here is well. Zina is able to indulge Lyonia, we're not suffering deprivation. Since the end of last autumn I've been translating Goethe's *Faust*, mainly the first part, but I'll have to add some passages from Part II. Both Fet and Bryusov came unstuck over this, but strange as it may seem, I'm succeeding. There's no fairness in life, and I don't expect it from anyone, but the way in which certain ideas and truths dear to me have rooted themselves so deeply in the hearts of a few, a very few individuals, is enough, it's a reward for everything, everything.

You have wonderful children, and one day we and our families will all meet together, I'm sure of it. I kiss you all very warmly. Is Raisa Nikolaevna Lomonosova still alive? Why do I never hear anything about her? My tenderest greetings to her and everyone I've mentioned or not mentioned.

Back to the novel. The poems (there will be more of them) are Yura's, and they'll appear as a block, forming one of the chapters of the future second volume, at the point following Yura's death in Moscow in 1929. The poems will be found among Yura's papers by his half-brother Evgraf.

I expect I'll get some children's books for Lydia's young children, though I suppose that's not necessary, you probably have complete editions of the classics in better condition yourselves. What wonderful letters Nicky and Rosochka wrote me. Lyonia is delighted and is preparing to reply, but I think he's dreaming of the time when he'll be able to reply in English.

It's a good thing that we're not in correspondence with each other; we'll have to carry on with this self-restraint until the era of suspicion comes to an end. The fact that I want to show my novel to you and a few other people is a risky departure from this principle. I could have avoided it if I hadn't written so much worthless rubbish in the past. The fact that, for good or ill, I have achieved recognition on the strength of nothing but this rubbish is an annoying absurdity which has to be straightened out so that things are put on a more proper footing. That's why I had to send you the novel. I conclude in haste. Kisses to everybody once again.

Borya

In the summer of 1948 Boris arranged for the part of *Doctor Zhivago* that he had completed to be copy-typed, and began handing it round to a wide circle of readers, sending it to his friends in a number of Soviet cities. Distribution of this first part of the novel was a risky undertaking, but Boris was anxious to share his work with people who might sympathise with it and would save it from oblivion, even if he himself were to perish. Savage repression had recommenced.

He would spend two or three months at a time doing translations so as to earn enough money to allow him to spend the rest of his time on the novel.

CHAPTER FOURTEEN
1956–1958

It was not until the summer of 1956 that Boris was able to resume his correspondence with his sisters in England, during Khrushchev's so-called 'Thaw'. Isaiah Berlin revisited Moscow and met Boris again. In his book *Personal Impressions*, describing his two visits in 1945 and 1956 (see above, p. 363), he recalls Boris telling him that *Doctor Zhivago* had been sent to Italy, and Zina begging him to persuade Boris to delay its publication until it had appeared in Russia. Boris's annoyance at this is echoed in the irritation of his next letter.

Isaiah Berlin probably also brought back the newly-published second edition of Boris's translation of *Faust*, which is inscribed: 'Dear Lida and Zhonia, read my and Goethe's *Faust* in Russian. I kiss you. Borya. 21 August 1956. Not far from where you were born'.

Boris Pasternak to Lydia Pasternak Slater, Josephine and Frederick Pasternak

14 August 1956. Peredelkino.

My dear Lida, Zhonia and Fedia!

I can't believe my eyes as I write down your names. A whole eternity has passed since I last wrote to you. It's a festival day for me to renew my correspondence with you. What can I tell you, so that it's a festival for you too?

I live better than anyone could have dreamed—not in the sense that anyone has done me some huge favour or made me happy, but that my life has been shaped by a chain of fortuitous events that I myself did not directly bring about or deserve, but that have brought me benefits and happiness despite being fraught with constant danger. I was very ashamed to discover that a few bits of futuristic nonsense whose consequences I had never thought of, had earned me something of a reputation a long way from here. Even without this disgrace, I had already renounced and felt ashamed of half of what I had written in the past; and then there came this absurd overvaluation. I didn't know where to hide for shame.

And I had Papa's example before me, this man who achieved so much, this artist of rare power and perfection, who for all his fame still remained undervalued.

I soon came to the natural conclusion that I ought to accept and make the most of my undeserved reputation, make use of the attention devoted to me, and justify the generous though inexplicable confidence expressed in me.

That's how I spent the post-war years, alternating between doing a lot of translations (*Henry IV*, both parts, both parts of Goethe's *Faust*, *King Lear*, *Macbeth*, a vast amount of lyrical poetry by the Hungarian poet Petőfi, etc.) and spending a number of years working on a long novel called *Doctor Zhivago*, the very beginning of which (one-fifth of the whole) I sent you, but that will have told you nothing at all, because you couldn't know how I intended it to continue, or how serious the subject was or where its exposition would lead me.

I won't go on about it. B[erlin] will bring it to you and you can read it.

Incidentally: Many people's lives, if not everybody's, progress in a series of strange coincidences. This has long been observed, but never explained. I had been planning to write to you, and started my letter three days before Berlin suddenly appeared. I had actually been holding back recently from writing to you, at Zina's request—she wanted me to wait until Lyonia was enrolled at university. Last year he failed the competitive exam for entry to the Higher Technical Institute simply because he was my son, because in certain official quarters my life is known in finer detail than I know it myself. And his mother didn't want me to prejudice his chances again by writing to you. He's now passed half his exams with excellent marks (he's applied to the faculty of physics and maths), and the other half, three exams in all, still lies ahead. But at the same time he's received his call-up papers, and in the intervals between exams he has to report to the military commission for medicals. Two powers are contending together for this poor boy, aggravating his exam nerves and interfering with his preparation between papers. If he doesn't achieve brilliant results in the exams, he'll be called up to the army at once. I don't know how all this will end, but I'll wait until everything is decided before I finish this letter and send it off with B[erlin].

To come back to the novel. You'll get to read it. You may not even like it, finding its philosophy tedious and alien, some passages boring and long-drawn-out, the first book too diffuse, and the transitional passages grey, pallid and ineffective. And yet—it's an important work, a book of enormous, universal importance, whose destiny cannot be subordinated to my own destiny, or to any question of my well-being. Its existence and publication, where that is possible, are more important and dearer to me than my own existence. That's why the arguments based on caution and common-sense which B[erlin] was putting to me, following certain things that had already happened with the book and which he'll tell you about, carry no weight with me. He has no idea what's at stake; he doesn't know what can be written about the life of our generation; the artistic habits and literary precedents that followed the Symbolist period haven't prepared him for this, or given him a suitable yardstick. (Let me add in parentheses that if you ever in the future want to write to me by post about your impressions, please write to say whether you liked the thing and how much you liked it, without going into too much detail about what it is.)

I'll give B[erlin] one copy. He promised me that the typescript would be transcribed in multiple copies in England (I should want no less than 12), accurately and correctly, and carefully proofread (incidentally, I haven't had time to check the last typescript). He'll look after this himself, you don't need to worry about it. When the copies are made, the novel must be given to the principal Russians over there—Katkov, Obolensky, Konovalov—and, very importantly, to Bowra. It may be that some time after the novel has appeared in Italian in Italy, in its full, unabridged version, it will become possible and necessary to have it translated and published in other languages, particularly English. The Italian publisher, Feltrinelli in Milan, will retain the initiative in all this. B[erlin] knows the details. I am not entrusting either him or you with any sort of commission, indeed to do so would be undesirable, and I am not asking you to do anything for me, except one single thing: when the time comes to publish an English edition, you must have good copies of the original in your own hands, or someone else's, and a very good translator must be found (an Englishman who is a gifted writer, with a perfect command of Russian), because this thing can't be translated any-old-how, amateurishly, using whatever resources come to hand. But even then, even if an ideal translator exists, with a perfect command of literary language, he'll still need advice from experts in Russian folklore and a variety of ecclesiastical nuances and texts, because there's a lot of this sort of thing in the novel, and it's not just in the form of passing references and borrowings which a dictionary or reference-book could explain, but of new formations arising in a live, creative manner against a real and authentic background, in other words everything that would be clear to a knowledgeable person, in a new perspective, different from what has gone before.

B[erlin] has mentioned the possibility of an invitation to your university, or to the Shakespeare celebrations next year in Stratford. Please don't do any of this. I shan't come. It's my dream to come to the West in two years or so, if I'm still alive, God willing. I terribly want to see you all. But to turn up in your country just for the sake of an encounter with you (however precious that would be for me), or in order to travel around and gather impressions—all that is really not enough. I would want some more active and wide-ranging contacts with other people, with exchanges of properly thought-out and mature ideas—not just imitations of them, as is generally the case. At the same time, the vast majority of these ideas of mine are in the novel, so it has to be published a long time before I go on my travels.

B[erlin] doesn't want to accept this, because he only looks at everything from the point of view of my safety and practical success. He sees the sequence of events in the reverse order. As he sees it, I must first get an invitation to England and make use of it, and after that I can allow translations of the novel to be published. According to our rules over here, publication of a work abroad before it comes out in the Soviet Union is an illegal act, for which I would be severely punished—I don't know how. But I can't imagine how or when the work could be printed here; and I didn't write it in order to hide it. And I accepted this risk, and however many times I were put to the test, I should take the same risk again. But to come back to the question of my visit. Over the past few years I've been very busy, I haven't read anything at all, and the little French and English that I once knew, I have well and truly forgotten. Maybe I'll polish it all up again. At all events, I don't at present possess the essentials required to perform improvisations on the subtlest and most intangible themes of the human spirit; so what would be the point of my coming?

After this extended letter, all on a single topic, I have to add that Lyonia is apparently going to be admitted to the university. Only a single mark, a written one, for composition, is still not known; the rest are all fives.[1] So this letter to you is going to be sent. Don't regard it as selfishness or indifference to everything else in the world if this long letter is filled with words not even about me myself, but merely about my latest work. It's the most important thing, not only for me, but objectively, in actual fact. All the rest you've probably been told by the others. Last year Olya Freidenberg died—you probably knew about that. Shura and his family live reasonably, they're always busy and overloaded with work. And what can I tell you about myself, at this level? It's better if I say goodbye and kiss you all, wishing both your families no less happiness and health than have fallen, and continue to fall, to my own lot. B[erlin] and others who have visited you in Oxford have told me a lot of good things about you all.

---

1. In other words, top marks.

Write to me whenever you like, and whatever you like, to my town address: Moscow V-12, Lavrushinsky Pereulok 17/19, apt. 72.

But I spend the whole year at the dacha; Zina has transformed it into a winter house with steam heating and every comfort.

In September 1956 Boris was visited at Peredelkino by Georgi Mikhailovich Katkov, an Oxford academic and friend of the Pasternak sisters. He offered Boris his help in getting the novel published in England.

The typescript of the recently completed autobiographical sketch 'People and Propositions' was brought to England by Isaiah Berlin.

Boris Pasternak to Lydia Pasternak Slater

21 October 1956. Peredelkino.

Dear Lida,

You're the mother of a family, you have the care of a whole household, and you're alone without help; and here I am bombarding you with letters. But I know your situation, I don't need anything from you, and you don't even have to read my letters as soon as you get them, you can do as I occasionally do, and put off reading them till a more convenient time (which of course never comes).

The difficulties of our correspondence, with its main topic being so unusual and inconvenient, and with so many other obstacles—all these are things that I honestly view as entirely normal. That's how life has to be, that's how I understand it and how it suits me—full of obstacles, striving towards mystery, withdrawn and difficult.

Was this why tragedy became the highest form of artistic expression for the Greeks—did they consider that the most essential function of art was to lament the poverty of earthly existence?

No, but the narrow constraints of tragedy concentrated and intensified the clarity and didactic richness of the content inherent in every destiny. That is how life must be. It must be a tragedy of fullness, a tragedy of productivity and happiness.

I've had a letter from G.M. [Katkov]. He's promised to write to me again when he's finished reading the last quarter of the novel. Then I'll write to him in person. But the letter that I have had from him is not the one I wanted to get.

I myself have a very complex relationship with my novel. I accept that it's uneven, diffuse, and defective as a work of art. I'm prepared to accept all kinds of opinions, even if they're extreme and mutually contradictory, and in my heart of hearts I agree with all of them.

But I am conscious that there are decisive turning-points in the history of ideas and of art the world over: I'm aware that it's no longer possible to carry on merely writing good literature; that all that means nothing and isn't interesting; that somewhere, in different parts of the world, people have to be taking certain steps—not in politics, but through the human creative spirit; and that my novel is one of these steps.

G.M. [Katkov] is well-meaning and obliging, ten times more so than I could possibly accept; but all that is entirely unnecessary. I was hoping he might have helped me, if he had been gripped by the work in the way that I've just been talking about; if he could have seen that it belongs to, and must be measured against, a different class of phenomena altogether, and if that had taken him beyond the stylistic assessments he writes about in his letter, very true and fair though they are.

And there are many other reasons too, for letting events take their natural course, without hurrying to meet them as I once thought. It's essential for the novel to be published here, at all costs. It will probably come out this winter, somewhat smoothed and softened.

I very much want G.M. to finish the book and write to me, and then I'll answer him. And it's no secret from him that I'm writing to you about his letter. He's right, his verdict is very understandable and well-deserved, but that isn't the point, and I've said what the point is.

Now you and he will deluge me with assurances of how overwhelmed you are and what a work of genius the novel is, and how I've misunderstood him. Please understand that considerations of gentleness and politeness have no place here.

I kiss you warmly, and all your family.

Your Boris

[...]

The State publishing house Goslitizdat was planning to expedite the publication of an edited version of *Doctor Zhivago* so as to forestall its publication in Italy. A contract with Goslitizdat was soon signed, and the editor started work.

Boris Pasternak to Lydia Pasternak Slater

4 November 1956. Peredelkino.

Dear Lida,

This isn't a reminder to you to write back to me. If you ever interpret anything I say as meaning that, I'll stop writing to you altogether. I don't in the least want to become a new burden to you, and there's no need for that whatsoever.

I'm enclosing a number of new poems of mine, primarily for Bowra. He may need them, or they may be of some other interest. I wonder when all this will reach you.

I don't know how to say this without appearing boastful, but with the more active contacts between the rest of the world and the Soviet Union over the past six months, I've been getting letters from all over the world, from the most unexpected places. And there are plans to publish collections of my poems in translation, in four different places—Yugoslavia, Hungary, Prague and Rome.

I've been delaying these publications in the hope that my autobiographical sketch and a new collection of my poems would be published in one of our journals here, *Novy Mir*, as they promised me long ago. The material in question is absolutely essential for the projected foreign publications—without it they'd lose half their interest, based as they would then be on old stuff that everyone is bored with. If the material were published over here, that would make it legal to republish it abroad. But what can I do, when this unfortunate interest in me from afar is regarded as a transgression for which they have to punish me by postponing or cancelling these publications here, though they enthusiastically accepted the material only six months ago?

There have been delegations here from the West, and some of them suggested that the autobiographical sketch would be suitable for a journal such as *Encounter*, or some French equivalent. Why hasn't that happened? Has the material been rejected as insufficiently interesting? If the autobiographical sketch, or selected extracts from it, were to be published in the West, that would greatly assist the projects I've just described, which I've been intentionally holding up until the editors have seen the autobiography. G.M. [Katkov] and his friend mustn't be surprised if they get requests for copies of it from unexpected parts of the world such as Bulgaria or Uruguay or Argentina.

Lidochka, my dear one, you probably think that I have nothing living left within me, that I've turned into a sort of literary machine, unconcerned with anything but getting all sorts of writings of mine printed and published in various places, and bringing different people together. But you'd be wrong. I'm still alive, too alive even, and life doesn't revolve round whether I have a grandson or a granddaughter, it means managing to say the most important things in time, and not leaving anything unclear, in this age of ours which is sustained by nothing but ambiguities and the fear of speaking out. I'm not a young man, and soon—we don't know when—all things will come to a resolution, and one such resolution will be death. So you, and all of you, must pardon me my haste; it isn't driven by fear but by boldness, and it's healthy, appropriate and timely.

Boris Pasternak to his sisters

23 November 1956. Peredelkino.

Dear Lida and Zhonia,

It's all getting more and more interesting, and the inevitability of death is completely unimportant. You're both terribly gifted. Thank you for your lively, thoughtful and rich letters. I pass over their details, not because they haven't aroused my interest. On the contrary—all Lida's acuity and Zhonia's description of style as a story retold a second time in a different way (that's exactly what happened—as I went from drafts to the final version, I wasn't copying out the text and making stylistic improvements, but writing from memory, often without looking at the previous version, but expressing its content in a drier and more condensed way)—yes, of course, I couldn't fail to observe such signs of your penetration, everywhere in your letters. But I'm not going to talk specifically about them, because half of the heartfelt things I have to say to you are always practicalities, needing time and space which then aren't available for other things. But before going on to them, tell me why I never hear a single word about Fedia? Doesn't he know that his life is just as dear to me as yours? I can't be wrong about this—I think I wrote my first letter to all three of you. And just a word more about your advice to me to be careful—though I'm afraid you'll think that I'm just talking and showing off. Perhaps it isn't always so, but in those cases when love and trust come to you from far away and make a name for you, you have to respond to them, otherwise the gift you have received becomes a theft. To limit your life to protecting yourself from danger is wrong, not because that makes your life seem grey and girls don't go crazy over you, but because this form of experience is too narrow—within its boundaries you don't discover the most important and essential things about life, those very things that you have to hand on to others in return for their love.

You have to live under the constant burden of your own guilt towards those nearest to you; you have to live a life that's darkened only by this kind of suffering; in constant horror at yourself, your deception and duplicity, and in all-consuming joy at your limitless rights, which you don't have to defend against anyone, nor receive from anyone, so innately special are they, so unique.
[...]

Your Borya.

The opening words of the letter that follows relate to the Soviet authorities' sudden decision not to publish either *Doctor Zhivago* or the *Essay in Autobiography*, or even a collection of Boris's poems.

Boris Pasternak to Lydia Pasternak Slater
[Original in English]

10 January 1957. Moscow.

Dear Lyda!

Things have changed in the old direction. I shall seldom write you the next future. But you be not restrained in the same way. Inform me, whenever you will, about matters of any literary or personal importance.

Thanks for your photographs, I have got them. You have charming fine children, I must felicitate you. As a non admirer of domestic tradition, inherited nature, family likenesses etc., I was glad not to find its despotic traces in the delighting smiling figures. On the contrary, I found in them happy signs of independent coming destinies of free choice in the matter of fate. Life is a voyage through time, deeds, works and posterity. In your sons and daughters you have made an astonishing great and far one. I am fond of your girls, I believe in the future of your boys.

I embrace you. Transmit my greetings to Zhonia and Fedia. Shura prospers with Irène and their household. Their son Fedia is on sea travel to antarctic pole. I fancy he will write you.

Your B.

You may write me Russian. This English letter is of no necessity but only a whim of me.

In March 1957 Boris fell seriously ill, and spent several months in hospital and in a sanatorium. It was not till the beginning of August that he could return home to Peredelkino and once again take up his correspondence.

Following the publication of extracts from *Doctor Zhivago* in the Polish magazine *Opinie* in August 1957 (the first publication of any part of the novel in any language, and therefore a matter of great concern to the authorities), Boris was summoned to appear before the Party's Central Committee and threatened with arrest unless he stopped all publications of the novel abroad. However, the telegrams he signed under duress had no effect, and preparations for publication continued.

A letter to Lydia dated 7 August has survived, but his next two letters were lost in the post—evidently confiscated. He therefore wrote to Lydia again in November, this time in English, and sent the letter via Rome with Sergio d'Angelo. The letter took a month to arrive. In the meantime, the first edition of *Doctor Zhivago* in Italian had come out on November 15, 1957.

Boris Pasternak to Lydia Pasternak Slater

[Original in English]

1 November 1957. Peredelkino.
The country house near Moscow.

My dear, we have started the disappearing of my letters in the case of their importance. This one will get to you on indirect foreign ways. That is the reason, why I write it in English.

The fulfillment of my secretest dreams, I hope, approaches; the publication of my novel abroad; only in translation at first, to my sorrow; in original, some day.

I had pressures to endure here of late, nuisance, menaces, in order to stop the appearance of the novel in Europe. I was forced to sign absurd, false, invented telegrams and letters to my editors. I signed them in the hope, which has not deluded me, that these persons, the unheard baseness of the counterfeit being so transparent, will disregard the feigned demands,—what justly they fortunately did. My triumph will be either tragical or unobscured. In both cases it is joy, victory, I could not have done it alone.

Here must be said about the share, about the part that takes in my last ten years life Olga Vsevolodovna Ivinskaya, the Lara of the novel, who has undergone four years imprisonment (from 1949) for the sole crime of being the nearest friend of me.[2]

2. An editor and translator, whom Boris Pasternak met in 1946, Olga Ivinskaya later became his lover. She was released from imprisonment shortly after Stalin's death, but when Boris died in 1960, she and her daughter Irina were again arrested and sent to labour camps.

She does enormously much in my behalf. She relieves me from the vexing negotiations with the authorities, she takes the blows of such conflicts on herself. She is the only soul I confer with on what is the tense of age or on what is to be done, or thought, or written, and so on. A translation of her from Rabindranath Tagore was erroneously ascribed to me: it was the only time I left the mistake unobjected.

Zeneide, the mild, terrible, calling forth perpetual compassion, childish-dictatorial and tearful creatress and authoress of the house and garden and the four seasons and our Sunday parties and our family life and domestic establishments is not the woman to suffer hard by another one or ever to betray herself of being aware of it and tolerating in.

And so life goes on, darkened by peril, pity and dissembling,—inexhaustible, fathomless, splendid.

You will be so ingenious as to guess, what to touch and what not to touch in your Russian post answer.

I embrace you most tenderly.

Your B.

Boris's next two letters to Lydia, written on 20 November and 14 December, 1957, were never posted; they remained among the papers of Olga Ivinskaya. Judging by their content, partly repeated in Pasternak's subsequent letters (cf. that of 18 December), they were soon superseded by others, and a month later Boris had to confess that he himself no longer remembered which letters he had actually sent.

In the first, written in English, Boris expressed the hope of soon coming to England, and enclosed his recent compositions 'Quietness', 'The Linden Avenue', 'Stooks' and 'Bacchanal'. He asked that they be shown to Zhonia and Fedia, and passed on to anyone who wanted to see them. He said that writing poetry had to go hand in hand with hard work on prose, for which he had once again come to feel a need. He ended by relating that his son Zhenia's wife, a granddaughter of the philosopher Gustav Shpet who had died in prison, had that week given birth to a son. He was called Petya, and Boris gave the family's address.

Lydia replied on 2 December 1957, describing how everyone was following the flight of the first Soviet satellite (Sputnik), and obliquely comparing it with the simultaneous appearance and 'travels' of *Doctor Zhivago*. Boris wrote on 14 December:

. . . 'How cleverly and well you write, my love. It was only yesterday that I reflected that my heroine and I are a third Sputnik fired into orbit—and then I find the same analogy in your letter.

I envy you for being able to collect these reports, and for being cheered by them. I have no access whatsoever to all this; I can only get indirect indications. For instance, these days I sometimes get official requests to receive foreign journalists. […]

In December 1957, after the Italian publication of *Doctor Zhivago*, Boris was obliged to participate in an arranged and supervised meeting and press conference with Western Communist journalists, the aim of which was to stop publication of the novel in the West. By naming the Scandinavian and British papers whose correspondents had visited him, Boris enabled his sisters to read the interviews and realise the situation he was in.

He also said that he had tried to persuade highly placed individuals to allow a censored version of the novel to be published in Moscow, and not to fear its publication in full abroad. Tolstoy's novel *Resurrection*, he said, had been published in this way at the time, and nothing terrible had happened as a result. After publication, the novel could be subjected to harsh criticism by Marxist and Communist critics in different countries, allowing them to point out his ideological errors.

Boris Pasternak to Lydia Pasternak Slater

17 December 1957. Peredelkino.

It's probably time for me to wish you a happy New Year, Lida. And what a truly and seriously new and decisive one it will be for me! Shura, our shared acquaintances, the so-called friends of the family, and even the members of my own family, have no idea of all these things, which are too close to me, too alive and important for me to talk about them. Some people I spare in order not to worry them; others are too mediocre, too long arrested in their development, too much gone to seed—I invite them to lunch on Sundays so that Zina doesn't get too bored. But the central path of my life passes them by, beyond their comprehension; it doesn't trouble them, and is known only to O.V. [Ivinskaya]. These are two different worlds, with no contact between them.

17 December 1957. Dear Lidochka, thanks for your letter which arrived on the 12th; it only took 10 days to get here. I'm terribly pleased that all this news, mostly unknown to me (I can only make indirect guesses at it), reaches you and pleases you so much. How strangely life has turned out, hasn't it? I'm alive and well and happy. You're clever to be collecting cuttings about the

Sputnik.[3] And it's probably just as well for me that I don't see them or know about them.

I kiss you warmly, and Zhonia, and Fedia, and all your families.

Your B.

I wonder if this postcard will reach you.

Boris's letters repeatedly voice his frustration at being deprived of any news about the novel's progress abroad and the impossibility of seeing comments about it in the international press.

Boris Pasternak to Lydia Pasternak Slater

18 December 1957. Peredelkino.

Dear Lida,

I had been thinking of answering your youthful letter, full of directness and wit, about the Sputniks and Yura in Italy, via the Union of Soviet Writers, but then I thought better of it and I'm using the old route, probably for the last time. Just imagine, all these comments and cuttings are out of my reach. I was only able to get an indirect idea of their quantity, when I was obliged to receive a number of representatives of the Scandinavian and British communist press. The *Daily Worker* correspondent spread out a handful of strips of paper in front of me, but wasn't able to leave them for me to look at, and immediately put them back in his pocket. They only related to a few English papers.

[...]

If, as people say (but this has happened before, and our representatives over here always refused and nothing ever came of it)—if, as some people think, I'm awarded the Nobel prize in spite of Soviet protests, then I'll probably be subjected to every kind of pressure here to refuse it. I think I have enough resolution to resist. But they may not allow me to travel to receive it. In that case, would it be possible to ask Fedia, using some sort of unofficial power of attorney from me (I can't for the moment think what this would be), to receive the prize for me and hand it over in trust somewhere until, as may happen, I'm able to come and visit

3. Lydia had employed a press-cuttings agency to follow Boris Pasternak and *Doctor Zhivago* through the press.

or give some indication of my personal wishes—would he agree to help me in this way? But all this would have to be done in the most private and confidential way from my side. I've also asked F[eltrinelli] not to transfer any money to me over here, but to look after whatever he plans to allocate to me until it becomes possible for me to travel and I can see him.

As a test to see whether they reach you, I'm sending you two postcards. The trouble is that if I write the sender's name on them, they risk being held up or lost. I embrace you warmly.

Your Borya

Boris was encouraged by the knowledge that he was an object of worldwide interest, and particularly by the attention paid to him in France. The readiness of his new French admirers to undertake the publication of his *Essay in Autobiography* and his new poems allowed him to relieve his sisters of the heavy responsibility of negotiating with publishers.

In the following postcard Boris extends the code of 'Yura' for *Doctor Zhivago*, and its imminent publication by Gallimard in France and Collins in England is figured as 'Yura's journey to Galya and Kolya'. The Soviet authorities were meanwhile actively engaged in trying to prevent publication.

Boris Pasternak to Lydia Pasternak Slater

23 January 1958. Peredelkino.

Dear Lida,

Thank you, and Zhonia and Fedia, for your card. Did you get the letter from your former teacher at the Gymnasium which I sent you, which she was moved to write after reading the article in *France-Soir* by Jean Neuvecelle?[4] Oh, how I wish that everything would happen quickly; how I long to see you all and exchange the thoughts that have piled up in such numbers over such a long time, about these important matters! You're probably surprised by my impatience to know that Yura has finally reached Galya and Kolya, and don't understand why I'm so

---

4. The letter from Lydia's French teacher was addressed to Boris at 'Peredelkino, near Moscow'— the address given by Jean Neuvecelle (Dmitri Vyacheslavovich Ivanov), the son of the Symbolist poet Vyacheslav Ivanov, in his despatches from Moscow. He had met Boris in the summer of 1957 and published an article about their meeting in *France-Soir* on whose staff he worked.

anxious at every delay in his journey. But even if his own people weren't responsible for all the machinations along the way, there could still be many unforeseen obstacles on his path, his journey could so easily be prevented—it's so difficult to foresee everything! But it's sinful of me to complain, I have been granted (and why me in particular?) such happiness! All of this should have happened earlier, while our parents were alive. Now that would have been a joy for them. And it would be nice if I could live a little longer, say another 5 years or so, to give me time to produce another great new work, embracing this last fresh experience of wide-ranging exchanges, these unbelievable events, the expressions of such emotion and understanding! I'm well, I kiss you all warmly. Tomorrow Z[ina] and L[yonia] are coming from town, and I have the feeling that there'll be news from you or one of your neighbours.

I embrace you.

The replies from Boris's sisters spoke of preparations for an exhibition of Leonid Pasternak's pictures in Oxford. Lydia sent her brother her new translations of his poems, for his opinion, and wrote that she had given a very successful reading of her translations at the Pushkin Club in London. 'The English don't understand the kind of poetry that's written in Russian', she wrote, 'but never mind—they'll get used to it'.

Boris Pasternak to Lydia Pasternak Slater

5 March 1958. Davydkovo [in hospital].

[...] During this relapse of the violent pains in my leg, I was once again (as last year) longing to die. Everything in my life, my activity, my fate, is so impossibly muddled and confused. You have no idea of the huge mass of letters from far away that reach me because of articles like those by Neuvecelle or Ruge.[5] How can I answer them? And yet thought cannot stand still, it has to develop and breathe. In my captivity and my silence, I turn into a sort of pretender, some kind of Khlestakov.[6] Oh, how difficult my life is, Lida. [...]

---

5. Gerd Ruge was a German journalist who visited Boris at Peredelkino; his account of their meeting was published in many Western newspapers in early 1958. Ruge went on to publish a 'pictorial biography' of Boris.

6. See above, p. 121, n. 5.

Boris Pasternak to Lydia Pasternak Slater

1 April 1958. Davydkovo.

[...] Your translations[7] are superb, but they confirm what I feel about the originals: that they are very uneven, and half of them boring and banal. Because of the French project, I had to look through them all last winter, and I discarded a lot, including, I think, 'Fairy Tale', 'July' and 'First Snow'. The qualities of your brilliant translations failed to save them, and it was only 'Candle' and 'When It Clears Up' that I didn't spoil for you. Your translations of these two are very good.

Nowadays I'm treated deviously, and in a fanatical way—with either downright hostility or undeserved and exaggerated kindness. I'm embarrassed to read some of the letters I get from abroad, full of ridiculous adulation.
[...]

Josephine wrote to Boris describing the exhibition of Leonid Pasternak's pictures at the Ashmolean Museum in Oxford. In its first few days it was visited by over 400 people, and it had to be extended by two weeks.

'What a fate for Papa!', wrote Josephine. 'War, illness and death deprived him of the chance to return to Moscow, yet he was so passionately anxious, in his last years, to have pupils again, and pass on to them his experience, his knowledge, the heritage of a duty that filled his life with toil and inspiration.'

The following two letters—to Lydia, dated 11 May, and to Josephine, dated 12–16 May—were entrusted to an Italian. They were delayed by five months: the Rome postmark on the envelope is dated 4 September 1958.

Boris Pasternak to Lydia Pasternak Slater

11 May 1958. Peredelkino.

Dear Lida,

I've just recently been discharged from hospital. This return to life is something tremendously powerful. If I sit for longer than an hour, my leg still hurts. But

7. Lydia translated many of her brother's poems, and her translations were later published as *Fifty Poems*, (London: Allen & Unwin, 1963). There is also an excellent parallel text edition of Boris's poems with English translations by various people, including Lydia—*Boris Pasternak: Poems*, compiled by Evgeny Pasternak (Moscow: Raduga Publishers, 1990)—in celebration of the centenary of Boris's birth.

life remains, as it always has been, a magical combination of successes and plans, and I'm terribly keen to write, but I have to put off working because I've accumulated a pile of letters from abroad that I want to answer.

I can imagine what Papa's exhibition must have been, in absolute and objective terms—what a place it must have occupied in your lives. When I tore out something like a hundred of his drawings from his albums and notebooks, and had them mounted and hung them on my walls, it wasn't so much the outward appearance of my rooms that was transformed, it was my whole life; starting from the day the pictures were hung, it was as if my life had been transported somewhere else, with a different sun and a different climate. I even wanted to name a book made up of things from that time—'A Room Hung With Pictures'.

This new re-confirmation of his everlasting success will no doubt have given you the feeling of a return of all your past experiences, and in a triumphant, self-affirming form, beyond what memory alone can ever achieve.

I don't know why, but I am now going to jot down for you two springtime trifles (when I speak of my longing to write, I have in mind more serious topics, along the lines of 'Bacchanal', 'Music', 'Night' etc.)

[Here he transcribes two short lyrical poems—'Beyond the Turning' and 'Everything Has Come True'.]

And now I've completely forgotten what I wanted to write about. O.V. [Ivinskaya] has a daughter who is a student, called Irochka Emelyanova. She has some friends who are students from abroad, and one of them is called Georges Nivat.[8] He has gone to Oxford, and writes to her from there. Apparently he has made the acquaintance of one of your boys. Which is it—Michael or Nicky? A rumour has been spread that Irochka is my adopted daughter—she is a beautiful girl, very brave and very gifted. Behind my back, she calls me 'Classic'. She is very well-informed about everything to do with me, and sometimes supplies her friends with typed copies of my manuscripts, uncorrected and full of errors. No doubt this Nivat is a very nice fellow, and O.V. maintains that I once saw him or he saw me, but I'm not sure of this.

I kiss you warmly, Zhonia, Fedia, and all your family.

Your B.

[...]

8. Georges Nivat later became a prominent French Slavist.

'A few years ago', Josephine wrote to her brother on 25 April, 'I decided to tidy up Papa's jottings. I started copying out everything he had written down, in notebooks, separate pages, notes or scraps of paper, without altering anything. It includes biographical materials, and Papa's views on art, and meetings with interesting people, and lyrical digressions. Lida insisted that I should send you at least a few lines, copied from the beginning of the first notebook, since they relate directly to you'.

Boris Pasternak to Josephine Pasternak

12 May 1958. Peredelkino.

Dear Zhonia,

Thank you for the excerpts you copied for me. You are Papa's Antigone, and you deserve honour and glory for that. All that Papa writes is tremendously touching. I seem to detect a note of regret in his thoughts about Mama, particularly after her death. He might have thought that she had failed to fulfil herself, that through his own fault and the family's, she had remained in the shade, not properly recognised . . .

Perhaps that was true, but it wasn't a mistake or a piece of neglect that should trouble one later on. The tragic element in life is its normal and natural condition; it has to be tragic to be real. When afterwards you shed tears over its testimonies, it's not because it cost too much and you paid dearly for it—you weep over its significance.

As a random example—it's just in the same way that (in spite of the additional catastrophic events) one can't help weeping over the records of the last days in the life of Schumann himself, and Clara Schumann's letter to her children telling them about their father's death. Even the knowledge that the daughters lived so long, and died as unmarried music teachers, one in 1928 and the other in 1938 in Switzerland at the age of 87, in some strange way moves one to tears.

Among your excerpts, one that was very important to me was where Papa says 'When and where was it that I first encountered it—my destiny?', and you say that 'he very much liked this way of putting it'. And there's also the fact that Papa resisted the literary temptation of presenting the answer to this question by recalling a dream that came to him that same night.

And it was also very important to me to discover that Mama played the Schumann quintet at the home of the Director of the British Museum one month before her death.

It's a fact that the first years in the life of our family were tied up with this quintet, before you were born. The quintet was the sound that filled the rooms and furnishings of the old apartments that you never knew. It's very good that you've deciphered and copied out these notes. I think that you yourself should carry on the work of abridging them further and arranging them in whatever way is best (even if only to make the material more transparent), since you have undertaken the work and carried it out. You don't need Lida to help. When you have sorted it all properly, it'll be clear what has to be done with it.

But you're right, of course, to treat me carefully as you do; no doubt I must seem to you and Lida to be heartlessly ungrateful and selfish, both towards our parents' memory, and Olya [Freidenberg] and her work, and all the destinies and people I've encountered on my way, and everyone around me and close to me. And I won't say a word here in my defence, except that I'm not, after all, defined only by my dereliction of family duty; there's probably something else there as well. And perhaps that something else is enough, and more than enough, to earn me forgiveness.

When D[octor] Zh[ivago] comes out in England, and if you read anything detailed, interesting and noteworthy about it, please send me cuttings and write a few words about anything you discover or hear about it (even if it's bad). Don't fear any consequences for me, excepting only the possibility that what you send may not reach me.

I kiss you warmly, and Fedia, and all your family. After these last two illnesses, and with the continuing pain in my leg and the constant possibility of an acute relapse, I have lost my confidence in the time I have left to me; I don't know how long I have got—not to mention the permanent (though just temporarily eased) political threat to my position, which also makes it impossible to imagine firm ground beneath my feet. But that's exactly why my life, at intervals and in bits and pieces, seems doubly magical and inexpressible, and I can't resist it or the way in which I'm undeservedly pampered.

Your B.

This attitude to life, this astonishment at how happy I am and what a gift my existence is —all this I have from my father. Reality and Nature enchanted him, and this was the guiding thread of his realism and his technical mastery of form. The member of the family who is most like Papa is Lyonia —a young man besotted by music, but so shy that he refuses to practise properly with his mother or an experienced teacher; thrashing about on his own, he has accumulated a repertoire going as far as Chopin's scherzi and ballades. He takes it tragically that he hasn't become a pianist like his step-brother—a drinker who's currently being treated for alcoholism.[9] The sad thing for me personally is that he so over-estimates the providential nature of music; surrounded as he is, if not directly then at one remove, by professional musicians, he doesn't see how many good musicians there are and how ordinary a thing music is. But of course, this isn't aimed at Mama.

16 May 1958

I'm afraid that my abrupt words may be misinterpreted, leading to misunderstandings and upsetting you.

Mama was a marvellous pianist. My recollection of her and her playing, her attitude to music and the very simple way she made room for it in her everyday life, put into my hands that demanding ideal which everything I've subsequently observed falls short of. It was against her talent that I measured my own claims and possibilities, and having failed in my own eyes, I gave up music. In the same way, the greatness of Papa's mastery, the fullness and inexhaustibility of everything he incorporated in the finished form of a drawing, and what he was able to achieve with the mere fact of a likeness—all this made it impossible for me, in all the succeeding years, to pose for anyone or to hang on my walls any pictures given me by other artists.

But it's impossible and unnecessary to talk about that. That's just an obvious ABC. I think that, just as Nature is governed by laws and tolerates no deviations from them, so too it is with art and the history of human creativity. Here the laws are represented by single works, by the exceptions alone, while the areas within which these exceptions arise only serve to make them stand out. And I consider that music, with its Schubert, Brahms and the whole mass of wonderful performers and teachers, is a huge, gigantic transgression committed by mediocrity, a transgression that has to be redeemed by even greater upheavals within itself, such as Chopin or Wagner, or (never mind how far one agrees with this) Tchaikovsky.

Over here, the Piano Competition was won by the young American pianist Van Cliburn, and everyone's in love with him and driven crazy by him and won over by him. Now that's something I understand. And then he'll leave, and there'll be no more music for ages.

I shan't write again for a long time. I have masses of letters to answer, which get in the way of my work. And I'm constantly dogged by 'unpleasantnesses'.

---

9. Stanislav Neuhaus (1927–1980), Zina's surviving son by her first husband. He was a noted pianist.

On 11 June Lydia wrote to tell her brother that she had given a public reading of her translations of his poems at Oxford. The poems 'July' and 'Winter Night' had been particularly well received.

Boris Pasternak to Lydia Pasternak Slater

10 July 1958. Peredelkino.

Dear Lida,

I believe *D[octor]* *Zh[ivago]* has come out in Paris, but I haven't yet received a copy and perhaps I never will, nor any reviews of it. The arrival or non-arrival of this sort of communications or of packages depends entirely on what the postal censors think of them. But some letters, some of them very interesting ones from very distinguished and important people, do reach me. [...]

My knee is hurting much less, but that's already happened once and then I suffered the horrors of a renewed relapse. So unless they do something radical (and even that may not help), something like an orthopaedic boot for my rather shortened right leg, and surgery to remove a meniscus from my knee, I shall never be safe from a third relapse. All this takes up so much of my time and causes me such pain. Without such a sure guarantee, I don't feel in control of my future—the lord and master of my existence is my right leg and knee, and they rule my life.

Perhaps this partly affects my projects. Unusually for me, I have no plans at the moment. I don't feel confident that I can afford to start anything long and wide-ranging, in prose, along the lines of *D. Zh*. But I'm not idle. Almost all my time is spent writing letters to foreign countries (it's bad for me to spend a long time sitting; I go for a two- or three-hour walk every day). Incidentally, if you ever get a postcard from me written in French or English, please don't think that I'm so stupid as to expose myself to ridicule by showing off my ungainly home-made foreign languages. The reason will lie in constraints and peculiarities of a nameless nature.

O.V. [Ivinskaya], like some other people, considers that my chief aim in life is poetry; she wants me to write fewer letters and more poems. At her persuasion, I've written five or six absolute trifles, which you'll get if she copies them out for you.

[...]

Boris Pasternak to Lydia Pasternak Slater

[Original in English]

11 July 1958. Peredelkino.

My dear, don't think I am so stupid as to boast of this broken language. The necessity is that sometimes I plunge myself in a foreign nameless form. The Dr seems to have been recently appeared in Paris. When you hear or read something concerning the matter, particularly in the near future when it will be published in E[ngland], try to send me newspaper cuttings in a letter or, be it too heavy and extensive, relate me the chiefest of its contents, far from tiring yourself and without too great a loss of your time, in the shortest abbreviation.

If you will get the English exemplary, in the case it will not make you great pains, send me it by bookpost through the Sov. Writer-Union Moscow G69 Vorovsky-str. 52, Foreign Commission. Or no, no, I release you from the trouble. It is C[ollin]s himself, who will take care of that. Je me porte comme un charme,[10] except the knee that aches me less but continuously.

There are three letters of me to you and J[osephine], especially in reply to her extracts out of father's diary, but they stay shelved without dispatch since April or May. Like Georgia almost thirty years ago, so it is now France which plays a strong, fervent, personal part in my life. What letters I receive from there, of what remarkable, significant people. It is not for the bragging but for the reason of the cordial strings touched by them, that I am telling it to you. Nous sommes quelques uns en France—m'écrit Alb. Camus—à vous connaître, à partager votre vie, d'une certaine manière . . . Il existe une force de création et de vérité qui nous réunit tous dans l'humilité et la fierté en même temps. Je ne l'ai jamais mieux senti qu'en vous lisant et c'est pourquoi—etc. etc.[11]

A French Oxford student Georges Nivat, the friend of O.V.'s daughter. He has made acquaintance of one of your sons, N. or M., strange coincidence, isn't it so? Let me know the receipt of this card to have verified this mode of communication.

But you write in your ordinary Russian manner to me.

The main reason why Boris wrote in English was that Russian letters frequently disappeared in the post. In addition, as he wrote, 'the need for an anonymous content'

10. 'I'm in the best of health'.
11. 'There are a number of us in France—writes Alb. Camus—who know you and in some way share your life . . . There exists a force of creation and truth which unites us all in simultaneous humility and pride. I have never felt this more strongly than when reading you, and that's why—etc. etc'.

obliged him not to sign his letters, and he preferred to write postcards, which he covered with tiny handwriting on both sides, leaving only a little space for the address. Most of these cards arrived safely and without delay.

In her foreword to a book of Boris's letters to Thomas Merton, Lydia commented on Boris's English, saying that he had spent many years studying Shakespeare and other early English authors, and had inevitably acquired their now somewhat archaic vocabulary. He had little familiarity with modern spoken English.

In the following letter, Boris expresses his indignation at the intrigues of Fedor Panferov, Secretary of the Soviet Writers' Union ('the other Fedichka'), who was determined to send him and Olga Ivinskaya to Baku and have him write about the heroic exploits of the workers drilling for oil from the Caspian seabed. This was first mentioned by Lydia in a letter of 12 July 1958, after Panferov had visited Oxford and met her, claiming to be a friend and well-wisher of Boris's. When he told her about the plans for a journey to Baku, she wrote to ask Boris about them, but at the time he overlooked her question and did not reply to it. Later, Olga Ivinskaya told him about Panferov's acquaintanceship with Lydia. Panferov was gravely ill, and Lydia was sorry for him. He had received treatment in England, and was supposed to repay the money spent on him by preventing Collins from publishing *Doctor Zhivago* in English. This he failed to do.

Boris Pasternak to Lydia Pasternak Slater

14 August 1958. Peredelkino.

Dear Lidochka,

I'm shattered by the news I have heard, which apparently relates to you, and which I have just heard about from O.V. [Ivinskaya]. I mean the other Fedichka and his trip. So his claws have extended to reach you too, poor thing. What an intrusive impertinence—just think! Of course, on his return he lost no time in summoning O.V., told her all about his exploits, and renewed his demands for us to go to Baku, threatening that steps would be taken if we refused; he intimidated her with his blackmail. It's striking to see that you view his suggestion in the same way as I have to. O.V. is also not trying to persuade me. Honestly, it's no joke—the mishaps with my leg over the last few years have taught me to be careful how I organise my days, alternating between movement and rest, and it's dangerous for me to change this for no good reason. How could I travel about like that, particularly with such a responsible task and with highly-placed eyes upon me! I myself have rejected the idea of an operation on my knee, and it's probably unnecessary anyway.

O.V. was indignant and called me a swine when she found out that I'd been asking you about Lomonosova, and wanting to give her some financial help through you if she was in difficulties. . . . . 'Lida has so many children, and she's on her own; and instead of finding out whether she needs help and offering her this money, you're using her to help you look after someone else.'

I still haven't received or seen the French Doctor.—I'm appalled to think that the long-delayed letters I wrote you in the spring will eventually succeed in reaching you, so that at the start of winter you'll be deluged with my April news.

Once again, there are rumours about the *pr*[*ix*] *N*[*obel*]. How I wish this could happen in a year's time, not before. There will be so many undesirable complications.

I am feeling well, and everything in my home and my soul is in the best of good order.

I kiss everybody.

All is well and unchanged in my family and my home.

Boris received a card from Josephine on 10 August, saying that she and Frederick had been on holiday near Munich, where they had met Fedor Stepun and his wife.[12] Stepun was full of praise for the translation of *Faust* which Boris had recently sent him; he also asked about *Doctor Zhivago* and said that in an indirect way he too was involved in its fate.

Boris Pasternak to Josephine Pasternak

22 August 1958. Peredelkino.

Dear Zhonia,

Thanks for your nice postcard. Please write and tell me how Fedia is. What a lot of Fedichkas there are in the world! Yours, Shura's, the one who was recently pestering Lida and claiming to be my 'friend',[13] and finally F. S[tepun]. How amazing that fate should have brought you together with him! The only thing that slightly alarmed me was your saying that he intends to get involved with *Zh*[*ivago*]. If that means plans for a discussion, an article or something of that

---

12. Fedor Stepun (1884–1965) was a Russian émigré philosopher and literary critic. He remembered Boris from the pre-Revolutionary years in Moscow, when Boris attended his philosophical group of young affiliates of Musaget, the Symbolist publishing house. In the 1950s he was involved in the preparation of the German edition of *Doctor Zhivago*.

13. Fedor Panferov.

sort, then nothing could be nicer. But if he's thinking of adding something to the German edition, the sort of thing that you over there might regard as a mitigating disclaimer, then that's totally unnecessary and very undesirable.

On the contrary—I was delighted by the uncompromising character of the French edition. Not a word along those lines. I only got to see the two publications this week.[14] A wonderful translation. There is a tendency to criticize it in certain circles, to present matters as though the author had something entirely different in mind, and his thoughts have been distorted by a bad translation. What a naïve subterfuge! Nine editions of this 'bad translation' over a single month, and I still can't read it without tears.

The same thing happened with the original, when I was finishing it off some three or four years ago, since when I haven't seen it again because I left myself without a single copy. It's a work that's so much greater than me, beyond my powers, beyond how I have grown used to seeing myself. A certain lady friend of mine (not O.V.) was right when she said to me at the time: '*Ne vous oubliez pas jusqu'à croire d'avoir vous-même écrit cette oeuvre. C'est le peuple r[usse], ses souffrances qui l'ont créée. Louez Dieu qui vous l'a mise sous votre plume.*'[15] That was a certain Katya Kr[ashennikova], a churchgoer.[16]

But as I've mentioned O.V., if you want to know what she looks like, look at page 190, the illustration of Margarete at her window—it's almost her likeness. *Montrez l'illustration à Georges, quand il rentrera, qu'il vous affirme la ressemblance.*[17]

I feel very well. How striking and how touching that, far away as you are, you realized what a bad idea it would be for me to travel to Baku. But what strength it takes to resist this compulsion coated in tenderness.[18]

Get Lida to write to me and say if she needs money.

---

14. *Le Docteur Jivago* and *Essai d'autobiographie*, both published by Gallimard (Paris) in June 1958.

15. 'Don't forget yourself to the point of believing that it was you who wrote this work. It was the Russian people and their sufferings who created it. Praise God for having expressed it through your pen.'

16. Ekaterina Krashennikova, a historian, met Boris in 1941. Some features of her personality are reflected in the figure of Simushka Tuntsova in *Doctor Zhivago*. She published her recollections of Boris in *Novy Mir*, 1997, No.1.

17. 'Show the illustration to Georges, when he returns, so he can confirm the likeness.' 'Georges' refers to George Nivat, who was a friend of Ivinskaya's daughter. Later in this correspondence Boris uses the name 'Margarete' to refer to Olga Ivinskaya, in order to protect her identity from Zina. The picture he refers to was by the artist Andrei Goncharov, published in Boris's translation of Goethe's *Faust*.

18. Olga Ivinskaya also tried to persuade Boris to take the trip to Baku. Her persuasion was harder to resist.

Josephine read *Doctor Zhivago* in the English translation she had just received, and on 3 August wrote to her brother:

'Yura has been here; he benefits from his foreign environment; it further brings out his exceptional nobility and musicality. His speech is like a piano improvisation. Do you remember how as a child I used to cry when you played the piano in the next room? And some of his tales are so painful they bring tears to your eyes. How much lies between those years and the present—how many worlds, an eternity.'

Lydia took up Boris's jocular reference to 'the French doctor', and wrote describing a 'medical congress' at which each delegate was more interesting than the last. This was an allusion to the first reviews of the newly published English edition of *Doctor Zhivago*.

The following letter from Boris is the last in this collection that he wrote in Russian; the letters presented hereafter were all written in English.

Boris Pasternak to his sisters

19 September 1958. Peredelkino.

My dears,

It looks as if a pile of rubbish from last spring (a number of my letters that had been held up) has landed on you or is about to do so. Don't dream of answering them—it upsets me that you'll waste your time to no purpose over them. The only consolation about them is that they relate to the distant past, to times that have been vanquished and overcome, and they show how much things have improved since then. I probably complained about my health at the time, but by now I've been better for a long time, and a lot of things that were still awaited then have now come to pass and are behind me.

I first thought the cover of the English edition rather garish, but I soon got used to it, and actually it's all fine.

Splendidly done, Lida, with your *Fairy Tale*.[19]

Sometimes people in Italy or France send me letters containing one or two press cuttings, and these reach me. At Pontremoli the book was awarded the Bancarelli prize. I don't know what it consists of. A director of the Stuttgart museum

---

19. Boris particularly liked Lydia's translation of Yuri Zhivago's poem 'Fairy Tale', which was included in the English edition of *Doctor Zhivago*.

wrote to me that the prize means that twenty thousand copies of the book are distributed to libraries in prisons, hospitals and hospices.

Thank you for your kind feelings towards Margarete. Lida was careful in referring to her, but Zhonia mentioned her initials on a postcard. Meanwhile everything at home is unchanged, everybody is well. M[argarete] is renting an apartment not far from here, in the next village. Yesterday in town she suffered a great misfortune, which so far has turned out all right. Her very gifted and beautiful daughter, the friend of Georges, is a wild, impulsive girl, engaged to Ch. (Georges knows him), a fellow student of hers at college. She was living alone in an apartment in town, and came home from her college, where Ch. had in some way deeply upset her. She spent a long time writing letters to me and her mother, then drank a bottle of essence of vinegar and swallowed ten Luminal powders. She was rescued and is now in hospital.

Is it true that an original Russian edition has also appeared? There are rumours that it's on sale at an exhibition in Brussels?[20]

I still haven't seen Shura after Malinovski handed over to him the watercolours by Papa that you had sent; I haven't seen them. He himself (Malinovski) came to see me at the dacha, and I liked him a lot.[21]

Thank you all for everything, your postcards are full of feeling and perceptive understanding. Thank you.

Boris Pasternak to Josephine Pasternak

[Original in English]

6 October 1958. Peredelkino.

[…]

I think your idea of our territorial placing here in P[eredelkino] is not exact enough through my fault. The house and garden in P with all its inhabitants (and myself inclusively) are in the same state as they were described in articles. It is my domicile with Z[ina] and L[yonia]. It has undergone no change. Z does not know that O[lga Ivinskaya] is renting a room in a peasant house of a neighbouring village. If the N[obel] prize of this year (as sometimes the rumour goes) will be assigned to me, and the necessity or the possibility for me comes to go abroad (all the matter is still absolutely dark to me) I can see no means not to try and not to want to take with

20. A pirated Russian edition of *Doctor Zhivago* was published in the Hague in August 1958, and secretly distributed at the Brussels World Fair.

21. Ivan Malinovski was the Danish translator of *Doctor Zhivago*, 'Luvers's Childhood' (1953) and 'A Tale' (1959).

me O. in the voyage, if the permission only is to be obtained, not to say about the probability of my own travel. But, seeing the difficulties, connected with the N. pr., I hope it will be conferred to other competitor, to A. Moravia, I believe.

16/X

[. . .] The danger of outward annoyances (almost imaginary at present), connected with the merited success of the novel is nothing, is a trifle in comparison with another, inner and much greater danger! The success will evoke idiotic editions and re-editions of my former nonentities in verses and prose (I speak of course of foreign undertakings). How the people don't perceive the gulf between all I made before and Dr. Zh.? It is more than disservice of dull (and therefore false) friends to remember in the face of the novel my 'poet's' past, pretending it to be one and the same with the authorship of the last writing. I cannot share this greedy interest and curiosity to one's first steps, origin, loves, home and family life. Our task and aspiration is not to be only not to remain faithful to ourselves, but to grow incessantly, to grow changed, to become transformed beyond recognition, to transmute themselves without rest in rich vitally lasting results.

[. . .]

CHAPTER FIFTEEN
1958–1960

Boris's dreams of a return to a calm and productive life were doomed. At the end of October 1958 he was awarded the Nobel Prize for Literature. The Soviet press called this an 'anti-Soviet onslaught by international reactionaries'. A political scandal ensued. The newspapers accused him of treason. Boris initially sent a telegram to the Nobel Committee thanking them for the award, but one week later, under pressure from the Central Committee of the Party and the Union of Soviet Writers, he was forced to decline. He was threatened with deprivation of his citizenship and exile abroad, but the active support of worldwide public opinion protected him.

Knowing his sisters would suffer for him during the relentless campaign of vilification, he sent them a telegram as soon as the furore had somewhat abated:

Boris Pasternak to his sisters
[Original in English]

10 NOVEMBER 1958. PEREDELKINO.
TEMPEST NOT YET OVER DO NOT GRIEVE BE FIRM AND QUIET. TIRED LOVING BELIEVING IN THE FUTURE
—BORIS

Boris Pasternak to Lydia Pasternak Slater
[Original in English]

11 December 1958. Peredelkino.

My dear,

It is my reply to your card from the nineteenth. [. . .] But don't exaggerate the importance of what you do or do not in my behalf: whether you write me or don't; whether you contrive at the general protestations or, in fear of the suppositional damage of them in my concern, try to restrain them and hold in check. Be aware that each your action of a certain kind towards me will be lost and disappear in a hundred of other manifestations, whose similar or opposite nature is impossible to foresee. And in my case, to do all, I think, is better than to do nothing. For instance all the letters I receive arrive minutely examined of course. But if their number reaches up to twenty daily from abroad (there was a day where there came fifty-four foreign letters at once), your free and frankly written missive will not add or diminish much to or of that pile. I would release you in that sense from your onerous and unnecessary precautions. I said to a Sw. correspondent I owe my saved life to my far worldwide friends intervening. You owe it, he retorted, to Lara, to her courageous activity. But don't think things have much changed. This official side of the business is too vast, mortally great and fatal to be much ruminated on. But there is another side of my continuing life or my spiritual existence, being in progress, things that should be directed by myself and rejoin in my hands and that slipped out of them. The publishers fury falling upon Safe Conduct, *short stories, ancient poems and other valueless stuff, after the success of* Dr. Zh., *the avidity after biographical minutenesses when there is an Autobiographical essay recently written by myself,— it is not a great tragedy for me, but it afflicts me as an objectionable disorder. I hide, I repudiate nothing, but when, for instance, I had to translate Shakespeare, an authority great and adult enough not to need my tutelage and licence, still there were passages of triumphant everlasting might that I put in full light, and there were other ones of the cheapest platitude and senseless rhetoric, that I put in shadow. How much more must one place his own loving life under the strict and perpetual censorship of beauty. And that is beauty in this true, not in the hairdresser's sense? It is a promise, a token of a free developing vital future, and evidence of its obvious germs. You were right to say in an interview: Mais mon frère n'aime pas cela! And the chance to see each other is gone!*

The next letter refers to Boris's defiant poem, 'Nobel Prize', which he gave to the *Daily Mail* correspondent Anthony Brown. It was published on 11 February 1959 with an imprudent commentary. Pasternak was ordered to leave Moscow for the duration of the visit by Harold Macmillan, the British Prime Minister, to prevent any unscheduled meetings with foreign journalists. On his return from his two-week journey to Georgia with Zina, he was summoned and interrogated by R.A. Rudenko, the General Public Prosecutor, and threatened with prosecution for treason against the State. His postcard to Lydia (below) was written on the day after this interrogation, which prompted his 'sense of dirt and . . . infamy' and profound humiliation.

Boris Pasternak to Lydia Pasternak Slater

[Original in English]

March 15, 1959. Peredelkino.

Here a set of casual house-photos for you. All your cards received, numberless thanks. An interruption in letter-writing can arrive for some time, don't worry yourselves about.

A tide of deep self-discontent, forgotten long ago, not experienced for the last years. Sense of dirt and infamy, of a life being the cause of perpetual, everyday torments for the next, for all.

I did not sufficiently estimate the weakness and humanity of our powers towards me, its being a rare exception. My fatal imprudence with the poor poem has to have sorrowful moral consequences in all friendly eyes, I suppose.

My broadly scattered, intricate, difficult life, I neither can nor will change or remake it. It was not done by my hands. But, letting it go its ways, I for myself, I shall bend my head deeper than last autumn and winter, in peace and humbleness, and try to undertake, a great new work, perhaps.

Don't influence yourself by my grumbling (about illustrations, about the title picture in your book). I have no firm opinions on that point. Let you not be misled by my complaints.

Three weeks ago I and Z[ina] flew to Tbilissi to avoid to be met by Engl[ish] journalists and reporters come along with McM[illan].

By a more proper time I shall retell you the few unimportant things contained in my evidently disappeared R[ussian] letter.

I embrace you all, pray forgive me my sadness and shortness.

At this time, another collection of Boris's works was published in England; it included *Safe Conduct*, some stories, the poem '1905', and a selection of other poems, some of which were printed in Lydia's translation. The foreword and the remaining translations were written by an old friend of Dmitri Sviatopolk-Mirsky, the poet and Slavist Alec Brown.[1]

---

1. *Safe Conduct: An Early Autobiography and Other Works* (London: Elek Books, 1959).

Boris Pasternak to Lydia Pasternak Slater

[Original in English]

April 18, 1959. Peredelkino.

[. . .]

Did I know your 'The air is full . . .'? It seems so familiar. You are an astonishing poet. I highly admire your foreword on 274. The conciseness, the judgement, the swift vivacity of style, everything that I am most liking in prose. The sentence, for instance: 'Those who are out for perfect English poems should read their own great poets (there are plenty of them waiting to be read).'

[. . .]

Lately I was shown an article of J. Lindsay on Zh[ivago] in Angl[o]-Sov[iet] Journal. The critic begins: 'I opened Dr. Zh. to admire.' In his place I would continue: 'But I remembered and realised what magazine I am writing for, and the book began to deceive my expectation.' He reproaches me the lack of characters, the diffusiveness, the absence of casual and logical connection, the motivelessness of actions and events.

I admit his disappointment to be quite sincere. And suddenly I understood clearer than ever before. Beside the political, poetical, ideological and other significances of the novel, Dr. Zh. is a kind of new prose, totally shut and closed for the halfpenny stock wisdom of Lindsay by the very novelty of the sort. It is the same incoherence, inaction, lack of movement, plot and consistency that Tolstoy incriminated to Tchekhov's plays, whereas just this indifference about passions, causes and consequences, past and present, this tendency to represent human dramatically interacting groups like only life landscapes and in no way more solemn, ponderous and immobile, this favourite manner of replacing and effacing lines and limits in descriptions, was exactly Tchekhov's chief strength and charm as a storyteller's, that ravished Tolst[oy] in Tch[ekhov's] tales.

It was not the bustle, the prizewinning, the actuality, the religious touch, that formed the destiny of the book and won souls (in W. Germ[any], for instance, to judge my correspondence, it became an object of adoration).

It is its novelty, not the struggling intended novelty of a proclaimed program-conform literary current or belief, but the involuntary novelty of its style and spirit, that works in the hearts of unsophisticated readers as their own modern sense and cannot gain the self confident experts of yesterday with their spoiled and narrow likings.

My conditions stop growing worse; it is not yet time to say if they will improve.

But it lost interest for me long ago. Mentally I am far away from this apparent present, which really is a lingering, stagnant agonizing past.

Please remit my thanks and admiration to Mr. Brown. Express also my gratitude to Mr. Elek while I try find leisure to write him. I embrace everyone in both your houses.

This letter caused Lydia great joy. Her verse translations of five of Boris's poems, in particular her excellent translation 'The air is full of after-thunder freshness', were preceded by a short note in which she expounded the principles by which she worked.

She said that in his poetry, Pasternak had inherited from his parents both painting and music—he had merely changed his instrument, finding expression for his music in language. To translate Pasternak without finding the same rhythms and melodies present in the original was inconceivable for her.

In her answer to Boris, written on 29 April, she told him she had been invited to read her translations in the USA. She spent a month in that country, meeting old friends who had fled there before the war, and also Kurt and Helene Wolff, who had published *Doctor Zhivago* in the USA the previous year.

Josephine and Frederick Pasternak visited Jacqueline de Proyart, Pasternak's French translator and trusted representative, in Paris. Proyart's account of their meeting is quoted in his next letter.

Giangiacomo Feltrinelli, the Italian publisher of *Doctor Zhivago*, refused to recognise Proyart's rights, and was distracting Boris from his work on a new play, started the previous spring. He had great hopes of this work, *The Blind Beauty*, which was to describe the fate of a talented nineteenth-century Russian actor and serf.

Boris Pasternak to Lydia Pasternak Slater
[Original in English]

July 31, 1959. Peredelkino.

Dear L., have you ever written to me after your return from your journey? If so, your efforts are lost in vain, I have had not a word from you. I know of your having written and wired to Sh[ura]. Both they are sojourning now in the Carpathians (west Ukr[aine]). Leonidas is driving Zina and Nina Tabidse in a car along the Baltic coast. Meanwhile Jenia (he) with his wife and their little Peter are staying at P[eredel]kino. I had signs of your having met with W[olff]s, of Mrs. Fisher having made the acquaintance of Charlie, of the visit paid by F[edia] and J[onia] to my

Paris friend. I am happy to know the chances, inaccessible to myself to be used and by the way rejoiced by you (perhaps without any pleasure to yourself, I don't know). But everyone is charmed. 'Elle vous ressemble un peu. J'en étais toute émue. Elle m'a demandé si vous fumiez et un tas d'autres détails de ce genre', etc.[2]

Oh, if only I could live ten or five years more! The disproportion between the made and the discussed and commented would not be so great as now, the stuff not so meagre, the evaporation not so large and diffused, I should have filled the gap with new things written and done, I am on the way to it. I have been eagerly zealous at my new work of late, I have ceased writing letters, when suddenly I saw myself compelled to interrupt the happy endeavour. I learned F[eltrin]elli to be risen in rebellion against my French guardian angel, he will complain to me of the obstacles she makes to him at every turn (out of her overdone and excessive foresight, I think). O[lga] esteems the things as alarming. The discord of the both named is death to me. F[eltrinelli] is also a true and noble friend, he deserves consideration. To settle the passions at such a distance is unfeasible and venturesome. Yet I try. And the unchained letter writing is come in full swing.

Oh, if only the other conditions should permit, I would be found able to stand the test of this blessed, unheard, thrilling, Goethe-like, strenuous and fruitful sort of existence. And I lead it indeed, though hidden, hampered to the utmost and unseen.

What are you now occupied with? Send me a few lines, if you can, or ask our sister to do it. Greetings to all.

Your B.

Boris Pasternak to Lydia Pasternak Slater

[Original in English]

November 4, 1959. Peredelkino.

My dear,

I guess your feeling of supposed unnaturalness by the first glance at my lines (the choice of language, the forced affected style etc etc) but you are wrong. You must be aware of the reasons and prerequisites of this my habit of corresponding with you in such artificial manner,—you don't know them.

---

2. 'She looks a bit like you. I was quite moved by that. She asked me whether you smoked, and a lot of other details of that kind.' Boris is here quoting Jacqueline de Proyart's reactions to Josephine.

A whole eternity has passed that I did not write you. I was quiet about the health and life of you all. From several sides I had news, mentionings, reports relative to you.

Money matters forced me to put aside my play writing a month ago. Within three weeks I translated El principe constante *for a Calderón edition. I did not write letters, I did not answer them. Now I can return to the play and to the rest.*

The only possible mode of living has clearly manifested itself the last years. Either life itself (in its historical conditions) must produce a new, incredible, fairylike chapter of reality; or it is me, who must bring about something similar and put it to paper. And so I live by these hopes.

I don't remember whether I ever sent you my short notice on Chopin I wrote shortly after the war. It was mean and unworthy to have left it undeveloped and undeepened as it was written in that remote time for a newspaper. Now Mr. St[ephen]. Sp[ender] has taken it for the Encounter. *Please read it and write me then upon.*[3] *Be it puzzling, hasty, simple and incomplete, it contains all I wanted to say. It has the statement or point of view on realism as an exceptionally highest degree of art (art's regularity, its whole domain being based on such rare exceptions and deviations), its custom and standard, its practice being romanticism, the easy superficial turning within a narrow circle of a certain culture or a certain taste, as for instance the French art and letters of the Rococo time, or our similarly conventional social-realism, or (with few exceptions) the typically-classical German music (and Brahms to the half) etc. etc. etc. And there are single solitary existences who want not art and beauty of their age, but worlds, world-creations in sounds, in tales, in colours, and madly and indefatigably, feed and saturate and supply their masterpieces with stuff and divinations nobody dreams of or exacts from them to make their works terribly lonely, great, independent, substantial universes for themselves. Of the refusal obtained by N[iva]t, I learned out of some Belgian clippings. Poor boy! It was even a much greater blow for Irene E[melianova] whose imagination ran high pending his arrival. Georges, having also been at first turned away, surmounted the obstacles and is visiting her every evening. I made at last his acquaintance. Your publisher Elek writes me about the play. It is too early to speak of a thing only begun and mostly still swimming in pure suppositions. He also asks about the book by Bertr. Russell he shall have sent to me, which never reached me. But let him not reiterate the attempt. Greet and thank him. Perhaps I will write him after I become a little freer.*

3. The poet Stephen Spender, editor of *Encounter*, did not publish Boris's article on Chopin. Lydia also failed to have it included in a book containing George Reavey's translation of 'A Tale' (London: Peter Owen, 1959). It was published after Boris's death, in *The Guardian*, on 15 September 1960.

I embrace you and you all tenderly.

Your B.

Please affirm me the receipt of this letter in few words without retardation. Say something essential that can interest me and be of use.

Boris Pasternak to Lydia Pasternak Slater
[Original in English]

January 24, 1960. Peredelkino.

My dear,

Georges [Nivat], I suppose, must have had written to you about his frequent visiting of the adjoining village, about his living for days and weeks there, about his meeting me at O.V. I[vinskaya's], who is renting a room in a peasant house of the same hamlet. He and Irene are great friends. Me seems he made or will make a proposal to her. Here is her photograph on that strip of land.

[...]

The only important is that I advance the play more quickly than I do, that I can bring it some day to the end. It moves so desperately slowly! The irreparable misfortune is that my present hindrances are seductions: pleasing cajoling letters, deep mutual meditations on fathomless world wide topics, and so forth.

But a sprout of reality has emerged in the manuscript and there is nothing in the world I could so long for as that this outset of an intended being should increase and grow. With all my forces I shall help it.

Boris Pasternak to Lydia Pasternak Slater
[Original in English]

1 February 1960. Peredelkino.

At last I have seen and enjoyed your August Encounter *letter 'P[asternak] and Wilson'. K. Wolff has sent me the clipping. You are a prodigy of endowment as ever, my dear. I was afraid you will be not polite enough against Mr. W. in your disputation. But pardon me my useless misgivings: your argument is a paragon of courtesy and refinement.*[4]

4. Lydia wrote a lively and down-to-earth letter titled 'Pasternak and Wilson' to *Encounter* XIII, No. 2 (August, 1959), pp. 84–85, criticising Edmund Wilson's essay 'Legend and Symbol in *Doctor Zhivago*', published in its June number, for its over-elaborate symbolic analysis. She pointed out that

I wrote you recently. I hope you will have received that letter. There is no news. The proportion between the unnecessary and inevitable on the one side and the desired and unattainable on the other remains the same.
Yours devotedly and affectionately

B.

Friday, Feb.5. Just now Sh. is bringing me your Hellmer Ashmore sending. Mind for the future: either you dispatch your letters of any sort you please simply through the ordinary post; or the people who undertake to transmit them must hand them over to the recipients themselves. But the second mode is absolutely useless I think.

St. Sp[ender] must be well groundedly disappointed on my account. The American translations showed him, T.S. Eliot and others I proved not to be they have been waiting for. Besides he and T.S. El[iot] must be hurt not having had from me comments or references in return to their sent collected poems, only short thanks for the fact of sending. But should I destroy the regular course of my day and sacrifice my year occupations, even then I would not find time sufficient for such a vast reading. They both are excellent and genuine poets. I wrote recently T.S. El[iot] at any rate.[5] *The tenet to like Chopin should be the sign of a bad taste or of ignorance is very old. The German* Goldene Buecher der Musik *of the beginning of the age did not even place him among the great composers. But St. Sp[ender] praised me the article in a letter and I knew that it will appear in March.*

Please calm Ashmore that he becomes quiet.[6] *He read in the* News Chron[icle] *I should have finished writing the play. He was reading it just in the period I was forced to interrupt the labour, ceding weeks and weeks to made-up, conventional, unreal requests of so to say needful, important rhymed translations I have been*

---

the Moscow street-names and houses in which Wilson disinterred hidden symbolic meanings were simply their real names, and when Wilson interpreted the posters advertising agricultural machinery by the firm Moro & Vetchinkin as a reference to Hamlet (*vetchina* meaning 'ham' in Russian), she protested: 'Is it at all conceivable that Pasternak should want to reduce his beloved Hamlet to a small quantity of boiled bacon? And what for? Just in order to let mystically-inspired, wide-eyed enthusiasts pick yet one more 'symbol', like a mushroom, and triumphantly place it in their already overflowing symbolic baskets?'

Stephen Spender had also asked Boris for a response to Wilson's article. In his reply, Boris avoided Lydia's robust polemic, but wrote a general letter about *Zhivago*'s relationship to recent literature and his own aims. In the summer of 1960, *Encounter* published three letters from Pasternak to Spender.

5. This letter was published by Lydia Pasternak Slater in *Quarto*, No.6 (May 1980), and deals with Eliot's poetry, Wagner, and Thomas Merton.

6. A Swedish paper had mistakenly reported that Pasternak's unfinished play was about to be staged. Basil Ashmore, a theatre director, wanted to commission Lydia to translate it, and Kurt Hellmer, a New York literary agent, was seeking the copyright for this hypothetical production.

unable to get rid of. Please mind another point. When, as I continue to hope, I shall have finished writing the play, F[eltrinel]li will immediately seize the centre, and the radii of all questions, those of translation, of publishing, of acting will scatter and run to all sides from him alone and in sole dependence on him. It is impossible to any one else or to a whole imaginary body (how to constitute it?) to regulate such an amount of world relations separately in pieces and parts. But how to master the life, the personal fate, the time to devote myself to this work, to belong to this task exclusively without hindrance? The impossibility of it is my constant gnawing privation. The desire to have it written (and I shall it have) is again a vehement longing for the great, for that great that has been animating the novel and has acquired me the sympathy and understanding of Th. Merton,[7] Ed. Wilson, and others.

My love and amitiés, and embraces and wishes of health and longevity for you all, for J[onia] and for F[edia].

Your poor B.

Inform me as soon as possible of the receipt of this letter, by a card, if you please, for not to waste your time.

There were made (and published in German newspapers) excellent snaps during the tour of the Hamburger Schauspielhaus in Moscow. I enclose one with the well succeeded Zen[aide] and Leonid.

Boris Pasternak's 70th birthday was celebrated on 10 February 1960. His sisters sent him a telegram of congratulations, and in a postcard sent the same day, Lydia wrote that in a newspaper photograph of the Hamburger Schauspielhaus production of *Faust*, Boris looked 'certainly no older than 36'.

But Lydia probably never received a reply. During the months before his last illness, Boris was completing the final version of the Prologue and Act I of his play, and in corresponding with Feltrinelli, who insisted on exclusive world rights to his entire oeuvre, past, present, and to come.

Pasternak bore the first symptoms of his illness—attacks of cardiac arrhythmia and pains below the shoulder-blades—by force of will-power. He did not consult a doctor. Several times a day he would stop work, lie down, wait for the pain to pass, and then sit at his desk again.

---

7. See Thomas Merton's book *Disputed Questions*, containing his articles in defence of Boris Pasternak during the Nobel Prize scandal (New York: Harcourt Brace, 1985), and the correspondence between Merton and Pasternak, with an introduction by Lydia Pasternak Slater (Lexington: The King Library Press, University of Kentucky, 1972).

He only took to his bed at the end of April, after copying out the first half of the play. Recognising the nature of his condition, he refused to go to hospital, and was cared for at home. News of his illness soon filled the European press.

[Original in English]

[17–18 MAY 1960. OXFORD.]
ZINA PASTERNAK PEREDELKINO NEAR MOSCOW
VERY WORRIED BORIS ILLNESS WIRE DETAILS ALSO ABOUT YOU. LOVING
PRAYING SISTERS FREDERICK

Shura's wife Irina, replied.

19 MAY 1960. MOSCOW.
BORIS INFARCT. TODAY ELEVENTH DAY ILLNESS ALL MEASURES TAKEN
SHURA CONSTANTLY WITH HIM HOPE NOT LOST FAVOURABLE OUTCOME
WILL KEEP YOU INFORMED DETAILS BY LETTER KISSES
—INA

But the doctors' diagnosis was wrong, and Boris's condition deteriorated.

21 MAY 1960 MOSCOW.
BORIS INFARCT SITUATION GRAVE THANKS TELEGRAM
—ZINA

[22 MAY 1960 OXFORD.]
ZINA PASTERNAK PEREDELKINO MOSCOW
GOD IS MERCIFUL PRAYING CONSTANTLY WITH YOU IN SPIRIT
—LYDIA

25 MAY 1960 MOSCOW.
CONDITION UNCHANGED MOSCOWS BEST DOCTORS TREATING ALL
NECESSARY DRUGS PROVIDED EARNESTLY REQUEST YOU REFUTE FALSE
BBC REPORTS OF BORIS UNSATISFACTORY TREATMENT DETAILS BY
LETTER
—ZINA LYONIA

[26 MAY 1960, OXFORD.]

PASTERNAK PEREDELKINO MOSCOW

ASTONISHED BY TELEGRAM BBC GAVE NO SUCH REPORT INDEED
NEWSPAPERS AND RADIO STRESS FIRSTCLASS TREATMENT HOWEVER
FORWARDED YOUR TELEGRAM TO PRESS GOD PRESERVE YOU

One of his nurses heard his involuntary cry: 'Zhonia, my beloved sister, I'll never see you again!'

Zina spent the family savings on his care. A mobile X-ray unit was brought to the dacha, and on 26 May the doctors diagnosed extensive lung cancer with metastases in the heart, liver and bowel.

Boris asked to see Lydia before he died. A telegram was sent:

27 MAY 1960 MOSCOW.

SITUATION HOPELESS COME IF YOU CAN
—SHURA

Lydia spent a week at the Soviet Consulate waiting for a visa.

28 MAY 1960 MOSCOW.

URGENTLY WIRE POSSIBILITY VISIT INFORM US IF NEED HELP GETTING
VISA
—LYONIA ZHENIA

They also sent a direct plea to Khrushchev.

29 MAY 1960 MOSCOW.

TELEGRAM TO PRESIDENT COUNCIL OF MINISTERS SENT 29/5 3 PM
—ZHENIA LYONIA

On the evening of 30 May, Boris had a last blood transfusion. Shura, who had spent the month by his brother's side, told him that Lydia was expected any moment. Later that same evening, Boris died.

Two days later Lydia's visa was granted. Forty years after her departure from Moscow, she returned. She slept in her brother's bed, and from his study windows looked out at the broad path beaten by the thousands who had followed his coffin, over the field and up to the churchyard where his body was laid.

For many years, Lydia continued to translate her brother's poetry, and to visit Moscow every year.

Leonid Pasternak's *Memoirs*, collated and edited in Oxford and Moscow by Josephine and Alexander Pasternak, were published in the USSR in 1975. Lydia and Josephine organised several exhibitions of Leonid's work in Germany, England and the USA. In 1979, thanks to Lydia's efforts, the Tretyakov Gallery held its first one-man exhibition of his work. That was the year of Lydia's last visit to Moscow.

She was preparing a parallel-text edition of Boris's poems and her own translations alongside. The plan was for this book to be published in Moscow and coincide with the centenary of Boris's birth, but she herself died on 4 May 1989, and the project was never completed.

Josephine survived her by four years. The gravestone in the Oxford Cemetery that houses their ashes, and those of their parents, bears a Russian inscription. It is the final quatrain from Boris Pasternak's 'August'.

Прощай, размах крыла расправленный,
Полета вольное упорство,
И образ мира, в слове явленный,
И творчество, и чудотворство.

Farewell, great span of wings unfurled,
The stubborn wilfulness of flight,
Words to illuminate the world,
Creation, wonder-working might!

ILLUSTRATION SOURCES

Photographs and illustrations are listed in the order in which they appear in the book. For cross-reference, captions are repeated. The photos are drawn from the Estate of Boris Pasternak and of the Hoover Institution Archives. Efforts have been made to locate the original sources, determine the current rights holders, and, if needed, obtain reproduction permissions. Upon verification of any claims to rights in the photos reproduced in this book, any required corrections or clarifications will be made in subsequent printings or editions.

FRONTISPIECE PHOTO:

Studio portrait of Boris Pasternak, Moscow, 1928. Hoover Institution Archives, Pasternak Family papers.

PHOTO SECTION I:

Boris Pasternak at Merrekül on the Baltic (in present-day Estonia). Oil painting by Leonid Pasternak, 1910. Estate of Boris Pasternak.

Leonid Pasternak in his studio in Moscow. Estate of Boris Pasternak.

Leonid and Rosalia Pasternak. Double oil study by Leonid Pasternak. Estate of Boris Pasternak.

Alexander Pasternak. Pencil and charcoal sketch by Leonid Pasternak, 1927. Estate of Boris Pasternak.

Albert Einstein playing the violin. Sketch by Leonid Pasternak. Estate of Boris Pasternak.

Rainer Maria Rilke. Sketch by Leonid Pasternak. Estate of Boris Pasternak.

The composer Alexander Scriabin. Estate of Boris Pasternak.

Pavel Ettinger (Pavetti). Estate of Boris Pasternak.

Leonid Pasternak with biochemist Boris Zbarsky, in Leonid's studio, 1917. Hoover Institution Archives, Pasternak Family papers.

Farewell picture in Moscow: Leonid, Alexander (Shura), Berta Kaufman, Boris, Rosalia, and Lydia (left to right), September 1921 (Josephine was already in Germany). Photographer: Galperin. Hoover Institution Archives, Pasternak Family papers.

Boris Pasternak. Oil painting by his wife Evgenia (Zhenia). Estate of Boris Pasternak.

Josephine Pasternak (left) and Ida Vysotskaya, 1912. Estate of Boris Pasternak.

Zinaida as a young woman. Estate of Boris Pasternak.

Lydia Pasternak, about 1921–22. Estate of Boris Pasternak.

Lydia Pasternak walking in Berlin, 1927. Estate of Boris Pasternak.

Stella Frishman, 1922. Estate of Boris Pasternak.

Portrait photograph of Rosalia, Lydia, Josephine (in front), and Leonid Pasternak in Berlin, 1921. Estate of Boris Pasternak.

Frederick and Josephine Pasternak, wedding photograph outside Berlin-Charlottenburg registry office, 1924. Estate of Boris Pasternak.

Frederick and Josephine Pasternak, 1924. Estate of Boris Pasternak.

Vladimir Mayakovsky, Boris Pasternak, Lili Brik, and Sergei Eisenstein (left to right), 1924. Estate of Boris Pasternak.

Boris with Zhenia and little Zhenichka. Studio photo, 1924. Photographer: Moisei Nappelbaum; FTM Agency, Ltd., Moscow. Estate of Boris Pasternak.

Zhenia and Zhenichka. Studio portrait, 1926. Estate of Boris Pasternak.

Zhenichka in a knitted suit, 1926. Estate of Boris Pasternak.

Boris, Zhenia, and Zhenichka aged 3, in their courtyard in Moscow, 1926. Photographer: Irina Ehrenburg. Hoover Institution Archives, Pasternak Family papers.

Rosalia, Lydia, Josephine, and Leonid Pasternak in Berlin, 1926. Estate of Boris Pasternak.

PHOTO SECTION II:

Boris reading Rilke's *Neue Gedichte*, 1933. Estate of Boris Pasternak.

André Malraux, Vsevolod Meyerhold, and Boris Pasternak (left to right) in Moscow, 1936. Photographer: Viktor Ruikovich; current copyright holder unknown; material rights claimed by Moscow House of Photography (MDF). Estate of Boris Pasternak.

Zhenichka with pigeons on street in Germany, 1926. Estate of Boris Pasternak.

Zhenichka (right) and his cousin Fedia (Alexander Pasternak's son), 1929. Estate of Boris Pasternak.

Pasternak family group in Berlin: (standing) Frederick, Leonid, and Lydia; (seated) Josephine and Rosalia, 1927. Hoover Institution Archives, Pasternak Family papers.

Frederick, Zhenichka, Zhenia, and Josephine (left to right), on a lake near Munich, 1931. Estate of Boris Pasternak.

Leonid Pasternak with Zhenichka, 1931. Estate of Boris Pasternak.

Leonid and Rosalia with (left to right) Charles and Helen Pasternak and Zhenichka, at a picnic in the German countryside, 1931. Estate of Boris Pasternak.

Helen and Charles Pasternak, 1935. Estate of Boris Pasternak.

Michael Slater (Mikey) in his playpen, 1937. Estate of Boris Pasternak.

Gilbert and Violet Slater, Lydia, Leonid, and Rosalia at the Slaters' home in Oxford, 1936. Estate of Boris Pasternak.

Boris's dacha at Peredelkino, where he lived from the late 1930s until his death. Estate of Boris Pasternak.

Boris Pasternak and Kornei Chukovsky at the Komsomol Tenth Congress, Moscow, 1936. Photographer: Boris Ignatovich; Union of Photographic Artists/Foto Soyuz. Hoover Institution Archives, Pasternak Family papers.

Anatoli Lunacharsky addressing the Union of Soviet Writers in Moscow (Boris Pasternak is in the third row), 1933. Hoover Institution Archives, Pasternak Family papers.

Maxim Gorky. Hoover Institution Archives, Joseph Freeman papers.

Boris Pasternak and Maxim Gorky at the Presidium of the First Congress of Soviet Writers, August 1934. Press-Cliché Bureau, Moscow. Hoover Institution Archives, Pasternak Family papers.

PHOTO SECTION III:

Boris writing, at Chistopol, 1943. Photographer: Viktor Avdeev. Estate of Boris Pasternak.

Boris at the front as a war correspondent, with the journalist Semyon Tregub, 1943. Estate of Boris Pasternak.

Boris Pasternak and Anna Akhmatova, 1946. Photographer: V. I. Slonimsky; Russian Information Agency/Novosti. Estate of Boris Pasternak.

Boris, his wife Zinaida (Zina), and their son Lyonia, at Peredelkino, 1946. Photographer: Viktor Slavinsky. Hoover Institution Archives, Pasternak Family papers.

Boris gardening at Peredelkino, 1946. Photographer: Viktor Slavinsky. Estate of Boris Pasternak.

Evgeni Pasternak in army officer's uniform, 1946. Estate of Boris Pasternak.

Boris's second son Leonid (Lyonia) with his nurse, 1940. Estate of Boris Pasternak.

Lydia Pasternak Slater with her children (left to right) Michael, Catherine (in front), Ann, and Nicolas in Oxford, 1945. Estate of Boris Pasternak.

Boris, Lyonia (on left), and the Georgian poet Georgi Leonidze, 1957. Hoover Institution Archives, Pasternak Family papers.

Boris with Olga Ivinskaya, 1957. Photographer: Alexander Less. Estate of Boris Pasternak.

Boris with his wife Zinaida (right) and Nina Tabidze, reading the telegram announcing his Nobel Prize, October 1958. Photographer: Max Frankel. Estate of Boris Pasternak.

The writer Kornei Chukovsky, with Boris and Zinaida (right) celebrating the Nobel Prize, October 1958. Photographer: Likhotal. Hoover Institution Archives, Pasternak Family papers.

Boris with Olga Ivinskaya and her daughter, Irina Emelianova, 1958. Estate of Boris Pasternak.

Irina Emelianova, daughter of Olga Ivinskaya, 1959. Estate of Boris Pasternak.

Boris after a performance in Moscow of Goethe's *Faust* by Deutsches Schauspielhaus Hamburg, with Gustaf Gründgens, who played Mephistopheles, 1959. Estate of Boris Pasternak.

Boris Pasternak in Peredelkino, 1959. Hoover Institution Archives, Pasternak Family papers.

INDEX OF NAMES

Blok, Alexander Alexandrovich (1880–
1921), poet, 38, 38n39, 81, 298, 368,
368n13
Blumenfeld (Anastasiev), Viktor Felixovich
(1888–1939, died in labour camp),
engineer, cousin of Heinrich Neuhaus,
244, 254
Bobrov, Sergei Pavlovich (1889–1971),
poet and translator, 10, 10n16
Bodarevsky, Nikolai Kornilievich (1850–
1921), painter, 228, 228n4
Bolshakov, Konstantin Aristarkhovich
(1895–1938, shot), poet, 226, 226n1
Borovsky, Alexander (1889–1968), Russian-
American pianist, 222–223, 222n12
Bowra, Cecil Maurice (1898–1971),
English literary historian, 368–370,
368n14, 374, 376, 381, 385
Brahms, Johannes (1833–1897), German
composer, 192, 398, 413
Brandukov, Anatoli Andreyevich (1856–
1930), cellist, 187–188
Braz, Osip Emmanuilovich (1872–1936),
painter, 132–133, 132n23
Brik, Lili (1891–1978), writer, wife of Osip
Brik, mistress of Vladimir Mayakovsky,
97
Brik, Osip Maximovich (1888–1945),
writer, 1
Brown, Alec (1900–1962), English writer
and translator, 409, 411
Brown, Anthony, English journalist, 408
Bryusov, Valeri Yakovlevich (1873–1924),
poet, 146, 377
Bubchik, see Solomon, Ivan
Bukharin, Nikolai Ivanovich (1888–1938,
shot), Soviet politician, 16n24, 265,
292–293, 295, 307, 311, 314n5, 316
Byron, George Gordon, Lord (1788–1824),
English poet, 322

Calderón de la Barca, Pedro (1600–1681),
Spanish writer, 413
Camus, Albert (1913–1960), French writer,
400, 400n11
Capablanca, José Raoul (1888–1942),
Cuban chess grandmaster, 279

Charles VI (the Mad) (1368–1422), King
of France, 313
Charles VII (1403–1461), King of France,
crowned by Joan of Arc in 1429, 313
Chekhov, Anton Pavlovich (1860–1904),
writer, 259, 267, 320, 410
Chernyak, Yakov Zakharovich (1898–1955),
literary historian, 104, 107–108, 113
Chopin, Frédéric (Fryderyk) (1810–1849),
Polish composer, 354, 364, 397–398,
413, 413n3, 415
Cliburn, Van (Harvey Lavan Cliburn)
(b. 1934), American pianist, 398
Cohen, Hermann (1842–1918), German
philosopher, Pasternak's professor in
Marburg, 45, 45n6, 171
Cohen, John Michael (1903–1989), En-
glish translator of Boris Pasternak's
poems, 370
Coleridge, Samuel Taylor (1772–1834), En-
glish poet, 297, 322
Conrad, Joseph (1857–1924), Polish-
English writer, 26–27, 30
Corinth, Lovis (1858–1925), German
painter, 44, 44n4, 107, 227–8
Craig, Edward Gordon (1872–1966), En-
glish actor and director, 281, 281n17

Dailis, Genrietta, Rosalia Pasternak's first
cousin, 89, 89n10
D'Angelo, Sergio (b. 1922), Italian journalist, 388
Dante Alighieri (1265–1321), Italian poet,
10, 94
Dickens, Charles (1812–1870), English
writer, 1, 3, 6, 31, 277–278, 298–299
Dima, nephew of Konstantin Bolshakov,
226
Dimitrov, Georgi (1882–1949), Bulgarian
communist, co-accused of Reichstag fire,
262–263
Diushen, Boris V., physicist and journalist,
9, 9n15
Dostoevsky, Fyodor Mikhailovich (1821–
1881), writer, 119n3, 298
Durylin, Sergei Nikolaevich (1887–1954),
writer and art historian, 276, 276n11

Efron, Ariadna Sergeyevna (1912–1975), artist and translator, daughter of Marina Tsvetaeva, 37n38, 345

Efron, Georgi Sergeyevich (1925–1944, killed in action), son of Marina Tsvetaeva, 345

Efron, Sergei Yakovlevich (1893–1941, shot), journalist, husband of Marina Tsvetaeva, 37n38, 345

Efros, Abram Markovich (pseudonym 'Roscius') (1888–1954), art critic and historian, 127, 127n11

Eglit, Robert Andreyevich, employee of the Commissariat for Internal Affairs, 2, 2n3

Ehrenburg, Ilya Grigoryevich (1891–1967), writer, 7, 7n11, 47, 259

Ehrenburg-Kozintseva, Liubov Mikhailovna (1900–1970), painter, wife of Ilya Ehrenburg, 136

Einstein, Albert (1879–1955), German physicist, 9n15, 94, 107, 228, 280

Elek, Peter, English publisher, 409n1, 411, 413

Eliot, Thomas Stearns (1888–1955), American-English poet, 415, 415n5

Emelianova, Irina Ivanovna (b. 1938), daughter of Olga Ivinskaya, 388, 388n2, 395, 400, 413–414

Engel, Ada Yulievna (Roginskaya) (1901–1970?), painter, 154

Erlikh, Volf Isidorovich (1902–1944), poet, friend of Sergei Esenin, 89–90, 89n11

Esenin, Sergei Alexandrovich (1895–1925, committed suicide), poet, 38–39, 38n39, 89–90, 89n11

Ettinger, Pavel Davidovich (Pavetti) (1866–1948), art critic and friend of the Pasternaks, 102, 102n5, 104–106, 109, 114–115, 120, 155, 203, 218, 231, 233–234, 250, 250n20, 279, 335–336, 348, 354

Favorsky, Vladimir Andreyevich (1886–1964), graphic artist, 154

Fedia, see Pasternak, Frederick; also see Pasternak, Fyodor

Fedin, Konstantin Alexandrovich (1892–1977), writer, 259, 278, 342

Feltrinelli, Giangiacomo (1926–1972, killed), Italian publisher, 381, 392, 411–412, 416

Fenia, Zhenichka's nanny, 15, 30, 70, 100

Fet, Afanasi Afanasyevich (1820–1892), poet, 146, 377

Fichte, Johann Gottlieb (1762–1814), German philosopher, 122, 122n7

Fischer, Brigitte Bermann (1905–1991), German publisher, 411

Fischer, Louis (1896–1970), American journalist, Moscow correspondent of the New York Times, 300, 300n13, 303

Flaubert, Gustave (1821–1880), French writer, 174, 298–299

Flohr, Salomon (Salo) (1908–1983), Czech and Soviet chess grandmaster, 279

Fonvizin, Denis Ivanovich (1745–1792), playwright, 313n4

Freidenberg, Alexander Mikhailovich (Sashka) (1884–1938, died in prison), engineer, son of Anna and Mikhail Freidenberg, nephew of Leonid Pasternak, x, xix, 255, 330–331, 331n14, 334, 334n17, 337

Freidenberg, Anna Osipovna (Asya) (1860–1944), sister of Leonid Pasternak, xix, 13, 15–16, 22–23, 33, 79, 85, 88, 115, 136, 160, 203, 206, 212, 225, 237–238, 245, 252, 284–287, 290–291, 314, 330–331, 334, 354, 358

Freidenberg, Olga Mikhailovna (Olya, Olyushka) (1890–1955), classical philologist, daughter of Anna and Mikhail Freidenberg, niece of Leonid Pasternak, xix, 13, 23, 44, 44n4, 121, 121n6, 124, 160, 160n1, 163, 212, 252–254, 257, 261, 284–286, 290, 292, 301, 312, 314, 330–331, 333–334, 354, 360, 382, 397

Freidenberg family, xix, 332n16

Frishman, Stella Samoilovna (m. Adelson) (1901–1988), neighbour of the Pasternaks in Volkhonka flat, 10n18, 14–15, 23, 46, 61, 74, 117, 156, 161, 188, 193, 272, 274, 297, 332

Boris Leonidovich Pasternak, Russian poet and writer, was the winner of the Nobel Prize for Literature in 1958. Born in Moscow, Pasternak is best known in the West for his monumental tragic novel on Soviet Russia, *Doctor Zhivago*. It is as a poet, however, that he is most celebrated in Russia. He fell out of favor with the Soviet authorities in the 1930s, but somehow was spared arrest and imprisonment. He died on May 31, 1960.

TRANSLATOR AND AUTHOR OF INTRODUCTION:

Nicolas Pasternak Slater is the son of Boris Pasternak's sister Lydia, to whom many of the letters in this collection were addressed. He has divided much of his life between work as a medical specialist in hematology and as a translator, publishing both scientific and literary translations including Boris Pasternak's autobiographical essay *People and Propositions*.

EDITOR:

Maya Slater, wife of Nicolas Pasternak Slater, is a widely published writer and a Senior Research Fellow of Queen Mary College, University of London.

FOREWORD AUTHOR:

Lazar Fleishman is Professor of Slavic Languages and Literatures at Stanford University. His publications include *Boris Pasternak: The Poet and His Politics* and *Boris Pasternak in the Thirties*.